P9-APE-150

Human Security and the UN

United Nations Intellectual History Project

Ahead of the Curve? UN Ideas and Global Challenges
  Louis Emmerij, Richard Jolly, and Thomas G. Weiss

Unity and Diversity in Development Ideas: Perspectives from the
UN Regional Commissions
  Edited by Yves Berthelot

Quantifying the World: UN Ideas and Statistics
  Michael Ward

The UN and Global Political Economy: Trade, Finance, and Development
  John Toye and Richard Toye

UN Contributions to Development Thinking and Practice
  Richard Jolly, Louis Emmerij, Dharam Ghai, and Frédéric Lapeyre

UN Voices: The Struggle for Development and Social Justice
  Thomas G. Weiss, Tatiana Carayannis, Louis Emmerij, and Richard Jolly

Women, Development, and the UN: A Sixty-Year Quest for Equality and Justice
  Devaki Jain

Human Security and the UN
A Critical History

S. Neil MacFarlane and
Yuen Foong Khong

Indiana University Press

Bloomington and Indianapolis

10151437

This book is a publication of
Indiana University Press
601 North Morton Street
Bloomington, IN 47404-3797 USA

http://iupress.indiana.edu

Telephone orders   800-842-6796
Fax orders   812-855-7931
Orders by e-mail   iuporder@indiana.edu

The paper used in this publication meets the minimum requirements
of American National Standard for Information Sciences—Permanence
of Paper for Printed Library Materials, ANSI Z39.48-1984.

Manufactured in the United States of America

Library of Congress Cataloging-in-Publication Data
MacFarlane, S. Neil.
  Human security and the UN : a critical history / S. Neil MacFarlane and Yuen Foong
Khong.
       p. cm. — (United Nations intellectual history project)
  Includes bibliographical references and index.
  ISBN 0-253-34714-9 (cloth : alk. paper) — ISBN 0-253-21839-x (pbk. : alk. paper)
1. United Nations. 2. Security, International. 3. Human rights—International
cooperation. 4. National security—International cooperation. 5. Internal security—
International cooperation. 6. Economic security—International cooperation.
7. Security (Psychology)—International cooperation. I. Title: Human security and the
United Nations. II. Khong, Yuen Foong, date III. Title. IV. Series.
  JZ4971.M33 2006
  341.7′2—dc22
                                                                    2005020912

1 2 3 4 5 11 10 09 08 07 06

To Anne and Pheak Son

The sovereignty of the community, the nations, the state . . . makes sense only if it is derived from the one genuine sovereignty—that is, from the sovereignty of the human being.

—Václav Havel

Contents

Foreword

It is surprising that there is no comprehensive history of the United Nations family of organizations. True, a few of the funds and specialized agencies have or are in the process of writing their institutional histories, but this is mostly a recent endeavor. Indeed, it is no more than what should be expected of all public organizations, especially internationally accountable ones, along with enhanced efforts to organize their archives so that independent researchers can also document and analyze dispassionately their efforts, achievements, and shortcomings. All this is an essential part of the record of global governance during the last half century.

Faced with this major omission—which has substantial implications for the academic and policy literatures—we decided to undertake the task of beginning to write an *intellectual* history; that is, a history of the ideas launched or nurtured by the United Nations. Observers should not be put off by what may strike them as a puffed-up billing. The working assumption behind our undertaking is straightforward: ideas and concepts are a main driving force in human progress, and they arguably have been one of the most important contributions of the world organization.

The United Nations Intellectual History Project (UNIHP) was launched in 1999 as an independent research effort based in the Ralph Bunche Institute for International Studies at The Graduate Center of The City University of New York, with a liaison office in Geneva. We are grateful for the enthusiastic backing from the Secretary-General and other staff, as well as from scholars and analysts and governments. We are also extremely appreciative for the generosity of the governments of the Netherlands, the United Kingdom, Sweden, Canada, Norway, Switzerland, and the Republic and Canton of Geneva; the Ford, Rockefeller, and MacArthur Foundations; the Carnegie Corporation of New York; and the Dag Hammarskjöld and UN Foundations. This support ensures total intellectual and financial independence. Details of this and other aspects of the project can be found on our website: www.unhistory.org.

The work of the UN can be divided into two broad categories: economic and social development, on the one hand, and peace and security, on the other. The UNIHP has committed to produce fourteen volumes on major themes in the first arena and a further three volumes if sufficient resources can be mobilized in order to focus on the latter. These volumes will all be published in a series by Indiana University Press. In addition, the project has completed an oral history collection of seventy-three lengthy interviews of persons who have played major roles in launching and nurturing UN ideas—and sometimes in hindering them! Extracts from these interviews appear in *UN Voices: The Struggle for Development and Social Justice*. Authors of the project's various volumes, including this one, have drawn on these interviews to highlight substantive points made in their texts. Full transcripts of the oral histories will also be disseminated in electronic form at the end of the project to facilitate work by other researchers and interested persons worldwide.

There is no single way to organize research, and certainly not for such an ambitious project as this one. This UN history has been structured by topics—ranging from trade and finance to human rights, from transnational corporations to development assistance, from regional perspectives to sustainability. We have selected world-class experts for each topic, and the argument in all of the volumes is the responsibility of the authors whose names appear on the covers. All have been given freedom and responsibility to organize their own digging, analysis, and presentation. Guidance from ourselves as the project directors as well as from peer review groups is provided to ensure accuracy and fairness in depicting where the ideas came from, how they were developed and disseminated within the UN system, and what happened afterward. We trust that future analyses will build upon our series and go beyond. Our intellectual history project is the first, not the last, installment in depicting the history of the UN's contributions to ideas.

Human Security and the UN: A Critical History is the eighth volume in the series—and in some respects one of the most challenging and wide ranging. S. Neil MacFarlane and Yuen Foong Khong bring to bear an enormous range of geographical and substantive expertise. With strong encouragement from us as the project's co-directors and editors of this series, they have sought to probe the history of an idea that is now an integral part of forward-looking international planning. For instance, human security suffuses the December 2004 report from the High-level Panel on Threats, Challenges and Change.[1]

What has happened over time to the notion of state security? "At the start of this new century, the protection of peoples is among the most important issues before us," summarized Lloyd Axworthy, who played a key role in the evolution of the concept as Canada's foreign minister. "Peace and security—

national, regional, and international—are possible only if they are derived from peoples' security."[2]

In fact, since the *Human Development Report 1994* presented a holistic approach to human security linked to human development, there has been a surge in analyses by economists and political scientists such as those MacFarlane and Khong document. There thus are strong reasons to give serious attention to human security today—reasons of theory, policy, practice, and process. Although there is no settled theory of human security, many of the building blocks for a healthy discussion have been laid.

Policy formulation raises the need to analyze relative costs, benefits, and trade-offs. Human security provides a broad analytical framework. To quote one notable and early example of such trade-offs, in 1977 Robert McNamara, then president of the World Bank, declared his conviction that the United States was vastly overspending on military and vastly underspending on non-military means, especially support for international development to strengthen its security.[3]

As regards practice, it seems too late today to put the genie of human security back into the bottle of traditional security analysis. Three widely cited international reports over the last decade have emphasized the need for broader concepts of security and have made recommendations for international action. Building on the work of the Commission on Global Governance and continuing with the Commission on Human Security,[4] the High-level Panel has made a persuasive case for "comprehensive collective security," which identifies six areas of threat where action is needed.

Finally, there are reasons of process. The UN's Security Council has already devoted sessions to HIV/AIDS and Sub-Saharan Africa and to the protection of children and women in conflict. The High-level Panel went farther, proposing that a permanent subcommittee of the Security Council be created, under a new under-secretary-general, to be responsible for peace-building, actions that it made clear would need to encompass economic and social reconstruction as well as political measures.

Of course anyone can insist, as Humpty Dumpty did in *Through the Looking Glass,* that "when I use a word, it means just what I choose it to mean— neither more nor less."[5] MacFarlane and Khong express some doubts about the "analytical traction" of human security for this reason, but to us it holds potential as an appropriate term for issues of comprehensive collective security in the early twenty-first century.

Indeed, what could be more crucial to national security than life itself? Axworthy wanted an answer to that question, especially in light of the furor surrounding another key moment for ideas when Secretary-General Kofi

Annan began speaking passionately about "the sovereignty of individuals."
Within an organization composed of states that take their sovereignty seriously, a controversial set of speeches at the end of the 1990s about humanitarian intervention was definitely ahead of the curve.[6] The moral pleas from the
future Nobel laureate that human rights transcended claims by states were put
forward more delicately later at the Millennium Summit. The reaction was
loud, bitter, and predictable, especially from China, Russia, and much of the
Third World. "Intervention"—for whatever reasons, including humanitarian—
remained taboo.[7]

Rather than going to members of the human security choir, we asked two
experts who are associated with the "bombs and bullets" tradition in international security studies to turn their attention to this essential, but elusive,
notion. We thought that it would be especially important to seek the hard-
headed views from two such analysts about what was good, bad, and indiffer-
ent about the changing and widening idea of human security. Although the
main purpose of the UN was to foster international peace and security, human security differs in two respects from what was foremost in the minds of
the Charter's framers. First, it reorients discourse on security away from the
state and toward individual human beings and their communities. Second, it
broadens the scope of analysis and policy beyond classical military concerns
and engages a much broader range of issues (from the domestic and political
through the environmental and economic to health).

Thus, a human security perspective has arguably been implicit since 1945
in much of the world organization's research, analyses, debates, and operations. However, taking this view too literally would overlook what constitutes
a substantial shift. The disappearance of the constraints of the Cold War and
the growth in civil wars has increased the UN's attention to substate, group,
and individual security concerns. The rise of gendered and human rights discourse has also contributed to the "humanization" of security, as has the evolution of the UN Development Programme's discussion of development and
security. Indeed, it is not surprising that two of our oral history interviewees,
Sadako Ogata and Amartya Sen, were co-chairs of the Commission on Human Security. Their 2003 report, *Human Security Now,* tries to place these
two notions—ensuring life as well as its minimal quality—side by side.

In this "critical history" of the idea, MacFarlane and Khong argue that the
discourse on human security has two dimensions: questioning the traditional
focus on the state in the security studies literature and focusing on the threats
to individual human beings; and widening the discussion of "threat" beyond
violence and toward economic, environmental, and other dangers. Regarding
the former, the authors contend that "the ultimate referent of security has to

be the individual," but with respect to the latter they argue that "[t]he over-riding problem is conceptual overstretch, i.e., the concept has been stretched to cover almost every imaginable malady affecting human beings; as such, it has lost much of its analytical traction."

This is bound to raise hackles with other analysts who are far more enthu-siastic about the policy relevance of the idea. For instance, in a set of essays in 2004 on the topic in *Security Dialogue*, a member of this project's Interna-tional Advisory Council, United Nations University vice-rector Ramesh Thakur, praised the multidimensional quality of human security and recom-mended that "realists . . . get real." Don Hubert, from Foreign Affairs Canada, who worked with former foreign minister Lloyd Axworthy in making his gov-ernment a champion of the concept, scratched his head and wondered about the value of analytical hair-splitting in light of human security's demonstrated policy relevance for banning landmines and establishing the International Criminal Court: "One might have thought that it was only French philoso-phers who rejected concepts that 'worked in practice, but not in theory.'"[8]

We are convinced that the UN story deserves to be better documented if it is to be better understood and appreciated. *Human Security and the UN* makes a significant contribution. As Secretary-General Kofi Annan wrote in the "Fore-word" to *Ahead of the Curve? UN Ideas and Global Challenges:* "With the pub-lication of this first volume in the United Nations Intellectual History Project, a significant lacuna in twentieth-century scholarship and international rela-tions begins to be filled."[9] This present volume is yet another step in closing the gap in the historical record.

We hope that readers will enjoy this account, at once a journey through time and ideas. As their subtitle promises, this is, indeed, *A Critical History*. As always, we welcome comments from our readers.

Louis Emmerij
Richard Jolly
Thomas G. Weiss
New York
February 2005

Acknowledgments

Our research and writing on the United Nations and human security have been greatly aided by friends, colleagues, and students who were always willing to engage our ideas in formation and who were unstinting in sharing their own ideas with us. In particular, we would like to thank the following individuals for giving us the benefit of their expertise: David Angell (Security Council dynamics); Lloyd Axworthy (Canada and human security); Mats Berdal (humanitarian intervention and evolving Security Council perspectives); Alexei Bogaturov (Russian perspectives); Jeff Crisp (the development of and problems with the refugee regime and perspectives of the UN High Commissioner for Refugees on human security); Shigeru Endo (Japanese perspectives on human security); Patricia Fortier and Jill Sinclair (Canadian perspectives on human security); Paul Heinbecker (the Security Council at the turn of the millennium); Don Hubert (Canadian perspectives and land mines); John Ikenberry (U.S. perspectives, or lack of the same, on human security); Tatiana Carayannis (Africa, children, and women); Nico Krisch (refining our notion of human security); Andy Knight (protection of children); Andy Mack (operationalizing human security); David Malone (perspectives on the Security Council); Larry Minear (humanitarian intervention); and Carolin Thielking (the evolving literature on human security).

We also want to express our heartfelt thanks to three very special groups of individuals. First and foremost, Tom Weiss, who put his faith in us and who was supremely patient and gentle even as we missed deadline after deadline. If we took longer than expected, it was in part because of the rigorous quality control that Tom and his superb team at the Ralph Bunche Institute exercised at each stage in the manuscript's preparation. Tom, Tatiana Carayannis, and the groups he assembled gave us excellent feedback; time and again, we found that we had to go back to the libraries or archives or reformulate our arguments. One of those groups, consisting of Richard Jolly, Rama Mani, Keith Krause, and Yves Berthelot, participated in the midterm review, and their feedback at that early stage was important and helpful. Finally, a third group, consisting of Louis Emmerij, Richard Jolly, Makoto Taniguchi, Ramesh Thakur, and Ann Tickner, read a first draft of the manuscript and showered us with generous praise as well as trenchant criticisms. Their detailed written comments encouraged us and gave us an opportunity to sharpen our arguments. Without the indulgence of the individuals in these three groups, this would have been a poorer book.

Colleagues at the University of Oxford—St. Anne's College, Nuffield College, and the Department of Politics and International Relations—have not only tolerated many iterations of our work in progress in various seminars and over countless teas or beers but have also responded with helpful comments and criticisms. Rosemary Foot (human rights), Andrew Hurrell (the unique logic of security threats), Adam Roberts (implications of human security for state sovereignty), Jennifer Welsh (historical and ethical aspects of humanitarian intervention), and Jonathan Wright (Germany) are reasons why we feel fortunate to be working in Oxford.

Successive cohorts of graduate students in Oxford's international relations program signed on as our research assistants, and without their well-honed research skills, we would have made more errors and missed more deadlines. We wish to thank Laura James, Adam Humphreys, John Lee, Jochen Prantl, Patty Chang, Taiye Tuankli-Worsonu, Pierre Gemson, Alexander Bristow, and Krishnati Vignarajah for their contributions.

The Geneva Centre for Security Policy (where Neil directed the Programme on New Security Issues) and Singapore's Institute of Defence and Strategic Studies (where Yuen is a senior research adviser) have also been most supportive of our work and we would like, in particular, to thank Barry Desker, Amitav Acharya, and Mely Caballero-Anthony.

With so much pre-publication help and advice from colleagues and friends, any remaining errors must be the responsibility of the authors.

For the members of our families who have put up with our unending disappearances into the office or study in the last few years, we say: here is proof that we were doing more than listening to Mahler (Neil) or Norah Jones (Yuen)! We dedicate this book to them.

Abbreviations

AAF	Army Air Forces
AIDS	acquired immune deficiency syndrome
ASEAN	Association of Southeast Asian Nations
AU	African Union
CCCW	Convention on Certain Conventional Weapons
CD	Conference on Disarmament
CHS	Commission on Human Security
CIA	Central Intelligence Agency
CoE	Council of Europe
CNN	Cable News Network
CSCE	Conference for Security and Cooperation in Europe
CSSDCA	Conference on Security, Stability, Development and Cooperation in Africa
CSW	Commission on the Status of Women
DDR	disarmament, demobilization, and reintegration
DPKO	Department of Peacekeeping Operations
DRC	Democratic Republic of Congo
ECOSOC	Economic and Social Council
EU	European Union
G-8	Group of 8
GDP	gross domestic product
GNP	gross national product
HDI	Human Development Index

HDR	Human Development Report
HIV	human immunodeficiency virus
HLP	High-level Panel on Threats, Challenges and Change
ICBL	International Campaign to Ban Landmines
ICBM	intercontinental ballistic missile
ICC	International Criminal Court
ICISS	International Commission on Intervention and State Sovereignty
ICJ	International Court of Justice
ICRC	International Committee of the Red Cross
ICTR	International Criminal Tribunal for Rwanda
ICTY	International Criminal Tribunal for Yugoslavia
IDP	internally displaced person
IFI	international financial institution
IGCR	Inter-Governmental Committee on Refugees
ILO	International Labour Organization
IRO	International Refugee Organization
MAD	mutual assured destruction
MONUC	Mission des Nations Unies au Congo (UN Mission in the Democratic Republic of Congo)
NAM	Non-Aligned Movement
NATO	North Atlantic Treaty Organization
NGO	nongovernmental organization
OAS	Organization of American States
OAU	Organization of African Unity
OECD	Organisation for Economic Co-operation and Development
OPEC	Organization of Petroleum Exporting Countries
OSCE	Organization for Security and Co-operation in Europe
P-5	permanent five
PrepCom	Preparatory Committee

RAF	Royal Air Force
SADC	Southern African Development Community
SALT	Strategic Arms Limitation Talks
SARS	severe acute respiratory syndrome
SIDA	Swedish International Development Cooperation Agency
UDHR	Universal Declaration of Human Rights
UNAMIR	UN Assistance Mission for Rwanda
UNCHR	UN Commission on Human Rights
UNDP	UN Development Programme
UNFICYP	UN Peacekeeping Force in Cyprus
UNHCHR	UN High Commissioner for Human Rights
UNHCR	UN High Commissioner for Refugees
UNICEF	UN Children's Fund
UNIDIR	UN Institute for Disarmament Research
UNIFEM	UN Development Fund for Women
UNIHP	UN Intellectual History Project
UNITAF	Unified Task Force
UNOSOM	UN Operation in Somalia
UNPROFOR	UN Protection Force
UNRRA	UN Relief and Rehabilitation Administration
USAID	U.S. Agency for International Development
WEU	Western European Union
WMD	weapons of mass destruction

Human Security and the UN

Introduction

- **Questions Addressed**
- **The Argument**
- **Defining Human Security**
- **The Structure of the Book**

> The state remains the fundamental purveyor of security. Yet it often fails to fulfil its security obligations. . . . That is why attention must now shift from the security of the state to the security of the people—to human security.
> —Commission on Human Security, 2003[1]

For much of the twentieth century, security was considered to be a concern of states. As former UN High Commissioner for Refugees Sadako Ogata put it, "Traditionally, security threats were assumed to emanate from external sources. Security issues were therefore examined in the context of 'state security,' i.e., the protection of the state, its boundaries, people, institutions and values from external attacks."[2] Security policy focused on the effort to sustain and promote the core values of states in their relations one with another. These core values were taken to be sovereignty and territoriality. The principal instrument of states in their quest for security was considered to be the military.

During the twentieth century, and particularly in its last twenty years, the meaning and content of security have been increasingly contested. The focus of this contestation has been the apparently straightforward question: "What is it that needs to be secured (both intellectually and practically) within the conventions of security studies?"[3] The traditional focus on the state has not disappeared. However, the discussion of security has expanded horizontally beyond military issues to take into account others, such as the economy, the environment, health, gender, and culture, in the context of an expansion of core values to include welfare and identity. It has also expanded vertically, questioning the rationale for exclusive focus on the state and suggesting that security might have other referent subjects. This latter expansion was both upward to encompass regional and global identities and downward to society and to distinct groups within it and, ultimately, to the individual human being.[4]

This book addresses one dimension of this expansion of discourse—the emergence of the concept of "human security," which one statesman suggested "has become a central organizing principle of international relations and a major catalyst for finding a new approach to conducting diplomacy."[5] The notion of human security is based on the premise that the individual human being is the only irreducible focus for discourse on security. The claims of all other referents (the group, the community, the state, the region, and the globe) derive from the sovereignty of the human individual and the individual's right to dignity in her or his life. In ethical terms, the security claims of other referents, including the state, draw whatever value they have from the claim that they address the needs and aspirations of the individuals who make them up.

In short, human security is distinct in its focus on the human individual as the principal referent of security. Many proponents of human security would go further to argue that it is also distinct in its recognition that the security needs of individuals go beyond physical survival in the face of violence to access to the basic necessities of life and to the establishment of the basic rights that permit people to lead lives in dignity.

Questions Addressed

This book is one part of a series of works commissioned by the United Nations Intellectual History Project. As explained in the initial volume of the series,[6] the fundamental purpose of this project is to examine the way the United Nations and its agencies have influenced how policymakers and others think about problems in international relations. In this context, we assess:

- The influence of the UN on the development of cognitive and normative frameworks pertaining to security
- The extent to which the UN's organs and agencies themselves initiated the reconstruction of understandings of security
- The extent to which UN bodies provided a forum where ideas regarding human security were disseminated by others
- The contribution of the UN and its agencies to the translation of ideas regarding human security from theory into practice

We agree with the project organizers that ideas have tended to be underemphasized in the academic study of international relations.[7] We take it as given that interpretive and normative frameworks do influence how policymakers and publics perceive and react to their environment.

Ahead of the Curve? suggested that the generation of ideas about human reality has been an important element of the UN's role in international politics. The authors also suggested that this role has been more successful in the economic and social areas than it has been in the "political and peacekeeping arenas."[8] This volume is distinct from others in the series in that it explicitly tackles the latter arenas.[9]

Although the focus of this book is on the UN's role, that role cannot be assessed in isolation from the broader historical and contemporary discussion of security. UN discussions of security are deeply rooted historically. The UN was not the only, nor necessarily the most significant, entity involved in reconceptualizing security at the end of the twentieth century. Assessment of the impact of the UN requires setting the organization's role against other significant potential elements of an explanation of where "new thinking" about security came from. One source is the global heritage of thought about the individual and his or her rights and security in the face of the state and organized violence. Others include particularly proactive states and regional organizations that may have pushed the envelope at the UN and in international relations more broadly. Nongovernmental organizations (NGOs) and the academic security studies communities are other possibilities. And, of course, all of these actors were reacting to change in the material and historical environment. Changing ideas, to the extent that they are meaningful, are rooted in changing realities.

The emphasis of the UNIHP is on the emergence of bold and unconventional ideas that change in fundamental ways how we think about human activity. "Human security" fits well in this framework. At the time of its emergence in the early 1990s, it certainly challenged conventional wisdom. Many would argue that it constitutes a fundamental revision of the way in which we look at the problem of security.

In examining the concept of human security, we address several questions. To what extent is the concept of human security rooted in earlier understandings of security? Is it a new understanding or a rediscovery and rearticulation of older ideas? How did the nation-state come to dominate discourse on security? What factors in the international system and within societies contributed to the erosion of the dominance of the state in discourse on security? This corresponds to the second concern of the UNIHP: "whether and how particular global occurrences have affected the development of new thinking."[10] Alternative sources of intellectual evolution include scholars and other opinion-formers operating nationally or in transnational epistemic communities,[11] state policy preferences, and the preoccupations of particular leaders. To what extent, and how, has the questioning of conventional understandings of security produced a redefinition of that concept that focuses on the individual and, and this is crucial, what role did the institutions of the United Nations play in this evolution of thought? Here we examine not only the central organs (the Security Council, the General Assembly, and the Secretariat) but also key specialized and associated agencies that are active in areas related to human security—notably the United Nations High Commissioner for Refugees (UNHCR) and the United Nations Development Programme (UNDP),[12] conferences organized and sponsored by the UN, and commissions established at the request of the Secretary-General.

To what extent has this apparent change in the way we think about security been embedded in the practice of international institutions and states and what role have the institutions of the United Nations played in this embedding? After all, in the current international system, the success or failure of UN revisionist thinking "depends on government perceptions of *raisons d'état* and the accompanying political will or lack thereof."[13] If one accepts that prevailing discourse both guides and constrains action, then the influence of ideas on practice may occur at the most basic level through the alteration of international public policy discourse. Other possible influences include the possibility that "ideas can provide a tactical guide to policy and action when norms conflict." This aspect of the question appears particularly significant in the case of human security: questions of state sovereignty have conflicted with numerous human rights norms, not least in the doctrine of military necessity in war but more obviously in the proscription of genocide and ethnic cleansing. The possibility that ideas may serve as a basis for the emergence of "new coalitions of political and institutional forces" also seems promising, given the emergence of the land mines coalition and the Human Security Network in the mid- and late 1990s. The evolution of attention to women and children in conflict and the broadening set of actors focusing on the problem of small arms suggest that human security may also be an apt illustration of another way in which new ideas influence practice: the setting of future agendas.[14]

And finally, given that this is a critical historical account, what are the benefits and costs of various approaches to redefining security along human lines and the various interpretations (broad versus narrow) of human security? Many would argue, for example, that despite the shortcomings of the state in addressing human security in the twentieth century, it remains the only structure that can credibly claim to be the basis for meeting the security needs of the individual.[15] If that is so, then one might be wary of reconceptualizing security and sovereignty in such a way as to prevent the state from doing this job, particularly since no other credible institutional alternative for addressing the protection of human beings appears to be emerging. Indeed, some might see "human security" not so much as a UN "idea" but as a "global challenge"; that is, a threat to a global political structure centered on sovereign states that in some respects, and recognizing its egregious failures in particular instances, has served humanity reasonably well.[16]

The Argument

> On ne peut saisir véritablement le sens et la portée d'une règle si l'on méconnait le contexte dans lequel elle a pris naissance et celui dans lequel elle produit ses effets.   —François Bugnion, 1986[17]

We start from the assumption that the behavior of states and of organizations of states—like the behavior of other human collectivities—is informed by ideas.[18] Policymakers interpret the world around them and the problems it generates in terms of cognitive constructs. These constructs allow them to separate data that are important from data that can be ignored and allow them to prioritize among significant bodies of information and focus on those deemed most important. These structures are constructed in particular social contexts. They supply the parameters within which debate on action occurs and beyond which it generally does not. Cognitive constructs may in turn be strongly informed by normative assumptions or logics of appropriate behavior. They may be accompanied by specific value preferences (what is right and what is wrong), which again are the product of shared historical experience and interpretation of that experience. In other words, behavioral outcomes are not merely the product of external stimuli. They also reflect subjectivity— how these stimuli are interpreted, what significance is attributed to them, and what might be seen to be an appropriate response to them.

Our colleagues raised in this context the question of whether the social context produces ideas or ideas shape the social context.[19] We agree with them that the relationship between the two is dialectical: the context generates the problems that evoke reflection, but the policies produced by that process of reflection and contestation in turn shape the social reality that theory claims to describe and explain.

The conceptualization of security (itself an important determinant of practice) has been profoundly influenced by the shifting historical context of international relations. The focus of security on the state is characteristic of the Westphalian system. It reflects specific problems faced by individuals (including individual sovereigns) at the time that system emerged in seventeenth-century

Europe. The consolidation of the state as the primary actor in international politics in the eighteenth and nineteenth centuries was accompanied by a gradual monopolization of security by the state. This was complemented, primarily in Europe, by the rise of nationalism as an understanding of community identity that often merged the state and its sovereignty with the national group and which, to a large extent, subsumed individual identity within that group. In international law, it was paralleled by the transition from natural law to positivist approaches. According to secular absolutist and constitutionalist theory, in any event, the state's ethical claim to primacy in security rested on a notional bargain whereby individuals traded their individual sovereignty for protection against both domestic and international anarchy. Since the state was the answer to individual security dilemmas, the individual accepted an obligation to contribute to the state's security and not to challenge the state in its quest to maximize a value that served individual and collective interest.

In the European-centered international system of the eighteenth and nineteenth centuries, the state's claim that its security concerns were paramount relative to those of its population was plausible. The states in the system were, on the whole, capable of providing internal order and preserving external sovereignty at a cost by and large deemed acceptable by the societies they governed. However, numerous processes in the late nineteenth and early twentieth centuries drew into question the state's capacity to sustain its side of the bargain. First, for much of the eighteenth century, war had been an elite occupation that involved small armies and had few direct effects on the population as a whole.[20] The emergence of mass conscription (first in France during the wars of the French Revolution) greatly increased the proportion of the population at risk in war. The emergence of guerrilla war in Spain in the early nineteenth century had a similar effect by blurring the distinction between civilian and soldier upon which the principle of discrimination was based.[21] What had been an elite and professional pastime became a mass affair.

Second, the industrial revolution dramatically changed the conduct of war and casualties within it. Modern production techniques enabled large numbers of men to be armed at reasonable cost. Modern transportation technologies facilitated their rapid deployment. Change in communications technologies (e.g., the field telegraph) greatly enhanced the capacity of commanders to control and maneuver larger groups of soldiers across large spaces. All of these developments entailed putting far larger numbers of human beings at risk in battle. Dramatic improvement in accuracy and rapidity of fire ensured that larger numbers of those exposed to combat became casualties. The casualty rates of the American Civil War and World War I in particular suggested that the human costs of maintaining state security in a changed technological environment had increased dramatically.[22] States effectively had to risk killing large numbers of their own populations in order to protect them.

In the interwar period, the emergence of strategic airpower made it possible to target concentrations of civilians well behind the front lines in war. Accompanying doctrine emphasized the potential impact of such attacks on the morale of the adversary, providing a strategic justification for the deliberate assault on noncombatants that occurred during World War II. This evolution culminated in the emergence of nuclear weapons. No state could protect its citizens from the possibility of mass extermination. Indeed, for the superpowers at least, "security" was based on the deterrence generated by planning for the mutual destruction of civilian populations and infrastructure.

The third issue impinging on the credibility of the state's claim to primacy in security arose from the killing by states of their own citizens and subjects.[23] As Kal Holsti put it: "Most of the mass killings of [the twentieth] century have been organised by states against their own citizens."[24] In this litany of brutality, the Holocaust played a particularly significant role; the deliberate effort to exterminate Europe's Jewish population stimulated subsequent efforts to embed fundamental human rights in international law. If the priority accorded to the state's security is based on a notional bargain whereby in return for the citizen's loyalty, the state undertakes to provide protection, then the phenomenon of state murder raises profound questions about the preferential treatment of the state's claims to security.

Decolonization also had an impact on the position of the state in security studies. As already noted, norms of national security arose in a system by and large composed of effective states capable of delivering normally expected services, including the protection of their citizens. With decolonization and the rapid expansion of international society, large numbers of new states emerged in the South. Although some (e.g., India and Singapore) rapidly demonstrated the traditional attributes of internal sovereignty, many had insufficient capacity to assert authority over their territories. Weak states were frequently captured by elites who used the state's resources in order to enrich themselves at the expense of the security and well-being of their citizens. These elites were protected from external interference by principles of nonintervention.[25] The effect was that the justification for the priority accorded to national security was further eroded.

The collapse of the Soviet Union and the end of strategic competition between the superpowers played their roles as well. During the Cold War, each superpower posed a profound threat to the survival of its adversary and its allies. The core relationship in international politics was confrontational and highly militarized. With the abortive reform and subsequent collapse of the USSR and the profound weakening of its successor state, the Russian Federation, such concerns receded into the background, leaving room for the articulation of alternative non-state-based understandings of security.

This rearticulation was also encouraged by increasing awareness of processes grouped under the rubric of globalization.[26] These also had an impact on the contract metaphor that accorded a special place to states in the consideration of security. In the first place, states are increasingly vulnerable to policies and processes that take place in other states. In such an environment, it is more difficult for states acting on their own to sustain the security of their citizens. This is particularly clear in the area of the environment. Deforestation in one state, for example, can affect water flows and climate in another.[27] In the area of health, the emergence of epidemic disease in one place can—via modern transportation systems—result in rapid global spread, as was suggested by the severe acute respiratory syndrome (SARS) epidemic of 2003.[28] More broadly, the deterritorialization of economic and cultural transactions has had significant impacts on the autonomy of many states in international society. The reduction in state autonomy in turn affects state capacity to address the aspirations of their citizens to security. Moreover, intrinsic to globalization is the expansion of categories of actors beyond the state to international firms and nongovernmental organizations, for example. To the extent that the emergence of a plurality of actors challenged the Westphalian primacy of the state in international relations, questions were raised about the statecentricity of the key concepts of international relations, among them security.

Finally, a number of aspects of the post–Cold War security environment highlighted the human impact of war in ways that encouraged the development of the concept of human security.[29] The proportion of civilian casualties in war (relative to combatant casualties) has risen continually through the twentieth century to a stage where the casualty rate of eight military personnel to one civilian that characterized the early twentieth century has been reversed. This has much to do with the increasing lethality of weapons and their increasing reach discussed above. But in the post–Cold War era, it also reflected the rapid proliferation of small arms, the growing salience of civil war, and the significance of ethnicity and identity in these wars. People were targeted for removal, torture, rape, and/or death because of who they were rather than what they did.

In addition, many of these conflicts occurred in territories with weak or collapsing state structures that were unable to cope with the effects of war on civilian populations. The combined effect was the radical increase in starvation, disease-related death, and mass displacement[30] that produced the term "complex emergency."[31] The development of more efficient means of transmission of information during the same period ensured that the suffering of these people was widely viewed, at least in the developed world.[32] Mass publics in the North were exposed to the profound suffering of individuals in zones of conflict. This greater awareness created pressure on governments to take the human security of victims of conflict into account in policy responses to threats to international peace and security.

The contextual factors of the seventeenth through the nineteenth centuries contributed strongly to the crystallization of the idea of national or state security. Equally, the evolving historical context of the twentieth century favored movement away from preoccupation with the state's security. One direction of this movement was upward, toward regional and global identities and the institutions that reflected these emerging identities. The other, and more significant from the perspective of this study, was downward (and backward) toward a refocusing on the security needs and aspirations of human beings.

At the core of this book is the question of how the impact of these changing contextual factors was translated into change in thinking about security and the role of the United Nations therein. We argue that the role of the UN was significant in this ideational change, although hardly determining. In the first place, as is clear in Chapters 4 through 6, the United Nations served as an incubator of key aspects of human security thinking. For example, the UNDP's Human Development Report Office was critical in initiating and elaborating discussion of the idea of human security. Second, UN organs served as a forum where changing understandings of security could be articulated by states and, with the passage of time, by nonstate actors as well. The evolving discussion of human rights in the UN system, for example, was significant in the questioning of the primacy of the state. The Security Council played an increasingly important role in this regard in the 1990s.

Third, the UN was instrumental in embedding the concept of human security in at least two respects. UN organs used their authority to define new norms regarding, for example, sovereignty and state responsibility. Many UN personnel (e.g., in the UNDP and the UNHCR) participated in epistemic networks that reconsidered the meaning of security and spread more human understandings of security in national bureaucracies.[33] Parts of the UN actively promoted human security through their publications and in their interactions with states.[34] The Secretary-General played an extremely important role in this regard, especially with regard to the protection of civilians and the notion of humanitarian intervention. In some instances (e.g., Canada, Japan, and Norway), states took up the concept as a useful conceptual focal point for their engagement in development and peacebuilding activities. In turn, these states' consideration of the concept and efforts to flesh it out in policy terms stimulated further evolution of the concept itself.[35] Finally, in their field programs, many UN agencies have been active in implementing the concept of human security.

In functional terms, we see in the UN's activities in the area of human security a good example of the bifurcated quality of the institution. On the one hand, it is an organization of states and serves as a vessel within which states can search for consensus and legitimate their policy preferences. On the other hand, it is a bureaucracy (or set of bureaucracies) with its own corporate personality, preferences, and resources for the promotion of ideas and for their implementation in the activities of agencies in the field.

Perhaps the real measure of the ideational impact of the United Nations in the field of security and, more specifically, its efforts to humanize security lies in the degree to which member states and other international actors have accepted the concept and adjusted their policy accordingly. Here the record is mixed. The term has been accepted only to a limited extent. The United Nations has not produced a uniform definition.[36] Yet the reports of several major UN-related commissions (the International Commission on Intervention and State Sovereignty [ICISS], the Commission on Human Security [CHS], and the High-level Panel on Threats, Challenges and Change [HLP]) take the concept to be central to the understanding of security issues in the contemporary world. Some states such as Canada, Japan, Norway, and Switzerland have embraced the concept and have used it in decisions about allocation of resources; many others have not. Still others actively resist the replacement or supplementing of state security by human security, since they perceive such a replacement to be a potential challenge to state prerogatives. The United States, Russia, and China appear to fall into this category, as do many countries in the South. It is not surprising in this context that no Security Council resolution has used the term human security. Some earlier enthusiasts among international organizations (e.g., the UNHCR) appear to have backed away from the term.[37] Others (e.g., the United Nations Children's Fund [UNICEF]) appear to ignore the phrase human security completely.

This said, it is perhaps more fruitful to focus on content rather than terminology. It has become increasingly accepted that the security claims of individuals are not necessarily subordinate to those of states. Many states and international organizations have accepted the notion that the security of human beings living within sovereign states is a legitimate international concern. As we shall see, this notion long predates the formation of the United

Nations. It has been present in the UN system in one form or another since its creation in 1945. The human rights aspects of this notion developed substantially, if haltingly, during and despite the Cold War. It became an increasingly important element of both UN and state practice after the Cold War. There is little reason to believe that it will be a victim of the return of "hard" security issues after 9/11 and the U.S.-led invasion of Iraq. It is equally clear that the United Nations has served as a focal point for, and promoter of, this questioning of the primacy of state security. The High-level Panel on Threats, Challenges and Change is perhaps the best example here in its effort to balance the security needs of states with those of individuals and to balance traditional (what some would call "hard") security issues with nontraditional security content (human rights and development).[38]

A similar evolution is evident in the consideration of development and its relationship to security. The notion that what counts in development is not so much national aggregates but individual quality of life and the capacity of individuals and communities to exercise a degree of control over their lives has also become increasingly accepted. These concerns have spread haltingly from agencies such as the UNDP and UNICEF to the international financial institutions (IFIs). The current World Bank preoccupation with poverty reduction is a good example. The 1990s witnessed a sustained effort to integrate economic and development issues into discourse on security. Again, UN agencies (e.g., the UNDP) played a major role in this process.

Defining Human Security

> Most people instinctively understand what security means. It means safety from the constant threats of hunger, disease, crime and repression. It also means protection from sudden and hurtful disruption in the pattern of our daily lives—whether in our homes, in our jobs, in our communities or in our environment.   —UNDP, 1994[39]

> In essence, human security means safety for people from both violent and non-violent threats. It is a condition or state of being characterized by freedom from pervasive threats to people's rights, their safety, or even their lives. From a foreign policy perspective, human security is perhaps best understood as a shift in perspective or orientation. It is an alternative way of seeing the world, taking people as its point of reference, rather than focusing exclusively on the security of territory or governments.
> —Commission on Human Security, 2003[40]

Before going further, it is worthwhile to consider the definitions of key terms of analysis in the book. What is security? Barry Buzan once noted that although the concept was widely used in the analysis of foreign policy and international relations, the literature on the concept was "unbalanced." There was a substantial empirical literature dealing with concrete practical problems. However, a parallel conceptual literature was largely absent.[41]

Dispute has persisted in the literature over most key elements of the concept. First, whose security are we talking about? As already noted, for much of the modern period, the state has been the principal, if not the sole, referent of security. Yet it is not immediately clear why that should be so, and much of the more recent literature on security contests this focus. Alternative candidates include the individual, the group (class or ethnic), the region, the international system (as in "threats to international peace and security"), and the globe. Moreover, many have argued that the exclusive focus on the state has intensified the security dilemmas that characterize world politics.[42]

Beyond this, there was, and is, considerable dispute over the substantive content of security. Most would agree that military affairs are intrinsically linked to the notion of security. However, there is good reason to argue that economics are central to security even as traditionally conceived, since the ability to generate and sustain military power depends on the economic capacity of the unit attempting to do so. Moreover, if what is being secured is the welfare of a community, then economic threats are potentially as significant as military ones. The decline of systemic bipolarity and the rise of economic interdependence highlighted this point, leading the Clinton administration in the United States, for example, to experiment with an Economic Security Council to parallel the National Security Council in the early 1990s. The ability of a state to translate power potential into useable military force depends on its capacity to effectively mobilize its population in support of war, suggesting that social and cultural factors fall within the ambit of the concept. And so on.

That a strong and generally accepted theoretical core of the concept of security is absent partly reflects the fact that the concept of security is essentially contested. It has an unavoidable and powerful evaluative content. Security is seen as a legitimate aspiration. Individuals and states—in casting what they do in terms of security—seek to appropriate the positive evaluative content of the term. In this context, Arnold Wolfers pointed out that the notion of security, "while appearing to offer guidance and a basis for broad consensus . . . may be permitting everyone to label whatever policy he favours with an attractive and possibly deceptive name."[43] Invoking the symbol of security in policy advocacy has significant justificatory utility in competition for public resources. Given the plurality of interests within and between societies, there will inevitably be disputes over what security means. The evolution of discourse concerning "human" security is itself an illustration of this essential contestedness. Many proponents of human security seek to privilege the claims

of individuals over those of states in the competition for attention and resources.[44] Those who resist this expansion of the concept frequently do so
because of its potential to erode the primary claim of the state to control over
security policy and undermine the statist conception of sovereignty. One might
also construe the disagreement between development- and rights-based approaches to human security to be an effort to orient public policy and public
resources toward the preferences of the competing advocates.

These ambiguities have impeded rigorous definition of the concept. Nonetheless, in most uses there appears to be a generally accepted central meaning.
Security implies the absence of, or the freedom from, threats to core values.
Core values generally include physical survival, welfare, and identity. When
we speak of human security, we are speaking of the absence of or the threat to
the core values of individual human beings.

A focus on the human being does clarify the referent object of security.
However, this move does not escape ambiguities similar to those discussed
above, since it fails to clearly answer the question of what is being secured. As
Fen Hampson has pointed out, there are numerous alternative conceptions
of the content of the package.[45] One has to do with the protection of rights
grounded in treaties and other instruments of international law. A second is
"freedom from fear," the protection of people from threats of violence. A third
engages the much broader notion of sustainable human development, where
human security involves economic, food, health, environmental, personal,
community, and political security.[46]

A further key problem is who defines the core values of the individual that
are being secured. This issue is presumably unproblematic with regard to
physical survival, but elsewhere there are trade-offs and significant differences
of opinion. The Johannesburg Summit (2002) and earlier conclaves on the
environment and development eloquently displayed significant differences
of view on the relative weight to be placed on sustainability versus development in the concept of sustainable development. These differences were evident not only between northern and southern countries, but also in northern
countries between agencies responsible for development and those responsible for environmental protection.

Discourse on human rights also suggests serious differences of view on the
content of identity to be secured. For example, what a person from one society
views as a violation of basic rights may seem to be a defense of human rights to
a person from a different culture. The seclusion of women in Islamic societies is
a case in point. In cases such as these, what for some might be seen as promotion of human security may be seen by others as a threat to it.[47] A similar problem is encountered in the consideration of identity as a core value. Are we talking

about the identity of the individual per se or about the identity of the individual as member of a distinct group? Preservation of the identity of the group may favor constraint on the individual's expression of her own identity.

In the chapters that follow, we discuss both development- and protection-based understandings of human security. For the moment, we take a deliberately broad approach to definition, considering human security to mean freedom from threat to the core values of human beings, including physical survival, welfare, and identity.

The breadth of the concept creates some difficulty in defining the boundaries of the subject treated here. Concern about basic protection of individuals draws us toward consideration of human rights and, more specifically, the rights of vulnerable groups (e.g., women and children). Successive conferences on women and children and the evolution of Security Council practice have increasingly placed the problems of both groups into the framework of security and protection from violence. Treating welfare as a security issue pushes the analysis toward development and sustainability. There are significant similarities between some approaches to the concept of human security and the development concept of "basic needs,"[48] not only in the sense that security from violence is itself a basic need but also because those adopting a development studies approach to the definition of human security would include the broad array of quality of life issues as aspects of, or prerequisites for, human security. Moreover, there might be reason to address disarmament issues and the role of the United Nations therein in that the proliferation of some kinds of arms (land mines and small arms) presents particular and serious threats to human beings attempting to go about the business of daily life but also because of the purported link between disarmament and development.[49] Several UN conferences (e.g., the World Food Conferences of 1974 and 1996) explicitly associated their objectives with the concept of security. A consideration of identity as an element of what is to be secured inserts the field of culture into the account.

There is a consequent risk of overlap with other studies in the UNIHP relating to rights, gender, and development. This is to some extent unavoidable, but what distinguishes this account is the optic of security. These related issues are treated not so much as self-contained areas of inquiry but in terms of their relation to evolving discourse on security in the United Nations and in international relations more broadly.

The Structure of the Book

The analysis that follows is divided into seven chapters. In the first part of the book, Chapter 1 examines the historical roots of the concept of security and the increasing focus of security discourse on the state and nation at the expense of the individual. It highlights the fact that the tension between the security of the individual and that of the state has been a long-standing artifact of international relations and domestic politics and stresses that the Westphalian privileging of the state is a product of a particular historical context (the consolidation of the nation-state and the ideological hegemony of nationalism) rather than a natural state of affairs. The last sections of the chapter outline the beginnings of the erosion of statecentrism in considerations of security in the period between World Wars I and II. The chapter also considers the roots of the functional broadening of security into the social and economic spheres in the nineteenth and early twentieth centuries. It concludes that many of the conceptual elements of what is now considered to be human security were reasonably well developed, at least in theory, by the end of the 1930s.

The second chapter examines precursors to the concept of human security in the Cold War era. It suggests that despite the limiting effect of the Cold War, much of the normative groundwork for the emergence of a human focus in security studies was laid prior to the 1990s. The development of international humanitarian law laid a strong normative basis for the protection of individuals threatened in or by conflict. In 1977 this was extended specifically to noninternational armed conflict. The Nuremberg process was an important first step in limiting impunity for war crimes and crimes against humanity. The Universal Declaration of Human Rights (UDHR) and the associated covenants furthered the process of establishing the rights of human beings as relevant issues in international relations. The Convention on Refugees and its 1969 protocol clearly established a regime of rights for those displaced across borders and the obligations for states receiving them. The evolution of discourse on basic needs and human development late in the period laid the basis for the economic and development aspects of human security that emerged in the 1990s.

After outlining ideational and normative developments during the Cold War, we step back in Chapter 3 to consider changes in the international system that may have contributed to the erosion of the centrality of the state in the theory and practice of security. The chapter suggests that the focus on the state as principal referent of the concept of security was increasingly challenged by technological, economic, and cultural change in the early and mid-twentieth century. The chapter then considers developments in the academic security studies literature, notably the evolving critique of the statist and military focus of conventional security studies. It chronicles efforts in the academic community to broaden conceptualization of security to take account of the changing context and the challenges it posed to the survival and welfare of human beings and their states.

The second part of the book focuses on the post–Cold War development of thinking about human security and the central role of the United Nations therein. Chapter 4 carries forward the discussion of the refocusing of development studies on human beings. It provides extensive discussion of the emergence of the concept of human development and relates that concept to human security. It then looks at how the long-standing recognition of the relationship between poverty and conflict was reproduced in discussions of the structural causes of conflict in the 1990s. It concludes with an examination of the 2003 report of the Commission on Human Security, which made a strong case for viewing human security as the protection of individuals from the vulnerabilities associated with sudden economic downturns.

The chapter highlights the influence of development economists and UN development agencies, the Secretariat, and the General Assembly in pushing development and sustainability on to the security agenda, in the effort to establish human development as a basic dimension of human security, and to deepen the appreciation of development issues as key aspects of conflict prevention.

In Chapter 5, we shift our attention from the development interpretation of human security to a focus on protection from violence. The chapter chronicles the evolution of Security Council consideration of the meaning of "threats to international peace and security" and their extension of the concept to cover threats to human security within states. It also discusses the insertion of protection into the mandates of UN peacekeeping forces. The chapter demonstrates the central role of the UN (particularly the Security Council) in qualifying the principle of nonintervention, linking it to the responsibility of states to protect their own citizens. It also considers the parallel efforts in regional organizations to address the issue of protection from violence. We argue here that there has been substantial normative change that has enlarged the purview of international organizations to intrude into matters of domestic jurisdiction where states fail to fulfill their responsibilities to protect those resident within their territory. The chapter also examines the emergence of judicial institutions designed to address impunity and the efforts of international society to regulate the proliferation and use of weapons that are particularly threatening to civilians. Chapter 6 goes on to look at normative and practical developments in the protection of particular groups; for example, children, women, and internally displaced persons (IDPs).

In sum, Chapters 4 to 6 identify a striking normative development that may redefine the rights associated with recognition of sovereignty and shows how these norms have been embedded in international institutional and state practice. It highlights the central role of the UN in this process as a generator of ideas, as a forum for advocacy and promotion, as an advocate in its own right, as a legitimizing device for state and regional activities, and as an implementer of new (human) understandings of security. It also underlines the central role of complex coalitions of transnational civil society actors and interested states that are focusing on particular issue areas (e.g., land mines, children in conflict, international criminal law, and international legal institutions) and how these coalitions interact with the United Nations to redefine security.

In Chapter 7 we assess the conceptual and policy payoffs and the pitfalls associated with the idea of human security. We see some positive gains, but we also point to a number of serious problems. We applaud the rebalancing between state and individual as referents of security. However, we judge the move to extend the domain of what counts as security issues beyond protection from violence to be ill advised. Characterizing economic, environmental, health, and other problems as security issues raises four questions. First, does the proposed alternative provide analytical traction? We suggest that it does not. Human development, for example, is a sensible concept in its own right. Conflating it with security produces conceptual confusion. Second, does the ideational change produce greater access to resources? There is to our knowledge no evidence that the rebranding of development as security, the environment as security, or health as security has produced a greater flow of resources toward the address of these extremely important problems. In this respect, such relabeling may produce false hopes. Third, more conventional functional understandings have their own merit. One danger of expanding the security agenda is that more conventional issues related to violence do not enjoy the priority they deserve. Finally, such reclassifications encourage military solutions to social and economic problems. We conclude by offering a more restrictive notion of human security that seeks to avoid these pitfalls.

The conclusion summarizes the principal findings. If one compares the end of the twentieth century with the end of the nineteenth, one sees substantial ideational change that has important implications for the status of individual human beings as subjects of international relations, for the meaning of sovereignty as a constitutive principle of international society and the rights it confers on states, and with regard to the obligations of international society where states fail to meet their obligations to human beings living within their borders. Although the responses to the attacks on the United States in September 2001 have placed pressure on this process of change, there seems little reason to believe that it will be decisively undermined.

The development of the idea of human security is a very broad and multifaceted process. In a volume of this type, it is impossible to do justice to all elements of this process. Inevitably, we have had to select and prioritize. With regard to actors, we do not provide a full analysis of the role of NGOs in the emergence of the idea, since this would merit a separate volume and since the series of which this book is a part focuses on the UN. We acknowledge that this results in a statist and multilateral bias. We do, however, discuss NGO roles where these have impinged most clearly on state and multilateral development of the idea (e.g., the land mines process discussed in Chapter 5). Moreover, we have had to choose among the many functional dimensions of human security. We have focused on the protection of human beings and on sustainable development. This results in what many readers may consider to be inadequate attention to, for example, the environment, health, and crime as human security issues. We recognize these shortcomings and the importance of these issues in further research.

Part I. The Archaeology of Human Security

The first part of this volume highlights the roots of human security as an idea that affected international relations. Although the general preference in this series is to examine ideas from the point that they intersect with the United Nations, in this case we are speaking more of the recovery of very old understandings of security rather than the generation of new ideas. Although the notion that sovereignty was linked to the state's responsibilities to protect those who live within its borders was considered by many to be a significant innovation of the 1990s, in fact it is rooted in the articulation of sovereignty and statehood in the early Westphalian era that was laid aside in the nineteenth and early twentieth centuries and recovered in the post–Cold War era. As we shall see, the United Nations played a considerable role in this recovery. But it was not so obviously the origin of the ideational development in question.

One basic element of the argument put forward in the Introduction was that understandings of security are in important measure a reflection of historical and sociopolitical context. There is little that is objective or natural in hegemonic understandings of security. They mirror the concrete problems people face at particular moments in time, the way they identify themselves, the structures within which people organize their lives or have their lives organized for them, and the perceived interests of those who dominate such structures. Yet hegemonic understandings have almost always been contested to one degree or another by alternative ways of seeing security.

For much of modern history, the hegemonic interpretation of security was statist (with regard to the referent of the concept) and military (with regard to the content of the concept). The security of individual human beings, in contrast, was largely ignored. Nor did threats other than military ones receive much consideration in writing and in policymaking on security, except inasmuch as the issue in question was perceived to be closely related to the accumulation and effectiveness of state power.

Yet Chapter 1 shows that there was a persistent historical tendency to view the purpose of the polity to be the protection and welfare of those individuals subject to it and to question the absolute rights of the state where its actions conflicted with its subjects' interests or core values. The question of whether the individual was obliged to surrender these values where they conflicted with state interests seems to be as old as reflection on relations between state and society. Even theorists of the absolute state accepted that in extreme circumstances, the failure of the state to honor its obligations to individuals relieved the latter of their obligation to obey.

The rise of nationalism and its fusion of state with nation and of nation with individual was contested by theorists and activists who emphasized individual (and group) political, civil, and economic rights. And the claim of states to absolute sovereignty was countered by some who argued that in circumstances where the state could not or would not protect its citizens or particular groups within the citizenry, outside actors had a right, if not a duty, to come to the assistance of victims. Likewise, states frequently recognized constraints on their behavior in war, the purpose of which was to limit the suffering of individuals, both soldiers and civilians. In these respects, Boutros Boutros-Ghali was right to question whether the theory of absolute sovereignty was ever matched by reality.[1] The evolution of social and political thought and practice in the later nineteenth and early twentieth centuries, moreover, brought an increasing appreciation that the obligations of states extended beyond physical protection to the mitigation of economic threats. In other words, even at its apogee, the reification of the state did not go uncontested in theory or in practice.

Chapter 2 addresses the place of individual human beings in international relations and security during the Cold War era. Under this rubric, it engages the UN directly. It demonstrates substantial internationalization of human concerns regarding protection, rights, and development at the normative level. It shows that the United Nations and its agencies played a fundamental ideational role in this process. The chapter also highlights a dramatic gap between this normative development and the practice of states and organizations of states, with the partial exception of European multilateral organizations. In this respect, the chapter highlights the power of sovereign states to resist intrusion into what they deem to be their space.

Chapter 3 provides a transitional contextual analysis. It accounts for the gradual erosion of a purely statist approach to security in view of the decreasing capacity of the state to ensure protection and welfare on its own and in terms of the abuse by states of their own power vis-à-vis their citizens. The basic point here is that although the bargain between states and individuals may have made sense earlier, it was gradually eroded by technological change. The last part of the chapter discusses the consequent problematization of the concept of national security in the academic literature on security, showing how a number of leading specialists in security studies came to question the hegemonic view of security as national and military. This sets the scene for the consideration of the emergence of human security in Part II.

1

The Prehistory of Human Security

- **The State and the Security of the Individual in the Premodern Era**
- **Absolutism and Constitutionalism in the Westphalian System**
- **State and Security in the Age of Nationalism**
- **Qualifications of the Dominance of the State in Security**
- **The Individual and Security between the World Wars**
- **Conclusion**

> Apologists for particular governments and for government in general commonly argue, precisely, that they offer protection from local and external violence. —Charles Tilly, 1985[1]

Ideas about society are the product of problems in social life, and few problems in life are new. Ideas are seldom "born"; they are recovered and modified in new circumstances. The concept of security is no exception.

Conventional analyses of the concept of security emphasize the state as the referent object of security; it is the state that is to be secured. The association of security with the state seemed natural for much of the nineteenth and twentieth centuries and reflected the dominant position of realism in the discipline of international relations.[2] This association is also, in many respects, the target of discourse on human security, an assertion of the rights and needs of the individual independently of, and sometimes in contradistinction to, those of the state.

Given the increasingly contested quality of the tight association between the state and security, it is useful to inquire just where it came from in the first place. Looking at the historical and ideational roots of national security may help us understand why, in the late twentieth century, the concept became increasingly contested and why the primacy of the state in discourse on security came to be challenged by other referent subjects, among them the individual human being.[3]

In taking a deep historical approach, we depart from the pattern in other studies in this series to take up an idea when it intersects with the UN (both as an organization of sovereign states and as a cluster of bureaucracies). The bulk of the analysis in this book focuses on the evolution of the UN's discussion of security. However, for reasons that we hope become clear in what follows, the roots of the emergence of human security lie in the justification of the state and its sovereignty and the manner in which changes in the social context of the late nineteenth and twentieth centuries drew that justification into question.

In addressing these roots, we first examine proto-ideas concerning the state and security in the classical and medieval periods. We then move to an extensive discussion of the normative theories surrounding the emergence of the modern state. This is followed by consideration of the rising role of nationalism and national security in the eighteenth and nineteenth centuries. We conclude with comment on the gradual evolution of norms and practices relevant to human security in the first half of the twentieth century. In this account, we are particularly interested in the views of theorists and statesmen about why the state was formed and what purpose it served and the ways they treated the question of sovereign rights and responsibilities with respect to citizens or subjects. Such indicators are useful in assessing the balance between prerogatives of state and individual security. In addition, we look at how the question of conduct in war (with respect to enemy combatants and civilians) was addressed and the extent to which constraints existed on the use of force that are related to individual security and rights.

In considering the relationship between theories of the state, its formation and consolidation on the one hand and the security needs of individuals on the other, we are not suggesting that the state was the product of a rational process of thought (i.e., that communities that realized a need for protection formed polities in order to achieve this end). Political communities coalesced for various reasons. Their coalescence reflected changing material conditions, power differentials and conflict, and leadership. Nonetheless, because uncoerced compliance is less costly than permanent and ubiquitous coercion, leaders and polities have generally sought to legitimize their positions by referring to normative claims to justify their rule. To the extent that these claims are accepted by the ruled, compliance with the preferences of the rulers is likely to be voluntary. If this quest for legitimacy is to be successful, authorities must make some effort to substantiate these claims. More concretely, leaders may not have formed states in order to provide protection to their citizens, but their provision of that protection promoted in their subjects some sense of obligation to comply with the state's requests and a degree of loyalty to the state and its purposes. This in turn enhanced the power of the state.

Much of the analysis in this chapter focuses on Europe. This is so because the current international system is an outgrowth of norms, institutions, and practices that evolved in Europe and then expanded outward.[4] In addition, the reification of national security is largely of European origin. It is by and large a product of historical and ideational processes that occurred in the European system from the rise of the absolutist state through the Thirty Years War, the Treaty of Westphalia, and the eighteenth-century balance-of-power system to the French Revolution and the rise of nationalism in the late eighteenth and nineteenth centuries. This said, insight on these subjects can also be gleaned from non-European thinkers from Kautilya and Confucius onward.

In examining the historical and normative origins of the concepts of state security and then national security, we acknowledge the risk of projecting contemporary concepts back into historical periods where they did not exist. This is a problem with all three of the constituent terms in play here. Most scholars would accept that the state as we understand it did not emerge until the fifteenth and sixteenth centuries.[5] This is less of a problem for us than it is for theorists of the state. For our purposes, when we discuss the state, we mean hierarchically organized political communities with varying degrees of autonomy and empirical sovereignty. As for the concept of "national," nations, as we understand the term, developed in postmedieval, Enlightenment, and post-Enlightenment Europe. The concept was largely alien to the medieval period,[6] as were the notions of legitimacy based on the concept. Finally, there was little if any use of the term "security" in analysis of "state" practice in the classical and medieval periods. As Emma Rothschild has pointed out, the Latin term *securitas,* from which the modern term is derived, referred to a sense of inner well-being.[7] It was an individual matter and was not used in reference to communities or states. Nor is there any frequent use of the term in reference to the polities of the medieval era. It was only in the Enlightenment that it came to refer to states and the protection of states and individuals from violence.

However, although the terms and concepts with which we discuss security have changed over time, the basic questions are as old as history itself. These concern the balance between the security of the state and that of the individual:

- Why does the state (or polity) exist and to what extent is its existence justified in terms of protection of its people?
- What claims can the state impose on its citizens in its effort to survive, what are the limits on these claims, and in what ways do these claims impinge on the security of individuals?

- Do states have a right or an obligation to interfere in the internal affairs of other states to protect individual subjects of the latter in the face of serious threats to their individual security?
- To what extent is the state's conduct in war constrained by notions about the protection of civilians and the appropriate treatment of enemy combatants?

We suggest that for much of the history of theorizing about the state, the latter has been conceived at least in part as an answer to individual and group security needs. This is generally accompanied by an implicit or explicit obligation of the state to protect its citizens. When the state fails to do so or when it becomes a threat to its own citizens, the state's claim to the loyalty of its population is diminished. To put it another way, the state has often been conceived as an answer to the human need for security, which is primary. Although the state's claim to a privileged position in matters of security grew stronger over time, it was rarely absolute and was generally accompanied by varying degrees of qualification by principles that defended personal space vis-à-vis the political community.

The State and the Security of the Individual in the Premodern Era

"States" and Security in the Classical Era

> For be sure of this: It is the city that protects us all; she bears us through the storm; only when she rides safe and sound can we make loyal friends.
>
> —Creon, in *Antigone*[8]

The emergence of the concept of state security is usually identified with the evolution of the international system from its medieval to its Westphalian variant. There were, however, reasonably clear antecedents to the notion in classical thought (Thucydides, Plato, Aristotle, and, in the later Roman period, Augustine).[9] Attention to these antecedents is useful intrinsically, but it is also useful because of the profound influence of these authors on later writers such as Thomas Aquinas, Jean Bodin, and Thomas Hobbes. Perhaps the clearest antecedent is the work of Thucydides, who was writing about a pluralistic state system in many respects similar to our own.[10]

The notion that the consolidation of the city-state was a precondition of civilized life is clear in his observation that in early Greek history all men carried arms to protect themselves against endemic violence, while later the

Athenians had no need to carry weapons because the power of the polis protected them. Once their basic need for personal security was satisfied, they could turn to more productive and pleasurable pursuits.[11] Or, as Aristotle put it later, the city is "the end and perfection of government: first founded *that we might live* [our emphasis], but continued that we might live happily."[12] It followed that the citizen was obliged to subordinate his ends to those of the polis when the latter was threatened because it was only in the polis that human beings could securely pursue their ends.[13] As Sophocles' character, the Theban king Creon, put it: "Never will I approve of one who breaks and violates the law, or would dictate to those who rule. Lawful authority must be obeyed in all things, great or small, just and unjust alike."[14] There is little indication in Thucydides' work or in that of other classical Greek writers of a belief that the security claims of the individual might trump those of the state where the two diverge.

This said, however, there are faint echoes of concern about the concentration of power in the hands of a sovereign in the work of some Greek authors. Plato, for example, noted that "no soul of man, while young or accountable to no control, will ever be able to bear the burden of supreme social authority without taking the taint of the worst spiritual disease, folly, and so becoming estranged from its dearest intimates."[15] The "self-caused blindness" associated with "irresponsible autocratic sovereignty" would sink the ruler and his community "in depths of ruin."[16] The fate of Creon after he had put his own sovereign authority above the religious beliefs of Antigone is a keen illustration of this understanding of the dangers of excessive concentration of power.

In addition, there was in Greek thought some recognition of the desirability of constraint in the organized use of violence against civilians in war. This view appeared to rest on a rudimentary idea of rights pertaining to the individual. For example, Plato suggested in *The Republic* that the enslavement of Greeks by Greeks should be abolished along with the stripping of corpses on the battlefield and the ravaging of land and the burning of fields in war.[17] Some have suggested that this is an early precursor of what later came to be called *jus in bello*.[18] More to the point here, these principles suggest some sentiment that the property and survival rights of individuals (or at least Greek individuals) were worthy of protection and that states should take this into account in their ways of war.[19]

Various doctrines in Roman law (e.g., *plenitudo potestas* and *princeps legibus solutus*) also tended to concentrate power, authority, and law in the hands of the ruler.[20] Since the state in the person of the ruler was the source of the law, the absolute, divine ruler could not be subject to the law. There was no obvious contestation of the primacy of the state's claims to security and the corresponding obligations of individuals to the state.

The question of individual responsibility to the state also arose in early Christian doctrine in several respects. One concerned the obligation to pay taxes to the Roman government. Here the Gospels are clear in their acceptance of obligation to the state.[21] More broadly, Peter's first epistle is clear in its insistence on Christian submission to the (pagan) state: "Be subject for the Lord's sake to every human institution, whether it be to the emperor as supreme, or to governors as sent by him to punish those who do wrong."[22] Augustine later admonished Christians to remember that they enjoyed human rights and secure possession of property because of the king, suggesting that these benefits implied an obligation to obey the king.[23] It was government that brought order and peace, from which Christians and others benefited.[24] In consequence, obedience to the state was Christian duty.

Given the teaching of the Gospels regarding violence, the issue of military obligation was particularly problematic. Was soldiering and participation in organized violence antithetical to the teachings of the Church? The answer was clearly negative. The Gospels refrain from condemning soldiers. Augustine discusses at length John the Baptist's response to the soldiers who came to be baptized,[25] concluding that "the natural order which seeks the peace of mankind ordains that a monarch should have the power of undertaking war if he thinks it advisable, and that the soldiers should perform their military duties *in behalf of the peace and safety of the community* [our emphasis]" and went on to note the a soldier had a duty to be obedient whether or not the command was "righteous."[26]

On the other hand, there are in Roman law certain principles that suggest an attenuation of the sovereign right of rulers. It was widely accepted that the ruler could not use his office for personal ends through, for instance, the sale of imperial property. Nor could he misuse his authority (the *leges imperii*). The principles of natural law in Justinian's codes bound the ruler to abide by promises and to respect the family (personal space). More important, perhaps, the doctrine of *lex regia* maintained that power derived from the people. In short, there is also in Roman writings evidence of consideration of the attenuation of sovereignty and a degree of obligation on the part of the sovereign toward those whom he ruled. Indeed, there were, at least from a Justinian perspective, justifications for resistance to unjust agents of authority. These principles reflected a strain of natural law thinking that may be traced from Aristotle to Cicero—the notion that "there existed a universal law of nature outside and beyond the *polis*."[27]

Turning to the issue of conduct in war, the Roman landscape is a depressing one; little appears by way of constraint (legal or other) on conduct in war, including with respect to wounded or captured combatants or enemy civilians. Early Christian thought, although focused principally on *jus ad bellum* (the justification of war), does display some concern regarding conduct in war. Augustine's work on the subject is illustrative. He considered the real evil in war to be the "love of violence, revengeful cruelty, [and] fierce and implacable enmity." The implication therein that restraint should be exercised toward the enemy, including civilians, is evident later in the same passage, where he suggests that "even in waging war, cherish the spirit of a peace-maker, that, by conquering those whom you attack, you may lead them back to the advantage of peace. . . . As violence is used towards him who rebels and resists, so mercy is due to the vanquished or the captive."[28]

The theme that order grounded in recognized authority is the precondition for human safety and fulfillment is also encountered outside Europe in the work of Confucius. Confucius developed his view on society and politics during a period of widespread violence associated with the collapse of the Chinese Empire into warring kingdoms. In his view, the fundamental purpose of government was the well-being of the people.[29] His concern with individual security is evident: "How true is the saying that after a state has been ruled for a hundred years by good men it is possible to get the better of cruelty and to do away with killing."[30] The "Rectification of Names" was an effort to restore the order that permitted normal life through a rigid hierarchical demarcation of the population into a ruler, nobles, ministers, and the common people in which members of each retained their status permanently. The existence of rigid hierarchy was accompanied by a strong sense of the ruler's (and others') responsibility. The existence of principles of conduct presumed a law that existed beyond the ruler. Each station carried obligations to others: benevolence, righteousness, humaneness, conscientiousness, altruism.[31] In other words, as in Greek thought, power is to an extent tempered by considerations of propriety, responsibility, and restraint.[32]

The Medieval Era

> For without the youth had found
> the fields were barren empty ground,
> within there was impoverishment;
> he found no matter where he went,
> the streets were empty in the town.
> He saw the houses tumbled down
> Without a man or woman there
> . . .
> The town was wholly desolate.
> —*Perceval, or The Story of the Grail*[33]

The collapse of the Roman Empire in the face of repeated invasions by migratory peoples resulted in a radical decentralization of power through the European system.[34] Transportation systems broke down and the Roman economy collapsed into localized fragments. Since the state as we understand it did not exist during the Dark Ages, the idea of loyalty to the state, or giving the ends of the state a priority greater than that accorded to those of the individual or group, was weak, if it existed at all.[35]

Secular scholarship regarding politics, as regarding much else, had been eradicated in the western world. What reflection there was proceeded in monastic communities and focused little on the day-to-day problems of the secular world. The Augustinian view that the world was one of violence and suffering because of man's fall from grace was common. Salvation was a matter for the next world, not this one.[36] Augustine's thought concerning authority in this world also enjoyed influence. Since government was a manifestation of the mercy of God in the face of the evil of human nature, human beings had an unqualified obligation to obey the sovereign. There was little effort to justify the claim of the sovereign to ultimate power on the basis of services (e.g., protection) provided to the people. Given divine sanction, there was little need to do so. This suggests little concern with the larger issues of individual security. However, as in the Roman period, there is considerable evidence in early Christian thought of a notion that the authoritative figures (the pope in spiritual matters and the emperor and his vassals in secular ones) were limited by obligations to their communities and the individuals that constituted them. These responsibilities derived from religious obligation.

It should be stressed that the European experience of collapse and anarchy was not typical of the larger history of the period. Perhaps the most significant development outside Europe, and one which had great implications for Europe itself, was the rise of Islam. Early Islamic thought bears in important ways on the themes covered in this chapter. Like their Christian counterparts, Islamic writers held that political leadership enjoyed divine sanction. In this respect, rule did not need to be justified in terms of benefits (such as protection) enjoyed by subjects of the polity. This had implications for the capacity of the individual to contest the actions of the ruler: "Hearing and obeying are the duty of a Muslim both regarding what he likes and what he dislikes, as long as he is not commanded to perform an act of disobedience to God, in which case he must neither hear nor obey."[37]

This did not mean that the caliph was unconstrained. The role of the caliph was recognized to be protecting (and expanding) the Islamic state, maintaining the peace within it, and securing the welfare of Muslims. Moreover, as just noted, he could not require a subject to disobey God. The latter stricture would appear to justify resistance to the state and qualification of sovereignty in the event that the sovereign violated the individual's (religiously defined) dictates of conscience. The rise of the *'ulama* created an institutional context for such expression of dissent. The legitimizing role of the *'ulama* served to an extent as a constraint on absolute power.[38]

Later Islamic writers, influenced to some extent by the Greek classics, developed a more rationalistic account of the polity. Ibn Khaldun's account of the reason for states, for example, bears considerable resemblance to that of Aristotle. He noted that aggressiveness is natural in human beings and that something was needed to control this impulse. This need was the basis for royal authority, embodied in a person who could restrain people from attacking one another, thereby making possible the productive activities that distinguished human beings from animals.[39] Khaldun emphasizes that although royal authority is based on power, the power itself is derived from feelings of group solidarity. Group feeling is manifested in virtues such as generosity, forgiveness, tolerance, hospitality, charity, patience, the faithful fulfillment of obligations, fidelity to religious law, and so on.[40] Success breeds decadence. The loss of virtue brings loss of authority. This produces vulnerability and political transformation. The waxing and waning of power and authority is thus an almost natural and inexorable process.

Therefore, the question encountered in later Christian writings—whether people have a right to question the authority of a prince ruling by divine right—does not really arise. Rulers who become decadent lose their divine sanction. Their replacement with others closer to the ideal is consistent with God's desires.

Early Islamic texts also have much to say about war. The Koran is ambiguous about *jus ad bellum*. On the one hand, it cautions against wars of aggression.[41] On the other, it appears to suggest an obligation to subdue non-Muslim communities that refuse to permit Islamic teaching. More important from our perspective, there is in the Koran a sense of limits on appropriate behavior in war, not least in the treatment of prisoners.[42] These are further developed in the first caliph's ten commands, which prohibited the killing of the old, women, and children; the destruction of agricultural property; the molestation of religious communities; and the confiscation of food (except when necessary).[43] In other words, the principle of discrimination in war was present in early Islam.

Returning to Europe, the chaos that followed the collapse of the Roman Empire gradually coalesced into medieval feudalism. The medieval system was characterized by a hierarchy of often overlapping loyalties, duties, and obligations and a considerable diffusion of power. The Church was deemed

universal in the spiritual realm, paralleling the secular structure of the Holy
Roman Empire. The empire, meanwhile, held relatively loose control over its
territories. Its position was increasingly contested by numerous monarchs.
Their position was challenged in turn by much-more-numerous powerful
vassals whose obligations to their suzerain (and vice versa) were often more
formal than real. Territory passed freely from one kingdom or duchy to another through marriage and private war. Conflict was endemic, the security
dilemma ever present. Society itself was highly militarized, and the rudimentary economy of the countryside was organized around maintaining local
military forces.[44] The creation of larger political units was inhibited by the
prevailing military technology in which defensive capabilities dominated offensive ones and by the primitive nature of transportation infrastructure.[45]

The fragmented quality of the system of states in medieval Europe was
accompanied by frequent localized lapses into chaos. Galbert de Bruges's account of the collapse of order after the murder of Charles the Good in Flanders
(1127), for example, recounts a descent into near-universal violence: "Now in
truth the whole land was so torn by dangers, by ravaging, arson, treachery,
and deceit that no honest man could live in security."[46] This instability contributed to considerable ambiguity in thinking about the relationship between
political authority and its subjects as that relationship impinged on security.
On the one hand, canon law embraced the Roman doctrine of *plenitudo
potestas* as a necessary aspect of sustaining a modicum of order and personal
security. The acceptance of "full power" to the sovereign reflected not only
considerations of divine legitimacy but also a sensitivity to the consequences
of challenge to the power of the sovereign. However, the question of who
possessed full power (the pope in spiritual and temporal matters, or the
pope in spiritual and the emperor in temporal matters) remained a matter
of some dispute and was one factor among several that contributed to the
centuries-long struggle for supremacy between papacy and empire between
1076 and 1268.

That the embrace of absolute notions of monarchical sovereignty and power
was incomplete was evident in the work of perhaps the most influential religious thinker of the period, Thomas Aquinas (1225 or 1227–1274). His major
contribution was the recovery of classical work on man and the state into
contemporary thinking about political organization. He differed greatly from
Augustine in his view of human nature.[47] For Augustine, the original sin made
man incorrigible and incapable of rational reflection. For Aquinas, drawing
on the classical natural law tradition mentioned above, the effect of original
sin was mitigated by man's rationality and, consequently, his capacity for improvement. In particular, man's rational capacity made it possible for him to

discern God-given natural law. The purpose of the state and ruler was to establish the good life: conditions in which the individual could improve himself. In this respect, the political community was instrumental "to securing
human goods which are basic (including other forms of community or association, especially domestic and religious associations) and none of which is
in itself specifically political, i.e. concerned with the state."[48] The purview of
the state's authority to regulate human conduct extended only to those actions that affected the public goods that were necessary conditions for the
pursuit of individual fulfillment: "the state's rulers cannot rightly intervene
in private relationships and transactions to secure purposes other than justice and peace."[49]

The existence of natural law implied restraint on the state and on its
authority:

> Underlying all legal arrangements were certain universal ethical and spiritual
> principles to be perceived by reason. What is significant in this early view of
> natural law is that within the reasonable framework of social life, there were
> rules and principles which even rulers had to obey.[50]

Such limitations clearly informed Aquinas's attitude toward tyranny. Because
tyrants governed in their own interest rather than that of the community as a
whole, people were entitled to disobey.[51] This was not just a matter of Roman
and canon law. Customary law also suggested that the monarch was not perceived to be "the" law or to be above the law but was to a degree subject to the
law. It was widely believed during the medieval period that sovereigns had
contractual duties and obligations to those beneath them. Henry Bracton's
discussion of the English Coronation Oath is illustrative. Here the monarch
promised to proceed by law and to limit his actions to his own jurisdiction.[52]

The Magna Carta (1215), meanwhile, made explicit the view that the
monarch's authority was conditional, depending on his or her performance
of defined duties and respect for established rights. The monarch's sovereignty
was attenuated or void if he or (rarely) she did not fulfill those duties. Indeed,
the document makes explicit provision for the right of rebellion in the event
that the monarch or his agents overstepped agreed bounds:

> If we, our chief justice, our officials, or any of our servants offend in any re-
> spect against any man, or transgress any of the articles of the peace or of this
> security, and the offence is made known to four of the said twenty-five barons,
> they shall come to us—or in our absence from the kingdom to the chief justice—
> to declare it and claim immediate redress. If we, or in our absence abroad the
> chief justice, make no redress within forty days, reckoning from the day on
> which the offence was declared to us or to him, the four barons shall refer the

matter to the rest of the twenty-five barons, who may distrain upon and assail us in every way possible, with the support of the whole community of the land, by seizing our castles, lands, possessions, or anything else saving only our own person and those of the queen and our children, until they have secured such redress as they have determined upon. Having secured the redress, they may then resume their normal obedience to us.[53]

A similar trend was evident late in the medieval period in the conciliar movement within the Church. The 1352 Church Council established the principle that papal election depended on the pope fulfilling certain duties. The effort to end the late-fourteenth-century schism at the Council of Constance also drew into question the absolute power of the pope. If, as the council decided, the pope was to be chosen by a council that represented the Church, then the council and the community that it represented were in some sense superior to the pope.[54] Later, and in the context of the Counter-Reformation, some Thomists rooted their analysis of the state firmly in notions of consent and the rights of the populace and opposed emerging absolutism. They accepted that tyrannicide might be justifiable in extreme cases. In other words, several strands of medieval thinking on politics suggest that those in authority were constrained in their actions by obligations to their subjects, a point that is essential to the current consideration of human security and the corresponding conditionality of the state's sovereignty.

Similar observations may be made about the very gradual evolution of norms of conduct in war in the medieval period. As we have seen, violence was widespread in medieval Europe. Knights and their retainers fought in service of their suzerain's cause or in that of the Church (the crusades); they also fought among themselves and often "brought violence to villagers, clerics, townspeople, and merchants."[55] They valued their privileged right to wage private wars. Knightly violence was perhaps the most significant source of concern with regard to public order. In turn, it was a major reason that monarchs, often strongly supported by the populace, sought to centralize their domains. The story of state formation in Western Europe is in large part a story of the suppression of private violence by centralizing monarchs.

Many consider the institution of chivalry itself to have been a form of constraint on violence directed at both fellow combatants and unprotected civilians. Evidence here is mixed. To judge from chronicles and romances, chivalric codes did encourage restraint among aristocratic combatants, with varying success.[56] Yet these accounts also suggest that the protection of animals (the knight's horse) was considerably higher on the agenda than protection of commoners, including civilians. Chivalry focused principally on conduct between knights. Commoners and their property appeared to be fair game. As Henry

V put it: "War without fire is like sausages without mustard."[57] The metaphor of war as a ravaging storm laying waste to the land and its people is common in medieval *chansons de geste*.[58] Such action is not treated critically; it often appears in paeans to particular warriors. The chronicles, however, display greater ambivalence; they report repeated instances of mass devastation, presenting the knights as a bane on social existence.[59]

The treatment of women in war (and in general) was likewise problematic. The romances report instances of rape by knights in a matter-of-fact, nonjudgmental fashion. Although there is discussion of knightly pledges to foreswear rape[60] and some effort to define in chivalric literature the circumstances in which it is legitimate to rape,[61] there was no consistent comprehension or acceptance that the act was itself wrong. And the discussion focused almost exclusively on the nobility; commoners were entirely beyond the scope of the debate.

It is worth emphasizing, however, that the chroniclers' accounts betray a normative judgment: mass violence against civilians was wrong. It caused suffering and removed the basic security necessary for people to live, let alone to prosper. A similar normative perspective is evident in some of the romances. They are full of examples of the torment of knights that used indiscriminate violence in an effort, perhaps, to convince knights of the potential consequences of their miscreance.[62]

It was left to theologians to articulate explicit norms that implied constraints on violence within and between the nascent states of Europe. The just war doctrine that evolved during this period accepted the necessity of violence in pursuit of order or for religious ends: "as the popular saying goes, 'wrong must be done to put an end to a worse wrong.'"[63] But it clearly argued for norms that limited the use of violence against civilians and their property, limitations based on principles of proportionality and discrimination in the use of force. Both views seemed based on the idea that although the interests of civilians might be damaged by war, those who waged war were morally bound to make efforts to limit that damage. In addition, the historical record suggests that as time passed, there was growing acceptance that specific threats to human security, such as rape, were unacceptable aspects of military campaigns and occupation regimes.[64] Although such principles were often deemed to apply specifically to war between Christians, Counter-Reformation thinkers of sixteenth-century Spain such as Francisco de Vitoria and Diego Suarez extended such obligations to the treatment of non-Christian populations on the basis of the universality of natural law. We have seen thus far how recognition of the rights of individuals tended to occur within the context of defined cultural communities (the Greeks, the Muslims, the Christians).

Counter-Reformation thinking challenged this directly in its emphasis on the unity of the human race:

> The human race, though divided into no matter how many different peoples and nations, has for all that a certain unity, a unity not merely physical, but also in a sense political and moral. This is shown by the natural precept of mutual love and mercy, which extends to all men. Wherefore, though any one state, republic or kingdom, be in itself a perfect community and constant in its members, none the less each of the states is also a member, in a certain sense, of the world, as far as the human race is concerned.[65]

Absolutism and Constitutionalism in the Westphalian System

Security and the Emergence of the Absolutist State

> Since the 17th Century, international security has been defined almost entirely in terms of national survival needs. Security has meant the protection of the state—its boundaries, people, institutions, and values—from external attack. —Commission on Global Governance, 1995[66]

As time passed, there was a gradual consolidation of political and economic structures, first on the Italian peninsula and then north of the Alps, into entities that began to resemble modern states and a commensurate abandonment of the *respublica christiana* in favor of a clearly anarchic and horizontal regional state system.[67] This consolidation has been explained in various ways. Some have suggested that it was a reflection of changing military technology that favored larger and more expensively equipped forces and, by extension, those political structures that were most capable of extracting resources to pay for these new capabilities. Such extraction, of course, presumed the existence of surplus, and others have argued that economic factors were paramount in laying the basis for the formation of the state. To the extent that it was not completely coercive, moreover, successful extraction presumed the provision of services, notably protection.[68]

Where the modern state came from is less important here than how this political transformation[69] affected thinking about the relationship between the state and the human beings who were its subjects. The consolidation of the state in Europe was accompanied by a considerable evolution in perspectives on sovereignty, the power of the sovereign, the constraints on that power, and what all of this meant for the individual subject of the state. The first effective normative challenge to imperial universalism dates to Pope Innocent III's recognition of the French claim to have no political superior (*rex imperator in regno suo*) in 1202.[70] The later process of state-building was accompanied by incessant conflict both between and, and this is just as important, within Europe's monarchies. Civil war convulsed England, France, and the Habsburg domains in the Low Countries. It had a profound influence on thinking about the state: "The Civil War experience, specifically in its religious context, led many to tie in justice and order with the mere survival of the State, and to reject claims that any Church, religious principle, or natural law had precedence over the continuity of civil law and the sovereign prince."[71]

These wars were in considerable measure religious in character. However, they also involved fundamental differences over the desired character of the European system; emerging monarchical states faced serious opposition both from above (the Habsburg imperial vision) and from below (the defenders of feudal privileges and the political fragmentation that they implied). This prolonged contest was accompanied by the development of relatively independent territorial units, the decline of the position of the Holy Roman Empire relative to the subsidiary units of the European states system, and the disappearance of papal influence over the affairs of European states. The outcome of the process was the modern state, possessed (in theory and often in practice) of internal and external sovereignty, controlling its domestic jurisdiction and having that control recognized as legitimate by its peers. The Peace of Westphalia, by establishing the legal equality of all crowned heads of state and their right to make their own foreign policies, completed the normative movement from a hierarchical to an egalitarian order among the great powers within Europe.

The internal and external violence of the period also produced an ideology that emphasized the concentration of power in the state, the doctrine of dynastic legitimacy as a basis for rule, and the absolutist theory of sovereignty.[72] In this body of thought we see the first reasonably unequivocal modern claim that the state, in the person of the monarch, is the primary referent in discourse on security. As Bodin viewed it, and in a clear departure from medieval natural law perspectives, the monarch as sovereign enjoyed *toute puissance*: the absolute power to make the law and to command all other groups and individuals.[73] The monarch, in effect, was the state. As Louis XIV put it: "*l'état, c'est moi.*" The state did not exist outside the monarch. He or she was not subject to law and his or her sovereignty could not be shared. It followed that the state/monarch's behavior toward his or her citizens was not, in the abstract, constrained by reciprocal obligations and established rights.

The two major strands in absolutism reflected very different approaches to the problem of legitimation. One was divine right—the proposition that the monarch ruled as God's agent and that just as God ruled the universe, the monarch ruled his or her domain.[74] In this variant, the divine authority of the pope and the emperor had shifted to the person of the king or queen. Power came from above and was not rooted in consent from below. Nor, given its origin, could it be contested from below. This view of sovereignty extended beyond Catholicism to reformists such as Martin Luther. He held that because the power of rulers was a gift from God, rulers were accountable only to God.[75] The monarch's subjects were obliged to obey and not to resist.

The second, and secular, strand was contractarian and was associated principally with the work of Thomas Hobbes.[76] Hobbes's *Leviathan* is the first major work that sets out the human dilemma in the modern terms of "security." As he put it: "The final cause, end, or design of men, who naturally love liberty, and dominion over others, in the introduction of that restraint upon themselves, in which we see them live in commonwealths, *is the foresight of their own preservation,* and of a more contented life thereby; that is to say, of getting themselves out from that miserable condition of war, which is necessarily consequent . . . to the natural passions of men."[77] His description of the "miserable condition" is well known but worth quoting at length:

> Whatsoever therefore is consequent to a time of war, where every man is enemy to every man; the same is consequent to the time, wherein men live without other security, than what their own strength, and their own invention shall furnish them withal. In such condition, there is no place for industry, because the fruit thereof is uncertain; and, consequently no culture of the earth; no navigation, nor use of the commodities that may be imported by sea; no commodious building; no instruments of moving, and removing, such things as require much force; no knowledge of the face of the Earth; no account of time; no arts; no letters; no society; and which is worst of all, continual fear, and danger of violent death; and the life of man, solitary, poor, nasty, brutish, and short.[78]

In Hobbes's view, men traded their individual liberty and natural rights upward to the state in return for the security that would permit them to live orderly lives. This act of contract was a one-time event. Individual sovereignty, once given up, could not be reclaimed in the event that the monarch did not abide by his or her side of the bargain. The sovereign possessed (or embodied) the natural rights of subjects. As a result, the notion that the individual could legitimately contest the actions of the sovereign on grounds of natural rights appeared to lack meaning.

Bodin's and Hobbes's views led to the doctrine of raison d'état. The ends of the state (especially the power of the state) were paramount. The ends of the state justified the means. The notion that the state could be constrained in its pursuit of these ends by moral considerations was ruled out. Raison d'état implied that "statesmen cannot be bound in public affairs by the morality they would respect in private life, that there is a 'reason of state' justifying unscrupulous action in defense of the public interest."[79] There is in the legal literature of the period a corresponding skepticism about the right of citizens to revolt against their sovereign.[80]

Once again, however, there are important qualifications in the theory of absolutism. It would be incorrect, for example, to suggest that the doctrine of raison d'état was devoid of moral content. After all, at least in the contractarian variant, the justification of the state's primacy was its protection of the "public interest" and of the citizens who, in an original sense, authorized it to govern.[81] As Lentulus said: "It is good to defend one's country in whatever way it be done, whether it entail ignominy or glory."[82] In its divine-right variant, the state's claim was rooted in a religious legitimacy with a profound moral content that focused on the human individual.

Moreover, in absolutist theory there were serious and ultimately unresolved problems in the relationship between the person of the sovereign and the state. Many proponents of this approach to government accepted the distinction between the person as sovereign and the office as sovereign. The individual ruler could "embody supreme authority," but the authority itself resided in the office, not the person. The power possessed by the monarch was not his or her property but was to be used to further the interests of the realm. Reminiscent of the legal limits on Roman imperial power, the monarch could not use the office for personal gain or alienate the state's property.[83] Despite his embrace of the absolute monarchy, Bodin nonetheless recognized the existence of important constraints on the exercise of power by the sovereign, including natural law,[84] customary obligations (with respect, for example, to property and taxation),[85] and fundamental laws that in some sense were prior to the legislative personality of the sovereign (viz., rules concerning succession and the nonalienation of state property).

Turning to contractarian absolutism, it is important to note two qualifications to Hobbes's view of absolute sovereignty. The first concerned the individual motive for entering into the contract, which is the fear of death. Although Hobbes generally took a once-and-for-all view of the act of consent, if the sovereign threatened the individual with death, then the contract was void. The second concerned the capacity of the sovereign to fulfill his or her end of the bargain. If the sovereign could no longer fulfill the function for which he or she was given power, then he or she "is no longer owed obedience, is no longer indeed a sovereign."[86] The similarity of this view to that of sovereignty as the "responsibility to protect"[87] is evident. What we have here is an early statement of the proposition that a sovereign's legitimate power is diminished in situations where the state is either itself a threat to the individual or where it is either unwilling or unable to defend the individual in the face of endogenous or exogenous threats.

In short, even in this tradition of thought that highlights the rights and powers of the state and the sovereign at the expense of their subjects, we see important qualifications of their omnipotence. These qualifications prefigure in important ways the contemporary discussion of human security.

Constitutionalist Theory and the State in Seventeenth- and Early-Eighteenth-Century Political Thought

> The movements opposed to absolutism sought comfort and countenance in ideas of inherent and indestructible human rights which were based upon the divinely appointed order of the Universe. . . . The doctrine of inherited sin has crumbled away; and its place has been taken by a convinced optimism in regard to human nature and reason and a belief that, if left to themselves, men will follow the lead of their natural interest in the community, and will solve every problem rationally by the standard of utility.
>
> —Ernst Troeltsch, 1925[88]

As we have just seen, even in its most extreme form, absolutism left some space for the consideration of rights other than those of the sovereign, rights that were linked in a fundamental way to the security of the individual. And absolutist theory, although essential for understanding the reification of the state in matters of security, was hardly unchallenged. The principal challenge to the untrammeled rights and power of the state that derived from its protective mandate lay in liberal constitutionalist theory.

Here too, the principal justification for the concentration of power in the state was the human need for security and protection. As John Locke put it, the state was "a voluntary society constituted for mutual protection."[89] As with Hobbes, the constitutionalist tradition is strongly contractarian. Individuals in their prepolitical state were assumed to be rational, to recognize the law of nature, and to be possessed of certain rights as a result of their humanity. These individuals entered into a contract to create the commonwealth—a state structure whose purpose was to serve the interests of these free and rational individuals and, in particular, to maximize their liberty and defend the commonwealth's security.[90]

Inherent in the concept of constitutionalism is the notion that the sovereign's authority and power are not absolute; they are constrained by rights and custom. This notion of constraint had important precursors in Roman (*lex imperii* and *lex regia*) and medieval thought (natural, canon, and common law).

Constitutionalism matured into an identifiable theory of the state and relations between the state and its subjects in the seventeenth and eighteenth
centuries. A key point in the evolution of constitutionalist theory was the
English Civil War and the need to justify Parliament's resistance to the Stuart
king. Here the discourse shifted (ironically) from religious to secular ground;
the rebels justified their position by referring to the "ancient constitution" of
England that constrained the power of the monarch. The constitutionalist
position was justified, therefore, largely in reference to a body of "basic, fundamental or customary law" rooted in the medieval period.[91] Alternatively,
the distribution of power and rights within a polity could be defined by a
written document (a constitution) to which legislators and judges deferred.

It was also in this period that theorists came to argue that the natural law
that implied constraint on the sovereign also implied natural or human rights
(justified claims held by human beings qua human beings and attributed to
all human beings on account of their humanity).[92] For Immanuel Kant and
John Locke, rights pertaining to individuals were seen to be limits on both
other individuals and political authorities.[93] For Locke, government existed
to sustain these individual rights (life, liberty, property). When a monarch
transgressed the boundaries of his or her jurisdiction or infringed on the rights
of individuals, people had a right to resist. For some, this right extended to
colonial peoples. Edmund Burke saw the American Revolution as a legitimate
rebellion against the metropole's effort to overstep the rightful boundaries of
power.[94]

Before going on, it is important to note that the contract and the natural
rights logic associated with it were not universal. These rights obviously did
not extend to slaves. And as Carole Pateman has convincingly demonstrated,
women were largely excluded; the contract was patriarchal.[95]

This leads us to consider what the rights and obligations of outsiders might
be in the face of a ruler's gross abuse of his or her subjects. This question,
which is so topical in current accounts of human security, had little meaning
in the pre-Westphalian context. It emerges with the growing acceptance of
principles of sovereignty in the Westphalian context and in the crystallization
of the associated principle of nonintervention in the works of Christian von
Wolff and Emmerich de Vattel. On the one hand, the doctrine of sovereignty
would suggest that such action was impermissible. On the other hand, natural law perspectives and their extension into natural rights[96] suggest a solidarity among human beings that may involve obligations to those in other states.

The same writers that questioned the right of people to revolt against their
rulers all accepted to varying degrees the right (although not the duty) of
sovereigns to intervene in other states on behalf of people being oppressed by

their rulers. Simon Chesterman notes in this context that Alberico Gentili (drawing from St. Ambrose) was "one of the first jurists to raise the notion of sovereign accountability."[97] Gentili argued the point on the basis of a fundamental human society, the existence of which gave each a concern for the fate of his fellows, including those in other jurisdictions. In *De Jure Belli ac Pacis*, Grotius similarly suggested that sovereigns had a responsibility not only to their own possessions and subjects but also (residually) to humankind. He suggested that war waged on behalf of the oppressed people of another state was a legal right. And Pufendorf argued that it was legitimate for sovereigns to defend another sovereign's subjects for reasons that those subjects could rightfully put forward but upon which those subjects were not in a position to act.[98]

More concretely, the Peace of Westphalia, which is widely considered to have laid the legal basis for the modern interpretation of sovereignty, also included provision for the rights of members of religious minorities in particular jurisdictions. To a limited degree, therefore, the founding acts of the international system contained some qualification of sovereignty in the event that the contract between state and citizens broke down or was incompletely fulfilled. Similar provisions were contained in the treaties of Nijmegen (1678) and Ryswick (1697) concerning the disposition of territories in the Netherlands between France and Spain.[99] Toward the end of the period, Kant's recognition of a universal right of mankind and his belief that the failure to respect rights in one jurisdiction would undermine these rights elsewhere would appear to justify intervention in defense of these rights. All seemed to be suggesting that sovereignty might not protect an abusive tyrant from those outside his state who might use force to defend the rights of those being abused.[100]

The final point to be made here concerns state and societal perspectives on the protection of civilians from violence in war. The long-standing concern over the treatment of civilians in war persisted through this period. Gentili, for example, argued that women, children, and priests should be spared in war on grounds of "humaneness." Grotius's notion of *temperamenta belli* betrays a similar sentiment in its plea for moderation in war with respect to the treatment of prisoners and enemy property.[101] Vattel, while considering all the population of enemy states to be enemies, argued that as a matter of justice and humanity, military forces had no right to molest women, children, the aged, and the sick when these groups did not resist. He echoed classical writers in his argument that peasants and their property should be spared if they took no part in hostilities and obeyed occupying authorities. He also suggested that the established laws of war, including the principle of humanity, should apply to civil and international conflicts: "It is very evident that the common laws of war,—those maxims of humanity, moderation, and honor, which we have already detailed in the course of this work,—ought to be observed by both parties in every civil war. For the same reasons which render the observance of those maxims a matter of obligation between state and state, it becomes equally and even more necessary in the unhappy circumstance of two incensed parties lacerating their common country. Should the sovereign conceive he has a right to hang up his prisoners as rebels, the opposite party will make reprisals."[102] There was also evidence from the conduct of military forces in this period of the emergence of norms concerning the protection of civilians in armed conflict.[103]

By way of conclusion, three aspects of the analysis should be emphasized. First, throughout the period of consolidation of the Westphalian system, the state was to varying degrees justified by its role in protecting the individuals within its territories. That is to say, it was recognized that the state had obligations to individuals within its territory. In due time, and particularly in liberal thought, this protective role was extended to the rights of individuals. State power was commonly perceived (Louis XIV notwithstanding) to be limited by custom and fundamental law to its own functional jurisdiction. Second, as the state grew stronger administratively, financially, and militarily, and as its claim to sovereignty in the sense of control over territories under its jurisdiction grew increasingly credible, the theoretical challenge to its absolute power in the form of individual rights and popular sovereignty increased in intensity.

Third, this discussion has focused on the relationship between the individual and the state and the comparative weight of the security claims of these two entities. Yet we are here talking of certain categories of individuals rather than of human beings per se. The contractarian discourse of the period was basically about men; women were excluded from political and social contracts. Summarizing prevailing attitudes of the period, Pateman comments: "Women cannot be incorporated into civil society on the same basis as men because women naturally lack the capacities required to become civic individuals."[104] This exclusion perpetuated severe security problems for women.

State and Security in the Age of Nationalism

> I vow to thee, my country—all earthly things above—
> Entire and whole and perfect, the service of my love;
> The love that asks no question, the love that stands the test,
> That lays upon the altar the dearest and the best;
> The love that never falters, the love that pays the price,
> The love that makes undaunted the final sacrifice.
>
> —Cecil A. Spring-Rice, 1918[105]

The doctrine of popular sovereignty reached its apogee in the revolutions of the late eighteenth century in France and the United States, to which this account now turns.

The mention of popular sovereignty immediately raises the question of who, exactly, constitutes the populace and how its interests are aggregated. How is collective action (in the pursuit, not least, of security) possible when sovereignty is limited by individual rights and consent; when, as Carl Friedrich put it, "The self is believed to be primary and of penultimate value"?[106]

Rousseau's answer to this question was to suggest that the sovereignty of "the people" was expressed in their decisions in a participatory democratic framework. Consonant with contractarian theory, the individual (free male) citizen consented to the political arrangement. Through participatory democracy, the act of consent was ongoing. The individual's sovereignty was thereby transferred to the collective, embodied in the state and the general will of the nation.

The link between popular sovereignty and nationalism is reasonably clear. As Liah Greenfeld has put it: "The specificity of nationalism, that which distinguishes nationality from other types of identity, derives from the fact that nationalism locates the source of individual identity within a 'people,' which is seen as the bearer of sovereignty, the central object of loyalty, and the basis of collective solidarity."[107] One sees here the beginnings of a conflation of state and community that grew in the nineteenth and twentieth centuries into the concept of the "nation-state." The security of the state became the security of the nation and of individuals as part of the nation whose identity was defined through their participation in that nation. Martin Wight has noted in this context that "it is a consequence of 19th Century nationalism that we personify a power, calling it 'she,' and saying that *Britain* does this, *America* demands that, and the *Soviet Union*'s policy is something else."[108] The state had become the person. Its subjects were deemed to be parts of the person. There was little scope for consideration of the security claims of individuals inside or below the state because the claims of state and people were seen as synonymous.

This conceptualization of nation and state carries obvious dangers to the individual and group security of minorities, political or other. Here there was no bargain between the citizens and the sovereign; the state was the citizens. The continual act of consent presumed an obligation to comply. To challenge a state based on the general will was to reject this obligation and to challenge the community itself. As the French Revolution demonstrated, the state, expressing what elites of the day claimed to be the general will, was not obviously subject to traditional or customary constraint.

The nationalism of the French Revolution is sometimes considered to have been civic in nature. People's membership in the nation-state was based on the act of consent and the acceptance of obligation to the polity. Those within a defined territorial space who accepted these arrangements were members of the political community. However, in both France and in Britain (another state whose nationalism was ostensibly civic in character), governments and cultural elites made sustained efforts in the eighteenth to twentieth centuries to imbue their nationalisms with cultural content. In France, the civic construction of the nation was contested by a conception of the French nation as existing prior to the French monarchical state. In practice, it was not as inclusive as the theory would suggest.[109]

In any case, in the Romantic postlude to the Enlightenment, the French Revolution, and revolutionary wars, nationalism and national identity developed in a more cultural direction, particularly in Germany but also farther south and east. Herder, for example, suggested that the nation—a group possessing common blood, culture, language, and historical tradition—was a natural phenomenon. It was only within this organic identity that the potential of the individual could be realized.[110] This tradition of thought relied on a mythologized original community that was purportedly ethnic in origin and was based on shared language, custom, and (often) religion. This conception of community was organic; the nation was a living thing that was embodied with mind, soul, and destiny and was entitled to statehood. When it was combined later in the nineteenth century with social Darwinism, relations between nations came to be seen by many as a permanent struggle for survival of the fittest. Conceiving the nation to be a living thing involved in evolutionary struggle also served to justify the imperial expansion upon which the Europeans embarked with gusto in the mid- and late nineteenth century.[111]

The relationship between the concept of the organic nation and the sovereign state was initially problematic, particularly for Europe's cosmopolitan monarchical class and in multiethnic societies. But in time, most came to understand the advantages of nationalism as a way to consolidate popular support and legitimacy and to mobilize the population for the purposes of state. The embrace of ideas of nationalism and popular sovereignty had given France a dramatic force multiplier during the Napoleonic Wars in the *levée en masse*. Industrialization created prospects for more efficient use of the demographic resources of the state in war. However, the capacity to realize this potential required an idea that would galvanize mass popular support, and nationalism was that idea. Moreover, as Karl Marx noted, nationalism was a useful device for deflecting emerging class contradictions within industrializing European societies.[112]

Increasingly widespread literacy, the growth of public education, and the development of mass newspaper media provided efficient ways to disseminate the idea of nationalism among a wide public. By the end of the nineteenth century, and despite the iconoclastic efforts of dissident socialists and liberals such as Richard Cobden, John A. Hobson, and Norman Angell, most citizens of the great powers saw little that was politically significant in the distinction between their personal interests and those of the state. As Karma Nabulsi convincingly and chillingly demonstrates, this was true not only of militaristic monarchies (e.g., Prussia and Germany) but also of such evolving liberal states as Great Britain.[113]

This conflation of the interests of person and state was not, however, merely a product of changing ideas. As is discussed further below, as the industrial revolution proceeded, states did more for their people—whether in the form of public education, regulation of the workplace, or the provision of pensions and social welfare programs. In other words, the consolidation of national identity was a matter of both ideas and perceived interests. The power of the idea in merging the interests and concerns of citizens into the agenda of the state was amply evident in the buildup to World War I in the behavior of the European socialist movement. Ostensibly devoted to transnational proletarian solidarity, Europe's major socialist parties voted for war credits, thereby permitting European states to finance their mobilizations. Their party members then went off to die in large numbers in World War I. As the quotation that begins this section suggests, the reification (or perhaps deification) of the state as a referent of identity and security appeared complete.

This bundling favored the emergence of modern realism as orthodoxy in international relations theory.[114] Realism in its recent formulation bases itself on several general propositions:

- The only significant actors in world politics are states.
- The international system is anarchic.
- In this pluralistic and anarchic environment, the principal concern of the state is survival.
- To survive, states must help themselves through the accumulation of power, the effort to construct and maintain balances of power, and the use of force.

The individual human being has no obvious place in this structure, except (in the classical sense of realism) in the role that leaders may play in the pursuit of power for their state. The conception of the state as the embodiment of popular sovereignty or as an organic union of the nation reflected in a general will justified and thereby facilitated what Martin Wight referred to as the personification of the state. This personification is an important underpinning of the edifice of the statist realism that dominated both the study of and policy in international relations for much of the twentieth century.

Qualifications of the Dominance of the State in Security

However, the growing dominance of the nation-state and military affairs in discourse on security did not completely eclipse concerns for individual human beings and their security. Seven of these concerns are considered here. Five concern the protection of civilians, the sixth the protection of individual combatants, and the seventh the further extension of the state's responsibility to protect into the economic sphere.

First, modern European states took their responsibilities to protect individuals increasingly seriously during the nineteenth century. The development of modern police forces reflected not only a concern to protect property and control opposition but also a desire to enhance the physical security of citizens.

Second was the gradual emergence of a prohibition on the slave trade and, to a more limited extent, on slavery itself. The leader here was the United Kingdom. Largely as a result of pressure from civil society, the United Kingdom banned slavery in the British Empire in 1807.[115] In 1815, it obtained agreement from the Congress of Vienna to condemn the trade in slaves. As Britain's preponderance in naval power grew in the 1800s, it attempted to end the transatlantic slave trade and then the slave trade in Africa.

As part of this effort, the UK negotiated a number of treaties with other powers conferring mutual rights of visit and search in midcentury, culminating in the General Act of the Anti-Slavery Conference (1890), which established an international organization aimed at suppression of the slave trade. In 1919, the Convention of St. Germain committed signatories to pursue the complete suppression of slavery and the slave trade.[116] In a strict system of state sovereignty, there was no obvious justification for such interference with trade and the domestic affairs of other recognized states and no obvious power-political reason to do so. The only basis for the action was a belief that basic human rights were universal and that states had the right, if not the obligation, to act internationally to promote the rights of noncitizens living in other jurisdictions. In addition, as Linda Colley has noted, the antislavery campaign served the British nationalist aspiration of asserting superiority over the United States, its upstart former colony, and was seen as an element of "national virtue."[117]

The antislavery effort was linked to the third concern—the effort in the late nineteenth century, specifically at the Congress of Berlin (1884–1885)—to oblige Leopold II to respect the rights of his indigenous subjects in the Congo as a condition of the great powers' recognition of his sovereignty over this territory. Article 6 of the Berlin Act of 1885 enjoined all powers that claimed rights in the Congo Basin to promote the moral and material conditions of the native population. Although colonial subjects did not have the same rights as citizens of states, "the very recognition of limits on a fellow sovereign's discretion in the disposition of his human assets was significant."[118] So too was the apparent belief that other powers had the *right* to establish such conditions.

The fourth concerned the efforts on the part of the Concert of Europe to address minority issues within other states. The settlements of the Napoleonic Wars at the Congress of Vienna (1815) continued the practice of limiting sovereignty on the grounds of minority rights. However, they took the practice forward in at least two important respects. First, in the provisions of the Vienna Final Act that dealt with the transfer of the people of Bern and the bishopric of Basel to the Canton of Bern and Basel, the people concerned were guaranteed "equal political and civil rights" in a significant extension of protection beyond religious freedoms. Second, in this act, the great powers also extended protections to national, in addition to religious, minorities (e.g., the Poles).[119]

Later in the nineteenth century, the attention of the great powers turned increasingly to the plight of Christian peoples in the Ottoman Empire. This history has been treated in some detail elsewhere.[120] Here, we recognize that the decisions of the great powers were profoundly colored by considerations of strategic interest[121] but that nonetheless they revealed a sense of obligation to suffering individuals within other jurisdictions. Moreover, and perhaps as important, they sought to justify their interventions in terms of the safety of subjects of another state. Ultimately, the Concert of Europe powers cooperated to complete the liberation of Greece and members of the Concert intervened to defend Maronite Christians in Lebanon in the 1860s. When new states began to emerge out of the rubble of the Ottoman Empire in Europe, the great powers stipulated in the Treaty of Berlin (1878) that states that were becoming independent had to provide for the respect of minority national and religious rights within their territories if they wanted their sovereignty to be recognized.

As Jennifer Jackson-Preece has argued, these provisions reflected the imposition of a "standard of civilization" that went well beyond the traditional minimalist criteria of recognition.[122] The great powers believed that the treaty gave them the right to intervene if these commitments were not fulfilled. Once again, this behavior suggests that in this period of the primacy of the sovereign state, concerns about security and protection of individual subjects of states were deemed to some extent to be legitimate in international discourse. Despite the generally accurate view that the powers imposed this restriction of sovereignty on "outsiders" while ignoring such issues in their own relations, there was limited evidence of similar limits on sovereignty in relations among the great powers themselves. The provisions of the Vienna Final Act regarding Poland are a case in point. Russian sovereignty over Poland was limited by protection of the rights of Polish people under Russian jurisdiction. It should be noted, however, that, as with earlier efforts to protect minority rights through treaty, these provisions lacked any serious or effective mechanism for enforcement.

Fifth, the concern over protection of individuals was also evident in the evolution of *jus in bello* during the nineteenth century. Although there was little progress in developing multilateral instruments to protect civilians in war, the period under consideration witnessed substantial efforts at the national level to regulate their treatment. The best known and most influential of these was Francis Lieber's *Instructions for the Armies of the Government of the United States in the Field* (1863). Here, the United States accepted an obligation to protect "religion and morality; strictly private property; the persons of the inhabitants, especially those of women" in areas under occupation. The Lieber Code prohibited "all wanton violence committed against persons in the invaded country, all destruction of property not commanded by the authorized officer, all robbery, pillage or sacking, even after taking a place by main force, all rape, wounding, maiming or killing of such inhabitants" under the penalty of death or severe punishment.[123] Adam Roberts and Richard Guelff point out that the Lieber Code was used as a model for the laws of war manuals of numerous other countries, including the Netherlands, France, Serbia, Spain, Portugal, and Italy.[124]

It is important to note that the frequently encountered distinction between "civilized" and "uncivilized" peoples persisted in the practice of the major western powers, particularly with reference to colonial subjects and indigenous peoples. The existence of military and legal constraints on the action of the U.S. military vis-à-vis civilians did not prevent it from participating in acts of genocide against the Native American inhabitants of its own country. Likewise, the spread of principles of civilian immunity in Europe did little to prevent the near-elimination of the Herrero people in German Southwest Africa (now Namibia) or, for that matter, the invention of concentration camps by the British in the effort to overcome their adversaries in the Boer War.

The evolution of norms and practice regarding soldiers wounded in war also bears upon our discussion. After the French Revolution, the medical services of European armies decayed. While in the eighteenth century, there had been a shortage of military personnel and they had been expensive to replace, the advent of conscription had eliminated the shortage. States could depend on a continual supply of new recruits; consequently, they reduced their investment in the care of existing forces.[125] As medical services declined, the number of victims increased. The results were graphically presented to Henri Dunant, a Swiss banker who had witnessed the carnage of the Battle of Solférino in 1859. He set about the task of convincing the major powers of Europe to grant protection to the wounded and medical personnel on the battlefield.[126] In 1864, his efforts culminated in the Geneva Convention on the Amelioration of the Condition of the Wounded and Sick in Armies in the Field, which recognized the neutrality of ambulances, field hospitals, and medical personnel while granting immunity to the wounded. The convention codified principles that had been customary through much of the eighteenth century but had weakened over the first half of the nineteenth. It also laid the foundation for the development of the International Red Cross movement. For our purposes, the key point here lies in the explicit recognition by states of obligations concerning the protection of citizens of other states in war.

The same recognition was evident in the efforts to eliminate particularly cruel forms of weapons. Although there had been efforts to ban certain weapons during the Middle Ages (e.g., the effort to ban the crossbow by the Lateran Council), the rapid evolution of military technology during the nineteenth century greatly increased the deadliness of war, stimulating a commensurate interest in controlling this lethality. The first product of this concern was the 1868 St. Petersburg Declaration Renouncing the Use, in Time of War, of Explosive Projectiles under 400 Grammes Weight,[127] which declared that the object of war "would be exceeded by the employment of arms which uselessly aggravate the sufferings of disabled men, or render their death inevitable." In consequence, "the employment of such arms would be . . . contrary to the laws of humanity."[128] The effort continued with Declarations 2 and 3 of the 1899 Hague Peace Conference, which limited the use of expanding bullets and projectiles containing asphyxiating gases.[129]

Moreover, trends in economic thought and social policy in much of Europe suggested a preoccupation with issues related to what we now consider the economic dimension of human security. As seen above, during the seventeenth and eighteenth centuries it was widely recognized that states had responsibilities to protect their citizens internally by maintaining order and externally by defending against attack. The focus here was on physical security. However, monarchs and their servants had always been aware that what we would now call individual economic insecurity had potentially disastrous implications for social peace and the security of the state. Had they needed any reminding, the French Revolution provided it. In this instance, the mass of urban unemployed and underemployed provided a large source of raw material for those who sought to challenge the monarchy and its successors.

As industrialization proceeded, increasing numbers of impoverished people crowded into the cities of Europe. Laborers and the unemployed frequently had inadequate means to sustain themselves and little economic protection against their employers, since notions of reciprocal obligation that were characteristic of rural life had weakened with increasing mobility and urbanization. Urban poverty had potentially serious consequences, not only for public order but also for public health.

The plight of the working class occasioned considerable reflection and proposals for reform. One protagonist in this effort was Robert Owen, an owner of a complex of textile mills in New Lanark, Scotland. He believed that attending to the material and emotional needs of the working class would not only address a fundamental social injustice but would also enhance productivity. Acting upon this belief, he created a model village and made himself a significant profit in the process. Perhaps his greatest practical legacy was the English consumer cooperative movement, but his vision of a more dignified life for the poor had a fundamental effect on the evolution of the British labor movement. And, as Robert Heilbroner has said, Owen and his utopian socialist colleagues made a fundamental intellectual contribution in suggesting that economic insecurity was not simply a consequence of unchangeable economic laws. People could be made more secure by enlightened action.[130] The point was carried further by John Stuart Mill, who suggested that the distribution of wealth was not a matter of economic law but a choice. This opened the way to consideration of how redistributive choices might enhance people's lives and, for that matter, contribute to the security of the state and society.

The utopian socialists and liberals were reformers. Their programs depended in considerable measure on the capacity to win elites over to an enlightened conception of their interest. This was not the case with Marxian socialists. Marx and his colleagues were deeply interested in the pauperization of the working class as the basis for a socialist revolution that would sweep away what they deemed to be the inherently exploitative capitalist economic system, laying the basis for real self-determination of the masses. They took the view that the reification of the state in theories of nationalism was a form of mystification that was designed to divert the proletariat from their objective interest in social revolution. Their agenda was explicitly coercive; the existing order had to be overthrown.

Just as the economic insecurity of the masses was fuel for the struggle of social revolutionaries, it was also a threat to the established national and capitalist order of Europe. Defusing the challenge to the state required co-opting the leadership of the working-class movement and mitigating the social distress that provided the social base for revolution. The result was a gradual evolution of increasingly elaborate and expensive systems of social protection (welfare systems, housing codes, workplace safety regulations, etc.) and the rapid expansion of state employment of workers, which constituted the application in policy of Mill's observation that distribution was a matter of choice rather than necessity.

Bismarck's Germany is a particularly interesting example of this trend. The German government in the late nineteenth century consciously encouraged the growth of heavy industry, accepting the rapid increase in urban population that resulted. In part in order to contain the potential social consequences, it embarked on the design of an impressive safety net. The number of teachers, doctors, nurses, and hospitals all grew substantially in 1880–1913.[131] The state adopted an elaborate social insurance system that included illness, accident, disability, and old age pensions in the 1880s. Part of this effort was practical: the state sought to create and sustain an educated and healthy labor force at a time when recruitment of labor was increasingly difficult. But it was also designed to limit class-based social discontent by tying the workers to the state.[132] Whatever the intent, these developments in Prussian and German policy constituted a recognition of the problem of economic insecurity and a steady and impressive effort to address it through the redistribution of wealth.

The Individual and Security between the World Wars

After World War I, the victorious powers decided at Versailles to establish the League of Nations as a collective security mechanism to promote peace in international relations. This is not the place for detailed examination of the League and its covenant. Several general points suffice. The League was a security organization, but its conception of security was overwhelmingly statist. The organization focused on preventing the resort to war by member states. There was little in the Covenant concerning human beings or their rights and their individual security.[133]

On the other hand, several aspects of the Covenant and subsequent League practice are important precursors of later developments in the realm of human security. Of particular note was Article 22 on the mandate system. Mandatory powers were to govern their new territories in a manner that recognized that the development and well-being of subject peoples was a sacred trust of civilization. In the first category of mandates were territories "formerly belonging to the Turkish [*sic*] Empire" that would exist as independent nations. These could be provisionally recognized as states and would receive administrative advice and assistance from the mandatory power, in whose selection the wishes of the people concerned would be considered. In the intermediate category of territories judged not to be ready for statehood (e.g., the Central African colonies of Germany), the mandatory administration was to "guarantee freedom of conscience and religion." The third category consisted of territories whose populations were deemed least developed. These could be administratively integrated with the mandatory power but with safeguards that protected the interests of the indigenous population. Mandatory powers in all three instances accepted reporting requirements that reinforced the conditional quality of their possession. These stipulations were combined with an annual reporting requirement. In Article 23, signatories also accepted obligations to "endeavor to secure and maintain fair and humane conditions of labour for women and children" and to secure just treatment of "native" inhabitants of territories under their control. The signatories also agreed to "entrust the League with the general supervision over the execution of agreements with regard to traffic in women and children," to confer on the League general supervision of agreements on control of drugs, and to endeavor to prevent and control the spread of disease.

None of this worked particularly well, but one could interpret the provisions on mandates as important precursors to later UN-based efforts to make colonial authority dependent on whether or not colonizers met standards pertaining to the rights of colonial subjects. After all, there was no obvious reason why conditions of this type applied to mandated territories should not also apply to colonial ones. In this sense, these provisions sowed the seeds of later efforts to make sovereign control over colonial territories conditional on state performance with regard to the citizens of the territories in question.

Two other aspects of League activities are worth mentioning as precursors to later thinking about the security of individuals and groups. As Tom Farer and Felice Gaer have pointed out, the effort of the victorious powers to characterize their struggle as one to defend and promote freedom carried with it at least some obligation to defend "individual and group claims against the state" once the war was over.[134] One manifestation of this was the effort to defend and promote minority rights in Central Europe. The Triple Entente made recognition or enlargement of Central European successor states contingent on their acceptance of guarantees of minority rights.[135] A number of treaties that were concluded with successor states protected minority rights and included provisions that made possible eventual reconsideration of the postwar territorial settlement on the basis of referendum (Upper Silesia, Saarland). The League created commissions to adjudicate claims regarding minority rights and was responsible for running referenda. What is interesting about these cases is the attenuation of state sovereignty involved in a state's acceptance of international obligations to particular groups within its borders. Although this was in some respects a continuation of practices evident in the nineteenth century, the mechanisms for implementation of these commitments were substantially more ambitious.

A second element concerned evolving norms and practice regarding refugees.[136] Prior to World War I, there was no international protection of refugees.[137] This changed substantially in the interwar period, owing to the transformation in warfare, the collapse of Eastern Europe's multinational empires, the consolidation of the nation-state with attendant implications for minority groups, and the Russian Revolution, which deliberately targeted particular classes for elimination.

In the latter context, the Entente powers faced a growing problem of flight from Russia, from which well over 1 million people were displaced. Bolshevik authorities exacerbated the problem by revoking the citizenship of many of these people, leaving them stateless. Those displaced people frequently landed without papers and lacked a formal legal identity. They also lacked access to consulates to obtain relevant documents. There was no legal regime to protect them. They had no right to work. Further travel was difficult, given tightening controls on cross-border movement and immigration.

In response, the League appointed a high commissioner for refugees, Fridtjof Nansen. He led the negotiation of a 1922 interstate agreement on legal protection for displaced Russians and persuaded governments to register refugees and provide them with documents. In addition, the fifty-one states that subscribed to the accord agreed to accept travel documents (the "Nansen Passport") issued by the high commissioner to stateless Russians. Nansen and his colleagues also played an important mediating and executive role in the response to the refugee crisis precipitated by the war between Greece and Turkey (1922). They negotiated agreements that allowed the exchange of some 1.1 million Turkish nationals of the Greek Orthodox faith and close to 400,000 Greek nationals who were Muslims. Nansen was also instrumental in getting the International Labour Organization (ILO) to form a refugee section, which focused on employment opportunities for refugees.[138]

Later, at the initiative of Franklin Roosevelt, a conference was convened in 1938 at Évian-les-Bains to consider the issue of Jewish refugees from Germany and Austria. Although few states ratified the convention that resulted, and—to state the obvious—the convention provided little or no protection to Jews caught up in the impending Holocaust, its specification of the rights of Jewish refugees was an important milestone in embedding principles of refugee protection in treaty law. The conference also decided to establish the Inter-Governmental Committee on Refugees (IGCR). During World War II, the purview of the IGCR's responsibilities was extended to refugees from the Spanish Civil War. After World War II, the IGCR, to a limited extent, provided protection to complement the assistance efforts of UNRRA (UN Relief and Rehabilitation Agency) with respect to uprooted populations in Europe. It disappeared, along with UNRRA, in 1947, a year after the League out of which it had grown was disbanded.

Four elements of these efforts directed at the problem of displacement deserve comment. One was that governments were responsible for implementing treaty agreements. The autonomous role of international institutions was correspondingly circumscribed. Second, governments exhibited considerable reluctance to grant rights to stateless and displaced persons. This reluctance grew with time and was particularly evident with regard to Jewish refugees, with tragic consequences.[139] Third, international mechanisms that addressed this problem focused on particular populations (the Russians or, later, refugees from the Third Reich); there was little effort to establish general principles of protection. Fourth, the activity of these organizations failed to prevent and, in the instance of UNRRA, actually facilitated a major repatriation of refugees in post–World War II Europe that was accompanied by massive violations of the rights of those returned to areas under Soviet control.

Nevertheless, the international effort to address the issue of refugees suggests an appreciation that the security of these individuals constituted a matter of legitimate international concern. As Robert Jackson has noted, it is hard to account for this concern in terms of state interest narrowly defined: "To address the problem of refugees, what is required is some moral notion, such as human rights, that transcends international boundaries and impinges on the freedom of sovereign states and citizenries."[140] After all, the states in question could simply have sent these people back to where they had come from or moved them elsewhere. However, the limits of this concern are also clear and significant. There was no substantial effort on the part of the League or its constituent states to address the problem of refugees at its source through diplomatic or other intervention.

The League was not the only institutional venue for consideration of the security of civilians affected by war. As discussed earlier, the International Committee of the Red Cross (ICRC) emerged in the 1860s in response to growing casualty rates in war, the suffering of wounded soldiers in battle, and the equally manifest inadequacy of military medical services and international norms to protect these services. In the late nineteenth and early twentieth centuries, the concern of the organization was extended to the treatment of prisoners of war. However, until World War I, there was little consideration, either by the ICRC or by states party to the conventions it promoted, of the situation of civilians in war. As Simon Chesterman has noted: "A century later, what is striking about these conventions is the near absence of provisions for the protection of civilians."[141]

In World War I, large numbers of civilians were arrested because they were citizens of enemy states. Others were detained as hostages to ensure the obedience of enemy populations in occupied territories. A third issue of concern was the problem of displacement discussed above. The plight of civilians in World War I and in postwar conflicts such as that between the Greeks and Turks encouraged further thinking about the responsibilities of belligerents and of the ICRC with respect to civilians. This began during the war in the effort to produce bilateral agreements on the basis of which the Bureau Civil of the Agence de Genève would generate lists of detainees and case files. These were helpful in transmitting documents and sending and receiving letters and parcels.[142] These arrangements were dismantled at the end of the war.

After the conclusion of hostilities, the ICRC continued with its efforts to codify rules regarding protection of civilians in war. In the 1920s, it produced a draft convention on the subject. However, its efforts ran into significant difficulty in the face of a lack of enthusiasm on the part of states party to the conventions. The 1929 ICRC conference failed to take the proposed convention further. It responded by preparing a more detailed convention on the protection of enemy civilians in territory controlled by a belligerent power, which was accepted at its fifteenth conference in Tokyo in 1934. The limitations of the parameters of this protection are worth stressing. Civilian populations targeted in their home country were not covered. Nor were actions of a belligerent power against elements of its own population covered. Movement toward more complete legal recognition of the rights of civilians and the duties of states derived from those rights was halted by the recurrence of war. And, in any event, the convention did not enter into force before war again intervened. World War II itself served as a principal catalyst for the development of legal instruments to protect civilians in war at Geneva in 1949.

The final area for consideration here is the evolution of perspectives on the relationship between economics and security, particularly as it relates to the individual. As noted above, the later part of the nineteenth century was marked by growing efforts of states to extend their protective obligations into economic life. This trend accelerated and became increasingly multilateral during the interwar period. The principal initial milestone was the formation of the ILO in 1919 as an agency affiliated with the League of Nations. The preamble to the ILO's constitution makes clear the link between security and individual welfare: it notes that "universal and lasting peace can be established only if it is based on social justice." With this in mind, the organization embarked on an ambitious program to regulate working conditions, promote the right to organize and bargain collectively, enhance the health of the working class, and protect women and children in the workplace.

The period's increasing preoccupation with economic security stemmed from a number of factors: the rising influence of social democratic parties in western democracies; concern over the possibility that social unrest might produce political instability; awareness that such unrest might spill over, undermining international order; and fear of the spread of communist influence among workers in industrialized states. But, as the preamble makes clear, the justification was not merely instrumental; the states parties cited not only the "desire to secure the permanent peace of the world" but also "sentiments of justice and humanity" as reasons for their collective effort.[143] The ILO's activities also extended to the promotion of rights of working people in dependent territories.[144]

This multilateral effort to enhance the welfare of the working class was accompanied by numerous programs at the national level that dealt not only with social security and workers' rights but also with public health, nutrition, and education for less-privileged citizens. The onset of the Great Depression accelerated these efforts. The New Deal programming of the United States operated from the premise that individual economic insecurity was the most fundamental problem facing the nation. As Franklin Roosevelt put it: "Our greatest primary task is to put people to work."[145] Two elements of American policy were of particular significance. The first was a radical expansion in social protection programs, which carried further the gradual evolution of the state's role in economic protection. The second was the advent of deliberately interventionist modes of macroeconomic management that were rooted in Keynesian economics and were designed to stimulate demand and thereby sustain or enhance employment. Notably, assuming that the essence of the problem that prevented recovery was a lack of savings to fund an investment-driven recovery or the unwillingness to release these savings, the public sector radically increased its capital spending.[146] This effort amounted to the use of the power of the state to manipulate the market in order to ensure the welfare of the population. Underlying this strategy, once again, lay not only a concern to forestall social unrest but a recognition of the obligation of the state to provide economic protection to its citizens.

In summary, the development of norms during the interwar period was of considerable significance to our subject in at least five respects. First, with regard to both the mandatory territories and minorities in Central Europe, we see the beginnings (or perhaps the beginnings of a recovery) of an approach to international relations that left some space for the rights and claims of individuals and groups as opposed to states. Second, the interwar period was an important precursor to the development of the post–World War II refugee regime, in that states became accustomed to the problem of mass displacement and to multilateral efforts to address it. In a perhaps more profound sense, they came to accept, albeit in a very limited way, the notion that persons who were displaced across borders and lacked the protection of their own state needed an alternative basis for their security. Third, there was slow progress in the effort to enhance the individual security of civilians caught up in armed conflict. Fourth, the period witnessed rapid growth in efforts to grapple with issues of individual economic security. And finally, this took place in the framework of a growing institutionalization of multilateral cooperation.

Conclusion

In the introduction, we identified a number of key themes or questions guiding this work. One was the extent to which the concept of human security is rooted in earlier understandings of security and social life. A second was how the nation-state came to dominate discourse on security. Several conclusions pertinent to these questions arise from the analysis in this chapter. The idea that the protection of citizens (or subjects) is a fundamental responsibility of the state is a very old one. Organized polities have generally been justified in terms of their role and capacity in the protection of human beings living within their borders. Even in instances of absolute (divine right or secularly based) claims to sovereignty, as in the Roman period or in the period of post-Westphalian absolutism, these claims were mitigated to some degree by the definition of functional jurisdictions, by the persistence of custom and fundamental law, and by recognized obligations to subjects.

The contractarian tradition makes these obligations rather more explicit. In the metaphor of the contract, citizens "trade" some portion of their rights and freedoms for protection and other services of the state. Unless one views this symbolic act of consent as final, it would imply that when the state failed to fulfill its side of the bargain (either by failing to protect or by becoming itself a threat to the security of the citizen), the validity of the contract would be in question and the justification for prioritizing the claims of the state to security would be in jeopardy. Even the extreme (absolutist) form of contractarian theory (such as that of Thomas Hobbes) recognized that considerations of individual survival trumped state sovereignty and that to the extent that a state could not protect its citizens, its sovereignty was correspondingly diminished.

The strongest claims to the primacy of considerations of *state* security came out of the nationalist tradition that merges the citizen into the nation and the nation into the state. Here too, however, the claim was frequently qualified by growing recognition of individual rights with respect to the state and by the evolving constraints on state practice, both externally and internally, in the laws of war. Between the two world wars, moreover, the primacy of considerations of state security was also mitigated to a limited extent by the concerns of international institutions (the League and the ILO) and nonstate actors such as the ICRC with respect to particular groups (national minorities, residents of territorial mandates, particular populations of refugees).

Turning from the referents of security to the functional content of the concept, in the late nineteenth and early twentieth centuries, the welfare of individual human beings, the mitigation of poverty, and the protection of the economic rights of the less privileged were growing preoccupations. Although the basis for this preoccupation was largely instrumental (i.e., the need to avoid unrest), basic concerns of social justice and humanity also played their part.

The question of what obligations and rights states might have in relation to systematic oppression or injustice within the border of other states also predates the modern era, although in a weak form. Although statesmen and theorists were often troubled by abuses elsewhere, the principle of nonintervention increasingly trumped any obligations of this type. As Henry Kissinger noted in reference to debates within the Concert of Europe on the treatment of Christians within the Ottoman Empire:

> Castlereagh did not deny that the atrocities committed by the Turks "made humanity shudder." But, like Metternich, he insisted that humanitarian considerations were subordinate to maintaining the "consecrated structure" of Europe, which would be jarred to the core by any radical innovation.[147]

In short, much of what has come to be seen as the normative agenda of human security has been present through history. What we now consider to be human security concerns grew significantly stronger in the nineteenth and early twentieth centuries, despite the primacy of the sovereign state. Moreover, emerging norms on, for example, the conduct of war, the treatment of minorities within other states, and the internationally recognized rights of individuals tended to be limited to the European states system for much of the period under consideration in this chapter. By the end of the nineteenth and early twentieth centuries, we see an unmistakable move toward the universalization of such norms.

On the other hand, the reluctance of international society to come to grips with situations in which states were unable or unwilling to address their citizens' needs for protection should be stressed. The norm in international society throughout the Westphalian period was strongly noninterventionist. The place of human rights in international law was quite limited. Where these rights were acknowledged and protected in international instruments, there was little effort to define mechanisms for effective international action in the event that such commitments were ignored. In practice, and despite the fitful normative evolution discussed above, the nineteenth and early twentieth centuries were littered with gross abuses of human rights, a subject to which we return in Chapter 3. We must turn to the post–World War II period (Chapter 2) and the post–Cold War period (Chapters 5–7) to discover any dramatic recognition of the significance of individual security and of the obligations of states and their organizations to address that security.

2

The UN and Human Security during the Cold War

- **The UN Charter and the Foundations of Human Security**
- **Human Rights and the Precursors of Human Security**
- **The Security of Refugees**
- **Individual Security and the Law of Wars**
- **Sovereignty and Nonintervention**
- **Humanitarian Intervention**
- **The UN and National Self-Determination**
- **The Human Element of Economic Development**
- **Conclusion**

> I am glad that the Charter of the United Nations does not deal only with Governments and States or with politics and war but with the simple elemental needs of human beings whatever be their race, their colour or their creed. In this Charter, we reaffirm our faith in fundamental human rights. We see the freedom of the individual in the State as an essential complement to the freedom of the State in the world community of nations. We stress too that social justice and the best possible standards of life for all are essential factors in promoting the peace of the world.   —Clement Atlee, 1946[1]

As we saw in Chapter 1, the state's position was largely justified by the claim that it protected individuals and communities. Individual claims to security could be bundled into national security for purposes of analysis. The "organic" linkage of state and nation implicit in the development of nationalism in the nineteenth century ostensibly eliminated the dichotomy between the state and the individual when it came to consideration of security. The latter part of Chapter 1 stressed that this organic linkage was never complete. By the end of the period under consideration there, there was evidence of a recovery of the individual and the substate group as subjects of international relations and security discourse. This chapter carries that theme forward into the period of the Cold War. We pay particular attention to the role of the United Nations in fostering discussion and development of norms in these areas.

It is useful to reiterate here that retroactively applying contemporary concepts to a past in which events and processes were not so conceived requires caution. The UN's discussion of the issues raised in this chapter seldom proceeded explicitly in terms of security. There was to our knowledge no significant use of the phrase "human security" in the United Nations during the Cold War. Nonetheless, if one takes the essence of the concept to refer to the protection of individual core values (physical security, welfare, identity), then there is much to discuss. The post–Cold War development of the concept of human security was rooted in, and built upon, a number of developments that occurred to a large extent within the UN and its associated agencies during the Cold War. In this respect, the institution—and the processes within it—played a significant role in promoting change in prevailing conceptions of security.

In examining this foundation, we address a number of questions:

- In what respects and to what extent was the individual deemed by international institutions to possess rights vis-à-vis the state?
- To what extent were individual claims to protection *within* states actionable by other states and multilateral organizations?
- Was intervention[2] deemed legitimate when states failed to honor whatever obligations they were deemed to have with respect to their citizens?
- To what extent was state conduct in war limited by concerns about the protection of individual human beings?
- To what extent did evolving thinking on development suggest a new focus on individual welfare needs?

Given the fact that explicit treatment of individual and community security was almost absent during the first forty-five years of the UN system, where should one look for precursors of the idea of human security? The principal possible indicators of movement toward an individualized conception of security lie in the first place in the evolution of international society's consideration of the rights of individuals in the face of potential threats from states. The most obvious foci of analysis here are the UN Charter, the UN Declaration of Human Rights (1948) and its associated covenants (1966), and conventions related to particular crimes (e.g., genocide) and the rights of particular groups (e.g., women, racial groups, and refugees). Movement in the direction of protecting human rights in the face of state repression would suggest growing concern with the survival goals of individuals, a central element of the

concept of human security, and a concomitant questioning of the prerogatives of state sovereignty.

Second is the cluster of issues related to the protection of civilians in war.
Here principal developments include the Nuremberg Trials and the 1949
Geneva Conventions and 1977 Protocols Additional to the Geneva Conventions. These instruments strengthened constraints on agents of the state with
respect to enemy civilians, those in occupied areas, and civilians threatened
by noninternational armed conflict. They also extended such constraints to
nonstate actors, suggesting that society's concern about protecting the needs
of individuals as opposed to the needs of the state was deepening.

A third cluster of issues concerns the changing perspectives of international society on development. To the extent that one can identify a transition
from statist development perspectives to those focusing on individual, family, and community needs, one might argue that this constitutes a reorienta-
tion of welfare objectives away from states and toward individuals and their
welfare, a "humanization" of development.

The fourth direction of inquiry concerns identity as a core value in the
definition of individual security. To the extent that one can identify a trend
toward more effective protection and promotion of community identities below the level of the state (e.g., the rights of minorities or subject peoples), then
one might conclude that this suggested a growing societal concern for the identity needs of individuals as members of these communities. In the period in
question, the key issue area is the evolution of societal norms regarding self-
determination, particularly, but not exclusively, in its anticolonial variant.[3]

These possibilities are considered in turn in the analysis that follows. Since
many of these issues are the focus of other volumes in this series, the treatment here is limited to examination of the implications of developments in
these areas for the evolving conceptualization of security.

A number of contrary indicators are also relevant to the analysis. Examination of the Cold War period suggests a paradoxical development. International norms regarding individual and group rights did grow stronger during
the period. However, so too did those concerning the sovereign rights of states
and the associated proscription of intervention in international practice. The
evidence to be considered here concerns the evolution of perspectives within
the United Nations regarding sovereignty and intervention in the context of
the growing influence of newly independent states in the General Assembly
and the deep resistance of the socialist bloc to dilution of the sovereign control of their territories in the face of an emerging human rights agenda.

The United Nations was hardly the only game in town. The activities of
the organization and its constituent bodies were sometimes complemented,

sometimes spurred, and sometimes inhibited by those of other actors in world politics. During the Nuremberg Trials, for example, the victors in World War II meted out their understanding of justice to the vanquished. Yet the introduction of the notion of individual criminal liability for the mistreatment of civilians by officials of a state did lay some of the groundwork for much later developments regarding the International Criminal Tribunal for the former Yugoslavia (ICTY), the International Criminal Tribunal for Rwanda (ICTR), and the International Criminal Court (ICC) in the post–Cold War era. The ICRC played a central role in promoting the development of international humanitarian law and extending it to noninternational armed conflicts. Regional organizations—notably the Organization of African Unity (OAU), the Organization of American States (OAS), the Council of Europe (CoE), and the Conference on Security and Co-operation in Europe (CSCE)—played a strong supporting role in developing and embedding refugee and human rights norms in the international system. Nongovernmental actors such as Amnesty International and the anti-apartheid movement spurred states toward new conceptions of the limits on state sovereignty and domestic jurisdiction in matters related to the protection of individuals and groups. In a similar vein, a rapidly growing international women's movement played an essential role in embedding gender as a central issue on the international human rights agenda.

The Non-Aligned Movement (NAM) and the Group of 77 played a somewhat contradictory role. On the one hand, they strongly supported the erosion of sovereignty and domestic jurisdiction where it concerned the colonial possessions of European powers and apartheid. They also promoted the international recognition and support of nonstate movements that claimed to represent colonial populations that had been denied the opportunity to determine their own future. On the other hand, nonaligned states made a strong effort to strengthen norms of state sovereignty and nonintervention in international politics as they pertained to recognized states. The record of the development of norms during the Cold War period was an amalgam of these sometimes complementary and sometimes contradictory efforts.

The UN Charter and the Foundations of Human Security

> The battle for peace has to be fought on two fronts. The first is the security front where victory spells freedom from fear. The second is the economic and social front where victory means freedom from want. Only victory on both fronts can assure the world of an enduring peace. . . . No provisions that can be written into the Charter will enable the Security Council to make the world secure from war if men and women have no security in their homes and in their jobs.   —Edward Stettinius, 1994[4]

The Charter grew out of the experience of the League of Nations and the collapse of the interwar system into a second world war. The framers of the Charter took the view that the war was in part a product of the inadequacies of the Versailles peace and the weakness of the League of Nations as an institution of collective security. The principal focus in the Charter was the creation of a system of interstate relations that would prevent war between states. In this respect the basic intent and focus of the Charter resembled that of the League Covenant, although the means and methods chosen to pursue the ends of international peace and security differed significantly.[5] In addition, as is evident in the epigraph that begins this section, the framers added a key point to the discussion; they recognized that freedom from want was a central consideration in the quest for international peace and security.

The UN Charter made substantially greater provision for the protection of individual rights and welfare than did its predecessor. Many of those involved in the drafting process saw the war in part as a product of the social and economic pressures of the 1930s depression. Massive hardship had played a role in provoking the political radicalism that enabled the Nazis to take power in Germany. The emergence of totalitarian regimes in turn created substantial threats to the political and civil rights of individuals. And it was widely believed that rights-abusing regimes tended to have aggressive foreign policies. To avoid such outcomes in the future, it was necessary to create and sustain the basis for individual economic security.

Appreciation of the link between individual and state security also grew out of the internal experiences of the democracies, most of which had experienced, or had narrowly avoided, considerable internal disruption emanating from economic discontent in the interwar period. It was widely believed that such discontents rendered capitalist states vulnerable to communist subversion. The New Deal was, in considerable measure, an effort to confront the prospect that economic and social insecurity could produce problematic political consequences. In some measure, the economic and social aspects of the UN Charter were an externalization of these American conclusions concerning domestic policy. Such considerations favored an interventionist role by the organization in the effort to prevent or remove social and economic conditions that might conduce to international tension.[6]

Both of these concerns were captured in the earliest significant declaration in the sequence that led to the UN Charter. The Atlantic Charter called for a peace "which will afford assurance that all the men dwelling in all the lands may live out their lives in freedom from fear and want."[7] The 1943 U.S. proposals at the Dumbarton Oaks meeting called for cooperation to solve international economic, social, and humanitarian problems, noting that the UN should seek cooperation in these areas "with a view to the creation of conditions of stability and well-being."[8]

Reflecting these considerations, the UN Charter balanced its recognition of sovereignty with an embrace of human rights and a concern for human welfare. In the Charter, sovereignty involved obligations as well as rights. Article 2 established that states were sovereign equals, but "all members, in order to assure to all of them the rights and benefits resulting from membership, shall fulfil in good faith the obligations assumed by them in accordance with the present Charter." Among these obligations was the promotion of human rights. The fundamental point of including human rights was that rights needed to be safeguarded "if the world was to be spared another catastrophe."[9]

Attempts were made early in the UN's history to prevent the accession of states (e.g., Bulgaria, Hungary, and Romania) that were deemed to be out of compliance with obligations regarding human rights.[10] The weak capacity of the UN to enforce these obligations in conditions of incipient Cold War was evident in the accession of these states despite their apparent noncompliance. In due course, and in view of decolonization and the emergence of large numbers of new states, the issue of compliance with Charter obligations as a precondition of membership became a dead letter.

Nonetheless, the embrace of human rights and the link between the violation of rights and human suffering on the one hand and threats to international peace and security on the other left open the interesting possibility that the council might identify threats to individuals and groups within states as threats to international peace and security. Article 2.7 of the Charter reserved the rights of the Security Council, acting under Chapter VII, to intrude into matters of essentially domestic jurisdiction if the council identified events within a state to be a threat to international peace and security. The possibility that the UN and coalitions of states could intervene to respond to threats to civilian populations is thus present in the Charter, although it was not acted upon during the Cold War.

Turning to human welfare, the Charter's first article identified the achievement of international cooperation "in solving international problems of an economic, social, cultural, and humanitarian character" as one of the basic purposes of the United Nations. On this basis, Article 7 called for the creation of an Economic and Social Council (ECOSOC) as a principal organ, the structures and functions of which were elaborated further in Chapter X. Article 55 (Chapter IX) clearly identified objectives related to individual welfare (higher standards of living, full employment, and conditions of economic and social progress and development) as preconditions for the attainment of peaceful and friendly relations among nations. The following article obliged members to take joint and separate action to achieve these objectives.

The concern over human welfare and human rights in the Charter extended into consideration of the obligations of members that administered non-self-governing and trust territories. The incipient effort to exert a degree of multilateral control over the treatment of colonial subjects evident in the discussion of the League in the previous chapter was expanded into substantial consideration in Chapters XI (the "Declaration regarding Non-self-governing Territories"), XII ("International Trusteeship System"), and XIII ("The Trusteeship Council"). In the first instance, the colonial powers accepted an obligation to

- Promote the well-being of the residents of these territories, including just treatment, protection against abuse, and respect for their cultures and their political, social, and economic advancement
- Develop self-government
- Promote development

In addition, they agreed to provide regular reports on conditions within their territories to the Secretary-General.

Similar obligations were accepted in relation to trust territories. Administering authorities appointed by the UN were obliged to provide annual reports on the basis of a questionnaire developed by the Trusteeship Council. The council meanwhile had the right to make periodic visits to the territories and accept petitions from their residents. In both instances, one sees a recognition that the conditions affecting the populations within administered territories were a matter of international concern, that the UN had some right to review performance in these areas, and that administering authorities accepted (at least in principle) the attenuation of their sovereignty in regard to these areas.

The logic of Chapters XI–XIII suggests that the authors of the Charter recognized the desirability of eventual self-determination. Adam Roberts and Benedict Kingsbury are right to note the Charter's caution in referring "not to the long-asserted but highly problematic principle of 'national self-determination,' but to the much vaguer formulation 'equal rights and self-determination of peoples,' which was less haunted by ghosts from Europe's history between the two world wars."[11] Yet if one obligation of the Charter accepted by the administering states was political development, one is entitled to ask the question: political development to what end?

Human Rights and the Precursors of
Human Security

The UN

Whereas the Charter's rationale for engagement with the needs of human beings was in important respects instrumental (the link between individual and international insecurity), the roots of the Universal Declaration of Human Rights lie historically in the genocide of World War II and ethically in the essentialist notion that human individuals have dignity and are entitled to be treated with respect.[12] In this view, human rights are intrinsic to status as a human being and are, therefore, inalienable.[13] The distinction between instrumentalist and essentialist embraces of human rights is important in this context, since the instrumental logic may be considered to apply only to instances where violations of rights are deemed a threat to peace, whereas the essentialist view is universal in application.

The Declaration provides a reasonably comprehensive rendering of what human rights may be. The later covenants on economic, social, and cultural rights and on political and civil rights translate the general principles of the Declaration into treaty commitments on the part of signatories. From our perspective, their importance lies in the international recognition that individuals might need to be protected from the actions of the states of which they were citizens or in which they were resident and in the effort of the UN membership to define the normative dimensions of the individual space in which the state should not interfere and set standards for the appropriate behavior of states with respect to people within their borders.

Just as important was the weakness of the UN-based international regime surrounding individual rights. The Declaration carried no specific legal obligations and provided no obvious international mechanism for ensuring compliance. Further development of the rights-based protection of human beings was substantially delayed by the deepening of the Cold War. The USSR and its allies were highly sensitive to political and legal principles that could potentially threaten their mode of governance. The United States, meanwhile, was not entirely comfortable with the elaboration of economic and social rights that might constrain the development of liberal capitalism. It took some eighteen years for the covenants to emerge.

Perhaps more important, neither camp was entirely reconciled to the derogation of sovereignty that might be expected in the establishment of a robust international human rights regime. This is evident in the mechanisms that evolved within the UN system to promote compliance with human rights norms. Until 1970, the UN Human Rights Commission did not even have right of access to individual communications to the UN on human rights issues. It was only in 1967 that it was granted the power to discuss human rights violations in specific countries.

When ECOSOC adopted resolution 1503 in 1970, which enabled the commission to conduct confidential investigations in response to individual communications that suggested a persistent pattern of abuse of human rights, the procedures it established were extremely complex and protective of state rights. The UN also established committees to supervise the two covenants that entered into force in 1976. A quick look at the UN Human Rights Committee that was established to address implementation of the Covenant on Civil and Political Rights suggested similar weakness. Cooperation by states under discussion was voluntary. Their representatives provided what information they chose. They answered questions when it suited them. There was no means to ensure timely submission of national reports. And the reporting process applied only to signatories of the covenant.

The Covenant on Civil and Political Rights includes an optional protocol that permits the Human Rights Committee to address complaints from individuals in states who have signed the protocol. This process is more one of monitoring than enforcement. The committee may investigate. It then reports its findings. It is up to the state in question to implement the findings. The majority of UN members—including the more obvious violators of human rights—were not parties to the protocol.

The United Nations pushed the envelope further in the area of human rights through the promotion of a number of conventions dealing with narrower rights concerns: the Convention on the Prevention and Punishment of the Crime of Genocide (1948), the Convention Relating to the Status of Refugees (1951), the Declaration of the Rights of the Child (1959), the Convention on the Rights of the Child (1989), the Declaration on the Elimination of All Forms of Racial Discrimination (1963), the International Convention on the Elimination of All Forms of Racial Discrimination (1965), the Declaration on the Elimination of Discrimination against Women (1967), the Convention on the Elimination of All Forms of Discrimination against Women (1979), and the Convention against Torture and Other Cruel, Inhuman or Degrading Treatment or Punishment (1984). All these documents were of universal application, except the refugee convention, in which the rights established pertained essentially to Europeans displaced across borders prior to 1951 (Article 1.2). The 1967 Protocol Relating to the Status of Refugees recognized the desirability of equality of status for post-1951 refugees and universalized the status established in the convention.

It was also in the Cold War that the foundations were laid for post–Cold War initiatives directed at women and children in conflict. In 1969, the Commission on the Status of Women (CSW) began to consider whether special protection should be accorded to particularly vulnerable groups, namely women and children, during armed conflict and emergency situations.[14] This led to an ECOSOC request to the General Assembly to adopt a declaration on the topic. In the meantime, awareness of the significance of sexual violence against women during conflict also grew as a result of experience in specific conflicts. In the early 1970s, for example, the UN's special rapporteur on violence against women reported evidence that rape was committed on a massive scale during the conflict in Bangladesh.[15] The result was the 1974 Declaration on the Protection of Women and Children in Emergency and Armed Conflict.[16] Here, it was recognized that women and children suffered particularly in armed conflict. The declaration urged states to comply with their obligations under international instruments (including the 1949 Geneva Conventions) as they concerned the protection of women and children. Although the declaration did not specifically mention sexual violence, it did make a general plea for compliance with the laws of armed conflict which directly address rape and prohibit degrading treatment; the Fourth Geneva Convention of 1949 is an example of such an instrument.

The significance of the UDHR and later additions to it is debatable. There were those like René Cassin, one of the drafters of the Declaration, who wrote in 1946 that he believed that "when repeated or systematic violation of human rights by a given state within its borders results in a threat to international peace (as was the case of the Third Reich after 1933), the Security Council has a right to intervene and a duty to act."[17] Others—principally diplomats— doubted whether the Declaration amounted to anything more than empty talk, given the reluctance to adopt enforcement procedures that would have given bite to its clauses and those of later instruments. However, as Michael Ignatieff has argued, a watershed had been crossed:

> Before the Second World War, only states had rights in international law. With the Universal Declaration of Human Rights . . . the rights of individuals received international legal recognition. For the first time, individuals . . . were granted rights that they could use to challenge unjust state law or oppressive customary practice.[18]

Regional Organizations

UN efforts to protect individual rights were complemented by numerous regional initiatives of variable significance. The strongest regional regime is that based on the Council of Europe, established by the Treaty of London in May 1949. The statute of the council *requires* member states to accept the rule of law and the fundamental human rights and freedoms of all individuals within their jurisdiction (Article 3). When European states (e.g., Spain and Portugal until the 1970s) did not respect these principles, they were excluded. When members were deemed to have departed from these principles (e.g., Greece in 1969), their membership was suspended (Article 8).[19]

Establishment of the council was followed in 1950 by adoption of the Convention for the Protection of Human Rights and Fundamental Freedoms.[20] It laid out a comprehensive list of protected civil and political rights and freedoms and provided for the establishment of a European Commission and Court of Human Rights (1954) to consider complaints by states and individuals and to refer admissible complaints to either the council's committee of ministers or the court.[21] After some delay, the court was established in 1959; it accepted submissions from both states and individuals and groups (when local remedies had been exhausted and when the state concerned had accepted the right of individuals to make complaints).[22] The court's decisions were final and binding. Enforcement mechanisms available to the CoE included putting pressure on the state in question, publishing the report and findings, and suspending or expelling the member. Associated treaty instruments, such as the 1987 European Convention on the Prevention of Torture and Inhuman or Degrading Treatment or Punishment, gave European bodies the right of mandatory inspection anywhere in the territory of member states. In short, at least in Europe, "human rights practices, which were previously an area of sovereign prerogative, are now subject to coercive regional enforcement."[23] The establishment of the CoE and its associated bodies was a major development in international protection of individuals against their own states.

The establishment of a robust international regime to protect individual rights within states in Western Europe was not replicated elsewhere. Although in "wider Europe," the mechanism of the Conference on Security and Cooperation in Europe included a human rights component, it lacked the means to implement any of its provisions.[24] The rights of human rights activists in Eastern Europe and the USSR were systematically violated by their own governments in the effort to suppress their activities, while other states and organizations remained silent or limited themselves to fairly ineffectual declarations protesting the violation of Helsinki principles.

In the Americas, the OAS Charter (1948) acknowledged member obligations under the UN Charter, recognized that justice and social security were important bases of lasting peace, and provided a detailed outline of economic and social rights, but it had much less to say about civil and political rights. In

Article 106, the charter provided for the creation of an Inter-American Commission on Human Rights but with little specification of its powers or role.[25] The regional regime was strengthened in 1969 through adoption of the American Convention on Human Rights (the Pact of San José). A comprehensive outline of personal, civil, and political rights was accompanied by a rather cursory section on "progressive development" (Article 26).[26] The pact also established the Inter-American Commission on Human Rights and the Inter-American Court of Human Rights.

The commission's mandate was to promote respect for and the defense of rights in the region and receive information from states on human rights within their territories. It was enabled to receive and take action on petitions from individuals and organizations in the region concerning state violation of the convention, review communications from states regarding violations of the convention by other states (but only when both had recognized the competence of the commission to do so), seek information and conduct investigations into claims, and seek friendly settlement of disputes. However, if no friendly settlement was forthcoming, the commission was limited to transmitting its report to the two parties. Neither of the parties was entitled to publish the report, but the commission could publish its report and findings after three months if no progress in acting on the complaint had been made or if the matter had not been referred to the Inter-American Court. The court could hear cases only after the procedures of the commission had been completed. There was no obligation on states to accept the jurisdiction of the court. Where states accepted jurisdiction, the court could rule against states but had no means of enforcing its rulings.

From the perspective of human security, the weaknesses of these arrangements are clear. The OAS General Assembly that selected the members of the commission consisted exclusively of representatives of states. States could refuse to permit the commission to review complaints brought by other states. States nominated candidates for membership on the court. Only states (and the commission) had the right to bring cases to the court. Although states parties accepted their obligation to comply with the judgment of the court, there was no mention of what would happen if they did not. And the foundational interstate agreements all made clear, repeatedly, the inadmissibility of intervention for whatever purpose.

Despite these protections of states rights, significant resistance remained in the Americas to institutionalizing and operationalizing even a limited human rights regime. It took ten years from the adoption of the OAS Charter for its article 106 (on the creation of a Human Rights Commission) to be implemented. The convention took nine years to come into force after it was ratified. Although the Inter-American Court of Human Rights began work in 1980, in its first decade it delivered judgments and opinions on only ten cases.[27]

The period of the Cold War was one of repeated and dramatic infringement of the rights that the region's states had embraced. A quick but incomplete list would include the Batista and Castro regimes, the Trujillo period in the Dominican Republic, the Duvalier period in Haiti, the repressions and disappearances in the Southern Cone in the 1970s, and the counterinsurgency campaigns in Central America in the 1970s and 1980s. Clearly practice fell a considerable way behind the development of norms.

In Africa, the OAU Charter also acknowledged the principles of the UN and the UDHR and accepted the promotion of international cooperation in human rights as one of its basic purposes. However, the principles of the organization were heavily weighted in favor of the rights of states and governments (human rights were not mentioned); it took eighteen years for the organization to agree to the African (Banjul) Charter on Human and Peoples' Rights (1981).[28] The enumeration of rights was paralleled by a list of duties, some of which drew into question the inviolability of rights. For example, Article 29 specified that every individual has a duty to preserve and strengthen national and social solidarity. When an exercise of the right to freedom of expression or association involved actions that might compromise solidarity, it would appear that the right was circumscribed.[29] In addition, numerous clauses were rendered "subject to law and order" concerns. Finally, it deserves mention that this was a charter of human *and peoples'* rights. The potential for tension between the two foci is obvious. The resulting ambiguity is not resolved in the charter.

The Banjul Charter established the African Commission on Human and Peoples' Rights, the function of which was to promote and protect human and peoples' rights in Africa. The protective function included a right to investigate "by any appropriate method." States that suspected violation of the charter by another state had a right to bring the matter to the attention of the allegedly offending state in the first instance. Where the matter was not resolved bilaterally within three months, the matter could be brought before the commission. Alternatively a state could bring such a matter directly to the commission. If the commission could not mediate an amicable solution, it would report (with recommendations) to the Assembly of Heads of State of the OAU. The commission also had the right to consider communications from actors other than states if a majority of its members agreed and if local remedies had been exhausted.

The commission was obliged to inform the state concerned prior to any substantive consideration of a particular communication. The commission could only recommend that patterns of abuse be investigated and was not empowered to investigate specific cases. In-depth investigation of particular situations required a request from the Assembly of Heads of State. All measures taken under provisions of the charter remained confidential, as did commission reports, unless the assembly decided to make them public. There was no specification of penalties that might be imposed on states in the event that they were found to be contravening provisions of the charter, and no court was envisaged in the Banjul Charter to adjudicate cases.[30]

In short, as in the Americas, states controlled who was on the commission. Members were nominated by states and were elected by the Assembly of Heads of State. States also controlled what the commission investigated and what was made public. Moreover, the charter made petition by individuals much more difficult than that by states. The requirement that the allegedly offending state be informed of accusations against it put plaintiffs at risk. Here too, although the body of principles that defended individual security was laudable (although qualified in disturbing ways), the framework for bringing these principles into practice was lamentably weak. The lack of substantial adjudication by the commission is a good measure of its irrelevance in practice. And state abuse of individual rights did little to suggest that these normative commitments were taken seriously in much of the region. As Christopher Clapham has noted:

> All in all, the African Charter constituted a formal admission on the part of the OAU and its member states that human rights within their own territories were a matter of legitimate international concern, while stopping short of any means by which they could be held responsible for any abuse of such rights.[31]

Yet both the Americas and Africa at least made progress in laying out regional normative frameworks for human rights that embodied and developed underlying UN principles. No such effort emerged in Asia. In general, the only region that made significant progress in operationalizing these principles and in holding states accountable in a practical sense for their behavior toward their own citizens was Western Europe.

Nongovernmental Organizations

The other development of the Cold War with implications for the later emergence of the concept of human security concerns NGOs. The Cold War period was one in which numerous transnational groups emerged that were devoted to the promotion of human rights and the protection of individuals being persecuted by their own states. Notable among these was Amnesty International. The case of Amnesty is of particular significance in this study in view of the systematic quality of its interaction with the UN. In this respect it is a fruitful example of mechanisms for the transmission of ideas between the UN, states, and NGOs. The UDHR grew out of state preferences and an interstate negotiation that created a new mandate for the UN. In turn, the UDHR was the basis for the formation of Amnesty in 1961. Its approach was deliberately transnational; by the early 1970s, 2,000 Amnesty groups had been established in thirty-two countries throughout the world.[32] The organization's point of departure was that it promoted the principles outlined in the UDHR through the development of standards.[33] In time, it developed a strong mandate to protect individuals as well. In both capacities, it sought substantial input to the UN, seeking and obtaining Category B consultative status with ECOSOC in 1964. The success of its efforts in promoting human rights standards at both the state and international levels and in shedding light on particular cases in which states infringed these standards for political reasons was recognized in 1977 when the organization received the Nobel Peace Prize.[34]

At the regional level, the Helsinki Final Act establishing the CSCE spawned Helsinki Watch (1978), which is devoted to monitoring compliance with CSCE principles and witness of their abuse. This was followed by the creation of similar watch groups in the Americas, Asia, and Africa in 1991–1998. These came together in 1988 to form Human Rights Watch. Amnesty International, Human Rights Watch, and other like-minded organizations formed the basis for a global civil society network of monitoring and advocacy of human rights issues during the Cold War.

A further, and perhaps stronger, example is provided by the emergence of a widespread women's movement. Persistent agitation for consideration of women's rights was a key factor in the emergence of a process to embed gender as a central aspect of international consideration of human rights, including the protection of civilians in conflict.

Conclusion

Despite the obvious weaknesses of the emerging human rights regime during the Cold War, the phenomenon is significant in this study in that it constituted a degree of international recognition of the rights of individuals vis-à-vis the state and attempted to set international standards for the protection of individuals. Both, as has been seen, are key elements of the later notion of human security. Given this study's focus on the role of the United

Nations in the evolution of the idea of human security, it is noteworthy that all the major regional human rights instruments take the UDHR as a major point of departure, as did the most prominent transnational nongovernmental organizations that focused on human rights during the Cold War.

The Security of Refugees

A further vector in the prehistory of the UN and human security concerned refugees. We saw in Chapter 1 how displacement following the Russian Revolution and the deepening problem of persecution of Jews in the 1930s stimulated efforts by the members of the League of Nations and the United States to develop a legal framework to protect these individuals. World War II restarted this process. The initial repatriation of persons displaced from Eastern Europe was halted relatively quickly in the face of considerable resistance on the part of those affected and as Cold War tensions emerged.[35]

As seen in the previous chapter, the UNRRA and the IGCR developed substantial responsibilities to protect and assist uprooted populations in Europe during and immediately after World War II. The two organizations were extinguished in 1947, in part because of American unhappiness with their role in the return of refugees to the USSR and Eastern Europe. In their place, the United States supported the creation of the International Refugee Organization (IRO). This proposal occasioned significant debate within the UN along incipient Cold War lines over whether the emphasis should be on return or resettlement of persons displaced by the recent war. The resulting compromise specified that in the first instance the focus should be on encouraging and assisting return but that the organization should also assist in resettlement when return was not possible. The mandate to resettle was sufficient to ensure the refusal of the USSR to join, and, as time passed, the focus narrowed to resettlement.[36]

Although initially the beneficiary population consisted of those displaced by war, after the 1948 Czechoslovak coup, IRO programs were expanded to include refugees from Eastern Europe; eligibility criteria were liberalized correspondingly. The establishment of the IRO was a significant step forward in establishing norms concerning the protection of displaced persons that is directly relevant to the roots of human security. Previous efforts to protect had focused on particular populations of displaced persons. As Gil Loescher points out, the IRO was the first organization that made status as a refugee dependent on the individual rather than a particular group, accepting "the individual's right to flee from political persecution and to choose where he wanted to live."[37] Yet the incipient regime was limited to Europe.

The IRO process was largely driven by the United States, which was increasingly animated by its desire to contain and discredit international communism. The UN played little role in the articulation and extension of the refugee concept in this period and was to some extent implicated in what was a self-interested policy agenda of a dominant state. In time, the cost of the IRO produced donor fatigue, and the UN context became politically complicated. The United States moved to the view that its interests in the refugee question could be managed better through bilateral or regional mechanisms under closer control.[38] Residual questions could be addressed by a much smaller and temporary agency.

These considerations ultimately produced the Statute of the UN High Commissioner for Refugees (which was adopted in 1950)[39] and the UN Convention on Refugees (adopted July 1951, entered into force April 1954). The convention defined refugee status, laid down minimum standards for the treatment of refugees; established the principle of nondiscrimination with regard to race, religion, or country of origin and the equally important principle of *nonrefoulement* and made provision to create a generally accepted travel document for refugees.[40]

The planned temporary nature of the UNHCR and the narrow terms of reference of the convention were highlighted by the limitation of the term "refugee" to persons covered under earlier agreements and/or the constitution of the IRO and to those who, as a result of events occurring prior to 1 January 1951 found themselves outside their own country and who were unwilling or unable to avail themselves of their home country's protection because of fear of persecution. A later clause made it clear that the events in question were those in Europe (except where states agreed to accept events elsewhere before 1 January 1951 as coming within the purview of the convention). In other words, the rights envisaged were geographically restricted. One practical result was that massive numbers of refugees outside Europe (other than those provided for by the UN Relief Works Agency and the UN Korean Reconstruction Agency) were left unprotected. On balance, neither the United States nor the Soviet Union had any particular interest in a strong, self-consciously multilateral refugee agency. Donor states denied the UNHCR funds for operations and initially limited the UNHCR to administrative functions. The U.S. preference for smaller, regionally specific ventures that it could control was evident in the creation of the Intergovernmental Commission for European Migration, which inherited the resettlement roles of the IRO. The UNHCR attempted to develop a limited relief role of its own through voluntary contributions, but this was stymied by lack of contributions until 1955, when the U.S. Congress appropriated a half million dollars for refugee operations in areas of U.S. strategic interest.[41] As Loescher has put it: "While creating and developing its own refugee institutions, the United States treated the UNHCR almost as a sideshow."[42]

Ultimately, the limitations on the UNHCR proved unsustainable. Recurring refugee problems in Asia (e.g., the problem of Chinese refugees in Hong Kong) and displacement from the Algerian war coupled with the increasing southern presence in the UN General Assembly led to a gradual expansion in geographical purview. The extension of the agency's activities was not accompanied by an enlargement of refugee status under law. Yet at the end of the 1950s the General Assembly authorized the UNHCR to use his good offices to provide assistance to refugees who did not come within the competence of the UN. By the early 1960s, the large-scale refugee problems in Asia and North Africa were joined by crises in Sub-Saharan Africa (e.g., the Angolan crisis of 1961, the Rwandan crises of the early 1960s, the exodus from southern Rhodesia, and the less dramatic, but over time nonetheless significant, flight from South Africa).

The result was the disappearance of the distinction between mandate refugees and "good offices" refugees in the 1967 protocol to the convention. The protocol removed the temporal and geographical limitations on protection of refugees, universalizing the status. With this instrument, which was concluded again within the UN system, the rights to protection and to *nonrefoulement* were extended to those fleeing across borders to escape persecution, whatever their region of origin.

Regional Organizations

Activities at the UN were complemented by normative developments in regional organizations. The CoE has no regional convention on refugees, a result of recognition of the universality and adequacy of the UN convention. Where European treaty law might be considered to impinge on refugee rights defined in the convention, the council has been careful to reiterate its commitments to the provisions of the latter.[43] It is not surprising, given the initial focus of the UN convention on Europe, that European institutions would see little need for further normative development. But the influence of the core UN discussion and document on subsequent European law and practice is obvious.

Africa, in contrast, did adopt a regional convention. The African convention acknowledges in detail the role of the UN (the Charter, the UDHR, the UN convention and protocol) in laying out the basic principles of refugee protection. It proceeds to confirm the UN convention's basic provisions. However, in a development of considerable potential significance to human security, it extends the UN definition of refugee beyond the criterion of fear of persecution, including, in addition, "every person who, owing to external aggression, occupation, foreign domination or events seriously disturbing public order in either part or the whole of his country of origin or nationality, is compelled to leave his place of habitual residence in order to seek refuge in another place outside his country of origin or nationality." The convention also specifies asylum obligations, prohibits prevention of entry and *refoulement,* and obliges states members to share asylum burdens when a particular country is having difficulty in meeting its obligations under the convention.[44]

In Latin America, normative development regarding displacement appears to have been largely absent until the 1980s, with one exception: the effort to lay out treaty law on territorial asylum.[45] The convention on asylum deals exclusively with the rights of states to grant or refuse to grant asylum and the mutual recognition of those rights. It does not address the rights of victims themselves. In this sense, refugee protection was a matter of sovereignty and state discretion. One suspects that this reflects rather strongly the politicization of refugee policy in the United States during the Cold War.

The crisis of displacement in Central America in the 1980s produced a significant initiative—the Cartagena Declaration (1984). In this effort to establish rules of the game for treatment of refugees from Central America's conflicts, the authors specifically called for accession of the states to the UN convention and protocol, the adoption in policy of its terminology and principles (and notably that of *nonrefoulement*), and support for the work of the UNHCR in the region. In addition, they recommended that the OAU's expansion of the category of refugee to include those displaced by violence be adopted with regard to Central American countries affected by conflict and that the provisions of the Inter-American Convention on Human Rights be applied to refugees by host states.[46]

Conclusion

As in the more general area of human rights, the evolution of the refugee regime suggests substantial progress toward international recognition of individuals' rights to security and international society's responsibility to protect individuals whose security is threatened. This occurred along several axes. Protection of refugees shifted away from the protection of specific groups and toward that of individual human beings. It extended from its point of origin (Europe) toward universality. While it began as a set of temporary arrangements to deal with a specific displacement crisis, it gradually acquired a degree of permanence in law and in practice.

However, it remained incomplete in significant respects. In its focus on fear of persecution, it failed to take full account of the security needs of people displaced for other reasons (e.g., war-related violence), although Africa and later the Americas moved in this direction. Betraying the continuing sovereignty concerns of states, it failed to properly address the protection of those displaced *within* borders. Although the principles of the UN convention came to be seen by many as universal, the degree to which they were accepted varied greatly across regions. Western Europe—at least at the normative level and to a considerable extent in practice—substantially embraced the UN's refugee principles. Africa went beyond them normatively to take into account the protection and assistance needs of those displaced by civil and international violence, while many African countries established laudable records of providing sanctuary for victims of the region's many conflicts. In contrast, movement was slower in Latin America. It was largely nonexistent in the Soviet bloc and Asia.

Moreover, the practice of refugee protection during the Cold War was frequently highly politicized. The establishment of an effective mechanism for protection of refugees was handicapped by the unwillingness of the major powers to undertake the significant financial burdens that such an effort implied. In the early years after World War II, the United States used refugee and asylum issues as a stick with which to beat the Soviet Union. Although the United States was the largest recipient of refugees during the period in question, the vast majority of those they took were from a small number of countries implicated in the Cold War. It never signed or ratified the UN convention and consistently resisted or ignored the convention's provisions as they applied to the Americas. Many other countries actively resisted their putative obligations to provide asylum for domestic political reasons.

Nevertheless, the adoption of the convention and the establishment and growth of the UNHCR during the Cold War laid the basis for an increasingly effective provision of protection to persons displaced across borders. In terms of the concrete number of beneficiaries and the nature of protection provided, there was considerably greater progress in this area than in most others relevant to the international protection of individual rights.

The fundamental contribution of the United Nations to this process was the normative commitments that were debated and adopted within the framework of the UN General Assembly. The UNHCR emerged as the key international agency for the promotion and protection of the rights of particularly vulnerable population of refugees, gradually replacing entities such as the IRO.

Subsequent regional arrangements concerning protection of and asylum for refugees drew heavily on UN instruments and practice. National legislation also betrayed the omnipresent influence of the UN.

Individual Security and the Laws of War

The issue of international protection of individuals extends beyond general universal and regional instruments dealing with human rights and the rights of refugees and into consideration of the evolving laws of war. The post–World War II process of prosecuting war criminals is particularly relevant to early thinking about individual security. It is also a major precursor to later efforts to use international criminal prosecution as a means of protecting individual human beings. As was seen in Chapter 1, the phenomenon of international tribunals to address the behavior of military and state personnel vis-à-vis enemy civilians and the residents of occupied territories dates back to the late Middle Ages. This practice had largely disappeared in the nineteenth and early twentieth centuries as the claims of the state to exclusive jurisdiction strengthened. Individuals acting on the authority of the state were not generally considered to be subject to international law.[47] This was not entirely implausible, since European states shared a common understanding of civilian immunity that served to limit atrocity in war between themselves. More particularly, there was prior to World War II little notion that agents of a state could be liable in international law for crimes committed against their own citizens.

This consensus broke down with the rise of fascism and Japanese militarism. The magnitude of the crimes of German and Japanese military and police officials committed against civilians, both citizens and residents of occupied territories, "shock[ed] the conscience of mankind."[48] If U.S. treasury secretary Henry Morgenthau, a close adviser to President Roosevelt, or British prime minister Winston Churchill had had their way, the surviving Nazi leaders would have been summarily executed. It was Henry Stimson, Roosevelt's secretary of war, who prevailed on the president to convene an international tribunal to try those responsible for the horrors of the Third Reich. Stimson's top lawyer in the Department of War argued that simply shooting Hitler would "do violence to the very principles for which the United States have taken up arms, and furnish apparent justification for what the Nazis themselves have taught and done." He concluded that "[n]ot to try these beasts would be to miss the educational and therapeutic opportunity of our generation."

At Nuremberg, the Nazi leaders in custody were charged with three crimes: launching an aggressive war, crimes against humanity, and violation of the laws of war. Of the three crimes, the last—violating the laws of war—was best understood as it was a time-honored principle. The Germans were in the dock for contravening the *jus in bello* principle of not harming noncombatants. That they had violated this principle by killing innocent civilians in occupied countries, sinking merchant ships at sea, and raining death on populated cities from the air is beyond contestation. It was also well known that the Allies also violated the *jus in bello* principle. The Allies' chief prosecutor, Telford Taylor, acknowledged that it was "difficult to contest the judgement that Dresden and Nagasaki were war crimes."[49] The Allies got around this problem by restricting the remit of the tribunal to judging German, and only German, actions. Even so, many have observed that the judges were especially circumspect about Germany's indiscriminate use of air power; they refused to convict German air chief Hermann Goering for the devastation of Warsaw, Rotterdam, and Coventry. As Kirsten Sellars put it, convicting Goering for destroying those cities would have looked like "a double standard too far."[50]

The charges of the crime of aggression and crimes against humanity were new in that they did not exist in international law textbooks: they were concocted against the enormity of the Nazi depredations and retroactively applied to the captured German leaders. Virtually all those who have written about Nuremberg take note of the novelty of these crimes and the retroactive application of justice; most also acknowledge that the way they were applied reinforced the impression of the trials as victor's justice. However, the majority has also appreciated the necessity of such a novel approach. Of special significance is the issue of individual responsibility: before Nuremberg, international law was binding on states, not on individuals. Leaders and officials had sovereign immunity and could not be tried for crimes committed by the state. In our terms, this was the reification of the state par excellence. In one stroke, Article 7 of the Nuremberg Charter, this principle of sovereign immunity was swept aside (albeit only momentarily). Without being allowed to hide under the covers of state protection, nineteen of the twenty-two Nazi leaders tried were convicted of committing crimes against humanity. Twelve of those found guilty were executed.[51] Along similar lines, the Tokyo trials, which took place from May 1946 to November 1948, found Japanese war leaders, including Prime Minister Hideki Tojo, guilty of aggression and war crimes. Seven of the defendants were sentenced to death; another sixteen received life sentences.[52]

The crimes covered by the Nuremberg Charter clearly covered genocide (see paragraph 6c of the tribunal's charter provisions). However, the UN quickly sought to strengthen the prohibition of genocide through the negotiation of a Convention on the Prevention and Punishment of the Crime of Genocide.[53] The convention entered into force in January 1951. Several aspects are noteworthy. First, it applied to peace as well as war. That is, it constituted a general protection against acts defined in Article II of the convention,[54] whether these acts occurred in war or not. Moreover, it applied to both the domestic affairs of states and their international actions. Third, Article II made clear that acts other than murder were covered by the prohibitions in the convention. This extended the protection of individual members of groups well beyond physical survival. Finally, it was universal in application, rather than being limited to any particular region of the world. In these respects, the convention constituted an important moment in the evolution of individual protection from violence.

However, the provisions for implementation of the convention were somewhat unimpressive: Article IV stated that persons committing genocide shall be punished. Article VI noted that persons charged with genocide would be "tried by a competent tribunal of the State in the territory of which the act was committed, or by such international penal tribunal as may have jurisdiction with respect to those Contracting Parties which shall have accepted its jurisdiction." Article VIII allowed "any Contracting Party" to "call upon the competent organs of the United Nations to take such action under the Charter of the United Nations as they consider appropriate for the prevention and suppression of acts of genocide or any of the other acts enumerated in Article III." In other words, in situations where there was no broad international agreement on the need to respond, no response would be forthcoming.

Nonetheless, the provenance of the convention is a useful example of the role of the United Nations in initiating, promoting, and implementing ideas. The convention emerged from a process that began with a request from three states (Cuba, India, and Panama) to the General Assembly to include the question on the assembly agenda. The assembly responded by declaring genocide a crime under international law and asking ECOSOC to prepare a convention on the subject. ECOSOC in turn requested that the Secretary-General prepare a draft for discussion. This draft was then discussed in an ad hoc committee established by ECOSOC, which prepared a further draft. After discussion, the draft was returned to the assembly in August 1948. In resolution 260 (III), the assembly approved the draft and suggested that it be forwarded to states for their ratification.[55] Here, in other words, the United Nations acted as a vehicle to legitimize and specify a widely held view of states. Although the organization was not the progenitor of the idea, it played a significant role in refining it, propagating it in international society, and legitimizing the outcome.

Another development occurred largely outside the UN framework and concerned the evolution of the laws of war (and their humanitarian components) in the ICRC. The evolution of the laws of war after World War II was a continuation of processes in the interwar period, but it strongly reflected the experience of World War II.

This evolution had two major phases—the adoption of the 1949 Geneva Conventions and the adoption of protocols thereto in 1977. The 1949 conventions were the product of proposals generated by the ICRC after the war and a thorough consultation in 1945–1948 which produced agreement on four conventions approved at the 17th International Conference of the Red Cross in 1948. These conventions were submitted to a diplomatic conference in Geneva in April 1949. Of the four 1949 conventions, the one that is most directly relevant in our account of the evolution of the concept of human security is the fourth (Convention Relative to the Protection of Civilian Persons in Time of War). Convention IV constituted a substantial expansion of the protection of civilians from violence in war. It extended this protection in a rudimentary way to noninternational armed conflict.[56] It singled women out for "especial protection against any attack against their honour," citing rape, enforced prostitution, and indecent assault as particular threats.[57]

The crucial innovations here, from the perspective of human security, were that the convention's Common Article 3 codified specific principles of international law regarding the protection of civilians in war and extended protection from declared war to any armed conflict, including interstate conflict, situations of occupation, and noninternational armed conflict. However, it was not entirely clear whether and in what respects Convention IV bound nonstate actors engaged in civil conflict. States (both signatory and nonsignatory to Convention IV) were sometimes reluctant to specify that internal disputes in which they were involved constituted armed conflicts, not least because they were unwilling to accept even this degree of international regulation of actions within their borders.[58] And it was generally felt that the protections afforded to civilian persons and property were insufficiently elaborated.

Such concerns led eventually to further developments in international humanitarian law through the 1977 Additional Protocols I and II to the 1949 Geneva Conventions. Further elaboration of the conventions was fostered by concern over Israel's role and conduct in the territories it had occupied in the Six-Day War (1967), by the worsening situation with respect to apartheid in South Africa, by lingering unhappiness with the impact of the war in Vietnam on civilians, and by the suffering of civilians in Nigeria's civil war. Protocol I, which applied to international armed conflicts, extended the protections of the conventions and protocols to armed conflicts over self-determination and those involving racism (Article 1.4) and made an effort to broaden the category of combatant to include participants in insurgent movements who might not be able to meet the identification requirements of previous conventions. This rendered individual members of such organizations eligible for protection on the basis of combatant status. More important, the protocol (Part IV) added greater precision regarding the definition of discrimination in war.

Protocol II (which dealt with noninternational armed conflicts), although much less exhaustive than Protocol I,[59] built upon Common Article 3 in a number of important ways by widening the category of persons to which the laws of war applied (Article 2.1); extending the list of prohibited acts to include collective punishment, terrorism, slavery, pillage, and the threat of any of the prohibited acts (Article 2.2); and stressing the special significance of the protection of children with regard to education, family reunification, nonrecruitment, humane treatment of child soldiers, and removal of children from the area of hostilities (Article 4). It also proscribed forcible displacement (Article 17). The protocol extended protection to humanitarian and medical facilities, shipments and personnel in internal conflict, and objects essential to civilian survival. It prohibited attacks on infrastructure, the destruction of which might create hazards for civilians (Article 15).

The development of international humanitarian law during the Cold War under the stewardship of the ICRC was a fundamental contribution to the subsequent emergence of the concept of human security. The rights of individual soldiers to protection were expanded and clarified. The rights of civilians to protection in war were substantially codified for the first time. And the laws of war (including issues related to the protection of armed civilians) were extended from interstate war to internal war.

The conventions and protocols discussed above established as law important constraints on the behavior of both state and nonstate actors with respect to civilians at risk of violence in war and those attempting to assist these victims. However, they rested on little more than moral suasion to ensure compliance. Protocol II was careful to protect the sovereignty of states and thereby to circumscribe the capacity of international actors to respond effectively to the abuse of civilians in civil conflicts. Article 3 specified that "nothing in this Protocol shall be invoked for the purpose of affecting the sovereignty of a State or the responsibility of the government, by all legitimate means, to maintain or re-establish law and order in the State or to defend the national unity and territorial integrity of the State." One might argue that the phrase "by all legitimate means" left a small window open for international action in the event that illegitimate means were used by a state. However, this window was slammed shut in the second paragraph of the article: "Nothing in this Protocol shall be invoked as a justification for intervening, directly or indirectly, for any reason whatever, in the armed conflict or in the internal or external affairs of the High Contracting Party in the territory of which that conflict occurs." The reasons for including this restriction were clear: the majority of states—and particularly states in the Third World and the socialist bloc—were unwilling to embrace legal principles that might give international organizations a right to intrude upon their domestic jurisdiction. The ICRC, meanwhile, was reluctant to advocate measures that might jeopardize its neutrality and alienate parties to conflict, thereby restricting its access to victims of war. That access was deemed to be based in part on the apolitical character of its activities. But at the end of the day, this resulted in substantial limitation on the capacity of international society to enforce compliance with principles regarding the protection of civilians in war.

Sovereignty and Nonintervention

In general, the statist orientation of international politics and security remained paramount during the Cold War, not least in the UN Charter, as noted earlier. As we have seen, the Charter's focus on peace and security among states had important implications for the international promotion of individual security. Article 2.1 established sovereign equality of members. Article 2.4 prohibited the use of force by states against other states and was generally taken to include a prohibition on intervention. The sole caveats were actions mandated by the Security Council under Chapter VII in response to threats to international peace and security and the recognition of inherent rights of states to self-defense (Article 51). These provisions, and similar ones at the regional level, established reasonably narrow limits on the legal basis for state or multilateral intervention to ensure the survival or the rights of individuals within other states, unless the council agreed under Chapter VII. Agreement on action based on Chapter VII proved rare during the Cold War.

Moreover, prior to agreement on the covenants to the UDHR, it was not entirely clear how binding the Charter obligations of states were regarding their general commitments to human rights. Although some believed that Charter Articles 1.3, 55, and 56 placed a direct obligation on states to respect human rights and fundamental freedoms, others took the view that no member state was "legally obligated to respect a particular right or freedom until it enters into an agreement recognizing the existence of the right and undertaking to respect it." The emphasis of the Charter in this area was on international cooperation in the promotion of human rights rather than on an individual state's compliance with general principles of rights. Until a state explicitly accepted such obligations, the UN had no right to concern itself with the state's conduct on the matter in question, given Article 2.7.[60] In this regard, it is pertinent to recall the origins of Article 2.7 itself. The article, which specifies the limits on the UN's capacity to intervene in the domestic jurisdiction of states, was explicitly intended to ensure that the economic, social, and rights issues included in the Charter would not give the UN power to intervene in the internal affairs of states.[61]

As noted earlier, one element of the apparent sacrosanct status of sovereignty during the Cold War was the abandonment of attempts to assess whether a state qualified for membership in the UN. This development was favored by the Cold War dynamic in which the great powers were careful to avoid alienating the growing Third World majority in the United Nations by applying conditions to the membership of new states in the international organization.[62]

In the meantime, Third World states, unsatisfied with the absence of explicit prohibition of intervention by states in the UN Charter, sought to entrench further the principle of nonintervention through action of the General Assembly.[63] To the extent that one takes General Assembly declarations passed by substantial majorities to be an indication of a consensus about the norms of international society,[64] the combination of Articles 2.4 and 2.7 and the succession of assembly actions in this matter appear to have created a remarkably robust normative regime of nonintervention by states, groups of states, or the United Nations itself. Developments at the United Nations were closely paralleled in regional organizations; the OAU and the OAS in particular adopted similarly watertight prohibitions on intervention.[65] This norm-setting by the combination of the General Assembly and regional organizations appeared to limit the possibility of forceful international action to protect civilians when the circumstances of their suffering fell within the expansive and ill-defined parameters of domestic jurisdiction.

The only major exceptions to this general prohibition concerned matters related to decolonization and racial discrimination (in postcolonial situations).[66] In the first instance, the Security Council on several occasions took up the matter of Portuguese administration of its African colonies, despite Portugal's rejection of international jurisdiction over what it deemed were its internal affairs.[67] The relevant resolutions[68] all suggest a concern on the part of the Security Council about Portuguese repression of individuals in territories under Portuguese administration and a desire to establish that these territories were non-self-governing "within the meaning of Chapter XI of the Charter" and therefore that General Assembly resolution 1514 of 1960—the Declaration on the Granting of Independence to Colonial Countries and Peoples—applied to these territories.

However, the operative paragraphs of the resolutions were extremely weak. The council did not invoke Chapter VII; its members confined themselves to deprecation of Portuguese policy, and "urgent calls upon Portugal" to cease repression and recognize the rights of the peoples of the territories to self-determination, and requested that states refrain from assisting Portugal in ways that enabled it to continue its repression. The council's efforts to deal with Portugal display some recognition of the link between rights, internal repression, and international security but a considerable reluctance to challenge Portugal's control of these territories directly. The reasons for this are clear in the lists of abstentions that followed each resolution, which each time included one or more of three permanent members: the United States, the United Kingdom, and France.

The second case deserving mention is that of the unilateral declaration of independence in Southern Rhodesia.[69] The council became seized of this matter in 1965 as the white government began its move toward independence. Again the principal concerns raised related to widespread repression and the infringement of the political and civil rights of the African majority in the territory by a racist minority. Nonetheless, the principal thrust of the resolutions (and one that was backed by the nominally administering power, the UK) concerned support for the UK in its efforts to cope with a rebellion that posed a threat to international peace and security. In this respect, the council's actions (which ultimately included invocation of Articles 39, 41, and 42 of Chapter VII in order to interrupt Southern Rhodesia's international trade, by force if necessary, and to isolate the territory diplomatically and financially) do not constitute a derogation of sovereignty on the basis of concerns over human security. After all, Southern Rhodesia was not a sovereign state and that state in which sovereignty was nominally vested (the UK) supported the resolutions. This said, however, the case serves as an interesting precursor to post–Cold War actions of the council in its identification of the denial of rights as a threat to international peace and security.

The tension with respect to sovereignty inherent in the pursuit of objectives now associated with human security was much clearer with respect to the council's treatment of South Africa and apartheid.[70] Here, on grounds that racism was an unacceptable practice, the United Nations was taking issue with a recognized state and member of the organization on an issue that arguably fell within traditional definitions of domestic jurisdiction. The council's major complaints were the denial of self-determination of the black and "coloured" majority in South Africa that was inherent in the doctrine of apartheid and the massive violation of political civil rights that was a result of the South African government's effort to maintain this system. The resolutions clearly state both essentialist (apartheid as "abhorrent to the conscience of mankind") and instrumental (apartheid as "seriously disturbing international peace and security")[71] arguments for engagement. Although the operative paragraphs of early resolutions generally involve exhortation of South Africa and member states, by the late 1970s, the position of the council had hardened. In part in response to the Soweto killings,[72] but also reflecting the concern of African states over South African military incursions into Angola, Mozambique, and Zambia and general unease over South Africa's nuclear program, it invoked Chapter VII to mandate an arms embargo against South Africa.[73]

The multiple causes of the actions of the council in this instance muddy the water. It is, however, doubtful that the council acted primarily as a result of threats to the rights of individuals and groups within South Africa, given the extent and seriousness of South Africa's acts of aggression in the region and the commitment of permanent members to nuclear nonproliferation. Nonetheless, the abuse of the rights (including the right to survival) of South Africa's majority population was clearly a significant contributing factor in stimulating the council's use of Chapter VII, not least because those permanent members who might otherwise have opposed such action were under significant pressure from civil society to distance themselves from the apartheid regime.

In short, there are clear (although limited) indicators of growing receptivity in the council to the dilution of the state's claim to security when that state is abusing elements of its own population or that of territories it administers. On a very limited number of occasions, such concerns evoked coercive action by the Security Council. These cases are also significant in their association of the concept of threats to international peace and security with the internal conduct of states vis-à-vis their own populations or territories over which they claimed sovereign jurisdiction. Later resolutions are also of interest in their recognition of the right of people within the jurisdiction of other states to attempt to overthrow current political arrangements and the right of other states to assist such people in this effort. This suggests a degree of dilution of the principle of nonintervention on human rights grounds. However, the caution with which the council approached these issues and the comparative weakness of the measures it took to address them indicate not only differences over the cases in question but also substantial lingering discomfort with the implicit derogation of the rights of states relative to those of individuals and groups within states.

The reluctance of the United Nations to address the issue of protection of civilians in conflict situations is also reflected in Cold War peacekeeping operations. In most instances, the issue of protection was not obviously raised because UN peacekeeping operations were deployed into interposition or observation roles by consent and after a cease-fire. The conflicts were generally between states. In two important instances, the UN accepted peacekeeping roles in internal conflicts where there were important protection needs. But here too, the Security Council avoided the question of protecting civilians from violence.

The first instance, intervention and civil war in the Democratic Republic of Congo (DRC), was an early example of the problem of state failure. In the face of a mutiny in the new Congolese army and military intervention by Belgium, the Secretary-General was mandated in Security Council resolution 143 of 1960 to provide the Congolese government with military assistance until such time as the national security forces were able to meet their responsibilities. The principal early focus was effecting the withdrawal of foreign forces, maintaining territorial integrity, and restoring law and order. Resolution 161 of 1961 further mandated the Secretariat to take measures to prevent the occurrence of civil war. The Security Council also made clear that it was not the role of the UN (or other outsiders) to determine the outcome of the DRC's internal conflict. This was a reasonably explicit indication of the UN's unwillingness to intervene directly on one side or another in the conflict between Congolese authorities and the emerging secessionist movement in Katanga.[74] However, from the perspective of human security, the civilian dimension of this war is more significant. This was an extremely violent conflict among parties who often had little awareness of, let alone commitment to, the laws of war. Military operations and general lawlessness generated massive civilian casualties. Yet significant in the resolutions is the complete absence of any reference to the suffering of civilian populations or of any UN role in protecting civilians from the depredations of foreign interveners, mercenaries, and often poorly disciplined local parties to the conflict.

The second instance—Cyprus—was an early precursor of a problem that bedeviled the UN system in the post–Cold War period, that of intercommunity conflict between defined ethnic groups. Here, UN peacekeepers were mandated to prevent the recurrence of fighting and to help restore and maintain law and order in Security Council resolution 186 of 1964. There was no reference in early resolutions to problems civilians faced as a result of the conflict and no consideration of the protection of civilians in the mandate of the UN Peacekeeping Force in Cyprus (UNFICYP).

In 1974, after a renewal of hostilities and foreign intervention, the mandate was effectively extended to the monitoring of a cease-fire line and buffer zone between the two parties. Council resolutions recognized the humanitarian consequences of the renewal of conflict and large-scale displacement of persons and called upon UN agencies to assist affected civilians.[75] Subsequently,

UNFICYP embraced certain humanitarian functions.[76] However, there was again no reference to protection of civilians in the mandates of peacekeepers and no apparent recognition of the possibility that the security of civilians might be a legitimate preoccupation of peacekeepers in the zone of conflict.

In both cases, it is entirely plausible that the presence of peacekeepers provided a degree of protection, in the sense that the presence of UN forces may have reduced the general level of conflict and lawlessness. However, this is a long way from the deliberate acceptance of a responsibility to protect. Peacekeeping more broadly was essentially statist in orientation. Its rules of engagement were extremely limited (generally to self-defense). The dearth of effort to uphold evolving human rights norms reflected several factors: the constraining effect of parallel normative developments regarding sovereignty and nonintervention, the emergence of a General Assembly majority that consisted of new states with a strong commitment to preventing the erosion of sovereign rights they had so recently acquired, the Cold War–induced immobility in the Security Council, and the preoccupation of the major powers with the balance of power and the bipolar competition for influence. International and UN action to protect individuals was rare and generally weak during the Cold War.

Humanitarian Intervention

The practice of state intervention in humanitarian crises provides another basis for assessment of the significance of norms regarding protection of individuals during the Cold War. Three cases are generally cited: India's intervention in East Pakistan in 1971; Vietnam's intervention in Cambodia in 1978–1979; and Tanzania's intervention in Uganda in 1979.[77] In each instance, it appears that the actions of outside powers in a civil conflict resulted in substantial improvement in human security. To what extent did these interventions reflect an embrace of norms concerning civilian protection against a predatory state and its agents? And to what extent did international society accept the propriety of action by states in the domestic jurisdiction of other states to promote such norms?

In each of these instances, the principal justification for action was not human security or human rights, but self-defense. In the case of India's action against Pakistan, India had been supporting an opposition movement (the Awami League) and an insurgent group (the Mukhti Bahini) in East Pakistan. Deepening state violence against the Bengali population there had produced a massive flow of refugees across the border into West Bengal. Pakistani air forces had attacked targets in India. India responded by attacking Pakistan and forcing its troops in East Pakistan to surrender. There is no doubt of the depth of Pakistani abuse of the civilian population in its eastern province. But the motives for action involved regional power and state security.

Nicholas Wheeler notes that India for a time attempted to justify its actions by referring to the profound humanitarian crisis in East Pakistan, citing Charter principles regarding human rights.[78] However, it did not press this argument, preferring instead to rely on self-defense justifications and on the security implications of the refugee crisis ("refugee aggression").[79] That it took this route reflects the lack of receptivity that it encountered in the council on the humanitarian point and, presumably, its awareness of the dangers of pursuing arguments justifying intervention in domestic affairs.

The UN, meanwhile, accepted the Pakistani view that the civil conflict in East Pakistan fell within Pakistan's domestic jurisdiction and hence under Article 2.7 of the Charter.[80] The council was deeply divided along Cold War lines by the conflict and found it impossible to take meaningful action. Noting the fact that "lack of unanimity . . . prevented it from exercising its primary responsibility for the maintenance of international peace and security," the council referred the matter to the General Assembly.[81] The assembly, in a clear rejection of the notion that human security concerns might attenuate state sovereignty, ignored humanitarian justification and called for an immediate cease-fire by a vote of 104–11–10.[82] Later in the same month, after India had unilaterally proclaimed a cessation of hostilities, the Security Council also demanded a cease-fire and offered the good offices of a special representative of the Secretary-General for a solution to humanitarian problems.[83] One can only conclude with Wheeler that "given the legitimating power of the rules of sovereignty, non-intervention, and the non-use of force, India's appeal that the Security Council treat its use of force as an exception to these because it was defending the 'justice part' of the UN Charter challenged existing norms."[84]

Seven years later, Vietnam's invasion of Kampuchea posed similar dilemmas for international society. The lack of human security in the face of massive state repression inside Kampuchea was well known. The regime had killed over a million of its own people. The repression had produced a flow of some 150,000 refugees into Thailand. The Vietnamese were also troubled by the close links between China and Kampuchea and their consequent vulnerability on two fronts. In late 1978, several Khmer Rouge divisions massed along the border. Vietnam responded with a limited incursion into eastern Kampuchea, where it established a client regime. Khmer Rouge forces collapsed in the face of Vietnam's attack, leaving the way open for Vietnam to take the capital. Vietnam justified its actions in terms of self-defense while claiming that the overthrow of Pol Pot had been achieved by an indigenous Cambodian resistance movement.[85] Vietnam's intervention—by removing a murderous government—greatly enhanced the security of the Cambodian population. Yet this felicitous consequence was largely ignored both in Vietnam's justification of its actions and the reaction of international society to the invasion. Humanitarian factors played little role either in Vietnam's diplomacy with respect to Kampuchea prior to its military action or its justification of its use of force to overthrow a recognized government. Indeed, Vietnam never formally admitted that its forces were inside Kampuchea.

The perspectives of the United Nations on the matter were clear in the organization's reaction. There had been no UN condemnation of the systematic abuse of human rights in Kampuchea. The general view of the Security Council with respect to the invasion was evident in the debates where China and western states vociferously condemned Vietnam, while the USSR and the Soviet bloc defended the Vietnamese position. The UN refused to seat the successor Cambodian regime. The reaction in the UN system to Vietnam's invasion suggests that arguments regarding human suffering and the rights of individuals within the jurisdiction of predatory states had little strength within the organization, despite the expanding framework of norms discussed above. The matter of humanitarian intervention was specifically and substantially discussed in the council in the Cambodian context. All North Atlantic Treaty Organization (NATO) member states represented there argued that Vietnam's intervention could not be justified. In particular, they rejected the notion that intervention could be justified by the reprehensibility of a regime's domestic policies. The Portuguese representative put it most succinctly:

> Neither do we have any doubt about the appalling record of violation of the most basic and elementary human rights in Kampuchea. . . . [Nonetheless], there are no nor can there be any socio-political considerations that would justify the invasion of the territory of a Sovereign State by the forces of another State.[86]

This opinion was also shared by Australia, the five Association of Southeast Asian Nations (ASEAN) members participating in the debate, and, more broadly, the membership of the NAM. The council ultimately produced a draft resolution calling for the withdrawal of foreign forces from Kampuchea. It was accepted by thirteen members but vetoed by the USSR, on grounds again having nothing to do with the humanitarian factor.[87] In short, in the Cambodian case, there is little evidence of acceptance of the proposition that where a state abuses its own population, other states may act to end the abuse.

A similar conclusion may be drawn from Tanzania's invasion of Uganda in 1978–1979. In this instance, the regime governing Uganda was widely known for its brutality toward its own population. Estimates of extrajudicial killings during Idi Amin's rule range between 100,000 and 500,000 people. Human rights violations in the country produced very blunt condemnations not only from nonstate actors such as Amnesty International and the World Council of Churches but also from the Commonwealth. In 1978, the internal security situation deteriorated as fighting between factions of the Ugandan armed forces spilled over into northern Tanzania. Idi Amin followed this up with a statement annexing the northwestern corner of Tanzania, an act that Tanzania condemned as tantamount to an act of war. In November 1978, Tanzania counterattacked, pushing Ugandan forces out of the Kagera Salient. The Ugandans responded with another attack into Tanzania in early 1979. Once again they were repulsed and Tanzania entered Ugandan territory. When Amin called for foreign assistance, Tanzania pushed further and Kampala fell in April 1979.

As in the case of Cambodia, Tanzania did not employ humanitarian or human rights arguments to justify its invasion, relying instead on self-defense. In contrast to previous cases, there was little international reaction to Tanzania's action, in part because of President Julius Nyerere's stature in the African community but also reflecting the growing impatience of both regional and international actors with the Amin regime. There was also little evidence that Tanzania sought strategic advantage through the occupation of Uganda. In this context, it is not surprising that Idi Amin's request to UN Secretary-General Kurt Waldheim for a Security Council meeting to discuss the matter was ignored, and there was no substantial discussion of the case at the UN.[88]

To summarize, the three major cases of state intervention in situations where a neighboring regime was jeopardizing the human security of its citizens provide little evidence that the growing basis for international concern about infringement on human rights within states had produced a willingness on the part of states to act in defense of the rights of "strangers" or that international society was willing to countenance such action. The states in question acted principally in response to perceived strategic threats or to take advantage of strategic opportunities.

It is noteworthy that in cases where civil war did not generate such threats or opportunities, there was little incidence of intervention, despite frequent massive human suffering. The classic case here is that of the Nigerian civil war,[89] where the encirclement of self-styled Biafra and the concentration there of large numbers of displaced Ibos created a massive humanitarian crisis that ultimately produced upward of a million civilian casualties. The war and its consequences for civilians occasioned much handwringing but little by way of intergovernmental action. The UN was hamstrung, not only by Cold War immobilization but also by the unwillingness of African states and the NAM more generally to countenance intervention in Nigeria's domestic jurisdiction. The war had no immediate negative implications for neighboring states, it was not linked to regional rivalries to any meaningful extent, and Nigeria was far stronger than potential regional adversaries. There was, consequently, little incentive for neighbors to intervene. Neither camp in the Cold War saw any substantial interest in engaging militarily (although the USSR and the UK did provide substantial military assistance to the federal forces). The result was that there was no intervention that might have forestalled human suffering and might have provided a greater degree of protection to civilians facing profound personal insecurity.

During the Cold War, in other words, although there was a development of norms related to human security, parallel normative developments focusing on sovereignty and nonintervention appeared to have a far stronger impact on practice when the two came into conflict. And, in a general sense, in reference to the Cold War era, there is little to argue with in David Rieff's observation that "while post-World War II documents like the Universal Declaration of Human Rights, the Genocide Convention, and the four Geneva Conventions of 1949 transformed both international law and the normative bases of international relations, the murderous 20th Century remained just as murderous."[90]

The UN and National Self-Determination

One important dimension of working out the balance of rights and duties between states and individuals that has been a persistent concern of international actors with respect to the domestic affairs of states has been the protection of minority communities within national boundaries. With the rise of the colonial empires, this extended into the question of the obligations of imperial powers regarding their colonial subjects and what role did the community of states play in ensuring that those responsibilities were fulfilled.

During the Cold War, international institutions, the United Nations included, were reluctant to address the issue of rights of minorities within states. The Charter waffled on the question. The UDHR also was not helpful. It accepted that discrimination on the basis of national origin was not permissible, it recognized the right of individuals to nationality, and it asserted that the deprivation of an individual's nationality was prohibited. The obvious meaning in the latter two instances was citizenship in a state. The Declaration steered wide of issues of minority identity and the rights that accrued thereto, with the exception of the negative right of nondiscrimination. The subsequent International Covenant on Civil and Political Rights (1966) embraced the principle of nondiscrimination and equality before the law as they related to nationality. It also recognized the right of minorities within states to enjoy their own culture, profess and practice their own religion, and use their own language. It recognized, moreover, that all peoples have the right to self-determination. However, it failed to define what a "people" was and what "self-determination" implied. The only instruction to states in the covenant (Article 2, paragraph 3) concerns the promotion of self-determination of non-self-governing and trust territories. The companion covenant on economic, social, and cultural rights repeats the Declaration's prohibition of discrimination on the basis of national origin and notes that all have a right to nationality and that no one can be deprived of nationality. The implied meaning, however, again relates to citizenship and not national identity.

The post–World War II discussion of self-determination at the UN was dominated not by issues relating to minority rights but by the cause of anticolonialism, which essentially involved the self-determination of territories rather than peoples. The organization played a significant role in the evolution of thinking and practice regarding national self-determination, at least with regard to the colonial possessions of the imperial powers.[91] It is probably the case that the colonial system was doomed by the end of World War II. The major colonial powers were exhausted and bankrupt as a result of the two world wars. Their position in the colonies was becoming more costly to maintain as nationalist opposition increased and as the notion that they had welfare obligations to their subjects took root. The rapid development of welfare systems and safety nets at home reduced the quantity of resources available to maintain the empire. Domestic electorates were increasingly skeptical of the legitimacy and practical benefits of colonialism. The colonies were less significant to the foreign policy of colonial powers as they turned to the challenges of reconstruction and regional integration in Europe. And both superpowers rejected the legitimacy of colonialism.

Although the outcome was perhaps inevitable, the UN did have a strong influence on the pace of decolonization by delegitimizing the institution in international society, by holding the colonial powers to account in uncomfortable ways (thereby increasing the diplomatic costs of the policy), and by isolating those colonial powers (e.g., Portugal) that resisted the evolving consensus.[92]

The General Assembly played the key part in this process; the anticolonial consensus there grew as the number of recently decolonized members expanded and the USSR under Nikita Khrushchev began to explore the possibility of alliance with the Third World against the West.[93] By 1960, the new majority had adopted the Declaration on the Granting of Independence to Colonial Countries and Peoples, asserting that colonial and other forms of subjugation of peoples were violations of fundamental human rights and were contrary to the Charter. The declaration reiterated the right of all peoples to self-determination and went on to reject lack of preparation for statehood as a pretext for denying this right and to call for the cessation of any acts of violence against colonial and dependent peoples attempting to exercise their rights. Further, it specified that immediate steps be taken to transfer power in trust and non-self-governing territories to their peoples.[94] In this respect, the General Assembly clearly asserted that subject peoples had the right to assert their identity through self-determination and that efforts by the colonial powers to resist the exercise of this right were unacceptable.

The assembly followed up in 1961 by establishing the Special Committee on Decolonization, which, following an expansion in membership in 1962, became known as the Committee of 24. The mandate of the committee was to assess implementation of the declaration. Membership of the committee was weighted in favor of Third World states, and it served as an effective thorn in the side of the colonial powers, arguably accelerating their exit from the colonies.

The success of the process of decolonization is evident in the fact that more than eighty former colonies have obtained their independence since the founding of the United Nations and only sixteen non-self-governing territories (the largest of which—New Caledonia—has a population of just over 215,000 people) remain for consideration by the committee.

From the perspective of human security, the sting in the tail here is that the United Nations has almost entirely failed to engage what had been the main substance of the discussion prior to its founding—the position of minorities within states, the rights accruing to them, and international rights and responsibilities to promote or to defend these rights when under assault by the state in question. Many of the most devastating conflicts in the post–World War II system (e.g., Nigeria and East Pakistan) had their roots in minority claims to self-determination. Such conflicts often occasioned massive civilian casualties, raising serious questions about the effectiveness of emerging efforts to protect civilians at risk. The United Nations remained aloof.

Action in support of the Charter's embrace of equal rights and self-determination of peoples was clearly limited by the endorsement of the principle of territorial integrity of member states in Article 2.4. Both Articles 2.4 and 2.7 limited the capacity of states and the UN itself to intervene in matters of minority rights. This would suggest either that the concept of "people" was limited to identification with recognized sovereign territory and, later, to colonial territories in their entirety or that the concept of self-determination (at least as it pertained to minorities within sovereign states) did not imply any right to secession and sovereignty. This understanding was confirmed in the Declaration on Granting Independence to Colonial Countries and Peoples, where it was noted that any attempt to disrupt the national unity or territorial integrity of a member state was incompatible with the Charter.[95]

The weakness of normative development regarding the self-determination of minorities was not surprising. The UN consists of member states. Many of these states had minority problems of their own. It was improbable that they would undertake actions that would draw into question their own territorial integrity. This sentiment was especially strong among recently decolonized states, as their national identities were frequently weak and contested. However, the sentiment extended to a number of permanent members facing challenges from territorially based minorities. At a more basic level, the effort by the League of Nations to pursue minority rights in the interwar period had produced numerous difficulties and had left a bad taste.[96] The question of group rights was much more problematic than that of individual rights, since the former had implications with regard to the principle of territorial sovereignty that underpinned the Westphalian international system.

The record of regional organizations in this matter was uneven but not substantially different. Although organizations varied in their receptivity to the promotion of individual rights within member states, in both North and South they displayed no receptivity to the notion of group rights to self-determination during the Cold War era.[97]

In short, to the extent that group identity was an element of human security, this dimension of the agenda remained underdeveloped during the Cold War.

The Human Element of Economic Development

> Every gun that is made, every warship launched, every rocket fired represents, in the final analysis, a theft from those who hunger and are not fed, who are cold and not clothed.   —Dwight D. Eisenhower, 1953[98]

> History has taught us that wars produce hunger, but we are less aware that mass poverty can lead to war or end in chaos. While hunger rules, peace cannot prevail. He who wants a ban on war must also ban mass poverty. Morally it makes no difference whether a human being is killed in war or is condemned to starve to death because of the indifference of others.
>
> —Brandt Commission, 1980[99]

The final issue for consideration in this chapter is the evolution of economic thinking in the post–World War II era. Initial consideration of the link between economics and security after World War II focused on the reconstruction of European states devastated by the war. Widespread deprivation and unemployment were widely perceived both in the United States and in Europe to create substantial potential for radicalization of the working class, growth in the influence of communist and allied forces, political instability, and, potentially, the erosion of the western position in Europe in favor of the Soviet Union. This economic dimension of emerging Cold War logic was one critical element in the elaboration of the Marshall Plan, whereby the United States provided massive amounts of capital for the reconstruction of Western Europe while encouraging incipient processes of economic integration there. In this respect, the initiative reflected a strong perception of the intimate link between economics and security and, more important, the link between individual economic circumstances and national and regional security.

In addition, consideration of economic well-being and the right to a decent life was a central component of the Universal Declaration of Human Rights. The preamble recognized the equal rights of men and women and affirmed the signatories' determination to promote "social progress and better standards of life in larger freedom." The Declaration further identified as inalienable individual rights the right to social security, the right to work and to equal pay for equal work, the right to "just and favourable remuneration," the right to leisure, the right to a standard of living "adequate for the health and well-being of himself and his family," and the right to education.[100]

As noted earlier, the specification of state obligations in this regard was delayed as a result of contestation of the human rights agenda during the Cold War. However, in the 1966 International Covenant on Economic, Social and Cultural Rights, signatories accepted obligations to promote and safeguard the right to work; to provide technical and vocational training; to establish equality of opportunity, fair wages, and decent living conditions; to establish safe and healthy working conditions; to protect the right to leisure; and to provide social security. The covenant also stipulated that women were to receive equal pay and enjoy equal working conditions. The covenant recognized the right to freedom from hunger and committed states to take adequate measures to its attain that goal. It stressed the right to "enjoyment of the highest attainable standard of physical and mental health" and committed states to take specific measures to ensure this right. Finally, states accepted an obligation to promote the right to education through universal, compulsory, and free primary education and open access to secondary and higher education. The agenda of what came to be known as "human development" was largely contained in the basic documents of human rights law that emerged from the 1940s to the 1960s.

As reconstruction proceeded successfully and the lines of the Cold War hardened in Europe, attention shifted to the South. This shift in focus was also encouraged by the beginnings of decolonization and the emerging bipolar competition for influence in the Third World. The first major development assistance program (President Truman's Point 4) was defined in Cold War terms: economic development in pursuit of freedom from want was perceived to be an essential element of the emerging global struggle against the communist threat.

The evolution of UN and related thinking on development is well treated in a companion volume in this series.[101] Here we are interested in one element of that evolution: the extent to which Cold War consideration of development reflected germinating ideas regarding the relationship between economics and individual security.

It has been accepted by most development economists, if not by state policymakers,[102] that the fundamental objective of economic development is the improvement in the quality of life of individual members of a community. As one distinguished member of the profession declared: "Economic growth was never regarded as the objective of development. . . . Poverty reduction was always at the heart of the concern."[103] The essential question was how to improve the quality of life. Was a focus on growth and related national aggregates (i.e., savings and investment) sufficient, on the assumption that gains in these aggregates would trickle down through the population, improving the lot of most or all of its members? Or were more targeted policies necessary to ensure that the benefits of development were widely shared? A second important question was whether development should be taken in isolation from related issues (e.g., rights and governance) or whether it had to be considered part of a larger project of change that empowered people not only economically but politically.

In the first years after the Cold War, the growth position held sway. The focus of development thinking and development assistance was on enhancing economic growth in the less developed countries. The targets were measures of state economic performance rather than individual well-being, on the assumption that growth not only was essential to the improvement of living standards and quality of life but that it would more or less automatically produce these desired consequences.[104] As Mahbub ul Haq put it: "After the Second World War . . . an obsession grew with economic growth models and national income accounts. . . . People as the agents of change and beneficiaries of development were often forgotten. . . . The delinking of ends and means began, with economic science often obsessed with means."[105]

It is important to note that this focus on national output aggregates was not universal. The UN itself produced a number of powerful critiques. A UN report issued in 1949 stressed the importance of the distribution of gains from development if the process was to increase the security and welfare of the masses of human beings.[106] In 1951, a UN expert group emphasized the importance of generating new employment opportunities as part of the development process and went further to argue that social justice (notably agrarian reform) was a necessary condition for successful development.[107] Yet the focus of the literature on national aggregates and on growth was evident. And its influence extended into the 1960s in the UN's First Development Decade.

The growth rates of many less developed countries were reasonably impressive during much of the 1950s and 1960s. But it became increasingly clear that growth in and of itself was not obviously producing the desired decrease in unemployment, underemployment, and poverty. As one observer put it much later: "GNP per head (an indicator of economic performance) and the human indicators of education (literacy rates) and health (life expectancy, infant mortality) are not very strongly correlated."[108]

The result was a broadening of the discussion that was important to subsequent thinking about human security. One dimension, reflecting the generally held view that a lack of investment capital was a significant handicap to development, was a growing interest in the relationship between disarmament and development. The proposals for the first UN Development Decade suggested that substantial reduction in military expenditure could reduce funds sufficient to double the growth rates of less developed countries.[109] A second was the growing appreciation of the human dimension of development; Secretary-General U Thant argued in 1961 that the improvement of conditions of life and the enhancement of the capacity of human beings to fulfill their aspirations were critical aspects of development.[110] Third, and more practically, several agencies, notably the ILO, devoted increasing attention to the issue of employment as an aspect of development, since it was through increasing employment that the benefits of development would reach the larger population beyond the elites.[111] This was linked to growing interest in income distribution as a target in development assistance. Fourth, greater interest in the development of human capital emerged. This was accompanied by discussion of the relationship between development and human rights.

These trends continued and strengthened in the 1970s in the Second Development Decade. By this time, the assumption that growth implied improvement in the standard of living of the mass of the population was severely contested. In mid-decade, the International Commission on Development Issues (the Brandt Commission) revived the link between disarmament and development, advocated a substantial transfer of resources to the developing world in a twenty-year "Marshall Plan," and called for a global program to ensure adequate access to food.[112]

One significant output of this process was the recommendation that a greater amount of national resources be devoted to improving the economic position of the working poor. This was linked to the emergence of a growing concern for basic needs.[113] Concern over poverty and basic needs was associated with increasing attention to rural areas and the need for land reform. It also opened a broader discussion of the role of women in development, fostered further discussion of the link between development and human rights, and provoked increasing consideration of the empowerment of civil society.

The shift to poverty programming and basic needs, although it more strongly reflected the basic point that development was about improving the lives of people, was not universally welcomed. Many aid recipients resisted it because it had the potential to be considerably intrusive in domestic affairs and distracted attention from other policy priorities such as the New International Economic Order (NIEO). Some suggested that the rich countries used the concept of basic needs to reduce development assistance.[114]

In spite of these obstacles, the gradual humanization of development was carried forward into the 1980s (the Third Development Decade) in the elaboration of a wide array of social goals to address poverty and give poor people a measure of control over their own lives.[115] Conventional targets such as growth, savings, and investment were supplemented by detailed objectives in the areas of nutrition, life expectancy and infant mortality, employment, and literacy. Moreover, outside the UN system, there was increasing attention to the link between development and security. The Brandt Commission called for a redefinition of security that went beyond military aspects to consider how to promote the basic conditions for peaceful relations between nations. This implied a need to address nonmilitary as well as military problems. As is evident in the quote at the beginning of this section, the commission stressed the connection between poverty and conflict. Noting that overseas development assistance was equivalent to 5 percent of global military spending, it also revived consideration of the link between disarmament and development.[116]

As the decade progressed, there was increasing attention to the link between development and environmental degradation, culminating in the Brundtland Commission's embrace of the notion of sustainable development, which linked development needs to the interests of future generations. The commission argued that today's development should not proceed at the expense of those not yet born.[117] The commissioners highlighted as key aspects of sustainable development the needs of the poor, the significance of equity in development, employment as the most basic of needs, and the importance of food and energy security for individuals. The commission also embraced the notion that defense spending diverted needed resources from the development enterprise: "The arms race—in all parts of the world—preempts resources that might be used more productively to diminish the security threats created by environmental conflict and resentments that are fuelled by widespread poverty." More important, the Brundtland report clearly securitized economic development issues, noting that "the real sources of insecurity also encompass unsustainable development."[118]

The interface between development thinking and development practice has always been problematic. It was particularly so during the 1980s as a result of the 1970s oil shocks and the consequent cascade of debt crises in developing countries. Recession in the developed countries had caused the demand for exports of primary commodities to decline. In the meantime, inflation in the developed world had increased the price of the manufactured imports of developing states. Consequently, the decade witnessed a dramatic decline in the terms of trade of developing countries. This made it increasingly difficult for them to service debt that had accrued during the 1970s as banks sought to recycle petrodollar deposits.

In response, while development theorists busily and constructively tended their garden, and in so doing, consolidated the trend of humanizing development, states and the IFIs moved development practice back toward a statecentric focus that emphasized national aggregates and institutional reform in national institutions. These reforms were designed to expand the space for private economic activity, reduce the role of the public sector in economic activity, and open developing states to the global economy. The associated stagnation of output and decline in public sector funding for safety nets and poverty programming produced frequent declines in per capita income and had extremely negative consequences for those who were marginalized in the project of neoliberal reform. These effects were exacerbated by the fact that fiscal stress and increasing defense expenditure in the developed world produced a decline in the share of developed-world GNP (gross national product) devoted to development assistance.

The shortcomings of practice and the intrusion of the Washington consensus notwithstanding, we see during the 1960s through the 1980s a significant evolution in development thinking away from traditional statecentric and growth-oriented conceptions.[119] The role of the UN in this process is evident here and has been fully documented by our colleagues in the series' study on the evolution of development thinking.

The significant aspects of this evolution from our perspective are

- The growing interest in the human dimension of development, particularly in the later Cold War and despite the interlude of the 1980s.

This evolution parallels, although more weakly, the expansion in recognition of the human being as a subject of rights in international relations.

- The nature of the link between development and security. It was increasingly accepted that security and development were related. Development was seen as contributing to security, underdevelopment to instability. However, the two concepts, for the most part, remained quite distinct. There was very little effort during this period to argue that development (or, for that matter, economic conditions in general) was a part of the concept of security.

- The call for disarmament that would fund development. In the 1970s in particular, it was argued that disarmament could fund a global transfer of resources to finance human development in poorer countries. The Brandt Commission in this respect is a clear ancestor of the 1994 Human Development Report discussed in Chapter 4.

- The clear gap between the evolution of norms in development theory and the behavior of states. In the later part of the Cold War, the proportion of GNP devoted to development assistance by the developed states declined. In the 1980s in particular, donor behavior was increasingly dominated by a neoliberal consensus that devalued the significance of human development indicators in favor of the reduction of public sector spending and reform of recipient economies to expand the space for private economic activity and global trade and investment. In other words, although the evolution of ideas in much of the development literature was toward the humanization of discourse on development, this had little impact on the behavior of donor states and the principal international institutions.

Conclusion

The Cold War era displays numerous traces of the human security agenda that would later emerge. In comparison with the interwar period, the security needs of individuals were far more substantially addressed both within the UN and outside it. Key norms were established that addressed the protection of individuals with respect to abusive state structures, war crimes, the treatment of civilians in war (both interstate and noninternational), and displacement across borders. Moreover, both these and the preexisting inherited norms were universalized, extending throughout the globe as international society expanded. The notion that there were norms for Europeans that did not apply to others largely disappeared. And, to an extent, the logic underlying these normative concerns moved toward recognition of the intrinsic value of human beings and their inalienable right as human beings to be treated with dignity and away from more strictly instrumentalist reasons.

The elaboration of norms concerning national self-determination, national liberation, and racism all had important links to human security in their address of the core value of identity. In addition, the development agenda displayed considerable movement toward the consideration of the needs of individuals and the protection of their economic welfare, as opposed to those of states, although the resurgence of neoliberalism in the 1980s drew this trend into question.

However, there were obvious limitations on the extent to which an orientation toward human security emerged during the Cold War. The mechanisms developed by international society to implement human rights norms were decidedly weak, with the exception of Western Europe, where, given the nature of domestic judicial structures, they were largely unnecessary. There was no evidence of any move on the part of the UN or international society more broadly toward the enforcement of protection when human rights were particularly grievously abused. The UN's use of military means was generally limited to the classical tasks of interposing, monitoring, and observing on the basis of consent from the parties. Interventions by states that had positive consequences for human security were widely condemned for the threat they posed to international order.

The period was also one in which contrary norms grew in strength, especially those concerning nonintervention and state sovereignty. The result was paradoxical. Emerging norms that might justify derogation of state sovereignty in the pursuit of human security were counterbalanced by a strong embrace of a view of sovereignty that maximized domestic jurisdiction and minimized still further the possibility for legitimate intrusion into the internal affairs of states.

The reasons for this tension are fairly clear. The impact of Cold War rivalry on the capacity of the Security Council to respond effectively to human security concerns was substantial and negative. The efforts of the superpowers to sustain their position within their spheres of influence gave them further reason to resist potential intrusion by international organizations operating on the basis of universal norms related to human security. In the General Assembly, the emerging Third World majority was deeply suspicious of efforts to diminish sovereign rights so recently obtained. The desire of the superpowers for influence over these new states diminished any prospect that general norms in the area of human security might be applied where such norms threatened the prerogatives of new states. Finally, although much of the groundwork was laid for the emergence of transnational civil society actors during the Cold War and while some NGOs made a considerable difference in the promotion of norms related to human security, bipolarity and the dominance of realist perspectives on security in the face of imminent threat left limited space for NGOs to contest the prerogatives of states in international security.

3

The Evolving Critique of National Security

- **Wars and Change**
- **Nuclear Weapons and Human (In)Security**
- **Developments during and after the Cold War**
- **The End of the Cold War and State Capacity**
- **Conclusion**

> [A]ny sweeping condemnation of Westphalia smooths out the ups and downs of history, and especially overlooks the extent to which the idea of the secular state was a significantly successful response to the torment of religious warfare in the seventeenth century, and indirectly fostered the ideas of self-determination for colonial peoples and co-existence between ideological adversaries in the twentieth century. Plausibly, it would be the re-empowering of the state as associated with citizens and territory that provides the best hope in the near future. —Richard Falk, 1999[1]

> [H]uman rights is not so much the declaration of the superiority of European civilization as a warning by Europeans that the rest of the world should not seek to reproduce its mistakes. The chief of these was the idolatry of the nation-state, causing individuals to forget the higher law commanding them to disobey unjust orders. The abandonment of this moral heritage of natural law, the surrender of individualism to collectivism, the drafters [of the Declaration of Human Rights] believed, led to the catastrophe of Nazi and Stalinist oppression. —Michael Ignatieff, 2001[2]

In the previous two chapters, we have seen how the emerging primacy of the claims of the nation-state concerning security was largely justified in terms of the state's provision of protection to individuals. It was generally accompanied by consideration of the rights of individuals and the limits these placed on sovereign authorities. Occasionally, theorists raised the possibility that state's failure to meet its obligations to protect citizens, residents, and subjects might weaken its claim to absolute sovereignty and permit intervention by outsiders to respond to the state's incapacity or venality. By the end of the nineteenth century, however, in Europe at least, such considerations had been drowned in the upsurge of nationalism and the union of the individual, the nation, and the state that this doctrine posited.

During the first ninety years of the twentieth century, the norms in international relations that protected individuals expanded in three respects. European understandings of individual rights were slowly extended to the rest of the globe. They slowly embraced groups (minorities, women, and children) that had historically been underprivileged or excluded in discourse on civil and political rights. And they deepened in substantive terms from survival to welfare and identity. On paper at least, states came to accept an increasing number of obligations in each of these areas—in declarations, covenants, and conventions on human rights and in the further elaboration of the laws of war.

In this chapter, we ask: What were the roots of this halting evolution? What developments in international relations fostered change in international society's understanding of the place of the individual in discourse and practice on security during the interwar and Cold War periods? What was the historical and material basis for the rapid change in thinking about security after the Cold War? In the first part of the chapter, we discuss a number of developments in the first half of the twentieth century that threw into question the settled nationalist understanding of the relationship between the state and the individual. In the second, we turn to the evolution of discourse on security during the Cold War, particularly the growing contestation of the statist, military conception of security that formed the intellectual basis for the subsequent emergence of human security.

Wars and Change

As we have seen, the nineteenth-century nationalist tradition, by merging the citizen into the nation and the nation into the state, left little room for anyone to contest the primacy of state security. Insofar as the lives of ordinary citizens were secure and insofar as custom and contractual understandings moderated the prerogatives of the state, the need to rethink or challenge state primacy was minimal. In the first half of the twentieth century, however, shifting power distributions, new ideological developments (including hypernationalism and fascism), and technological advances all worked to undermine this equilibrium between citizen and state. This chapter examines how the two world wars, strategic bombing, the Holocaust, and the advent of nuclear weapons called into question the ability of the state to hold up its end of the bargain by providing for the security of its citizens.

The two world wars sent almost 100 million civilians and soldiers to their premature deaths.[3] The cruel and inhumane way in which millions of these victims died—through firebombing, gas chambers, starvation, and execution—

shocked the conscience of those who survived. The massive casualties and inhumanity inflicted on humans by other humans caused many, in the aftermath of World War II, to ask whether the primacy accorded to state security had been excessive. This emerging critique of national security was manifested in the refusal of the Nuremberg judges to exempt the Nazi leaders from individual responsibility for their actions and in enumeration of specific individual rights vis-à-vis the state in the Universal Declaration of Human Rights.

The emerging critique of state or national security is closely related to the rise of a human rights discourse. Another way of saying this is that the critique of national security and the rise of the notion of human rights are two sides of the same coin: as consciousness rose about the state's inability to provide the physical and existential security desired by its citizens, so did attempts (by the same citizens or humankind) to reclaim the rights that had been metaphorically "transferred" to the state. The UN Charter, the Declaration of Human Rights, the Convention on Genocide, and the Geneva Conventions may all be interpreted as the successful wresting back of individual rights from the state, a recall made necessary by the tragic events dealt with in this chapter. This wresting back of human rights in the late 1940s and early 1950s was real and not metaphorical. As we have seen, the rights recalled became enshrined in international documents. But that did not mean that human rights began to trump state rights in domestic or international politics. After all, these conventions were adopted by states. And on most issues and for most areas of the world, human rights would repeatedly take a back seat to the rights of states until the 1970s.

The World Wars

In 1899 and 1907, the major powers met in The Hague to discuss arms reduction, avoidance of war, and the laws of war. No agreements on arms reduction came out of these Hague conferences, but important conventions on civilizing warfare were adopted. Signatories of the 1899 Hague Convention agreed to outlaw the dropping of explosives from balloons, the use of projectiles to discharge asphyxiating gases, and the expanded use of dumdum bullets.[4] As Adam Roberts has pointed out, many of these conventions were brushed aside in World War I. The opening act, Germany's invasion of Belgium, violated Article 1 (of the 1907 Hague Convention V on Neutrality in Land War), which was unambiguous: "The territory of neutral Powers is inviolable." More ambiguous was the combat status of those who resisted the German occupation. Neither of the Hague conferences made much headway in clarifying this point, and Germany exercised little restraint against Belgian resisters. In April 1915, Germany used poison gas against the Allies; Britain replied in kind with chemical weapons five months later at the battle of Loos. The prohibition against bombing from the air ("balloons") did not stop the emerging air forces of the major antagonists from bombing each other's military and industrial assets. Tami Davis Biddle has argued that since airplanes were not balloons, no one felt constrained by the "no bombing from balloons" rule; quite the contrary, all sides were anxious to test the military prowess of the nascent air forces.[5] In general, the belligerents tried to aim at military targets, but the accuracy of the bombers was so low that populated and undefended cities were inevitably hit.

Biddle has observed that the war "also saw emergent forms of strategic bombing—bombing done well behind the lines of battle in order to undermine an enemy's war economy and will to fight."[6] She cited Germany's use of zeppelins on the English coast and London, French raids against Germany, and British bombings of industrial centers in Germany toward the end of the war as emerging instances of strategic bombing.[7] The latter, as we will discover, would become a major issue—in terms of the laws of war and civilian casualties—in World War II. The key prohibitions in World War I were on the bombing of "undefended" cities and villages and attacks on hospitals, churches, and buildings devoted to arts and sciences. Adam Roberts has argued that while violations of the Hague conventions were found everywhere, one must not lose sight of World War I's "greatest and most difficult challenge to the laws of war": "the terrible military slaughter caused by great armies engaged in machine-gun, shell, and trench warfare."[8] This was the most difficult challenge because the slaughter was not contrary to the laws of war; soldiers fighting soldiers was consistent with the accepted principle of the 1868 St. Petersburg Declaration "that the only legitimate object which States should endeavor to accomplish during war is to weaken the military forces of the enemy."[9] The difference was that World War I was a total war, where entire "societies had been massively mobilized for war, industry had produced the means of waging war in vast quantity, and the poor conscript soldiers in the front line had been overwhelmingly the targets and victims."[10] This observation about total war and its principal victims, set in the context of a discussion about the laws of (land) war, is normatively and empirically on the mark because it highlights the changing nature of war and its horrific human consequences. From a condition where the state was able to provide its citizens some insulation from the ravages of war, World War I ushered in an era where the state would be increasingly unable to perform that protective function.

World War II, the second total war of the twentieth century, was almost four times more destructive than World War I, judging by the number of lives lost. Fifty-five million perished, of which more than half were civilians.[11] Three developments during the war are especially relevant to our analysis: strategic bombing, the Holocaust, and the advent of nuclear weapons. These developments reinforced and amplified a trend that was already obvious during World War I: the increasing inability of the state to provide the physical and psychological security expected by its citizens. Nowhere was this phenomenon more obvious than in the European states conquered or dominated by Nazi Germany: Jews from these lands were herded into ghettos and transported to concentration camps where they joined Jews from Germany for the eventual slaughter that came to be known as the "final solution" to the "Jewish problem."

Strategic Bombing

Strategic bombing refers to the aerial bombardment of the adversary's industrial and civilian centers in order to undermine the adversary's morale and will to fight. Strategic bombing thus aims less at the physical destruction of front-line soldiers and their war equipment than the industrial capacity and psychological will of the adversary. Advocates of strategic bombing assumed that once a certain threshold of aerial bombardment of the enemy's industrial and civilian targets was reached, the enemy would "crack." General Hugh Trenchard, the first head of the Royal Air Force (RAF), justified Britain's bombing of Germany's industrial centers in 1918 in terms of its impact on morale. As he put it then, "The moral effect of bombing stands undoubtedly to the material effect in a proportion of 20 to 1."[12] Historians have derided Trenchard for pulling his statistic out of thin air; they have been more respectful of Italian General Guilio Douhet's theory of aerial warfare. Douhet published his influential *Command of the Air* in 1921, which argued that future wars would be won or lost by air power. For Douhet, the decisiveness of air power lies in its intended target:

> Mercifully, the decision will be quick in this kind of [air] war, since the decisive blows will be directed at civilians, that element of the countries at war least able to sustain them. These future wars may yet prove to be more humane than wars in the past in spite of all, because they may in the long run shed less blood.[13]

Douhet's claim to fame as the father of modern strategic bombing rests primarily on this attempt to mix the moral with the strategic. Air power was the wave of the future; when directed against civilians, it would shorten wars and lead to less bloodshed. Trenchard was just as convinced about the ability of strategic bombing to crack the morale of the enemy, but he was less forthcoming about whether it was the more humane course. Douhet's theory was the subject of intense debate in military academies in the interwar period, but like all academic debates, it would be settled by events in the real world.

At the beginning of World War II, Britain, France, and Germany acceded to a U.S. plea to restrict bombing to military targets. That restriction was observed until May 1940, when Germany bombed Warsaw and Rotterdam indiscriminately. In August, German bombers accidentally hit London; the following night, Britain responded by attacking Berlin from the air.[14] Thus began the slide into the Douhet-Trenchard mode of strategic bombing: the indiscriminate or "area" bombing of cities in search of the all-important (and ultimately elusive) political objective of crushing the morale of the adversary's civilian population. In effect this meant killing as many of them as possible (as in firebombing) in the hope that those who escaped would be too hurt or demoralized to support the war effort.

The U.S. Army Air Forces (AAF), which had joined the battle in Europe in 1942, refrained from bombing civilian targets in the first two years of air operations against Germany and Italy. The AAF stuck to its preference for "precision bombing" of military targets until late 1944, when the availability of more planes and the insistence of civilians that the war be ended quickly caused it to join the RAF in "area" bombing of Germany.[15] Britain and Germany's Douhetian warfare had inflicted severe damage on London, Berlin, Coventry, and Hamburg. U.S. collaboration with the RAF in area bombing began in earnest in early 1945 with Operation Clarion (which hit Heidelberg, Gottingen, and Baden-Baden), followed by Operation Thunderclap (which hit Berlin), culminating in the firebombing of Dresden.[16] The Allied bombing of Dresden, a city of great beauty but no military assets, has been singled out as one of the most ghastly episodes of the war: the firestorm created by the bombing incinerated tens of thousands of refugees running from the ground war. As one historian described the annihilation, even "air-raid shelters became suffocating incinerators which cooked those inside until their bodies were charred hulks and their body fats formed a thick layer on the floor."[17] Biddle went on to argue that Dresden "foreshadowed what was to come in the Far Eastern theater." One month later, the firebombing of Tokyo began, claiming 80,000 lives; sixty-six other Japanese cities would suffer the same fate before President Truman unleashed the power of the atomic bomb at Hiroshima and Nagasaki in August 1945.[18]

Strategic bombing, or at least the Douhet-Trenchard variant practiced during World War II, came to be seen as a strategy of dubious morality. It blurred the distinction between combatants and noncombatants, thereby making it impossible to apply the *jus in bello* strictures that had governed civilized warfare for centuries. Perhaps just as important, it caused dispro-portionate loss of lives without delivering the knock-out punch to the adversary's morale promised by Douhet's theory. Postwar assessments of stra-tegic bombing generally cast doubt on its effectiveness in crushing the morale of the German people. The moral case against strategic bombing has been ably made by Michael Walzer and Geoffrey Best. Both contend that under conditions of supreme emergency, as obtained between 1939 and 1944 for Brit-ain, strategic bombing was not unjustified; however, by mid-1944, when Brit-ain was no longer in mortal danger and had obtained the technical capability to conduct precision bombing, it was manifestly unjust to continue—in fact, to accelerate—the bombing of German cities.[19] The killing of hundreds of thousands of German civilians—including 100,000 at Dresden—at this point in the struggle was gratuitous.

The legal case against strategic bombing is more ambiguous, primarily because the law of war on bombing cities was itself ambiguous prior to World War II. At Nuremberg, the prosecution adopted a light touch when it came to trying Hitler's generals for indiscriminate bombing, in part because of this ambiguity and perhaps even more because Allied forces were also implicated in that method of war fighting. In his seminal book *Humanity and Warfare,* Geoffrey Best concluded his analysis of warfare in the first half of the twenti-eth century by lamenting that "it [his analysis] has been mostly about civil-ians. Objectively and quantitatively, they constitute the category of human beings for whom the law of war was most found lacking." The law of war was found lacking in protecting the civilian because in World War I, and espe-cially in World War II, "the line of material distinction between 'soldier' and 'civilian' became more blurred."[20] Best's book dealt with the factors behind this blurring of the distinction between combatant and noncombatant, of which strategic bombing was a major one. The significance of strategic bomb-ing for our narrative is the moral questions it raised, especially in light of post–World War II evaluations of its effectiveness as a strategy. Geoffrey Best, one might say, did have his eye on the big picture: indeed, his analysis is mostly about civilians and, we might well add, and it is also about the inability of the state to protect them from harm.

The Holocaust

While the worry of most individuals is about the ability of their state to protect them against the depredations of other states, Jews in Germany were subjected to the depredations of their own state in the 1930s and 1940s. As

Germany invaded its neighbors, the Jewish population of occupied countries such as Poland and France were rounded up and transported to concentration camps to be exterminated as part of Hitler's "final solution" to the "Jewish problem." Six million Jews lost their lives in this premeditated and systematic genocide that we have come to call the Holocaust. Although the Nazi regime also persecuted and killed the infirm, socialists, communists, gypsies, and homosexuals, the term "Holocaust" is most often used to describe Germany's policy, between 1933 and 1945, of exterminating the Jewish people of Europe. Three phases leading to the final solution may be discerned. From 1933 to 1939, Jews in Germany were stripped of their civil and political rights, verbally demonized, physically assaulted, and made to flee from work and home. Between 1939 and 1941, an additional 1.5 million Jews (not counting the half-million German Jews) fell under Nazi control; many were herded into ghettos in occupied Poland and France pending a "territorial solution" which included exiling them to Madagascar, the French colony which Germany assumed would be ceded to it soon.[21] It was in the third phase, which began with the attack against the Soviet Union in 1941 and lasted until the end of the war in 1945, that Hitler embarked on the genocide of the European Jewry.[22]

That the Holocaust could be perpetrated by "a people steeped in Western culture and rich in scientific knowledge"[23] came as a shock to many. The manner in which the Hitlerian state appropriated the methods of science and public administration to streamline and render ultra-efficient the murder of the European Jewry is a major blight on the achievements of modernity. In trying to account for what made the Holocaust possible, Ian Kershaw has pointed to what he sees as the "frontal and total" attack on liberal values:

> The individual was to count for nothing, but was to be subordinated wholly to the interests of the racially defined nation, the Volk. Groups excluded from the 'national community' were automatically to lose any citizenship rights.... [T]he Nazi Program of 1920 could state openly: "Only members of the nation [Volksgenossen] may be citizens of the State. Only those of German blood ... may be members of the nation. Accordingly, no Jew may be a member of the nation."[24]

In his moving but relentlessly argued tome, Daniel Goldhagen tried to come up with reasons why so many Germans succumbed to this attack on liberal values. His answer was German anti-Semitism, which he saw as the ideological impetus that transformed many ordinary Germans into becoming "Hitler's willing executioners" during the Holocaust. While his thesis remains controversial, his observation about the disconnect between ordinary Germans and Jews is on the mark:

Had the Nazis been faced with a German populace who saw Jews as ordinary human beings, and German Jews as their brothers and sisters, then it is hard to imagine that the Nazis would have ... been able to proceed, with the extermination of the Jews. If they somehow had been able to go forward, then the probability that the assault would have unfolded as it did, and that Germans would have killed so many Jews, is extremely low.[25]

This plea for underscoring our common humanity was a central lesson of the Holocaust. The postwar planners institutionalized this lesson in two ways. On the reactive side—involving punishment and deterrence—they established the Nuremberg and Tokyo trials. Here, as noted in the previous chapter, the notion of sovereign immunity as cover for the systematic violation of the rights of human beings was drawn into question in significant ways. On the proactive side, they enshrined our common humanity in the United Nations Charter and later in the Universal Declaration of Human Rights and a host of other international conventions that protected the (noncombatant) individual. As Best put it, the Nuremberg Trials and the Declaration of Human Rights constituted the two pillars of the Allies' "Temple of Peace": "the human rights program representing the values of the future, and the war crimes trials symbolizing the destruction of the evil forces of the past."[26]

Although the impact of these normative changes on international (and domestic) practice was limited during the Cold War, it is clear that the human rights instruments of the late 1940s and early 1950s were major salvos directed at the reified state; they aimed to restore to the individual his/her innate rights which had been prejudiced (*in extremis* for many) during the first half of the twentieth century, especially during World War II and the Holocaust. The importance of this change in ideas and norms cannot be overemphasized. When the state was reified or put on a pedestal for the public goods—including security of its citizens—that it was supposedly supplying, it was difficult and perhaps even unnecessary to advance a discourse based on individual rights. What World War II showed with its strategic bombing and especially the Holocaust was the enormous peril in which humanity was placed in the absence of such a discourse. While it was possible to describe the atrocities committed against Jews, gypsies, socialists, prisoners of war, and other civilians, no vocabulary existed to effectively counter and condemn the depredations of the state. The advent of such a vocabulary and discourse—centered on the idea of human rights—in the aftermath of World War II is thus one of the most precious outcomes of the tragic period. For those living outside Western Europe, the existence of this human rights discourse probably did not mean very much in its first twenty-five years (the 1950s to the mid-1970s). The Cold War and the rivalry between the two blocs held in abeyance the implementation of these aspirations and relegated them to the back burner. But the critical thing is that the idea had been planted.

Nuclear Weapons and Human (In)Security

World War II, strategic bombing, and the Holocaust all point to the dangers and inexcusable atrocities associated with the idolatry of the state. Nuclear weapons, however, occupy a more ambiguous position in the emerging critique of national security. The form of nuclear strategy that persisted during the Cold War—deterrence through mutual assured destruction (MAD)—was premised on each opponent holding the other's population hostage to a most horrifying death. The United States and Russia each sought to prevent a war between themselves and their allies by threatening to decimate the industrial and population centers of the other. To be precise, "assured destruction" was defined by the Pentagon in 1965 as "one-fourth to one-third of the Soviet population and two-thirds of Soviet industry."[27] Even the archrealist Henry Kissinger, Nixon's national security adviser and later secretary of state, has described MAD as "the most inhuman strategy for conducting a war."[28] Such an approach to peace obviously places all of humanity under risk and renders it insecure. One only has to recall the "duck under the desk" exercise that millions of American schoolchildren were subjected to at the height of the Cold War.

Yet there is evidence to support the argument that the existence of nuclear weapons and in particular the strategy of MAD played an important role in preventing the two superpowers from coming to blows during the Cold War.[29] Nuclear weapons, in other words, restrained two ideological and powerful adversaries from settling their differences in the way that previous great powers have normally used: a major war. Such a direct clash—and the world came very close to such a precipice in 1961 and 1962—would probably have dwarfed the scale and destruction of previous wars and in the extreme would have had eliminated a large part of humanity. The available evidence suggests that during both the Berlin Crisis of 1961 and the Cuban Missile Crisis of 1962, each side went out of its way to avoid backing the other side into a corner.[30] The nuclear sword of Damocles hanging over the heads of decision-makers has been established as a major explanation for their caution and restraint during these and other crises. In situations where the nuclear factor was irrelevant and in areas where the two superpowers were not involved in face-to-face confrontations, they were less cautious and restrained: witness the invasion of Hungary (by the USSR) and military interventions in Korea and Vietnam (U.S.), Czechoslovakia (USSR), the Dominican Republic (U.S.), Afghanistan

(USSR), and Grenada (U.S.). For most international relations scholars, these empirical observations and the theoretical insight that previous bipolar systems have tended to end in major wars demonstrate that MAD has been a major factor in upholding the general peace.

Yet critics of this smug "nuclear security" would be remiss not to point out the psychological/existential insecurity of living in such a tightly wound nuclear world. Stanley Kubrick's antinuclear movie *Dr. Strangelove* captured the sentiments of those who felt anything but secure. Similarly, the famous political advertisement put out by the Lyndon Johnson administration with the little girl in the garden juxtaposed against images of a mushroom cloud was widely believed to have contributed to the defeat of his Republican contender Barry Goldwater: the advertisement implied that a trigger-happy Goldwater presidency was likely to bring America closer to nuclear war. The insecurities of MAD were far from absent from the political consciousness of the global public.

Moreover, while international relations specialists study the successful nuclear brinksmanship exhibited by President John F. Kennedy's Executive Committee during the Cuban Missile Crisis, recent revelations suggest that the United States and the Soviet Union came much closer to the nuclear precipice than is commonly thought. One of the Soviet submarines subjected to the U.S. Navy's depth charges was rocking so unbearably that two of the three officers with the authority to fire nuclear-tipped torpedoes ordered that the torpedoes be loaded. They had surmised that war had already begun. Only the third officer by the name of Vasilii Arkhipov (whose recent death in the Soviet Union allowed this story to be told) retained his cool and persuaded his colleagues not to launch the nuclear-tipped missiles against the U.S. warship harassing them from above.[31] For skeptics of nuclear security, this episode illustrates the potential of factors such as the unknown and local commanders and their psychological breaking point in triggering a nuclear confrontation. The United States did not know then that Soviet submarines possessed nuclear-tipped torpedoes; in fact until the Arkhipov account surfaced, this fact was not generally known. The firing of a nuclear-tipped torpedo would likely have escalated the crisis to unimaginably violent heights.

After being forced to back down in Cuba, Soviet president Nikita Khrushchev vowed "never again" to be caught in a position of military inferiority to the United States. The hotline and the Limited Test Ban Treaty notwithstanding, Russia spent much of the 1960s in an arms race with the United States. Strategic parity was reached in the early 1970s, which made it possible for both sides to sign the Strategic Arms Limitation Talks treaty (SALT I). SALT I, however, did not prevent both sides from increasing and improving their nuclear arsenals. The Soviets continued to build such that by the late

1970s, they had amassed more intercontinental ballistic missiles (ICBMs)—
though of a poorer quality—than the United States, which brought back a
strong feeling of nuclear insecurity in that country. That insecurity was manifested in what two physicists, tongue-in-cheek, labeled the MAD vs. NUTS
debate: proponents of the former maintaining that the requirements of deterrence are met with the possession of second strike capability and advocates
of NUTS arguing that the capability to fight a nuclear war—including the
ability to match one's adversary at every step of the escalation ladder—was
essential to successful deterrence.[32] The debate about nuclear arms was trig-
gered in part by the policies of the Ronald Reagan administration. Reagan
had surrounded himself with specialists on the Soviet Union who were convinced that it was planning to fight and win nuclear wars. America had to
prepare and arm itself to respond in kind. This approach to nuclear strategy
alarmed not only the MAD thinkers but the U.S. and European public as well.

This strong push by the Reagan administration to confront the "evil empire" in what many observers labeled as Cold War II—of which the acrimoni-
ous debate about the winnability of fighting nuclear wars was a part—was
instrumental in galvanizing a mass antinuclear movement. Demonstrations
in the West against the reigning nuclear policies of the superpowers were common occurrences in the early 1980s. Scientists weighed in with theories about
nuclear winter; their computer simulation models showed that the explosion
of 500–2,000 warheads would bring about a subsequent "nuclear winter"—
irreversible climatic and ecological damage—that would be enough to end
the world.[33] For the first time since 1962, there were genuine public fears in
the United States and Europe that the policies of the superpowers were edg-
ing them closer to nuclear war. In 1984, the *Bulletin of Atomic Scientists* moved
the clock on the magazine's cover to three minutes before midnight, the hour
of the nuclear holocaust.[34]

The Catholic Church, with its illustrious tradition of writings about just
war, joined the nuclear debate with its Pastoral Letter on War and Peace.[35]
Written by the U.S. National Conference of Catholic Bishops, the pastoral
letter began by declaring that humanity was confronting "a moment of supreme crisis in its advance toward maturity." The crisis had to do with "the
threat which nuclear weapons pose for the world and much that we hold dear
in the world." It was because the bishops had "seen and felt the effects of the
crisis . . . in the lives of people we serve" that they felt impelled to issue their
moral evaluation of the nuclear situation.[36] Combining Catholic moral reasoning with a deft understanding of the details of nuclear policy, the bishops
argued that the possession of nuclear weapons for deterrence purposes was
conditionally acceptable, the condition being that the possessors should be

working toward progressive disarmament. Hence deterrence was moral only as a transitional policy. The bishops rejected targeting strategies that aimed at civilians and all notions of nuclear war as morally unacceptable. They also came out against the notion of nuclear superiority, arguing that sufficiency was the less unacceptable strategy for purposes of deterrence.[37]

While the Catholic bishops critiqued the morality of nuclear deterrence and nuclear war in terms of Christian moral precepts, Jonathan Schell's *The Fate of the Earth* advanced a secular but impassioned plea about the urgent need to bury nuclear weapons lest they bury us all in a nuclear holocaust.[38] Schell argued that since the nuclear age, humankind had refused and resisted thinking about the consequences of a nuclear war. Schell's book embarked on a blow-by-blow account—synthesized from the latest scientific findings—of the effects of a full-scale nuclear war. Against those who speculated about escalating the nuclear ladder or fighting limited nuclear wars, Schell argued that the outbreak of a nuclear war would indeed end life on earth as we know it. Comparing the impending nuclear holocaust with the Holocaust of the 1940s, Schell wrote:

> We don't want to believe [the gas chambers of Auschwitz]. . . . But our wishful disbelief is stopped cold by the brute historical fact that it happened: we are therefore forced to believe. But extinction [by nuclear war] has not happened, and hides behind the veil of a future time which human eyes can never pierce. It is true that the testimony of those who survived . . . [about] Hiroshima and Nagasaki offers us a vivid record of devastation by nuclear arms, but this record, which already seems to exhaust our powers of emotional response, illumines only a tiny corner of a nuclear holocaust, and, in any case, does not reach the question of extinction.[39]

Schell's pained and repeated haranguing of his reader about their emotional numbness to the nuclear question gave the bestseller its edge. In the concluding chapter, Schell argued that "the choice" was either to abolish nuclear weapons or to face the probability of extinction. Written at the height of Cold War II, Schell's book found a receptive audience among all those who were concerned that the Reagan administration's policies might drive the United States and Russia into a major confrontation. Although we can now say that Schell was perhaps on the alarmist side, his book remains one of the most eloquent and passionate arguments against being lulled into a false sense of nuclear security. That his argument was based on the importance of ensuring the existence of the human race puts him closer to being a promoter of our "right to life, liberty and the security of person" than is commonly understood.

Whether a U.S. administration less bent on the arms race and confronting the Soviet Union would have galvanized world public opinion about the dangers of nuclear war in the same way is hard to know. But our reading of the debates of that period suggests that it was more than just the Reagan administration. More than three decades after the explosion of the first nuclear device, a sense of ennui and fear emerged among the informed public in the West, which also came to believe that living under the threat of nuclear devastation was not a given. The human rights policies of the Jimmy Carter administration helped legitimate views that looked beyond state security and raised questions about the actual psychological and potential human costs (in the event of war) of nuclear deterrence. The plans and scenarios for fighting a nuclear war advocated by the Reagan administration added a certain shrillness and urgency to these reconsiderations, but the pervasiveness of the antinuclear movement and its longevity suggest that it was not merely a response to the administration's nuclear war–fighting cries.

The antinuclear movement did not peter out after the Cold War. The latest manifestation of this concern was the request by the General Assembly in 1994, over the objections of the United States, France, and the United Kingdom, that the International Court of Justice (ICJ) advise whether international law allowed the threat or use of nuclear weapons. Many of the nonaligned states testified that international humanitarian law forbade "the use of excessively injurious weapons . . . and that the effects of nuclear weapons do not distinguish between combatants and noncombatants."[40] The ICJ issued its finding two years later and took the position that in general, the use or threat of nuclear weapons was "illegal" although it was conflicted about its legality in the extreme case of a state fighting for its very survival.[41] States that threaten or plan to use nuclear weapons will of course justify their action as an "extreme case" involving their very survival, but the significance of the opinion of the ICJ is that it has placed the onus on the state concerned. Hitherto none of the nuclear states has had to justify their threat or use of nuclear weapons to the international community. Whether the U.S. use of nuclear weapons in Hiroshima and Nagasaki would pass the "was the survival of the United States at risk" test is an interesting question. Perhaps just as important as the ICJ's finding is the evolving opinion within the General Assembly that nuclear threats are illegal and the associated tactic of applying international law to the wielders of nuclear weapons.

Around the same time, the Canberra Commission on the Elimination of Nuclear Weapons, which was created by the government of Australia, issued its findings on the utility of nuclear weapons in the post–Cold War era. The commission's members resembled an international who's who of those who think about, make, and implement military strategy. Its report called for the elimination of nuclear weapons on three grounds. First, nuclear weapons were so destructive that they could not be used for military purposes; they could only be used for deterrence. The commission felt that nuclear weapons could not be used, in part because to use them against a nonnuclear state was considered to be "politically and morally indefensible." Second, the commission argued that the continued deployment of nuclear weapons entailed too high a risk that they would be used accidentally. Finally, it argued that if the states that had nuclear weapons refused to give them up, nuclear proliferation, which reduces the security of all, would be inevitable.[42] What gave these conclusions force and credibility was that they were the consensus of a group of individuals who had made and implemented nuclear policies and who had thought about them as political decision-makers or nuclear strategists.

The abolitionist sentiments of the ICJ and Canberra Commission are likely to encounter strong skepticism from the nuclear powers. While the end of the Cold War has taken the edge out of the nuclear arms race and in fact has led to serious negotiated reductions in the arsenals of both the United States and Russia, a new insecurity associated with nuclear weapons and other weapons of mass destruction (WMD), such as chemical and biological weapons, has emerged. The threat that these weapons will fall into the hands of terrorists and that "rogue" states will develop them is replacing MAD as the new source of insecurity. These fears have been exacerbated by the events of 9/11. For all the weaknesses and dangers of MAD, counting on the rationality of the adversary—that it valued its own survival more than its desire to cause death and obliteration of the opponent—to make deterrence work was not unreasonable. Current worries that terrorists will explode a crude nuclear device or release biological toxins in a crowded city are based on the fear that the terrorists do not subscribe to such mundane cost-benefit calculations: those likely to be involved in detonating WMDs are willing to sacrifice their own lives on earth in exchange for a better life in the afterworld, so long as they succeed in inflicting maximum damage on their adversaries' civilians.

If human insecurity during the MAD era stemmed from our being unwitting hostages in the delicate balance of terror, it was a trade-off that states with nuclear weapons were willing to countenance in the name of national security. These nuclear states believed that adopting the correct strategy in dealing with other nuclear states would minimize the probability of nuclear war. The psychological insecurity associated with such strategies was part and parcel of living with nuclear weapons. The danger of nuclear war has receded with the end of the Cold War, but states—both nuclear and nonnuclear—are confronted with a new WMD challenge that they find equally dangerous and less tractable: the proliferation of WMDs and the possibility that they will fall into the wrong hands. Terrorists and rogue states do not subscribe to the traditional rules of the game. The United States felt compelled to wage preventive war against Iraq to eliminate the (nonexistent) WMD threat posed by Saddam Hussein. After September 11, the state seems to be at its wits' end about how to protect its citizens not just from rogue states but also from WMD-wielding terrorists. States are devoting enormous energy and resources to prevent fissile material from falling into the hands of terrorist groups, but many experts believe that it is only a matter of time before such groups obtain enough material to build and use several small nuclear devices. In 1997, for example, Russia could not account for 84 of the 132 suitcase-sized nuclear devices in its arsenal.[43] Exploding such a nuclear device in a crowded city may not kill as many as an ICBM exchange, but the probability that it will happen seems higher, in part because states cannot be 100 percent successful in preventing terrorists from gaining access to nuclear material and in part because the terrorists' not-of-this-world cost-benefit calculations make them undeterrable. Despite the end of the Cold War and the best efforts of the state, nuclear weapons continue to be a major source of human insecurity.

We began this chapter by juxtaposing Richard Falk's historical appreciation of the state with Michael Ignatieff's evaluation that it was the idolization of the nation-state that made the Holocaust and Stalin's pogroms possible. Neither is wrong. Falk can safely concede that the reification of the state made possible the excesses of Nazi Germany and Stalinist Russia. Ignatieff is unlikely to reject the achievements of the state, including re-empowering the properly constituted state to handle future challenges. The events of the twentieth century indeed raise serious questions about the state and about equating state security with individual security. For even if Falk is right about the role of the secular state in protecting the individual and his or her faith from the depredations of others (who are presumably of different faiths), the two world wars, the advent of strategic bombing, the experience of the Holocaust, and the policy of mutual assured destruction did push many ordinary men and women into harm's way and put them in a state of severe existential insecurity.

Yet realizing that fascism and technological "advances" have raised serious questions about the state's ability to protect does not mean that the state was relegated to the margins of international relations. There is no better evidence of the reification of the state than the legalist paradigm, or the notion that the referent of international law remains the state. It was only when human beings acted as beasts—as the Nazis and their supporters did during the Holocaust—that World War II's victors made an exception to statist principle and tried and convicted the Nazi leaders as individuals. An opening had been made, to be sure, but it was a tiny opening. The state would prove to be a remarkably resilient creature. While cognitively there was increasing recognition that idolizing the state was a risky enterprise, there was also general recognition of Falk's points about its stabilizing and positive features. The institutional innovations that were introduced after 1945—the Nuremberg and Tokyo trials, the Declaration of Human Rights, and the genocide convention—to chip away at state idolatry would all be in place by the early 1950s, but with a few exceptions, they would remain in disuse for the next forty years.

Developments during and after the Cold War

> However defined in detail, the idea of "human security" springs from the same values that during the second half of the twentieth century led to the greater articulation of norms for securing human rights, civilizing the conduct of war, and protecting the vulnerable.   —Astri Suhrke, 1999[44]

In the previous chapter, we chronicled the halting development of international norms regarding the security of individuals, suggesting that much of the ideational basis for the subsequent development of human security was laid down during the Cold War. In the first section of this chapter, we discussed how historical events and technological developments favored reconsideration of the place of the individual human being in security. Although the events of the first half of the twentieth century had severely dented the notion that the state was there to protect the individual, the idea that the individual needed to be "secured" against the state had to wait another forty years—almost till the end of the century—before becoming part of the mainstream discourse. In the interregnum, we observe many developments that helped inch the human rights agenda forward, and the purpose of this section is to trace the most important of these developments. In particular, we focus on the arguments of a group of thinkers who sought to chip away at the dominant paradigm of security as "military security." Their attempts to broaden and redefine the notion of security to include economic, environmental, and demographic threats paved the way for the emergence of the concept of human security. Their ideational offensive against state and military security, we also argue, was greatly aided by the shifting international context—the end of the Cold War—and the internal wars that followed.

Thirty Inglorious Years

"Thirty inglorious years" was how Geoffrey Robertson characterized the period between the signing of Universal Declaration of Human Rights and the coming into office of the Carter administration.[45] The mid-1940s to the mid-1970s were inglorious for Robertson because neither the spirit nor the

letter of the Declaration was heeded by most states. As he put it: "Any prospect of a New World Order based on the Universal Declaration was swiftly
shattered."[46] What shattered that prospect was the Cold War. The onset of the
East-West rivalry in 1947 and its intensification in 1949 with the explosion of
the Soviet atomic bomb and the "fall" of China to communism, ushered in a
series of military crises, "limited" wars, and overt and covert interventions by
the major protagonists—the United States and the Soviet Union—to prop up
clients in danger or depose hostile leaders in the Third World.

Given these pressures, it is not surprising that "national security" remained
narrowly state based and military in essence. This understanding of security
was most compatible with the realist and neorealist doctrines that were then
dominant in academic and foreign policy discourse.[47] When the state as a
whole was perceived as being subject to an immediate existential threat in an
intense bipolar conflict involving a nuclear arms race, a human security perspective seemed irrelevant. However, it does not follow that the notion of
protecting individuals disappeared altogether, even during the years when the
Cold War was at its most intense. The ways in which the very existence of
nuclear weapons prompted certain thinkers to draw a distinction between
individual and national security were discussed in the previous section.

Just as important, the human costs of the Cold War became increasingly
evident during this period. Even though none of the nuclear crises moved
beyond the precipice, they highlighted the precariousness of human survival.
The Korean and Vietnam wars claimed over 5 million deaths, all sides considered. In the peripheries, dictators from Erich Honecker to Ferdinand Marcos
to Anastasio Somoza literally got away with murder and other human rights
abuses as long as they remained aligned with, and had the protection of, one
of the superpowers. The domestic polities of the principal antagonists were
also not exempt from reverberations of the Cold War: Mao Zedong's Great
Leap Forward sacrificed 20 million Chinese in the name of catching up with
the imperialists, and the McCarthy years stirred up a consuming anticommu-
nism in the United States that blighted the political landscape, infringed on
the political and civil rights of many, and, in some cases, destroyed the lives of
innocent Americans.

The détente years may have led to a relaxation of tensions between the two
superpowers, but they did not improve the prospects for a human rights agenda
in America's foreign policy. As late as 1974, when Secretary of State Henry
Kissinger discovered that his ambassador to Chile had broached the issue of
human rights with the Pinochet regime, he ordered his staff to "tell [U.S.
Ambassador] Popper to cut out the political science lectures."[48] But this policy
of not asking questions about human rights abuses under Augusto Pinochet—

coming in the aftermath of CIA involvement in the overthrow of the demo-
cratically elected Salvador Allende—was the tail end of an approach that was
increasingly out of step with the times. Angered by Richard Nixon's domestic
antics and disillusioned with the excesses of his amoral realpolitik foreign
policy, the American public voted for a change in 1976. They picked Jimmy
Carter, whose campaign had decried the unethical domestic and foreign policies of the Nixon-Ford years.

Although the years 1946–1976 were a bleak period for individual security
in general, there were three bright spots. First was Europe. As noted in Chapter 2, human rights policies gradually became more significant and more comprehensive in Europe throughout the decades following World War II. The
European Convention for the Protection of Human Rights and Fundamental
Freedoms entered into force in September 1953, monitored by the European
Human Rights Commission and enforced by the European Court of Human
Rights. Especially novel was the right of individual petition whereby individuals who felt that their rights had been violated could petition the commission directly. If the petition was found to have merit, the commission could
then refer the case to the European Court, whose ruling would be binding on
member states. Europe's laudable role in implementing "selected rights" from
the Declaration may be explained by the fact that it was at the center of the
carnage associated with World War II and the Holocaust. European leaders
perceived a direct relationship between the abuse of human rights within a
state (as in Nazi Germany) and the propensity to wage aggressive war. Human rights therefore complemented Europe's economic and political integration as a way to prevent the recurrence of war.[49]

A second bright spot was the rise of human rights NGOs such as the International Commission of Jurists (founded 1952), Amnesty International (1961),
and Helsinki Watch (now Human Rights Watch).[50] But even before the rise of
dedicated human rights NGOs, other more broad-based organizations such
as the World Council of Churches, Lions International, and even the American Federation of Labor were among the forty-two NGOs invited (by the U.S.
Department of State) to the San Francisco conference of 1945, where they
played a role in insisting that the human rights clauses be included in the
Charter of the United Nations.[51]

Amnesty International, however, emerged as the most famous human rights
organization of its time in part because of its untiring and unflinching efforts—
during all phases of the Cold War—to document political prisoners held by
governments of all complexions and shame these governments into taking
the human rights of their political dissidents seriously. Amnesty's human rights
work is especially noteworthy because it began and continued in a political

context where liberal states such as the United States and Britain consistently turned a blind eye toward the worst abuses of their allies. Successive U.S. administrations felt that they could not question the human rights record of their allies in the Third World because Washington needed their support in countering Soviet and Chinese expansionism during the Cold War. NGOs such as Amnesty held up the torch of human rights in these "inglorious years."

The third bright spot was the short-lived, but nevertheless important, human rights policies of the Carter presidency. The thirty inglorious years of human rights neglect ended in 1976 for Geoffrey Robertson because the next year Jimmy Carter was inaugurated as president. Eager to distance his administration from the amoral diplomacy of the Nixon-Ford-Kissinger years, Carter incorporated a human rights component into his foreign policy. Critics have argued that Carter's human rights policies were incoherent and inconsistent, thus preventing the United States from occupying the moral high ground while putting U.S. national interests at risk.[52] There is some truth in these criticisms: weak allies in strategically less significant places such as Argentina, Bolivia, Guatemala, Uruguay, and Thailand were held accountable for their human rights record while others (allied or not) such as South Korea, Iran, China, and the Soviet Union were let off the hook. Military or economic aid to those on the accountable list was cut if their human rights record failed to improve. Although success was hard to document while the policy was in action, subsequent accounts by political prisoners such as the Argentinean journalist Jacobo Timmerman suggest that Carter's policies did have some impact.[53]

Even though Carter began to have doubts about his human rights policies by the second half of his term, he had advanced the cause in a critical and long-lasting way. By setting up the Bureau of Human Rights and Humanitarian Affairs in the State Department that was headed by an assistant secretary, he institutionalized human rights in the U.S. foreign policy agenda. This, coupled with congressional initiatives requiring the State Department to report on the human rights record of aid recipients, meant that the apparatus for monitoring human rights abuses, and for crafting responses, was in place. When the Reagan administration tried to nominate Ernest Lefever, an academic who had questioned the wisdom of an external human rights policy, to head the Human Rights Bureau in 1981, he was ignominiously rejected by the Senate.[54] Human rights had become a very salient issue by the early 1980s, and a constituency had been created in the executive-legislative nexus. After Carter, even those officials who were dubious about the role of human rights in American foreign policy felt compelled to speak the human rights language even if, once confirmed, they might not have accorded it the priority that Carter's officials did.

These three bright spots in a generally bleak human rights landscape are important because they kept the human rights flame alive and they each institutionalized concerns about, and policies on, human rights on the agendas of the European integration process and the foreign policy of the United States. They were also a constant thorn on the sides of major as well as minor predator states. When Carter's successor Ronald Reagan did away with détente and revived the Cold War in the early 1980s, sentiment in the United States and Europe showed a certain weariness about the psychological, material, and human costs of the unending struggle. Many in the United States and Europe felt that it was time to reevaluate the human and material costs of conducting the Cold War.

Reevaluating National Security:
Security Against What?

The conventional conception of security always had its detractors, but it was not until the later years of the Cold War that mainstream thinkers and policymakers began to voice their dissatisfaction with the military security obsessions of the Cold War. Three developments facilitated the effort to "redefine security." The first development was the relaxation in tensions—"détente"—between the superpowers. Despite their checkered histories, détente and the Helsinki process opened up intellectual space to articulate alternative conceptions of security. One of the most famous documents issued during this period was the report of the Independent Commission on Disarmament and Security Issues (which was chaired by Olaf Palme), *Common Security: A Blueprint for Survival* (1982). The report advocated an alternative way to reduce the likelihood of war by asking states to adhere to norms such as self-restraint, renunciation of the use of force to settle disputes, arms reduction, and delinking arms control negotiations from other political issues. Pointing to the CSCE processes as a model, the report stressed the necessity of "seeking common ground even with adversaries in the interests of mutual survival."[55]

Second, the rise of economic interdependence, which was welcomed by most as being conducive to global economic welfare, also raised concerns that states might be vulnerable to the economic maneuvers of others. The Organization of the Petroleum Exporting Countries (OPEC) oil embargo against supporters of Israel—principally the United States—in the wake of Arab-Israeli War of 1973, convinced some that the link between economics and security was underappreciated. The industrialized countries were vulnerable to disruption in energy supplies, and when such supplies were used as a weapon or bargaining tool by the suppliers, the strategic options available to the West (such as supporting Israel in the Arab-Israeli conflict) might be limited. Consciousness of this link between economics and security would pave the way for the formulation of policies such as conservation and reducing dependence on foreign oil in order to make the state less vulnerable to disruption of supplies in future crises. Thinking outside the military box and incorporating economic issues into one's conception of security were seen as necessary moves in the era of economic interdependence.

Third, military security was not perceived as the most urgent security issue in much of the Third World. Nuclear deterrence and fighting a nuclear war, for example, could not be more irrelevant to most Third World policymakers. These individuals and their countries were essentially bystanders in the nuclear debate. Conventional deterrence and war were certainly more important, but they did not exhaust the concerns of policymakers. Third World leaders realized early that once their country obtained statehood, internal challenges to their legitimacy and regime were usually more pressing.[56] In meeting these challenges, the military was only part of the solution (and often the undesirable part, as when it is used to put down rebellions). Security, for the state as well as for the regime, needed to be more comprehensive. The term "comprehensive security" came into existence.[57] The approach focused on the societal and economic underpinnings of security. Focusing on military security was inadequate because young states experienced problems of internal legitimacy that could be solved only by having economic policies that delivered. Moreover, many of these societies were ethnically heterogeneous, requiring public policies that were acceptable to the various ethnic groups. In Southeast Asia for example, ASEAN demonstrated this comprehensive approach to security by articulating the importance of "national resilience," which was in turn seen as the prerequisite for "regional resilience."[58]

Barry Buzan's *People, States, and Fear* was one of the early attempts to bring together these themes into a coherent framework. Buzan deconstructed the notion of "national security" and rebuilt and extended its purview beyond the military arena.[59] In addition to state or national security, Buzan identified three other relevant units to which the concept may be applied: the individual, the region, and the international system. Thus, to the question of security for whom, Buzan answered that it could be the state, the individual, the region, or the international system.[60] And in addition to the military and political sectors privileged by the traditionalists, Buzan proposed that the societal, economic, and environmental sectors are also part of the security *problématique:* "The 'national' security problem turns out to be a . . . security problem in which individuals, states and the system all play a part, and in which economic, societal and environmental factors are as important as political and military ones."[61]

Buzan's addition of new sectors to the traditional security discourse was prescient; it anticipated subsequent works by writers such as Richard Ullman and Jessica Tuchman Mathews that sought to "redefine" security. For the purposes of our narrative, however, it is Buzan's prioritization of his "levels of [security] analysis" that is more interesting. Despite the title of his book, which appears to suggest that "people"—the human individual—would emerge as the ultimate referent of security, he ended up privileging the state. His justification is that "at the end of the day national security policy still has to be made by states." And since "security policy-making is very largely an activity of states, there is an important practical sense in which national security subsumes all of the other security considerations found at the individual and systemic levels."[62]

Despite its focus on American national security, Richard Ullman's 1983 article "Redefining Security" went further than Buzan in elevating the importance of "people" as the referent of security.[63] Ullman argued that from the onset of the Cold War, Washington had defined American national security "in excessively narrow and excessively military terms."[64] According to Ullman, this one-sided definition of national security gave a "false image of reality."[65] Such images misdirected states to focus on military threats while neglecting other potentially more harmful threats; they also militarized international relations in ways that are not conducive to improving global security. Ullman felt that there was an urgent need to redefine the notion of national security by broadening it to include nonmilitary threats.

Ullman agreed with Thomas Hobbes that security was perhaps the most fundamental good the state is supposed to provide. But he disagreed with Hobbes that security was an absolute value. Security often coexisted in tension with liberty, and in liberal democracies, the trade-off between the two was a matter for negotiation. In a rather prescient passage, Ullman suggested that

> The tradeoff between liberty and security is one of the crucial issues of our era. In virtually every society, individuals and groups seek security against the state, just as they ask the state to protect them against harm from other states. Human rights and state security are thus intimately related.[66]

Ullman recognized that national security was potentially in conflict not only with liberty but with other cherished values as well, given the scarcity of national resources. He redefined national security in a way that appeared to be capable of prioritizing these values:

A threat to national security is an action or sequence of events that (1) threatens drastically and over a relatively brief span of time to degrade the quality of life for the inhabitants of a state, or (2) threatens significantly to narrow the range of policy choices available to the government of a state or to private, nongovernmental entities (persons, groups, corporations) within the state.[67]

Ullman had little difficulty listing threats in the first category: external wars, internal rebellions, terrorist attacks, blockades, boycotts, and natural disasters (such as earthquakes, floods, droughts, and epidemics). He had greater difficulty identifying threats in the second category that did not also degrade the quality of life. His examples of the disruption of flow of critical resources, environmental degradation, Third World poverty, and dissatisfaction all narrow the range of available policy options and degrade the quality of life (albeit over a longer period of time). Two qualities of Ullman's definition stand out. One, as the above examples indicate, his redefinition was very expansive. Two, his definition of national security came close to according coequal status between the individual and the state.

Though far from universally accepted, Ullman's article was one of the earliest and was perhaps even the seminal statement on a people-centered approach to security. To be sure, he continued to couch his analysis in the language of national security. But a careful reading of the article points to a distinctively human-centered conception of security in two respects. First, he saw the individual human being as the primary referent object of security. The purpose of national security was to safeguard not that abstract entity, the nation-state, but the state's "inhabitants." Second, and less directly, he viewed the insecurity and oppression of foreign nationals, particularly in the Third World, as having an important negative effect on U.S. national security. Hence the security of human beings across the world comes to be seen as a legitimate matter of concern—if not necessarily for its own sake.

A second influential attempt at "Redefining Security" was Jessica Tuchman Mathews's 1989 article in *Foreign Affairs*. Mathews began her article by declaring that "the 1990s will demand a redefinition of what constitutes national security."[68] Mathews, who had worked on global issues in the Carter administration's National Security Council, argued that "global developments now suggest the need for another . . . broadening definition of national security to include resource, environmental and demographic issues."[69] Driving her analysis were demographic trends: world population would increase from 5 to 6 billion in the decade between 1990 and 2000 and 90 percent of the added billion would be in the developing countries. This would create intense pressures on the earth's natural resources such as forests, water, oil; the unthinking exploitation of these resources would lead to environmental degradation.

Unlike Ullman, who sought to advance a general definition of national security that could encompass a new range of threats, Mathews's main objective was to add "the environment" to existing understandings of national security. She focused on detailing the causal sequences behind environmental disasters, and it was her mastery of these sequences that gave the article its urgent tone. Tropical forests, for example, were "fragile ecosystems" that could easily unravel if disturbed. Deforestation disturbs the nutrient cycle, causing the soil to lose its fertility; plant and animal species find it hard to survive in such habitats and some may become extinct. Another consequence of deforestation is soil erosion, which silts up downstream rivers, bringing floods and droughts. Hence, "traced through its effects on agriculture, energy supply and water resources, tropical deforestation impoverishes about a billion people."[70] For Mathews, it was this impoverishment of large numbers of people in the Third World that turned the environment into a security issue:

> Environmental decline occasionally leads directly to conflict, especially when scarce water resources must be shared. Generally, however, its impact on nations' security is felt in the downward pull on economic performance and, therefore, on political stability. The underlying cause of turmoil is often ignored; instead governments address the poverty and instability that are its results.[71]

Mathews did not elaborate on this link between poverty and instability, but she warned that existing modalities of diplomacy that assumed national sovereignty to be coterminous with national borders were outdated because environmental issues usually transcended national boundaries. In an increasingly ecologically interdependent world and in a world where ecological strains have repercussions on state security, Mathews saw the need for "a new diplomacy . . . new institutions and regulatory regimes."[72] Without this new manner of thinking and working—in which redefining security was the first step—the survival of humankind itself would be imperiled.

Our analysis of the reconceptualization of security in the late Cold War would not be complete without mentioning the role of the charitable foundations, based principally in the United States. During the Cold War, organizations such as the Ford, Carnegie, and Rockefeller foundations played crucial ancillary roles to the state in sponsoring studies on the developing world, nuclear deterrence, crisis management, and cognitive/psychological profiles of America's adversaries. As the Cold War was winding down, many of these foundations switched their priorities to an analysis of security that is less focused on the state and the military. Among the most influential of these was the MacArthur Foundation's Program on Peace and Security in a Changing World, which was administered through the Social Science Research

Council. Consistent with the premonitions of writers such as Buzan, Ullman, and Mathews, the MacArthur Program sought to encourage young scholars to go beyond traditional ways of analyzing security. Through a series of prestigious two-year pre- and post-doctoral grants, the MacArthur Foundation helped nurture a new cohort of security analysts who came from a variety of disciplines, including those not normally considered as part of "security studies," such as anthropology, sociology, and economics.[73]

Not surprisingly, these nontraditional security analysts went well beyond focusing on military hardware or strategy; instead they trained their eyes on topics such as norms, ideas, trafficking of women and drugs, and truth commissions, which they saw as security issues. Between 1984 and 2000, the MacArthur Foundation devoted about US$15 million to the program. When an accounting of achievements was called for at the end of the program, one member of the Social Science Research Council's Committee on International Peace and Security suggested that a major achievement was the "success in appropriating the term 'security.'" As evidence, he pointed to an essay by a leading traditionalist called "Should Strategic Studies Survive?" in which the author basically conceded the term "security studies" to the "broadeners" and regrouped those who are keen on focusing on military strategy under the rubric of strategic studies or international political military studies.[74]

Two points about these attempts to reconceptualize security are noteworthy. First, they entered the debate in the 1980s, well before the Cold War ended. Whether they were reactions to what many perceived as the excessively militaristic approach of the Reagan administration or anticipations of a new dawn is not central to our purposes. Probably both factors were important. What is more pertinent is that these writers performed important conceptual legwork that would later facilitate the acceptance of these new ideas by informed opinion and national and international policymakers. The fact that Ullman and Matthews were card-carrying members of the foreign policy establishment gave their views a certain gravitas in academic and policy circles. They advocated a broader approach to security that allowed policymakers to view the pervasive civil and internal conflicts of the 1990s as serious security issues in need of security responses. Once issues such as the safety of civilians and refugee flows are viewed as "security" issues, it became possible to bring them to the attention of the Security Council and, where appropriate, for the council to characterize them as "threats to international peace and security." Chapter VII of the UN Charter provides for measures by the international community, including the use of force, in order to "maintain or restore international peace and insecurity." As we shall see later, Chapter VII was invoked in the majority of UN interventions, including Somalia, Bosnia, Rwanda, Haiti, and Sierra Leone. If the conflicts of the 1990s had been primarily of the Iraq-Kuwait kind (interstate war), the vocabulary provided by the "redefiners" would not have made much headway.

Second, the relevance of these extensions of the security agenda to the development of the concept of human security is clear—these new issues are threats to individuals first and foremost. Although this point is implicit in the writing of all of the authors discussed above, most did not dwell on the point that the individual was the ultimate object to be secured. Buzan, who included the individual as one of the contending referents of security, eventually subsumed the individual under "the state." Ullman probably came closest to privileging the individual, while Mathews was more concerned about multilateral cooperation among states. But their efforts to extend the notion of security beyond the military arena cannot help but train one's eyes on the individual. When the issue was protecting one's country from military attack, the congruence between individual and state/military security was obvious. When the issues are earthquakes, global warming, and economic privation, it is not at all obvious that the object to be secured is the state. Moreover, the state may not even see these issues as security problems (as in Ullman's critique) or if it sees it, may not be able to do much on its own (Mathews's Bangladesh scenario). Yet the malfeasance of the state is likely to have the result of rendering its citizens vulnerable to these threats. In other words, once the concept of national security is broadened to incorporate nonmilitary factors, the individual becomes a very strong contender—vis-à-vis the state—as the ultimate "thing" to be secured. The end of the Cold War and the political dynamics unleashed would make the need to protect individuals even more urgent.

The End of the Cold War and State Capacity

If the exigencies of the Cold War stacked the deck in favor of the state, as opposed to individuals, and emphasized military security instead of the other dimensions of security, its sudden demise in 1989 unleashed forces that seemed to confirm the arguments of those who urged switching the referent of security away from the state to human beings and extending security's domain to include societal upheaval brought about by internal war, economic privation, famine, ecological devastation, and refugees. The Cold War overlay—that is, economic and military domination or support by either of the superpowers—propped up or held together many weak or failing states. When that overlay was withdrawn in the early 1990s, many states imploded or just failed to function: they found themselves incapable of providing basic security and economic and social necessities.

In that sense, the first major international incident of the post–Cold War period, Iraq's invasion of Kuwait, was less a harbinger of things to come than a last gasp instance of interstate war, in this case an unvarnished instance of one state (Iraq) using aggression against another (Kuwait). When the U.S.-led coalition succeeded in ejecting Saddam Hussein's forces from Kuwait, President George H. W. Bush heralded the coming of a "new world order." Bush has received much flak for his statement but he was right in one sense: interstate aggression of the kind inflicted by Iraq on Kuwait would not be allowed to dominate the post–Cold War world. What took Bush and the international community, including the United Nations, by surprise was the disorder in the years to come, much of it associated with internal wars in Africa, the Balkans, and Asia.

The war in Somalia, one of the first of these post–Cold War internal wars, was more indicative of shape of things to come than the Gulf War of 1990–1991. It also had a deleterious impact on subsequent events. The origins of the breakdown of government and order in Somali have been documented elsewhere and need not detain us. David Laitin provides one of the most succinct descriptions of the anarchy that many will remember from their television screens:

> By late 1991 not only was there an interclan war for control over Somalia, but an *intraclan* war for control over Mogadishu. Throughout the south, and in Mogadishu especially, warlords . . . claimed control over bands of well-armed youths, who with their armed Land Rovers . . . roamed the cities and roadways plundering, extorting, and killing. By late 1992, due to the civil war, the entire infrastructure of the country was ruined, mass killing, starvation, and disease afflicted much of the population, there was no central government that could negotiate on behalf of the state, and international relief workers were nearly as vulnerable to attack as the Somali population.[75]

The United Nations authorized a Chapter VI peacekeeping operation (UNOSOM I) in April 1992 with the aim of delivering humanitarian assistance to the victims of the civil war. The first contingent, however, was not deployed until months later, and the situation continued to deteriorate. On 3 December 1992, the Security Council passed resolution 794, which authorized a U.S.-led humanitarian intervention with 38,000 troops. The Unified Task Force (UNITAF) ultimately consisted of 26,000 U.S. troops and 10,000 from twenty-two other countries. UNITAF, also known as Operation Restore Hope, was authorized to use force to ensure the delivery of humanitarian relief to Somalis. It was followed by UNOSOM II in May 1993. That summer, supporters of clan leader Mohamed Aideed ambushed UN forces, killing twenty-four and wounding fifty Pakistani soldiers. In retaliation, the UN called upon the

U.S. Rangers to go after the perpetrators of the crime. The hunt for Aideed and his supporters climaxed in a firefight in October that claimed eighteen U.S. lives and wounded seventy-eight others.[76] We now have reason to believe that Al Qaeda was involved in assisting Aideed's forces in the attack, but back then, the U.S. troop casualties in a humanitarian mission was enough to persuade President Clinton that the game was not worth the candle.[77] He ordered the phased withdrawal of U.S. forces from Somalia. This would later be known as the Mogadishu effect, referring to the unwillingness of the United States and some other states to take casualties in the course of performing their duties in UN peacekeeping missions or, for that matter, to participate in such operations at all.

Somalia heralded the arrival of a kind of internal or civil war that would plague the post–Cold War international scene. These internal wars were usually caused by the fragmentation of weak (or "failed") states, which resulted in violent competition for power among rival clans or groups. In the case of Somalia, religious or ethnic cleavages were irrelevant because the Somalis were culturally homogenous: they shared a similar faith, Islam, and spoke the same language, Somali. Yet once the center was exposed as hollow, anarchy reigned and it became a violent free-for-all. The competing groups differentiated themselves on the basis of the clans to which they belonged, even though there were also intraclan power struggles. It is the human consequences of these struggles that concern us. The human toll exacted by the Somali tragedy points to the new shape of human insecurity in the 1990s. Innocent civilians were caught in the crossfire between clans or ethnic groups, masses of people were displaced in their own country, and thousands of refugees fled warfare and persecution. Fifty thousand people have died in this internal conflict. It was scenes of such large-scale human misery—existential insecurity, if one wants to use the term—beamed nightly into our television screens by CNN and the international media that persuaded the international community that something had to be done.

The internal wars of the early 1990s—in Croatia, Bosnia-Herzegovina, Rwanda, Chechnya, and Kosovo, to mention only the most prominent examples—had, in addition to the dimension of the struggle for power or territory, another core fissure that rendered them even more vicious and deadly: religious and ethnic cleavages. If the "othering" in the Somalia case was based on clans, the "othering" in these later cases was based on ethnic and religious differences. As one of us put it in a recent monograph on military intervention in the contemporary era:

> The explosion in civilian deaths and mass displacement was tied to the fact that the pursuit of civil war was widely spread across populated territories.

Furthermore, in multi-ethnic societies ... these wars involved not merely political and military groupings, but entire communities and their identities. The
objectives of war frequently included not only the conquest of territory and/or
control of government but also the destruction or the removal of the adversary
population. ... The result was humanitarian crisis, if not genocide.[78]

As these identity and ethnic wars generated one humanitarian crisis after
another, many threatening to spill over to neighboring states, the international community—represented by the UN—was often faced with the question of whether to intervene. UN interventions in Haiti, Cambodia, Sierra
Leone, and East Timor have been considered qualified successes. However,
there have been many failures as well; Rwanda and Srebrenica are the most
infamous.[79] In Rwanda, the Security Council refused to reinforce its UNAMIR
(United Nations Assistance Mission for Rwanda) forces despite receiving credible reports in early 1994 about the Hutu government's plan of genocide against
the minority Tutsi population. When the plan was implemented in April and
May of that year, the United States and Britain at first refused to describe the
killings as genocide and the Security Council "went repeatedly into secret
session ... cowering over the Mogadishu factor which prevented action as the
death toll mounted to more than 800,000."[80]

The failure of the international community of states to halt mass atrocities
was also stark in the case of Srebrenica—a Muslim enclave amid a largely
Serbian countryside—which was designated a "safe haven" by Security Council resolution 819 and protected by UN troops (Dutch in this case). That, however, did not prevent the Serbian forces under General Mladic from attacking
it in 1995. Encountering no NATO air attacks (an option the Dutch government rejected for fear that its peacekeeping force would be taken hostage or
hurt) or resistance from UN peacekeepers, General Ratko Mladić's soldiers
took the city in July 1995. In plain sight of UN forces, they executed 7,000
Muslim men and youths and relocated 23,000 women and children.[81]
Robertson explained the fall of Srebrenica in the following way:

> Srebrenica was allowed to happen because of the Mogadishu factor: states in-
> tervening from humanitarian motives refused to risk the lives of their own
> soldiers to make that intervention effective. ... The Dutch government pre-
> ferred to dishonour promises and to allow Muslims to die in their thousands
> rather than to suffer one more Dutch casualty.[82]

Since World War II, the world has witnessed twenty-five interstate wars
and about 122 civil wars. The death toll from the interstate wars is around 3.3
million; that from the civil wars 16.2 million.[83] Interstate wars have become
even more rare with the end of the Cold War; internal wars have claimed the

lion's share of fatalities, the overwhelming majority of which have fallen on civilians. While lives lost represent the most harrowing aspect of these wars, the war refugees and the internally displaced persons generated by these wars have also reached staggering proportions. One study reports a sixfold increase in refugees worldwide between 1975 (2.4 million) and 1995 (14.5 million). Similarly, in 1982 there were 1.2 million IDPs spread over eleven countries; the figure for 1997 was 20 million, found in over thirty-five countries.[84]

Because most of these internal wars (all situated in the Second or Third World) were sparked off by the unraveling of the state, the notion of the state as the protector and guarantor of security has been severely undermined. "State security" in these instances became an oxymoron: the state in question and its coercive organs were up for grabs, and groups hijacked the state apparatus and turned the state into a predator against civilians (on the "wrong" side). The result was civil war and, in many cases, intervention by the international community to stem the unfolding humanitarian disasters. The prevalence of these wars and the casualties they caused in the 1990s helped remove the last defenses around which the reification of the state was built. In the last decade or so, state sovereignty has become more contingent upon the state's ability to provide for the basic security of its citizens; when the state is barely existing or when it fails to provide the security goods, it has become fair game for international intervention. The dominant description for these efforts by the international community was humanitarian intervention. That the purpose of these actions was to protect the rights of threatened individuals or their security was obvious even though the vocabulary of human security did not command wide usage until the mid-1990s.

Conclusion

In this chapter, we have attempted to do two things. First, we have considered in what respects the experiences of total war, strategic bombing, and the Holocaust drew into question the validity of states' claims to primacy in the discourse of security on the basis of their role in protecting human individuals. Where states were no longer capable of protecting their citizens from attack well within their borders, it was unclear why their security claims should be paramount. Where states killed large numbers of their own citizens, it became clear that the state could itself constitute a major security threat to individuals within it.

We noted that the consequent reconsideration of individual rights in international relations that followed World War II constituted a critical challenge to the statist emphasis in discourse on security. The full implications of this challenge were not realized during the Cold War, given the serious rivalry between the two blocs in which raison d'état seemed to be a major impetus behind much of their policies. Nonetheless, the development of norms continued and human rights became an important aspect of, and to some extent constraint upon, the policies of some major states (e.g., the United States under Carter). In the meantime, NGOs and other transnational human rights activists began questioning the treatment of individuals by the governments, and the influence of such groups grew. In a broader sense, economic, technological, and environmental developments associated with globalization raised further questions about the state's capacity, acting on its own, to defend and promote the security of individuals within it. These were taken up in a number of influential critiques of conventional thinking about national security, critiques that directly or indirectly privileged threats to individuals (or to humanity as a whole) in discourse on security. The heavy overlay of bipolarity, however, constrained any significant policy adjustment.

The end of the Cold War removed the overlay and cleared the way to rebalance security discourse in favor of individual human beings. At the same time, the rapid growth in the number of incidents of internal conflict—and the grievous consequences for human beings caught up in them—focused international attention further on the security needs of people. Somalia illustrated how failed states left their inhabitants at the mercy of clans and bandits; Bosnia showed how identity conflicts in disintegrating states endangered the lives of the weaker party and highlighted the rapaciousness of the predator state (Serbia). National security cannot be at stake when there is no nation to begin with. In the final analysis, the referent of security can be no other than the human individual. The result was the emergence of a dynamic discourse on human security and a further adjustment of international norms and practice, to which this analysis now turns.

Part II. The Emergence of Human Security

> Despite the growing safety net of the world's states, people in many areas now feel more insecure than ever.
>
> —Commission on Global Governance, 1995[1]

> I believe the distinctive feature of the new emerging international order should be assigning the highest priority to the human being, and placing the human being at the centre of international activity.　　—Juan Samovía[2]

In Chapter 2, we showed that much of the normative basis for embedding human security in international relations was laid during the Cold War. We also argued that the United Nations was one principal venue in which this development occurred and that UN officials played a significant role in this process. Although regional organizations, states, and nongovernmental organizations also played a large part, their efforts consciously built upon the foundation of norms laid by the United Nations. The analysis in Chapter 2 also showed the key role of UN agencies in "humanizing" development by encouraging the shift from national aggregates to a focus on individual needs and empowerment. However, we suggested that in both human rights and development, there was a wide disparity between this evolution of norms and state practice.

As we argued in Chapter 3, the end of the Cold War fundamentally changed the international context in which the development and implementation of norms proceeded. At the same time, the threat to individual security was highlighted by the growing incidence of civil war. The human consequences thereof (ethnic cleansing, genocide, mass rape, the systematic abuse of children, and levels of displacement unmatched since World War II) added a new urgency to the issue of individual and group safety from violence.

In the early 1990s, there was considerable optimism that a more people-centered order could be achieved, that the principles that had developed in the Cold War could be translated into practice. As Secretary-General Boutros Boutros-Ghali put it:

> In these past months a conviction has grown, among nations large and small, that an opportunity has been regained to achieve the great objectives of the Charter—a United Nations capable of maintaining justice and human rights and of promoting, in the words of the Charter, "social progress and better standards of life in larger freedom."[3]

Another key participant related this development more specifically to understandings of security: "We have the extraordinary opportunity of being able to think about a new world order, or about new security concepts, without this world order or these new security concepts being the result of the military victory of some nation or group of nations over others."[4]

During the post–Cold War era, considerable development took place along all of the axes of individual security that we have been tracking. The discussion of human development merged into an evolving discourse on security. Key contributions outlined the salience of economic threats to the security of individuals, the significance of economic privation as a source of instability and conflict, and the importance of empowerment through development to the well-being of people. For many, the economic well-being of individual human beings came to be seen as a core element of individual security. Along similar lines—and in the context of the HIV/AIDS epidemic—there was an ever-more-explicit debate about health as a fundamental aspect of security.

The 1990s and the early years of the twenty-first century also witnessed substantial, although not universal, reconceptualization of the relationship between the state and the individual in the realm of physical security from violence and a growing emphasis on the contingent character of state sovereignty. Norms concerning the protection of civilians in war deepened dramatically and extended more clearly to internal war. International actors became increasingly preoccupied with the question of intervention in the internal affairs of states that lacked the capacity or the will to defend their own citizens. There was growing consideration of the extension of the protections afforded refugees to individuals displaced within borders by conflict and instability. Growing attention was paid to the security needs of particularly vulnerable groups (e.g., women, children, and indigenous peoples).

And it was in the early 1990s that the concept of human security emerged as an intellectual device that brought together these disparate considerations of individual protection, rights, and welfare and as an instrument of advocacy in international society.[5] The discussion of human security not only became explicit but also expanded dramatically, taking in large numbers of different actors (international organizations and specialized agencies, states, nongovernmental organizations, and independent commissions), many of whom were competing for ownership of the concept. Particular individuals operating within these institutional contexts (e.g., Boutros Boutros-Ghali, Mahbub ul Haq, Lloyd Axworthy, Kofi Annan, Frances Deng, Graça Machel, Mohamed Sahnoun, Gareth Evans, Amartya Sen, and Sadako Ogata) played a substantial role in leading and shaping the discussion. Literally thousands of documents on, or related to, human security emerged during the period under consideration. How should one make sense of this extraordinarily complicated and multifaceted process?

Our principal approach is thematic and institutional. In Chapter 4, we assess the vibrant discussion of the link between welfare, human development, and human security with particular attention to the work of the UNDP[6] and the Commission on Human Security.[7] To what extent and in what ways was individual economic security seen to be a precondition for national and international peace and security? To what extent was freedom from economic threats seen as an essential component of human security?

In Chapter 5, we focus on the evolution of a rights-based and protection-oriented view of human security. Perhaps the most substantial articulation of a rights and protection view of human security was the report of the International Commission on Intervention and State Sovereignty.[8] In unpacking this dimension of human security, we devote particular attention to the Security Council and General Assembly but also to other UN institutions (e.g., the UNHCR and the UN High Commissioner for Human Rights, UNHCHR), the humanitarian and human rights communities, regional organizations, and the initiatives of interested states. We also outline the emergence of international judicial institutions that deal with crimes committed against civilians in war and conclude with an examination of the efforts of international society to control, if not to eliminate, weapons that are particularly threatening to civilians in conflict. In Chapter 6, we turn to a number of more specific themes related to the evolving concept of human security, looking in some detail at processes related to children, women, and IDPs as particularly vulnerable groups with special needs.

We note that our coverage of the humanizing of security is not comprehensive. For example, issues related to health are treated as part of the broader discussion of sustainable development and security. In addition, we say little about the environment and human security. We also have little to say in this chapter about identity and security. These decisions reflect in part limitations on space. However, they also reflect the fact that the core of the debate on human security revolves around development and protection. In writing the story in the way we do, we believe that we are faithful to the principal lines of contestation regarding human security.

We recognize that the distinction between the development and protection approaches to human security is somewhat artificial. The major contributions on the development side acknowledge that physical protection from violence is important not only to human security but also to the development enterprise. Likewise, those focusing on protection acknowledge the importance of human development and the economic sources of conflict. The difference is one of emphasis.

For the development approaches, the physical security of human beings is one among many aspects of human security, and generally not the most important. The secondary significance of physical security in these approaches is well illustrated by Amartya Sen, the Nobel laureate in economics who co-chaired the Commission on Human Security and who is perhaps the most prominent proponent of the development interpretation of human security: "We have to recognize the fact that insecurity is not just concerned with poverty. The insecurity in the lives of human beings caused by violence and conflict deserves a fuller recognition."[9] His remark suggests that the issue of physical protection has not received adequate attention in the analysis of human security. This is a statement that may make sense to someone cocooned in the economic discourse on security. To those who focus on protection from violence as the central component of human security, it is breathtaking in its detachment from what they perceive to be the center of the security *problématique*. For these groups, physical security against threats of violence is a precondition for addressing other elements of the security equation; development may be an important contributor to but is not part of human security.

Our analysis demonstrates that the United Nations played a fundamental role in this transformation of international thinking about security. In the first place, units of the organization played an important agenda-setting function by laying the concept on the table and generating discussion of it. The Secretary-General was a central player at key points in catalyzing serious reflection about both the development and protection aspects of the human security agenda. UN-sponsored conferences provided multiple forums for the articulation of the idea. The organization's central institutions—especially the Security Council—played a seminal role by inserting human security concerns into the discussion and definition of threats to international security and by building norms around these concerns. The unauthorized and illegal interventions in Kosovo and Iraq notwithstanding, the council developed a fundamental role in the legitimation of action within the domestic jurisdiction of states to address human security concerns. In these respects, the issue of human security is a classic example of the UN's role in the evolution of ideas in international relations and foreign policy practice.

4

The UN and Human Security: The Development Dimension

- **Human Development Revisited**
- **From Human Development to Human Security**
- **Conflict Prevention and Human Security: The Structural Causes of Conflict**
- **The Return of Development and Security:** *Human Security Now*
- **Conclusion**

One principal aspect of the effort to broaden the concept of security concerned the relationship between development and security.[1] In pursuing this theme, we first examine the ongoing discussion of human development and its growth into a developmentalist understanding of human security. The development vector of human security faltered at the 1995 World Summit for Social Development and appeared to have been eclipsed for a time by the burgeoning discussion of protection discussed in the next chapter.

However, consideration of the economic dimension of human security continued in the flourishing discussion of conflict prevention. The recognition of the economic sources of conflict has a long history. In the 1990s, discussion of the economic root causes of conflict evolved rapidly in the context of substantial consideration of conflict prevention in NGOs, the UN, regional organizations, and states. The discussion of root causes focused on development shortcomings and was clearly informed by the assumption that poverty and hopelessness (i.e., a lack of individual security from economic threats) encouraged violent behavior. It followed that addressing human development concerns mitigated the risk of violence.

The chapter concludes with extended consideration of the conception of human security promoted by the Japanese-sponsored Commission on Human Security. The report made a substantial, if contestable, contribution to clarifying the relationship between development and human security.

Human Development Revisited

The humanizing of development that was evident in the 1970s and 1980s continued into the 1990s, involving an impressive array of academics, policymakers, and activists. One key early role was played by the North-South Dialogue of the Society for International Development. In 1990, the roundtable held a high-level meeting called The Economics of Peace in Costa Rica. Participants included former president of the World Bank Robert McNamara, Olusegun Obasanjo of Nigeria, UNICEF executive director James Grant, Inga Thorsson (the Swedish minister for disarmament well known for her earlier work on the relationship between disarmament and development), Brian Urquhart, and Richard Jolly. They were hosted by Costa Rica's president Oscar Arias.

The roundtable called for a new concept of global security that focused not on military security but on "the overall security of individuals from social violence, economic distress and environmental degradation" and sought to focus attention on the obstacles to "realization of the full potential of individuals." It revived the link between disarmament and development raised earlier by the Brandt Commission, calling for the use of the post–Cold War peace dividend to fund accelerated human development while addressing environmental imbalances. In these respects, the choice of Costa Rica as a venue was appropriate. Costa Rica had abolished its national armed forces in 1948, instead devoting national resources to consolidating democracy and enhancing human development.[2]

The writings of prominent development economists were also critical to the development of the proto-idea of human security in the early 1990s. This intellectual activity centered on the UNDP, which in 1990 inaugurated a series of human development reports (HDRs)[3] under the leadership of Mahbub ul Haq with substantial intellectual input from, among others, Nobel laureate Amartya Sen. The first report discussed the nature and measurement of human development, highlighting the importance of equity in growth if the latter were actually to improve the lives and enhance the opportunities of individual human beings. Perhaps most significant, it proposed an index to measure national performance in human development—the Human Development Index (HDI)—which was derived from data on life expectancy, educational attainment, and gross domestic product (GDP) per capita.[4]

The measurement of human development has always been a contentious matter. If we take human development to be "a process of enlarging people's choices,"[5] then one might wish to include levels of political freedom as part of an index. If the precondition to exercising choice is having enough to eat, why not food security? If we accept that the choices of particular groups (e.g., women) are especially constrained, then perhaps measurements of gender equity should be a part of the overall HDI. Yet adding further measures to the index raised serious problems not only with regard to the availability and comparability of data but also with regard to how one measured an issue such as political freedom. Subsequent reports addressed many of these issues. The preference of the organization was to keep the basic set of variables reasonably simple and finite. As Mahbub ul Haq put it:

> More variables will not necessarily improve the HDI. They may confuse the picture and blur the main trends. It is best to recognize that the HDI will remain a partial reflection of reality. And there is some virtue in keeping the index sharp and simple, studying other legitimate concerns alongside the HDI rather than trying to integrate everything into the HDI.[6]

The 1991 and 1992 HDRs turned to the financing of human development and the international dimensions of human development. In a portent of what was to follow, the 1992 volume raised again the possibility of diverting some portion of the peace dividend to development.

The issue of resource reallocation was further explored in a 1993 HDR Office working paper by Keith Griffin and Terry McKinlay, who noted that spending on social services at the base of the pyramid of public expenditure had higher returns than spending at the top; it reduced the need to rely on the questionable trickle-down effect from economic growth at the national level. As the authors put it, "It is by now widely understood that there is no one-to-one correspondence between material enrichment (measured, say, by GNP per capita) and the enrichment of human lives (measured, say, by the human development index). The human development approach thus implies the dethronement of national product as the primary indicator of the level of development."[7] The parallel to contemporaneous reasoning on security—that security at the state level had no one-to-one correspondence to security at the individual level—is striking.

From Human Development to Human Security

The 1993 HDR brought a third basic theme in the human development discussion to the fore: participation. It stressed that the empowerment of people was essential both in the state and in markets not merely because popular participation improved outcomes but because development was about helping people take control over their lives. What is critical from our perspective was that this point was extended explicitly into the realm of security:

"The concept of security must change—from an exclusive focus on national security to a much greater stress on people's security, from security through armaments to security through human development, from territorial security to food, employment, and environmental security."[8] This observation was followed, again for the first time in the series, with a set of suggestions that tied security policy explicitly to development: facilitation of the transition from defense to civilian production, an acceleration of disarmament in the developing world, and the creation of new alliances and mechanisms for peace, all with a central focus on conflict prevention.

This merger of development and security discourse was carried further in the *Human Development Report 1994*, the subtitle of which is *New Dimensions of Human Security*.[9] What had been one tentative theme in a report focusing on people's participation in processes and institutions became the centerpiece in a sustained effort to redefine security along human development lines. The report offered the first substantial definition of human security: "Human security can be said to have two main aspects. It means, first, safety from such chronic threats as hunger, disease, and repression. And second, it means protection from sudden and hurtful disruptions in the pattern of daily life."[10]

The authors embraced both human development and human security as universal values that emanated from the essential dignity of all human beings. They defined human security as the summation of seven dimensions of security: economic, food, health, environmental, personal, community, and political. Although the basis of the report's discussion of human security was essentialist, the authors recognized that both human development and human security had instrumental value in the pursuit of peace as well: "Without peace, there may be no development. But without development, peace may be threatened."[11] Taking this point further, they argued that world peace depended on individuals having security in their own lives, noting the predominance of internal war in the contemporary international system and the roots of such war in socioeconomic conditions.

On this basis, the report asserted that the path to peace was sustainable development. To put it another way, sustainable human development and human security were mutually constitutive; the two together were the basis for peace. Although the report focused on human beings in general, it also devoted attention to the security needs of particular vulnerable groups, especially women:

> Among the worst personal threats are those to women. In no society are women secure and treated equally with men. Personal insecurity shadows them from cradle to grave. In the household they are the last to eat. At school,

they are the last to be educated. At work they are the last to be hired and the first to be fired. And from childhood through adulthood, they are abused because of their gender.[12]

The report stressed that human security was threatened not only by conditions of deprivation, inequity, and instability within states but by the globalization of threats, noting in particular the impact of population growth, illegal migration, economic disparities between states, the drug trade, pollution and environmental degradation, and terrorism. Achieving sustainable development and human security required a global reallocation of resources that were available as a result of the post–Cold War peace dividend.

The report had a profound impact on the evolving discussion of security, if not within the academic security studies community, then among multilateral organizations coping with conflict, postconflict normalization, and development more broadly. Together with its 1993 precursor, it made a conceptual leap that is central to this book. As we have seen, for many years, discourse on development had focused on the ultimate ends of development: improving the quality of life of human beings and empowering them to control their own lives in the face of ubiquitous economic threats. This was accompanied by the development of an increasingly persuasive critique of traditional (state-oriented) development objectives, since often they were not directly relevant to the needs of human beings and since improvement in national aggregates was sometimes detrimental to the needs and purposes of individual human beings.

Outside the development literature, there was during the late Cold War and early post–Cold War periods a growing questioning of the obsession of security studies and security policy with military threats and military responses (evident in the Brandt Commission report discussed in Chapter 2 and the work of Richard Ullman and Jessica Tuchman Mathews addressed in Chapter 3) and an increasingly persistent objection that acting upon this understanding of security could undermine the security of people. The UNDP reports brought these two strands together by proposing an approach to security that not only focused on individuals rather than states but also moved away from earlier understandings of security that emphasized military threats to highlight nonmilitary threats to human survival and well-being. The report argued clearly that the threat of physical violence was only one aspect of the human security equation. Going further, it suggested that the threat of violence was not necessarily the most significant element of human security; it emphasized instead welfare and quality of life.

The motivations underlying this conceptual move are reasonably clear. As we have seen, for many years the argument had been made in development circles that disarmament (or, in the post–Cold War era, the peace dividend) could serve as an important source of resources for development that benefited the poor. Advocacy along these lines had not been particularly successful, in part because of the counterargument that the (traditional) security needs of the state required allocation of substantial resources to defense. This argument could be defused by reinterpreting the very concept of security with which defense spending was justified. If the referent of security was the individual and not the state and if the content of security was not primarily defense against physical threat from violence but safety from the threats of hunger, disease, and repression and sudden and hurtful disruptions in daily life, then it followed that spending on human development was spending on security, that human development policy was security policy. In the introduction to this book, we argued that security was an essentially contested concept. Security was perceived to be a strongly valued social good. By appropriating the word, those who argued that human development was intrinsically connected to security appropriated the word's value content; this act served as a potentially powerful justification for diverting significant resources toward the (development) policy preferences of this group.

The UNDP's evolving thinking on human security was paralleled in other significant venues. One of the most notable was the Commission on Global Governance. The commissioners noted what they considered to be the increasing irrelevance of traditional security preoccupations and policy to the real security challenges of the end of the twentieth century. They argued that the traditional focus had numerous negative consequences, among them the creation of hypertrophic national military systems, the justification of budgetary policies that favored defense over domestic welfare, and the encouragement of measures that severely restricted citizens' rights and freedoms. Noting the increasing unlikelihood of interstate war, they argued: "Other increasingly important security challenges arise from threats to the earth's life systems, extreme economic deprivation, the proliferation of conventional small arms, the terrorizing of civilian populations by domestic factions, and gross violations of human rights. These factors challenge the security of people far more than the threat of external aggression."[13] This led them to embrace the concept of the security of people and of the planet.

The *Human Development Report 1994* was written as a basis for UNDP input to the 1995 Copenhagen World Summit for Social Development.[14] In the 1994 HDR, the UNDP proposed an ambitious agenda for the summit, calling on conference participants to embrace the idea of human security and adopt a substantial series of measures, including a new world social charter, targets for human development, and a global human security fund to address

common threats. It also asked them to establish an economic security council
to operate in parallel with the existing Security Council.[15] The report suggested in its agenda for the summit that savings from reduction in military
expenditure could be credited to a demilitarization fund to reduce budget
deficits, finance military conversion, and fund human development and security. Much of the focus of this finance would be national, but the report
called for western industrialized countries to devote the human security component of the fund not only to domestic human development but—through
the global human security fund—to similar efforts in poorer countries.[16] In a
broader proposal, the UNDP suggested a 20:20 formula for promoting human development, whereby developing countries would devote 20 percent of
public spending and donor countries would devote 20 percent of assistance
flows to human development.[17]

The Social Summit recognized that social justice and social development
were preconditions for peace (and vice versa). It accepted that violence was
rooted to some extent in poverty, unemployment, and social disintegration.
States that participated in the summit also accepted obligations regarding the
safety of people within societies and the protection of vulnerable groups. In
general, the summit deliberations and documents returned to the original agenda
of the UN General Assembly resolution calling for the summit (enhancement
of social integration, particularly of marginalized and disadvantaged groups;
alleviation and reduction of poverty; and the expansion of productive employment).[18] In the preparatory stages, there had been considerable discussion of human security in language that paralleled that of the UNDP. However,
this disappeared well before the summit itself. The ambitious UNDP agenda
for action that focused on human security was largely ignored; the delegates
preferred vague formulations (e.g., the total eradication of poverty) that did
not specify what commitments of resources were necessary to achieve them.[19]
The effort to capture the peace dividend also disappeared.

Resistance to the human security agenda at the summit may be explained
by several factors, most of them relating to the unabashed liberal universalism that pervaded the UNDP analysis. Its emphasis on universality (particularly on issues such as gender rights), whether rightly or wrongly, challenged
other cultural perspectives on rights. Its implicit contestation of sovereignty
was deeply problematic for many southern states and for Russia and China.
Its strong emphasis on the development side of security met with little enthusiasm in other UN bodies (e.g., the Department of Political Affairs, the Department of Peacekeeping Operations [DPKO], and UNHCR), and in the
human rights community. Its advocacy of reform of UN institutions risked
diluting the power of the permanent members of the Security Council and

threatened numerous vested interests within the UN. Its effort to capture the peace dividend ran afoul of the defense policy and fiscal preferences of both developed and less developed states. Finally, the sheer breadth of the agenda the report embraced was deemed impractical, if not impracticable, by some states.[20]

Despite the summit's retreat from the language and the specifics of human security, the effort of the UNDP to refocus international society's consideration of security had a fundamental effect on subsequent thinking and action. The later development of discourse on human security and the reconsideration of state security prerogatives implicit in the concept are rooted in the UNDP's reimagining of the meaning of the security.[21] The UNDP laid down the baseline.

Conflict Prevention and Human Security: The Structural Causes of Conflict

> Extreme poverty and infectious diseases are threats in themselves, but they also create environments which make more likely the emergence of other threats, including civil conflict. —Kofi Annan, 2004[22]

> We fight against poverty because hope is an answer to terror.
>
> —George W. Bush, 2002[23]

The security-as-development argument receded in the mid- and late 1990s in the face of the compelling physical threat civil conflict posed to human survival. Such conflict, however, fostered a sustained discussion of conflict prevention. There were several elements in this discussion. One, reflecting the fact that international institutions had been taken surprise by the rapid onset of conflicts in Southeastern Europe and the former USSR after the Cold War and the collapse of the USSR, was consideration of mechanisms to provide early warning of potential conflicts. Another concerned the role of diplomacy in defusing emerging crises, including fact-finding missions, and political confidence-building measures.[24] A third focused on preventive military deployment to forestall the transition of tense situations into active conflict; the UN Preventive Deployment Force in Macedonia is the classic example. It is the fourth—identifying and responding to the structural causes of conflict—that concerns us here. Among the key structural causes of instability and conflict identified in this literature were poverty, inequality, and lack of economic opportunity. In this respect, the evolving conception of conflict prevention embraced the significance of individual economic insecurity as a source of conflict. The response to the problem of individual economic insecurity was human development.

In 1992, Boutros Boutros-Ghali underlined the significance of "economic and social developments that may, unless mitigated, threaten international peace and security" and called for ECOSOC to develop mechanisms for early warning in this area.[25] The theme was picked up by the UNDP in its 1993 HDR, which noted that although diplomacy and military forces might be useful in the short-term effort to defuse crises and maintain the peace, long-term solutions to the challenge of conflict prevention required economic development and greater social justice.[26] It was also a significant element of the Secretary-General's *An Agenda for Development* (1994), which emphasized the dialectical quality of the relationship between development and security. Peace and stability were necessary for development; they could not endure in the absence of a human welfare and freedom.[27]

In another significant contribution, in 1994 the Carnegie Foundation responded to the emergence of post–Cold War conflict by establishing the Carnegie Commission on Preventing Deadly Conflict. The commission's task was to clarify the nature of the problem of deadly conflict within or between states, to analyze how the international community should respond to the prospect of such conflict, and to determine what the structure of the response should be. It produced twenty-seven published and five unpublished reports and ten books. Several of its products (e.g., the work by Edward Laurence, Michael Klare, and Jeffrey Boutwell on small arms)[28] played a seminal role in developing particular aspects of the discussion of human security.

The Carnegie Commission's final report noted the increasing incidence of civil conflict in post–Cold War world politics and highlighted the threats posed to civilians, especially to women and children, in such wars. In its analysis of the causes of such conflict, the commissioners recognized the significance of sudden economic deterioration and resource scarcity. In considering ways to prevent the outbreak of civil conflict, the commission emphasized the generation of economic opportunities and, prefiguring the 2003 analysis of the Commission on Human Security, the strengthening of social safety nets. The commission also noted the central importance of economic recovery in preventing the re-emergence of conflict once settlements had been achieved. It drew attention to the need to address root causes of conflict and called upon governments and leaders to "ensure fundamental security, well-being and justice for all citizens." At a structural level, the report highlighted the importance of ensuring well-being (access to necessities, including food, health services, education, and employment) as a key aspect of conflict prevention. The commission shared the thrust of the human development literature regarding growth, emphasizing that while it was important, it was imperative to ensure that the gains from growth were equitably distributed. Growth without equity could exacerbate societal tensions, reducing individual and national security, particularly when economic status and opportunities varied along ethnic lines.[29] The report also called for a more systematic and substantial UN role in conflict prevention, suggesting an agenda for change in the organization to allow it to fulfill this role effectively and calling for closer cooperation between the political bodies of the United Nations and IFIs to marshal the latter's resources to more effectively address the economic root causes of conflict.[30]

The UN Secretariat pursued the matter. Kofi Annan came to his post with a strong commitment to replacing what he considered to be a culture of reaction in the UN with a culture of prevention. One early initiative was his 1998 response to a Security Council request for an analysis of the security and conflict situation in Africa.[31] This report is significant not least because we see the Secretary-General explicitly embracing the concept of human security and arguing that "ensuring human security is, in the broadest sense, the cardinal mission of the United Nations."[32] More to the point here, he underlined the importance of sustainable human development to conflict prevention. Recognizing resource scarcity, low levels of growth, inequitable development, and the impact of structural adjustment as important sources of tension in African societies,[33] he emphasized the importance of growth coupled with economic reform in the search for stability in the region.[34] He stressed the significance of social development (investing in human resources, improving the provision of public health care, fostering social justice, and eliminating gender discrimination).[35] Annan also emphasized the need to foster positive international conditions for sustainable development through debt relief and the reform of the international trade regime.[36]

The General Assembly also took up the matter of development as an aspect of conflict prevention and management. In its 1998 "Declaration and Programme of Action on a Culture of Peace," the assembly recognized the significance of anti-poverty strategies, the assurance of equity in development, and the pursuit of food security as elements of peacebuilding.[37]

In 1998–1999, the focus of consideration of conflict prevention shifted to the Security Council. This began with the council's discussion of the Secretary-General's report on Africa. In a series of presidential statements and resolutions, the council recognized the seriousness of the challenge of conflict in Africa and the need to build capacity both in the UN and at the regional level to address not only peacekeeping and peacebuilding but also conflict prevention. Here the close link between economic and social development and peace and the significance of poverty eradication and sustainable development as elements of conflict prevention were emphasized.[38] The council established an ad hoc working group to develop recommendations on how to implement the Secretary-General's report.[39]

After an open debate on conflict prevention in November 1999, the president of the Security Council issued a statement outlining the role of the council in this area. Although the bulk of the statement dealt with issues that fall more clearly within the organ's remit (early warning, preventive diplomacy and deployment, targeted sanctions, postconflict peacebuilding), it also stressed the significance of root causes (including social and economic problems). In this context, it called upon all UN organs to "assist member states to eradicate poverty and to strengthen development cooperation" in addition to addressing human rights concerns.[40] In July 2000, the council followed up with a further statement in which it called upon ECOSOC to take a more active role in structural conflict prevention.[41] It also suggested that conflict prevention be integrated more effectively into development assistance strategies and called for the Secretary-General to produce an analysis of and set of recommendations for conflict prevention.[42]

In response to this request, the Secretary-General developed his ideas on conflict prevention further.[43] In a report heavily influenced by the findings of the Carnegie Commission, he reiterated his commitment to moving the UN from a "culture of reaction to a culture of prevention." He also stressed again the mutually reinforcing character of conflict prevention and sustainable development. He dwelled in particular on the importance of dealing with structural causes of conflict, including socioeconomic factors,[44] arguing that structural conflict prevention was in essence sustainable development. The bulk of the report was devoted to an elaboration of the role of the United Nations in conflict prevention. His recommendations were wide ranging. Of particular significance here was his repetition of the Security Council's call for ECOSOC, given its mandate to address socioeconomic root causes of conflict, to take a more active role in the UN's efforts to prevent conflict. He stressed the need for UN development assistance to "focus on decreasing the key structural risk factors that fuel violent conflict, such as inequity—by addressing disparities among identity groups; inequality—by addressing policies and practices that institutionalize discrimination; . . . and insecurity—by strengthening accountable governance and human security."[45] He recommended that UN resident coordinators set up conflict prevention groups in their countries to identify and address key structural risk factors.

The Secretary-General pursued the economic dimension of security in other venues as well. In his Millennium Declaration, he stressed that an adequate livelihood was a basic right but also stressed the connection between poverty and conflict:

> Extreme poverty is an affront to our common humanity. It also makes other problems worse. For example, poor countries—especially those with significant inequality between ethnic and religious communities—are far more likely to be embroiled in conflicts than rich ones.[46]

On this basis, among others, he called for global poverty to be halved by 2015.

Reflecting change in its membership (notably the departure of Sweden in 1998 and Norway in 2002), the Security Council's consideration of the issue of conflict prevention has diminished in recent years. The reduction in attention also reflects the salience of other issues (e.g., terrorism). However, the agenda had moved from formulation of principles (in which particular entrepreneurs such as Sweden played a key role) through elaboration and on to institutionalization and implementation. The period of 1998 to 2002 witnessed a substantial embedding of the issue in the UN system, in the programs of UN agencies, and in training of personnel.[47]

The themes of structural causes of conflict and development as conflict prevention were highlighted in the report of the High-level Panel on Threats, Challenges and Change. Noting the correlation between poverty (measured by GDP per capita) and conflict, the panel suggested that when poverty was combined with ethnic or regional conflict, grievances were compounded. It noted the significant impact of environmental degradation on people's livelihoods and the devastating effects of HIV/AIDS and other infectious diseases on the societies and economies of vulnerable countries. Curiously, it made no effort to link the latter to security per se, although the chapter in which this analysis occurs was entitled "Collective Security and the Challenge of Prevention."[48]

Before leaving the issue, it is appropriate to mention that this process of reflection in the UN was paralleled in governments of states and in regional organizations. The Swedish Foreign Ministry's 1999 study on conflict prevention noted that poverty was a central component of the evolving conception of security and called for the integration of conflict prevention with development cooperation.[49] The Swedish International Development Cooperation Agency (SIDA) allocates significant funds for efforts in this area.[50] In 2001, the UK Department for International Development mounted a substantial program on conflict prevention in cooperation with the Ministry of Defence and the Foreign and Commonwealth Office. The combined funds to prevent conflict both globally and in Africa spent over £600 million from 2001 to 2004.[51]

With a strong push during the Swedish presidency of the European Union in particular, the European Commission recognized the significance of poverty reduction as an element of conflict prevention, highlighted the role of development assistance and cooperation in pursuit of this objective, and called for the mainstreaming of conflict prevention in development assistance.[52] The security strategy of the Council of the European Union suggested that there was a direct link between widespread poverty and the incidence of conflict.[53]

This effort to embed the development logic of conflict prevention is not limited to the liberal European powers. In the context not only of interpreting post–Cold War conflict but also its war on terror, the United States embraced the relationship between human suffering and social and political violence. The Bush administration's *National Security Strategy of the United States of America* recognized the need to deal with the underlying conditions that "spawn terrorism" and argued that global prosperity enhanced U.S. national security. The president recognized that disease, war, and desperate poverty in Africa threatened America's strategic priority of combating global terror.[54] More broadly, as suggested in the quotation that begins this section, President Bush acknowledged that hopelessness was a source of terror and that poverty alleviation was one means of providing hope. This was one reason among several for the president's call for a 50 percent expansion in U.S. core development assistance through the Millennium Challenge Account.[55]

The structural conflict prevention logic penetrated into the strategy of the U.S. Agency for International Development (USAID). In a 2003 report on the relationship between foreign aid and the national interest, the agency underlined the significance of root causes of conflict and the strong correlation between economic stagnation or decline and the incidence of conflict. It suggested that previous programs had been insufficiently attentive to implications (positive and negative) of development assistance for security and conflict. While poverty and suffering in and of themselves did not produce conflict, they did create a fertile environment for conflict to emerge. In particular, USAID noted the potentially destabilizing impact of youth unemployment. When this group has no hope, they are vulnerable to political entrepreneurs who seek change through violence. In addition, they might be attracted by the economic opportunities social violence provides. According to the agency, development assistance (e.g., education and the generation of jobs) targeted at improving economic opportunities for this group would mitigate the potential for conflict.[56]

Perception of the relationship between human development and conflict prevention was not an exclusively northern affair. The African Union's (AU) legislation establishing a peace and security council recognizes the interdependence of socioeconomic development and the security of states and peoples as a basic principle of the council.[57] The Conference on Security, Stability, Development and Cooperation in Africa (CSSDCA) process emphasized the importance of acknowledging and acting upon the unavoidable relationship between sustainable development and security.[58] The CSSDCA process is also significant for this volume because of its definition of the security component of its activities:

> The concept of security must embrace all aspects of society including economic, political, social and environmental dimensions of the individual, family, community, local and national life. The security of a nation must be based on the security of the life of the individual citizens to live in peace and to satisfy basic needs while being able to participate fully in societal affairs and enjoying freedom and fundamental human rights.[59]

This amounts, rhetorically anyway, to an embrace of the broad logic of human security by African heads of state and a recognition that dealing with individual security needs—especially their "basic" economic needs—is a central aspect of conflict prevention.

The crises in Somalia, Rwanda, and other areas in the mid- and late 1990s gave further impetus to consideration of the economic aspects of conflict prevention; many analyses highlighted the role of inequitable development and dysfunctional development assistance in fostering these conflicts.[60] This realization produced a major shift in thinking about the humanitarian and development enterprises. Whereas for many years the dominant approach had been to stress the apolitical character of assistance activities, donors and implementing agencies came to recognize the need to take into account the relationship between economic decline and conflict and to consider the potential in the design and delivery of assistance to promote conflict. Correspondingly, there was a growing stress on the role of such assistance in conflict prevention.[61]

The evolving discussion of structural conflict prevention stressed the significance of poverty, inequity, and lack of economic opportunity as important factors contributing to instability. This development in the post–Cold War era echoes the much older recognition that human deprivation could contribute to insecurity. It follows that security policy, broadly defined, needed to include development activities designed to address these root causes of conflict. The United Nations played a central role in establishing (economic) root causes of conflict as a significant security policy issue, not least in the Secretary-General's insistence on the need to move toward a culture of prevention but also in the application of this insight in particularly conflict-prone regions, such as Africa. The process within the Security Council was pushed by particular states (e.g., Sweden and Norway) but was strongly informed by analytical and prescriptive inputs from the Secretariat. The question of root causes of conflict—and the associated implication that ensuring security within the international system requires addressing the economic threats faced by the poor—has gained prominence in the policies of UN development agencies. It has also spread to significant donors such as the United States, the Scandinavian countries, the UK, the European Union (EU), and the Organisation for Economic Co-operation and Development (OECD). The normative and institutional development of the African Union and the CSSDCA reflects this understanding. Consideration of the underlying causes of terrorism has given further impetus to consideration of the human security dimension of conflict prevention.

The Return of Development and Security: *Human Security Now*

As we have seen, the effort to define human security along economic and development lines faltered in the mid-1990s and its position was increasingly challenged by the discussion of physical protection during the later 1990s. However, the shift to a focus on protection in discussion of human security was not universal. The discussion of root causes as an aspect of conflict prevention is one example. Moreover, the UNDP, a large section of the community of development economists, and certain states continued to pursue thinking on the development dimension of security. Certain key events in international relations in the late 1990s, especially the 1997–1998 Asian financial crisis,[62] highlighted once again the significance of economic threats to individuals. Millions of people lost their livelihoods in conditions where safety nets were weak or nonexistent. The result was widespread and deep human misery.

One prominent contribution to the reassertion of the development dimension of human security was the work of Amartya Sen. In the last half of the 1990s, he moved his earlier work on human development toward a substantial consideration of the relationship between development and freedom, defining development itself as "a process of expanding the real freedoms that people enjoy."[63] The broader argument heavily emphasizes the importance of transparent and representative (i.e., accountable) governance not only as a constitutive dimension of development but as a means of ensuring that people's other needs are addressed.[64]

One of the principal instrumental freedoms upon which he focused was "protective security":

> [A]verting famines and preventing calamitous crises . . . is one important part of the process of development as freedom, for it involves the enhancement of

the security and protection that the citizens enjoy. The connection is both constitutive and instrumental. First, protection against starvation, epidemics, and severe and sudden deprivation is itself an enhancement of the opportunity to live securely and well. The prevention of devastating crises is, in this sense, part and parcel of the freedom that people have reason to value. Second, the process of preventing famines and other crises is significantly helped by the use of instrumental freedoms, such as the opportunity of open discussion, public scrutiny, electoral politics, and uncensored media.

He used the Asian financial crisis and its decimation of the lives of millions of people as a key example that supported his argument.[65] Although the argument inextricably links development and civil and political rights, the vision of security (i.e., what threats people are to be protected from) is strongly economic in character. The threats identified are starvation, epidemics, and sudden and severe deprivation. The threat of physical violence, in contrast, receives little emphasis in this work.

Among states, Japan's embrace of sustainable human development—and of the importance of empowerment and self-help—dated back into the early 1990s in the TICAD (Tokyo International Conference on African Development) process, which was launched in 1993. Later in the 1990s, Japan was a very close observer of Asia's economic near-meltdown, a process that strongly affected key markets and destabilized regional partners such as Indonesia. Japanese foreign minister Keizo Obuchi articulated his country's acute sensitivity to the human consequences (such as loss of livelihood and withdrawal of children from schools) of the Asian financial crisis.[66]

In December 1998, as prime minister, Obuchi embraced human security as an element of Japanese foreign policy and announced the establishment of the UN Trust Fund for Human Security, to which Japan contributed over $203 million between 1999 and 2002.[67] The programming of the Trust Fund departs from the observation that "[h]uman security aims to protecting [sic] people from critical and pervasive threats to human lives, livelihoods and dignity, and thus to enhancing [sic] human fulfilment."[68] The principal purpose of the fund is to make grants to UN agencies and affiliated organizations to finance activities that promote human security. The activities that were funded (programs to alleviate poverty, provide food security, enhance the welfare of returning refugees, rehabilitate schools and hospitals, provide vocational training to ex-combatants, control disease, promote reproductive health, enhance public health services, replace crops in the struggle against narcotics, and control trafficking in women and children)[69] suggest a clear emphasis on human development as the central thrust of human security.[70]

The Japanese government announced a new approach to development assistance in 2002 at the Johannesburg Summit on Sustainable Development. Its representative stressed the need for peace as freedom from the threat of violence. The representative also stressed the need for security, which included "social security that allows 'normal life' for ordinary people." Combined with structures of governance that protected basic human rights, these conditions would "give ordinary people 'predictability' and 'political and economic participation,'" allowing sustainable development and fostering conflict prevention.[71] Accordingly, the Japanese "people-centered approach" to security acknowledged the need for protection from violence but embedded that emphasis in a much broader definition of security that stressed the need for people to develop means of protecting themselves from a broad array of threats to their livelihoods and rights through education, equality of economic opportunity, adequate health care, and the mainstreaming of gender.[72] Sustainable human development again was a central means of providing such protection.

Japan's embrace of a primarily developmentalist understanding of human security reflected not only the evolution just described but also the country's discomfort with the seemingly interventionist thrust of the evolving discourse on human security. The link between protection and intervention was unacceptable to a number of key states in the region (notably China) with whom Japan had complex relations.[73] Japan's unhappiness was exacerbated by the emerging consensus of the International Commission on Intervention and State Sovereignty on "the responsibility to protect," the title of its 2001 report (see Chapter 5).

When Kofi Annan called for further efforts to achieve "freedom from fear" and "freedom from want," Prime Minister Yoshiro Mori responded by reiterating Japan's embrace of human security as a key aspect of its foreign policy and offered to fund and support an international commission on human security. With Japanese support, Kofi Annan established the Commission on Human Security in 2001. The CHS was led by Nobel laureate Amartya Sen and former UN high commissioner for refugees Sadako Ogata. It brought together an impressive group of scholars and practitioners to develop an agenda to promote human security. In contrast to the approach taken by the International Commission on Intervention and State Sovereignty, the CHS deliberately took a broad view of human security, stressing the need to address deprivation as well as violence and conflict. Its report is the definitive statement of the development approach to human security.

Although it recognized the fundamental role that states play in fostering human security, the commission stressed that states frequently fail in this obligation. In consequence, the new security agenda had to be focused on people. It acknowledged the significance of safeguarding human beings from physical harm but emphasized the empowerment of individuals and communities to take control of their lives. In reinserting empowerment into human security, the report suggested that ultimately, the protection of communities rested in important measure with those communities themselves. The challenge for international agencies was to enhance the capacity of communities to address threats themselves instead of replacing community capacities to address these threats.[74]

The people-centered concept of human security brought together physical protection, rights, and development. The report defined human security as "the protection of the vital core of all human lives in ways that enhance human freedoms and human fulfilment. . . . It means creating political, social, environmental, economic, military and cultural systems that together give people the building blocks of survival, livelihood and dignity."[75] Reflecting tensions within the commission and more broadly within international society, it resisted the temptation to define what was contained in this vital core, arguing that the answer might well differ from one society to the next. The relationship between state security and human security was complementary, not competitive, it argued. Stable, representative, and responsive institutions were necessary conditions for human security. Fostering human security contributed to the stability of the state and its institutions.[76]

Elsewhere, the report emphasized that "[h]uman security is concerned with safeguarding and expanding people's vital freedoms. It requires both shielding people from acute threats and empowering people to take charge of their own lives. Needed are integrated policies that focus on people's survival, livelihood and dignity, during downturns as well as in prosperity."[77] Despite the ostensible balance between development and protection, the last part of this definition suggests a strong emphasis on economic welfare and its safeguarding as a fundamental component of human security. In this sense, there is a strong link between the logic here and that of the UNDP's *Human Development Report 1994*, which placed an equally strong emphasis on threats to economic well-being as a basic security problem and characterized human development as an expansion of people's choices and an enhancement of their ability to control their own lives.

Human security was seen to complement both human rights and human development. In the former case, while human rights were universal and authoritatively defined in the UDHR and other foundational documents (e.g., the 1993 Vienna Declaration), the lens of human security assisted in identifying what rights were at stake in any given situation. While human development was a forward-looking concept that stressed the expansion of people's opportunities, human security was more about limiting downside risk. One sees in the CHS report an almost explicit rejection of the narrower focus on protection from violence and physical threat manifested, for example, in the report of the International Commission on Intervention and State Sovereignty discussed in the next chapter, and an insistence that it made little sense—when discussing security—to ignore broader social, economic, and environmental threats to human well-being. Reflecting Kofi Annan's remark cited above, the approach to human security had to be integrative rather than selective.

Conclusion

In this chapter we have explored three themes related to the economic dimension of human security. The first is the "humanization" of development. As we saw in Chapter 2, during the late Cold War, there was among development economists an increasing discomfort with defining development in terms of growth and measuring it in terms of national aggregates, such as GNP, savings, and investment. The discomfort originated in the recognition that trends at the national level had no necessary effect in improving the lives of people. As a result, development economists and development agencies focused increasingly on how to measure human well-being and how to deliver on improving people's lives, especially the lives of the poor, through employment and poverty alleviation policies. In this respect, reconsideration of the referents of development parallels that concerning referents of security. In both cases, there was a downward movement from the state to the individual human being in her community.

This trend continued and deepened in the post–Cold War period. UN organizations played a very important role in this process. In particular, the UNDP's effort to develop measures of human development and rate states in terms of their performance on these measures, although perhaps imperfect, did encourage recipients of development assistance to focus on income distribution, the quality of life, and meeting basic needs in their approaches to development. Such considerations also became increasingly embedded in the policies and practices of multilateral development agencies and major donor states.

Second, we saw in Chapters 1 and 2 that there has been a long-standing recognition of the relationship between economic well-being on the one hand and the security of states on the other. Enhancing stability and security, therefore, called for efforts to promote "freedom from want." During the post–Cold War period, this became a major theme in the efforts to address both the internal conflicts that characterized the period and, after 2001, terrorism. Although the literature on conflict prevention retained a strong focus on measures outlined in Chapter VI of the UN Charter (preventive diplomacy, preventive deployment) and Chapter VII (sanctions), we have shown that there was also increasing recognition that the failure of development was a root cause of conflict and that to forestall violence in the first place and prevent postconflict societies from slipping back into violence, assistance programs should take into account their potential impact on conflict.

Here too, the UN played a substantial role. The Secretary-General led the way with his call to replace a culture of reaction with a culture of prevention and his seminal report on the causes of conflict and the promotion of durable peace in Africa. So too did both the General Assembly (in its consideration of the culture of peace) and the Security Council (in its prolonged consideration of conflict prevention as an aspect of security policy). Both the UNDP and the World Bank have made substantial efforts to integrate conflict and conflict prevention into program design. These efforts have extended, both normatively and in policy implementation, into the activities of donor states and regional organizations (especially the EU). American analysis of the threat of terrorism has encouraged efforts on the part of USAID to address what are considered to be the root economic and social causes of terrorism. The similarity of American and UN agency analyses of root causes suggests that the UN has influenced the development of understanding of the structural causes of conflict in U.S. official agencies.

Finally, consideration of human development produced a merging of discourse between development and security. The 1994 *Human Development Report* and reports of the 2003 Commission on Human Security and the 2004 High-level Panel all emphasize that human well-being and the capacity of communities and individuals to protect their economic welfare are key considerations in the broader account of human security. This reflects a recognition, which was clearly articulated in the much earlier Brandt Commission report, that economic threats to human beings can be just as fatal as physical threats from violence. One may argue about the merits and demerits of broadening the core concept of security accordingly (as we do in Chapter 7), but it is unquestionable that this conceptual development has encouraged a much deeper and more detailed consideration of individual economic well-being as an unavoidable aspect of the promotion of human security.

The United Nations and its agencies and the prominent individuals (e.g., Mahbub ul Haq and Amartya Sen) associated with those agencies also played a fundamental role in this evolution of ideas. The UNDP laid the concept of human security on the table and highlighted its economic dimensions. All subsequent discussion of human security has this report as its point of origin. The Secretary-General repeatedly used the notion of freedom from want to encourage a focus on the economic dimensions of security. The CHS and HLP, whose respective 2003 and 2004 reports represent the culmination of the broadening approach to security, were established by Kofi Annan and were led by individuals with strong connections to the United Nations. Again, though, the role of states was also crucial. That the CHS was established and could carry its work to term was largely the result of the sustained interest of the Japanese government in the concept of human security and in the need to give pride of place to development as an aspect of human security.

5

The UN and Human Security: The Protection Dimension

- **The United Nations and the Responsibility to Protect**
- **Sanctions and Human Security**
- **Civilian Protection and Regional Organizations**
- **Addressing Impunity**
- **Human Security and Disarmament**
- **Conclusion**

> The question whether a certain matter is or is not solely within the jurisdiction of a State is an essentially relative question; it depends upon the development of international relations.
>
> —Permanent Court of International Justice, 1921[1]

> Through its foreign policy, Canada has chosen to focus its human security agenda on promoting safety for people by protecting them from threats of violence. We have chosen this focus because we believe this is where the concept of human security has the greatest value added—where it complements existing international agendas already focussed on promoting national security, human rights and human development.
>
> —Government of Canada, 2002[2]

In the mid-1990s, and in view of the egregious violations of basic human rights characteristic of much post–Cold War internal armed conflict, some concluded that the focus on development of the UNDP's approach to security distracted attention from increasingly serious problems of basic protection of human beings involved in war. While acknowledging the seminal and constructive role of the agency's *Human Development Report 1994* in focusing the concept of security on "people" and in highlighting "non-traditional threats," one influential analysis suggested, for example, that the agency's approach to the concept "made it unwieldy as a policy instrument." Moreover, it took issue with the report's emphasis on threats associated with underdevelopment and suggested that this led the UNDP to ignore "the continuing human insecurity resulting from violent conflict."[3]

This approach did not ignore development questions but suggested that human security, conceived as safety from violence and from abuse of rights, was a prerequisite for human development: "If people lack confidence in society's ability to protect them, they will have little incentive to invest in the future. . . . Human security provides an enabling environment for human development."[4] We see here the crystallization of a division in the understanding of the concept of human security between a development perspective that sees safety from economic threats as an essential aspect of human security and a rights and protection perspective that sees physical safety as distinct from, and prior to, the address of economic problems. This alternative view is illustrated eloquently in the title the Canadian government chose for its 2002 human security policy framework: *Freedom from Fear: Canada's Foreign Policy for Human Security.*[5]

With these considerations in mind, this chapter turns to examination of a narrower interpretation of human security that focuses on the protection of human beings from violence. One central theme throughout the early part of this volume was what rights and duties outsiders, be they states or organizations, have when the rights of individuals are being massively violated within the territory of a recognized member of international society. During the Cold War, although the international framework of norms around individual human rights developed impressively, action against states that would not or could not conform to basic and universal principles concerning such rights was made difficult in two respects. Decolonization was accompanied by a strong articulation of the principle of nonintervention, and structural bipolarity impeded action within the jurisdiction of states outside the spheres of influence of the two superpowers.

In the post–Cold War era, the latter effect disappeared. Moreover, states and multilateral organizations became increasingly aware that the state itself— owing to incapacity or malevolence—might be the most significant threat to the safety of its own citizens and that violations of rights within states could have powerful spillover effects. These growing realizations brought sustained reconsideration of the meaning of sovereignty and the rights it bestowed on states. Recognition of the threat to individuals emanating from internal conflict and from the state itself was, and remains, a constant refrain during the post–Cold War period.[6]

With the end of the Cold War, and in the context of early euphoria regarding the nature of the post–Cold War system, these factors came together in an explosion of norm-building regarding protection of civilians threatened by conflict. Part of this process was haphazard, involving ad hoc responses to crisis. Part was deliberate. In both cases, the United Nations was a central player in producing and promoting ideas, in providing a venue in which this conversation could proceed, and in serving as a mechanism for legitimating, and sometimes implementing, changing understandings of the place of the individual in security.

We begin with an account of the interplay of UN organs and agencies and states in consideration of the protection of civilians in general. In order to assess the weight of the UN's role and to determine the extent to which UN-centered discourse was more broadly accepted in international society, we supplement this analysis with an examination of the evolving perspectives of regional organizations and key states on human protection. Finally, we turn to the effort to develop norms and institutions to address impunity in the violation of the rights of human beings and to control specific types of weapons that constitute a particularly severe threat to human beings.

The United Nations and the Responsibility to Protect

> Sovereignty can no longer be used to shield gross violations of the security of people from international action.
>
> —Commission on Global Governance, 1995[7]

As just noted, during the Cold War the role of the Security Council in civilian protection was strongly circumscribed not only by division within it but also by the narrowness of their definition of threats to international peace and security. Intrusion into the jurisdiction of states by the council was limited to a number of cases of decolonization (e.g., Southern Rhodesia/Zimbabwe), anomalies arising from the mandate and trusteeship systems (e.g., Namibia), and apartheid. None involved the use of force to promote the security of individuals or groups within the states in question.[8] There was little consideration of protection of civilians in mandates of peacekeeping forces.

Matters changed substantially in the early 1990s. This process arguably began with northern Iraq in the spring of 1991, where a humanitarian crisis was rapidly developing as Kurds were driven from their homes by advancing Iraqi forces. Turkey was unwilling to allow them to cross the border. The Security Council expressed its grave concern over the repression of Iraqi civilians and noted that the movement of Kurds had occasioned cross-border incursions that the council considered to be a threat to international peace and security.[9]

Several aspects of this resolution are pertinent here. First, it did not invoke Chapter VII of the Charter, which would have given the council the power to override Article 2.7 dealing with domestic jurisdiction. In fact, the resolution specifically mentioned the latter article in the preamble, emphasizing the council's respect for Iraq's sovereignty, territorial integrity, and political independence. Second, it was not the movement of displaced persons per se that was identified as a threat to peace and security. Instead, it was the problem of cross-border incursion. In other words, at this stage the council shied away from the notion that an internal humanitarian crisis emanating from the violation of citizens' rights by their own state fell within its remit. Cross-border incursion was much safer ground because it was inherently international and not domestic. And third, there was no threat of UN or UN-mandated action (other than humanitarian) to address the root of the problem within Iraq. The rather weak wording of the resolution and the lack of robust implementation clauses reflected the reluctance of a number of council members to provide a broad power of intervention in domestic jurisdiction.

It must also be acknowledged that members of the Security Council were the principal moving forces in this initial reinterpretation of UN responsibilities toward civilians at risk. Three permanent members were contemplating active intervention in Iraq on behalf of the Kurds and the Shiite population in the south before the council acted. Arguably, council action was the product not so much of the UN's commitment to protection shared by its members as it was an effort to forestall unilateral measures by states impinging on the sovereignty of a member of the UN, whether it was a defeated belligerent or not. It is noteworthy in this context that three permanent members of the Security Council—France, the UK, and the United States—created and sustained an air exclusion zone over both northern and southern Iraq, ostensibly to protect civilian populations at risk from the potential use of Iraqi air power.

The action in Iraq mandated by Security Council resolution 688 was significant in one further respect. It raised the question of whether those displaced within borders were entitled to preventive protection, a concept the UN high commissioner for refugees made much of and which laid the basis for the approach of the UNHCR to internal displacement in Bosnia-Herzegovina later in the decade.[10] The idea here was that those displaced within borders had a right to remain within their country and international agencies and other states had a corresponding duty to ensure the security of these groups.

The Security Council approach to human security evolved further in response to the humanitarian crisis in Somalia. The collapse of the Somali state and the deepening conflict among various factions within the country had produced mass starvation. The council's reaction began with an acknowledgement of the situation that underlined the possible threat it posed to regional security. The council appeared to be suggesting that the spillover of the internal conflict created dangers for neighboring states. In this case, Chapter VII was initially invoked as the basis for a council-mandated embargo on the shipment of weapons to the various factions.[11] Several resolutions later, the council determined that the situation within Somalia constituted a threat to international peace and security, noted the remaining obstacles to the delivery of humanitarian assistance and the dangers to relief personnel working there, declared its determination to create an environment that was conducive to mounting humanitarian operations, and, acting under Chapter VII, authorized a military action led by the United States to foster such conditions.[12] Once UNITAF had achieved a modicum of security in the country, it was replaced by a peacekeeping force (UNOSOM II) operating under Chapter VII with a similar mandate.[13]

The unfortunate outcome of the operation notwithstanding, the recognition of human tragedy as a threat to international peace and security in and of itself was a striking development. It is worth stressing that the crisis in Somalia, although it was appalling in its human dimension, did not actually threaten international peace and security. What appeared to have happened here was that the council exploited the underspecification of what such threats were in order to override Article 2.7's protection of domestic jurisdiction for essentially humanitarian reasons.[14]

The Security Council invoked Chapter VII a second time in 1992 to address a humanitarian crisis in Bosnia. Various resolutions in the spring and summer of that year identified the humanitarian crisis in that country as a threat to international peace and security, deployed a peace operation (United Nations Protection Force; UNPROFOR) to assist in the delivery of relief and protect humanitarian personnel and shipments, imposed an embargo on shipments of arms to the former Yugoslavia, mandated a naval blockade of the Yugoslav coast, and banned military flights in response to attacks on humanitarian flights.[15] Later, the council called on member states to freeze the assets of the Yugoslav government held abroad and established a broader sanctions regime.[16] In addition, the council specifically condemned the mass rape of Muslim women in Serb detention camps.[17] As the depth of crimes against civilians grew clearer, the council called for the establishment of an International Criminal Tribunal for the former Yugoslavia.[18] Later, UN protection was extended to the Muslim enclave of Srebrenica.[19] Five other safety areas were added a month later.[20]

The failure of all of these efforts to achieve peace or human security in the former Yugoslavia and the implications of this failure not only for the credibility of the UN but also for that of regional institutions led the United States and its NATO allies to adopt a more active military and diplomatic role in

1995 with regard to Bosnia. Ultimately, U.S. diplomatic efforts, coupled with changes in the military balance between the Serbs and their adversaries, produced the Dayton Accords and the transfer of military responsibilities from UNPROFOR to NATO's IFOR (Implementation Force).[21]

The case of Rwanda, while it is notable for the indecisiveness and irresponsibility of the council, also contributed to this evolution. In the later stages of the crisis, the council, once again determining that a humanitarian crisis constituted a threat to international peace and security and acting under Chapter VII, mandated a French-led intervention to protect civilians in the south of the country and to assist in the delivery of humanitarian relief.[22] Following the precedent established with regard to the former Yugoslavia, the council also established an International Criminal Tribunal for Rwanda to call the principal *génocidaires* to account.

What was striking about all three of these cases, particularly in contrast to earlier peacekeeping operations, was the explicit extension of UN military functions to the protection of civilians from harm, both international personnel involved in humanitarian operations and the victims themselves.[23] In addition, although the cases of Iraq, Bosnia, and Rwanda (or, for that matter, the later case of East Timor) did not obviously raise Article 2.7 concerns since the authorities assented to UN activities,[24] the Somali case did involve intervention for humanitarian purposes without the consent of the state concerned. In that case, the lack of a government or state to deliver consent drew into question the precedentiary value of the international intervention without consent.

The series of decisions just discussed, along with others concerning, for example, efforts to restore democratic governance in Haiti and in Sierra Leone, suggest some movement toward the principle of privileging the rights of civilians to protection in internal conflicts where these rights are being abused. This was accompanied by evidence that the council sought to hold the agents of states engaging in these violations accountable before the law. In a number of instances in the second half of the 1990s (e.g., Bosnia, Kosovo, and East Timor), such actions led to the partial or complete suspension of state sovereignty by the United Nations. In other words, the 1990s show reasonably clear movement toward privileging the individual and his or her security over that of the state and its security.

However, several caveats are appropriate. One is that in all three cases just discussed, the unique and nonprecedentiary nature of the crisis in question was highlighted in relevant council documents. This clearly reflected the reluctance of some permanent members (e.g., Russia and China) to move toward general norms and their rearguard action in defense of the sovereignty of states. The discomfort of some council members regarding the decision on northern Iraq was evident in the strong reservations of China, Cuba, Yemen, and Zimbabwe about the general implications of resolution 688 and by the abstentions of India and China in the vote on the resolution. In the case of Somalia, the skeptics were careful to underline the unique character of the situation in order to minimize the prospect that the action would be taken as a precedent elsewhere. In many instances, the resolutions reaffirmed the sovereign nature of the state in question. Although one might argue that the accretion of "unique" cases does suggest a shift in the general rule regarding nonintervention, the slow and gradual quality of Security Council action was further evidence of the organ's caution in treading this ground. The unwillingness of the council to mandate intervention in the case of Kosovo, the consequent decision of the United States and its allies to exit from the UN process, and the widespread outrage that greeted NATO's action[25] also suggested the incompleteness of this normative evolution in the broader society of states.

The partial quality of the embrace of a right and obligation to protect civilians within the borders of sovereign states is also evident in the selectivity of the international actions discussed. The human security grounds for intervention in the civil war in Sudan or in the Democratic Republic of Congo were as compelling as those that provoked UN action in the cases just discussed. No forceful action to protect civilians was forthcoming. In the case of Rwanda, despite early warning, the Security Council reacted to evidence of deepening crisis by reducing the strength of the peacekeeping force in place rather than by expanding its mandate to permit more robust action in defense of civilians at risk or reinforcing the force with better-equipped troops. Council members deliberately avoided the discourse of genocide in this case in the effort to avoid any apprehension of obligation stemming from the illegality of genocidal acts.

Many have suggested that the selectivity of Security Council behavior in the area of protection indicates that the embrace of protection may be nothing more than a justification for action taken for self-interested reasons. This conclusion is perhaps too harsh. It is hard to find self-interested geostrategic reasons for the American-led action in Somalia, for example. And, more broadly, such arguments ignore the substantial impact of domestic opinion in eliciting state responses to humanitarian crises.[26] However, there appears to be a general pattern in which states, while taking humanitarian challenges seriously, generally need a further reason to put their military personnel at risk. This is not necessarily a bad thing. The morality of leaders of a state putting the lives of their citizens in danger where the event to which they are responding poses no threat to their polity may be questioned. The principal obligations of national leaders are presumably to their citizens—those whom they have been selected to serve and to protect. In other words, the tension between the solidarist impulse and the obligations associated with more particular forms of identity has hardly disappeared.

All of this said, viewing the matter historically, there did seem to be a rather substantial shift in the Security Council's view of security toward centering the concept on people rather than states. This is quite significant. It would not be surprising if it had been nonstate actors (e.g., human rights and humanitarian NGOs) that pushed this agenda—their position was not at stake. For a body composed of states and dominated by the great powers to take this route, however hesitantly, suggests that many states themselves perceived a need to qualify sovereignty in matters of human security.

Although movement on protection in the Security Council was the most prominent element of the evolution of ideas in and the changes in the norms of the UN system during this period, by the mid-1990s other parts of the UN system were also embarking on a more explicit consideration of the implications of the concept of human security. Aid agencies, especially the UNHCR, were strongly influenced by their practical experiences of operating in war zones. Their concern about protection of civilians from violence in war was strengthened by particular experiences in the mid-1990s (e.g., the genocide in Rwanda and the drawn-out discrediting of the UN in the former Yugoslavia).[27] General discomfort within the humanitarian community over the potential consequences of delivery of humanitarian assistance without protection and a corresponding disillusionment with the narrowness of the mandates and rules of engagement of peacekeepers in many humanitarian crises increased the discomfort. One aid worker in Bosnia noted the obvious irony in UNPROFOR's rules of engagement: "The UN troops were instructed to use force to protect the aid supplies—but they were prevented from using force to protect people."[28] More generally, the UNHCR has noted that "it has become all too clear that humanitarian action can play only a very limited role in protecting human rights and safeguarding human security in situations of ongoing conflict. As the tragic events in Srebrenica and Zepa demonstrated in 1995 when the 'safe areas' established by the UN Security Council were overrun by Serb forces, more assertive forms of action are required to safeguard the physical security of vulnerable populations."[29] Reflecting the general disillusion, one of the agency's former officials put the point more directly: "You don't reply to fascism with relief supplies and you don't counter ethnic cleansing with reception centres for the displaced."[30]

In 1997, the UNHCR chose to structure its annual report *State of the World's Refugees* around the concept of human security, noting that displacement was a product of individual insecurity and that everyone had a right to both security and freedom. The report reviewed the broadening of the concept of security in the post–Cold War era, highlighting the significance of the Security Council's 1992 recognition that "the non-military sources of instability in the economic, social, humanitarian and ecological fields have become threats to peace and security," and that there was an ineradicable connection between the "security of states and the welfare of citizens." Its analysis was grounded in the *Human Development Report 1994* and it acknowledged the UNDP's fundamental point of departure: "Human security has two principal aspects: safety from chronic threats such as hunger, disease and repression, and protection from sudden and hurtful disruptions in the pattern of daily life."

The focus of the UNHCR's report was squarely on the particular protection problems faced by populations displaced by violence and repression. There is no substantial discussion of the development dimension of human security stressed by the UNDP report. Instead, the UNHCR focused on the problems of defending refugee rights, the nature of and responses to internal displacement, the issue of return and reintegration, the difficulties of sustaining the asylum system, and the continuing difficulties faced by stateless persons.[31] In this respect, this second UN-family adoption and promotion of the concept strongly reflects what Fen Hampson referred to as the human rights interpretation of human security.

One reason some UN organizations embraced the application of human security to their activities was that a number of states had adopted the concept as an organizing principle for elements of their foreign policy during this period. In this respect, one could interpret the UNHCR report to some extent as an effort to appropriate the language of human security in order to appeal to the growing number of donors who advocated for the redefinition of security in human terms. One prominent example was Canada. In the mid-1990s, the Canadian government found itself promoting a rather broad agenda that included human rights, governance, child soldiers, women in conflict, land mines, peace operations and peacebuilding, and the development of international criminal law. It faced criticism regarding the diffuse quality of this agenda, and human security provided a useful umbrella concept for these disparate activities.[32]

As noted in the introduction to this chapter, the Canadian approach to human security was rooted in a critique of what was perceived to be the excessive breadth and consequent lack of policy focus in the UNDP's conception of human security. Canada's focus in the era when Lloyd Axworthy was foreign minister was the human costs of violent conflict and the safety of people involved in such situations. Canadian policymakers took the view that the security of the state was not an end in itself but was a means of ensuring security for people within its borders. Ensuring human security strengthened the legitimacy and stability and, therefore, the security of the state. Because of the increasing interdependence of states, concern for the safety of people extended beyond borders. Just as the security of each state depended on that of other states, "the security of people in one part of the world depends on the security of people everywhere."[33]

Similar preoccupations by like-minded states produced the Human Security Network, founded in 1999 on the initiative of Canada and Norway.[34] The network seeks to define concrete policies in the area of human security as a basis for coordinated action and attempts to serve as a catalyst that raises awareness of new issues in the area as they arise. Its concerns include the universalization of the Ottawa Convention on Anti-Personnel Landmines, the establishment of the International Criminal Court, the protection of children in armed conflict, the control of small arms and light weapons, the fight against transnational organized crime, human development and human security, human rights education, the struggle against HIV/AIDS, efforts to bridge gaps in implementation of international humanitarian and human rights law, and prevention of conflict. Although the network was established explicitly outside UN frameworks, its members strove to promote the human security agenda within, and in association with, the organization.

The role of independent commissions in furthering the notion of protection of people as a key element of the security agenda was not limited to the Security Council, UN organizations, or particular states. It gained additional prominence through the efforts of the Commission on Global Governance. Publishing its report a year after the horrors of Rwanda and as the crisis in Bosnia was coming to its dénouement, the commission noted that "in many countries the security of peoples has been violated on a horrendous scale without any external aggression or external threat to territorial integrity or state sovereignty" and that confining the concept of security to the protection of states ignored "the interests of the people who form the citizens of the state and *in whose name sovereignty is exercised* [our emphasis]." The report argued that although the state's need for security against external attack could not be ignored, "the international community needs to make the protection of people and their security an aim of global security policy." This had clear implications for the Charter's protection of sovereignty. The commission warned that Article 2.7 should not be treated lightly but suggested that it was "necessary to assert as well the rights and interests of the international community in situations within individual states in which the security of people is violated extensively."[35] In this respect, the commission clearly prefigured key elements of the later normative developments, to which we now turn.

Toward the end of the 1990s, and in the context of consideration of the UN's inaction in Rwanda, its ineffectiveness in Bosnia, and the decision of the NATO states to act outside the UN Security Council process in Kosovo, the Security Council's approach evolved further. In the case of Srebrenica, the General Assembly requested in 1998 that the Secretary-General commission an independent report on the massacre in 1995.[36] In the case of Rwanda, the Secretary-General himself commissioned a similar report.[37] Both reports indicated that the United Nations and its member states had failed badly in fulfilling their responsibility to protect communities in danger of physical destruction.[38] In neither case was there a problem with early warning. In both instances, UN forces were present when the atrocities occurred and either had no mandate to intervene (Rwanda) or chose not to (Srebrenica).

The publication of these damning reports coincided with the arrival of Canada as a nonpermanent member of the Security Council. Canada had been developing a human security focus in its foreign policy since 1996, not just because of the predilections of its foreign minister. One of its most senior army officers had been commander of the Rwanda operation during the genocide, and Canadian policymakers were well aware of his reports from the field.[39] In 1996, moreover, Canada had attempted to lead a multinational force to protect refugee camps in eastern Zaire threatened by advancing forces of the Banyamulenge, backed by the government of Rwanda.[40] The operation was overtaken by events in its preparatory stages,[41] and major contributors of troops withdrew their support. Both events enhanced Canada's sensitivity to the issue of protection. Canadian diplomats made protection not only the central theme of their own approach to human security but the focus of their term on the council.

At the time of Canada's election to the Security Council, its Department of Foreign Affairs and International Trade held an internal strategy meeting to discuss what the country's priorities should be during its tenure. Most of the suggestions were related to human security, broadly defined. The group decided to embrace protection of civilians in war as the central theme of Canada's term. At Canada's initiative, the council held an open meeting to discuss the general issue of protection of civilians in war in February 1999. In the presidential statement at the meeting, the council linked the issue of protection directly to its primary responsibility for peace and security and "expressed its willingness to respond, in accordance with the Charter of the United Nations, to situations in which civilians, as such, have been targeted or where humanitarian assistance has been deliberately obstructed."[42] It requested that the Secretary-General produce a report recommending actions it might take to enhance the physical and legal protection of civilians in armed conflict.

Kofi Annan delivered the report in September 1999.[43] He outlined several dimensions of the threat, focusing on armed attacks against civilians, forced displacement, the intermingling of combatants and civilians in refugee camps, the denial of humanitarian assistance and access, targeting of humanitarian and peacekeeping personnel, the widespread availability of small arms and antipersonnel land mines, and the humanitarian impact of sanctions. He also drew specific attention to the special needs of children and women in armed conflict. He went on to remark—without reference to particular cases—that the Security Council recognized "that massive and systematic breaches of human rights law and international humanitarian law constitute threats to international peace and security and therefore demand its attention."[44] In short, the notion of international responsibility to protect individuals and groups whose security was physically threatened in armed conflict had become, in the mind of the Secretary-General, a generalizable proposition that was not limited to specific crises on an ad hoc basis. He concluded his report with a broad-ranging set of recommendations, a number of which will be touched upon in discussion below. In this context, the most important was his recommendation in a section on intervention that "in the face of massive and ongoing abuses, [the council] consider the imposition of appropriate enforcement action."[45]

The council responded to the Secretary-General's report with two resolutions. In the first, it condemned the targeting of civilians, urged compliance with international humanitarian and human rights law with respect to the treatment of civilians, called on states that had not ratified major humanitarian and human rights instruments to do so, emphasized the responsibility of states to end impunity, underlined the importance of safe access for humanitarian personnel and the need for parties to conflict to ensure the safety and security of UN personnel. It recommended consideration of how peacekeeping mandates might better take into account the protection of civilians in armed conflict, and noted the special circumstances of women and children in armed conflict. Most important from this perspective, the council responded to the Secretary-General's recommendation concerning intervention by expressing "its willingness to respond to situations of armed conflict where civilians are being targeted or humanitarian assistance to civilians is being deliberately obstructed, including through the consideration of appropriate measures at the Council's disposal."[46]

The resolution also established a working group to consider the council's response further. The working group's efforts were embodied in Security Council resolution 1296 of 19 April 2000. Here, the council noted "that the deliberate targeting of civilian populations or other protected persons and the committing of systematic, widespread and flagrant violations of international humanitarian and human rights law in situations of armed conflict may constitute a threat to international peace and security, and, in this regard *reaffirms* its readiness to consider such situations and, where necessary, to adopt appropriate steps." Later in the resolution, it extended this observation to situations where humanitarian assistance was being deliberately obstructed and which might constitute a threat to international peace and security.[47] The use of the language of threat to international peace and security places these issues within the remit of Chapter VII of the Charter. That in turn raises the possibility of waiver of the principle of nonintervention in Article 2.7. Notwithstanding the admonition in the first operative paragraph that the council should approach the issue of protection on a case-by-case basis and taking into account the particular circumstances of the case, these two resolutions appear to suggest the halting emergence of a generally accepted norm that permits intervention in the event of grievous lapses in the protection of human beings.

Similar preoccupations were evident in the *Report of the Panel on UN Peace Operations* (the Brahimi report), which was issued in August 2000. The report noted that the protection of human rights was essential to effective peacebuilding and stressed the need to provide human rights training for peacekeepers.[48] It declared that "peacekeepers—troops or police—who witness violence against civilians should be presumed to be authorized to stop it."[49] During this period and subsequently, protection began to creep into the mandates of peace forces.

The Secretary-General also played a significant advocacy role in the General Assembly as the UN digested its evaluations of the events in Rwanda and Srebrenica. He considered threats to human security in successive reports to the assembly in 1999[50] and 2000.[51] In the former, he signaled his own embrace of the evolving human security perspective[52] and noted the importance of focusing on people's needs and fears in the effort to prevent conflict while delicately navigating the growing controversy among human security proponents about whether protection or development should be prioritized:

> First, the international community should do more to encourage policies that enhance people-centred security in conflict-prone States. Equitable and sustainable development is a necessary condition for security, but minimum standards of security are also a precondition for development. Pursuing one in isolation from the other makes little sense.[53]

He also suggested (implicitly) that when gross violations of human rights occurred, concerns about sovereignty should not be taken as a reason for inaction.[54] He followed this a year later in *We the Peoples* with a fundamental, if troubling, question. After acknowledging widespread opposition to humanitarian intervention, he asked: "If humanitarian intervention is, indeed, an unacceptable assault on sovereignty, how should we respond to a Rwanda, to a Srebrenica—to gross and systematic violations of human rights that offend every precept of our common humanity?"[55] In the 2000 report to the General Assembly on the work of the organization, he adopted the language of human security, explicitly[56] noted the 1999 and 2000 reports on Srebrenica and Rwanda, and repeated this question.[57]

Overall, this evolution in the Security Council, the General Assembly, some UN organizations, and within some member states suggested growing international acceptance of the obligation to protect civilian victims and humanitarian workers in the face of conflict-related threats to human security. Once again, the historical process was complex. Circumstance played a significant role in stimulating normative change. Both the General Assembly and the Secretary-General were instrumental in deepening the debate. Interested states such as Canada were significant in bringing the matter in a sustained way before the Security Council, played a key role in the working group processes that produced the resolutions, and were instrumental in building a coalition in the council sufficient to assure adoption.

However, a number of questions remained unanswered. What was the threshold for action and how was international society to respond? In particular, under what conditions was "humanitarian intervention" justified? In an effort to respond to these questions, Canada sponsored the establishment of the International Commission on Intervention and State Sovereignty.

The Responsibility to Protect

The ICISS was created in 2000 by the Canadian government with support from a number of major U.S. foundations. In the context of the debates surrounding inaction in the face of genocide in Rwanda, failure or mixed results in Somalia and Bosnia, and highly contested unmandated action in Kosovo, it addressed the question "when, if ever, it is appropriate for states to take coercive—and in particular military—action, against another state for the purpose of protecting people at risk in that other state."[58] In so doing, it sought not to diminish sovereignty as a constitutive principle of international relations but to reconcile that principle with the solidarist imperative of protecting human beings at risk in conflict. The twelve commissioners wrestled with these questions for a year before delivering their report in September 2001.

The central point in the report was that states had a responsibility to protect their own citizens. This obligation was deemed inherent in the concept of sovereignty. The notion that sovereignty involves responsibilities to protect is a very old one. But it was most clearly revived in the 1990s in work by the influential expert on IDPs, Francis Deng, which predates the formation of the ICISS.[59] When this obligation was not met, the state's claim to sovereign rights was correspondingly diminished. Both Deng and the ICISS maintained that when states could not or would not protect their citizens in the face of avoidable catastrophe, the responsibility to protect shifted to the broader society of states.

According to the ICISS, international responsibility in such situations had three elements: to prevent, to react in the event that prevention failed, and to rebuild societies where protection had failed. Of these, the commissioners deemed prevention to be the most important dimension. They held that preventive options should be exhausted before reactive ones were considered. The report declared that military intervention to protect civilians should be exceptional and that a threshold of just cause had to be crossed. It defined the threshold in terms of "large scale loss of life, actual or apprehended" and or "large scale 'ethnic cleansing,' actual or apprehended." The ICISS also proposed that a number of precautionary principles needed to be satisfied before an intervention should proceed: right intention (the primary purpose of the intervention had to be the halting or averting of human suffering); last resort (other nonmilitary options had to be exhausted before the military option was selected); proportional means (the scale, duration, and intensity of the intervention should be the minimum necessary to secure human protection); and reasonable prospects (the existence of a reasonable chance of success in halting or averting suffering and the reasonable likelihood that the consequences of action would not be worse than the consequences of inaction).[60]

The commissioners strongly preferred Security Council mandates as authorization for such action. They called for agreement among the council's permanent members not to use their veto power in cases where their vital interests were not engaged. In the event that the Security Council rejected a proposal or failed to act, they suggested that other options be explored: consideration of the issue by the General Assembly under the "Uniting for Peace" procedure and Chapter VIII action by regional organizations before they sought subsequent authorization by the Security Council. They noted the need for the council to take into account the possibility that if it failed to discharge its responsibilities, states might not rule out other means to meet the situation, which would draw the credibility of the UN into question.

The report is distinguished by its effort to tackle this highly sensitive issue in a practical way and to give concrete guidance to the United Nations in answering the Secretary-General's fundamental question. The report is distinct from many of the other contributions to the debate on human security in its specificity. Rather than attempting to address the wide range of human rights and development issues linked to the concept, it establishes a clear focus: the physical protection of individuals and communities experiencing or at risk from physical violence. It then addresses a discrete issue: when and how should international actors should intervene to defend these people when their government is unable or unwilling to fulfill its protection responsibilities.

The report is also striking for its focus on the state. Much academic discussion of human security focuses on people and ignores the state or considers it to be a major source of threat to human security that needs to be transcended.[61] While explicitly acknowledging the possibility that the state could constitute a major threat to human security, the report argued that the state was also the preferred solution to the problems of protection. However, the report firmly endorsed the 1990s trend toward the qualification of sovereignty, associating this concept with the responsibility of the state toward those residing within its own borders. To the extent that this responsibility was not fulfilled by the state in question, the state thereby attenuated its own rights that went with sovereignty, and the responsibility for protection shifted to the international community. Yet in the view of the commissioners, the "rebuilding" phase involved reconstituting the state in such a way that it could fulfill its protection responsibilities.[62]

This said, problems remained. The report said little about how to operationalize the threshold beyond which intervention is permissible. The embrace of both actual and apprehended violations of rights made this problem worse. How much apprehending is enough and what are the criteria for apprehending? The notion of right intention is highly problematic, since motives are generally mixed where force is used. It is often not easy to see how one could determine whether the motive of intervention was primarily humanitarian. The report also did not provide a clear basis or method for judging whether there were reasonable prospects for success. Its embrace of the proposition that peaceful alternatives should be exhausted before intervention did not take adequate account of the urgency that characterizes such situations. Exhausting alternatives takes time. In the meantime people die, as was obvious in the dithering regarding Darfur in 2004. Similar comment might be made concerning the report's discussion of right authority. The Security Council is not known for the efficiency of its decision-making procedures or for the timeliness of its decisions. One of the principal regional interveners, NATO, does not recognize its status as a Chapter VIII regional arrangement.

Finally, the report recognized that humanitarian intervention is not feasible when the abuse of rights is being conducted by a great power or when the interests of that great power are vitally engaged in such a way as to predispose it to oppose international action. This view was eminently pragmatic, but it left the authors open to the charge that humanitarian intervention motivated by the responsibility to protect was limited to targeting weak states. This position inevitably undermined the legitimacy of the argument they attempted to make.[63]

The report is an intriguing illustration of the complementarity of the roles the UN and states play in the emergence of new ideas. The initiative underlying the report came from the Secretary-General who, in response to the failures of his organization (and of its members) in the 1990s, "insistently raised the question of how the international community should respond" to the human need for protection occasioned by crises within states.[64] General commitments to protection could be obtained within the UN (resolutions 1265 and 1296 are good examples). But the statist nature of the organization and the jealousy with which many states within it guarded what they perceived to be their sovereign prerogatives precluded agreement on concrete conditions under which sovereignty could be derogated for reasons of human protection. Therefore, the question was taken up by an interested state. That state constructed a broadly representative commission (although we note that there was no Chinese member) to push the envelope. The report did that, notably in its explicit embrace of the linkage between protection and the claim to sovereignty that has been a persistent theme in this book. Subsequent to its completion, the report was taken back to the UN, forming the basis of informal (and so far largely fruitless) discussion both in the Security Council and in the General Assembly.

One sees here a familiar sequence. Global events demand a UN response. The response and the problems therewith occasion reflection within the UN. The process of reflection generates questions that promote further development of ideas within and outside the UN system. The products of these processes then reenter that system in the quest for universal propagation and legitimation. That further progress on the responsibility to protect remains stalled is a product in part of historical circumstance, notably the attacks of September 11, 2001, on the United States. It also reflects profound continuing resistance among states to the attenuation of sovereign rights. This should not be taken as evidence of failure. Changing ideas is a long and complex process. As one of the ICISS co-chairs put it after a rather inconclusive Security Council consultation on the subject in 2002: "*Personne ne s'attendait à ce qu'au bout de deux jours de discussion la question de l'intervention humanitaire soit résolue. . . . Le débat était un exercice de prise de conscience.*"[65]

The discussion of humanitarian intervention tends to obscure the fact that the protection of civilians in war is a much broader matter. Whatever the fate of the ICISS process will be, the work of the council regarding protection continued beyond resolutions 1265 and 1296. In 2002, the president of the council took up the matter again, producing an aide mémoire.[66] Here the council laid out in detail the implications of its evolving understanding of the protection of civilians in conflict for the design of council-mandated peace support operations. The president noted the document's potential applicability to situations "where the Council may wish to consider action outside the scope of a peacekeeping operation." The aide mémoire consists of a set of primary objectives, issues for consideration, and precedents (i.e., Security Council resolutions) in relation to a number of topics central to the problem of civilians in war: humanitarian access; the separation of armed and civilian elements of a population; justice and reconciliation; security, law, and order (focusing principally on police and judicial institutions); disarmament, demobilization, reintegration, and rehabilitation; small arms and mine action; the training of security and peacekeeping forces to sensitize them to the problem of protection of civilians; effects on women and on children; the safety of humanitarian personnel; media and information; natural resources; and the humanitarian impact of sanctions. Together they constitute a reasonably comprehensive roadmap for how to respond to the council's concerns regarding civilian protection in the mandates of the forces it authorizes.

The basic evolution discussed above is amply reflected in the treatment of sovereignty and responsibility by the High-level Panel on Threats, Challenges and Change that reported to the Secretary-General in December 2004. The panel argued that when they signed the Charter, member states accepted a degree of qualification of sovereignty. In so doing, they accepted certain responsibilities, notably those concerning the protection of individuals living within their borders: "There is growing recognition that the issue is not the 'right to intervene' of any State, but the 'responsibility to protect' of every State when it comes to people suffering from avoidable catastrophe—mass murder and rape, ethnic cleansing by forcible expulsion and terror, and deliberate starvation and exposure to disease." When states fail to fulfill these responsibilities, the collective security logic of the Charter dictates that "the international community" should take up some portion of those responsibilities to provide protection and enhance the capacity of the state in question to do so. In this context, the panel highlighted what it perceived to be a growing acceptance that the Security Council, under Chapter VII, could act to redress internal wrongs if it defined these as a threat to international peace and security.[67]

Sanctions and Human Security

The second major effort by the Security Council to address protection concerned the humanitarian impact of sanctions. During the course of the 1990s, and particularly in the context of long-term sanctions against Iraq, the humanitarian community had become increasingly vocal about the impact of general sanctions on the most vulnerable populations of targeted states.[68] The UN attempted to set up mechanisms for exemptions to sanctions on humanitarian grounds, the most complex (and problematic) being that regarding Iraq. Nonetheless, it was widely felt that the generalized sanctions were a blunt instrument with almost unavoidable humanitarian consequences. Humanitarian problems were also encountered with regional sanctions, as was made clear with sanctions regimes against Sierra Leone and Burundi.[69] The Secretary-General went further in his Millennium Report of 2000:

> When robust and comprehensive economic sanctions are directed against authoritarian regimes, a different problem is encountered. Then it is usually the people who suffer, not the political elites whose behavior triggered the sanctions in the first place. Indeed, those in power, perversely, often benefit from such sanctions by their ability to control and profit from black market activity, and by exploiting them as a pretext for eliminating domestic sources of political opposition.[70]

Such concerns were also evident in the treatment of the issues of women and children in war.

The Security Council acknowledged these concerns in its resolution on the protection of civilians in war and established a working group to address the general impact of sanctions on civilian populations.[71] One sees the results of this reflection in the increasing use of targeted sanctions (as in Libya, Angola, and Afghanistan) and in council requests to monitor and assess humanitarian impacts of sanctions where these are imposed (as in Afghanistan in 1999 and 2000 and in Liberia in 2001 and 2003).[72] The council's interest in targeted sanctions spawned a number of nationally based efforts to refine sanctions regimes. One was the Swiss-led Interlaken Process (initiated in 1998), which focused on the design and implementation of targeted financial sanctions.[73] A second (the Bonn-Berlin Process, initiated in mid-2000) focused on arms embargoes and related initiatives and on travel bans.[74] A third (initiated in 2001) was the Stockholm Process, which emphasized implementation of targeted sanctions, particularly sanctions directed at individuals.[75] By 2004, the Security Council had essentially abandoned comprehensive sanctions, focusing instead on targeted options.[76]

In short, the council and other bodies within and around the UN moved both to make the protection of civilians and humanitarian assistance a potential reason for Chapter VII action against a state that was not fulfilling its responsibilities and to adjust the UN's own actions in order to take account of their implications for civilians in target states.

Civilian Protection and Regional Organizations

The evolution of ideas and norms centered on the United Nations was paralleled at the regional level. In Europe, at the beginning of the 1990s, and reflecting the rapid changes at the end of the Cold War, the CSCE (now the Organization for Security and Co-operation in Europe) began to develop the "human dimension" of its activities. The origin of this movement was a decision by the Vienna Follow-Up Meeting in 1989 to establish an ongoing conference on the human dimension of the Helsinki Accords. Here the CSCE established a rudimentary mechanism of accountability in the area of human rights. Signatories agreed to respond to requests for information concerning human rights and fundamental freedoms from other member states, to hold bilateral meetings with other members when such issues came up, that states could raise such issues with the CSCE as a whole, and that members could raise issues related to information exchange and bilateral meetings at meetings of the Conference on the Human Dimension and at full CSCE follow-up meetings.

This was followed in 1990 by agreement on the Copenhagen Document, which restated in much more specific terms the shared commitment to the promotion of human rights and fundamental freedoms and to justice and the rule of law.[77] The document is germane also in its initial elaboration of common standards for the protection and promotion of freedom and rights and in its agreement on a role for the CSCE (e.g., in observations of elections) in monitoring implementation of these standards within member states. Although the meat of the Copenhagen Document lies principally in the areas of democracy, the rule of law, and human rights, several components had specific application to physical protection of individuals. For example, in paragraph 13, members recognize the need to provide special protection to children from threats of violence and exploitation. In paragraph 16, the members commit themselves not to use or tolerate the use of torture under any circumstance (an irony in view of the embrace of torture in the war on terror by the George W. Bush administration, a key member of the organization[78]). And although there was no specific qualification of sovereignty in the document,[79] in paragraph 11 it did recognize the right of individuals (or groups acting for them) who felt that their rights were being violated to communicate with international human rights bodies. More broadly, the document is in itself a recognition that domestic human rights issues are matters of international concern, a point made explicitly in the follow-on Moscow Document[80] (the name is another irony in view of Russia's systematic resistance to international oversight of its abuse of the people of Chechnya).

The Moscow Document tightened the mechanism defined by the Vienna Follow-Up Meeting. It reduced the deadline for member response to queries on human dimension issues to a maximum of ten days and the deadline for organization of bilateral meetings to no more than one week. It also provided for the creation of a pool of experts to deal with human dimension issues as they arose. States could invite a panel of experts to their territory to assist in resolution of human-dimension issues within their borders. Signatories guaranteed that individuals who came before panels could speak freely and confidentially without fear of retribution. More ambitiously, the Moscow Document gave states the right to ask the CSCE to request agreement from another state to invite a mission of experts to address specific human-dimension issues within the latter's territory. If that state declined or if the outcome of the mission of experts was deemed unsatisfactory, the requesting state (if it was supported by five other members) could request the creation of a CSCE rapporteur mission to establish the facts, report on them, and give advice on possible solutions to the issue. In the event that a requesting state considered that a particularly serious threat to fulfillment of human dimension commitments had arisen, with the support of nine others it could immediately engage the same procedure. Both the Copenhagen and Moscow documents substantially limited the rights of member states to suspend or to qualify human rights in declared emergencies.

These agreements appear to be an impressive enhancement of the regional accountability of states in matters pertaining to human security. Member states acknowledged that their counterparts had a right to hold them to account for their treatment of their own citizens. Mechanisms were established for intrusive monitoring and for ensuring the transparency of findings. The CSCE established a substantial institutional capacity for implementation of the human dimension—the Office for Democratic Institutions and Human Rights—in 1992.

It is noteworthy that there has been no sustained effort to take advantage of the challenge provisions of the Moscow mechanism,[81] despite numerous instances in which states were apparently violating their Copenhagen and Moscow commitments. These included instances, such as those in the former Yugoslavia and the former Soviet Union, when such commitments were being massively violated in internal conflicts with frequently tragic results for the people whose rights the Conference on Security and Co-operation in Europe/Organization for Security and Co-operation in Europe (CSCE/OSCE) purported to be protecting.

The second European dimension concerns NATO, one of the principal alliance structures of the Cold War era. It was designed to deter (and, if neces-

sary, repel) a Soviet attack on Western Europe. Until the 1990s, it was config-
ured for heavy conventional war with a potential for limited nuclear escalation. The end of the Cold War rendered its strategic objective moot. NATO's
adjustment to changing strategic realities began in earnest with the London
Declaration.[82] While stating its intention to "remain a defensive alliance" (paragraph 5) and to retain nuclear and conventional capabilities appropriate for
that purpose (paragraph 15), the NATO Council recognized the need for a
fundamental adaptation of the doctrines and activities of the alliance to take
into account the end of the continental confrontation. NATO went further in
Rome in 1991, when it adopted a new strategic concept.[83]

Several points in the concept are relevant here. In the first place, NATO
argued that the dominant threats the alliance faced were now those associated with the "adverse consequences of instabilities that might arise from the
serious economic, social and political difficulties, including ethnic rivalries
and territorial disputes, which are faced by many countries in Central and
Eastern Europe." These could produce crises that might draw in outside powers or spill over into NATO countries (paragraph 10). In consequence, it was
deemed necessary for NATO to embrace a broader approach to security that
involved political, economic, social, and environmental elements in addition
to the basic defense function.

Despite the widening in the alliance's understanding of security and its
mission, there was at this stage little consideration of civilian protection functions for NATO forces. This changed as the crises in the Balkans deepened in
1992. In June 1992, NATO for the first time declared its readiness to participate
in crisis management and peaceful dispute settlement, offering to support
peacekeeping activities under the CSCE.[84] This change of direction occasioned
a substantial effort to develop peace-operations doctrine and to exercise it, in
the contexts of both NATO and its Partnership for Peace.[85] As the Bosnian
war progressed, NATO became directly involved in the provision of support
to UNPROFOR through its policing of air exclusion zones. This was in support of a mission with an explicit protection component that focused on the
security of humanitarian access. As the Bosnian situation unraveled in 1995,
NATO forces entered the country to enforce the Dayton Accords. Although
the focus of the deployment was deterrence and stabilization rather than the
protection of civilians per se, it seems clear that NATO's presence did contribute substantially to the security of civilians in Bosnia. Moreover, NATO forces
assisted (somewhat reluctantly, it must be said) in the apprehension of persons under indictment by the ICTY.[86]

Finally, NATO went to war over Kosovo with an explicit mandate to protect human beings—halting the abuse of that region's Albanian population

by Serbian security forces.[87] The organization, acting without UN Security Council authorization, used air power to coerce the government of the Federal Republic of Yugoslavia to halt its attacks on Kosovo Albanians and to surrender its operational control over the territory to NATO and associated states. The next iteration of the alliance's strategic concept—adopted at Washington during the war—went further than previous texts in explicitly linking its commitment to regional stability to putting "an end to human suffering."[88]

Elsewhere,[89] the Washington concept specifically identified the abuse of human rights as a potential cause of local and regional instability and cited human suffering in war as a matter of concern to the alliance, not least because of its potential to create spillovers that affect the security of other states. With this in mind, the concept accepted the possibility that NATO might respond to crises with "non-Article 5" military operations and stressed the need to develop and maintain forces appropriate to such operations.[90] These developments at the diplomatic level were paralleled by training and exercises to enhance NATO capacity to coordinate with the wide array of political and humanitarian actors engaged in the response to crisis.

NATO's actions in Kosovo are fundamental to this work. Here a subset of international society claimed a right to use force to address the protection needs of a community within the domestic jurisdiction of another state. They claimed that right without any explicit UN mandate from the Security Council in an action widely deemed to be "illegal but legitimate."[91] In so doing, NATO raised the stakes dramatically, suggesting that states or groups of states could claim the right to act to defend people in other states in the absence of legal authorization where such authorization could not be obtained. NATO's action was particularly controversial since it was directed at a country that was not a member of the western alliance.

For these reasons, the Kosovo affair had a fundamental effect on the deliberations of the ICISS discussed above. The commission, which was grappling with the question of what was legitimate in the absence of Security Council authorization, noted the obvious tension between the implications for international order of bypassing the Security Council and the equally damaging implications of failing to act in the face of the slaughter or ethnic cleansing of human beings. While avoiding a definitive conclusion on the right course of action, the commissioners concluded that where the council was incapable of acting, it was "unrealistic to expect that concerned states will rule out other means and forms of action to meet the gravity and urgency of these situations."[92] In this respect, we see a clear example of the actions of a regional organization that pushed the envelope of ideas.

The final European institution to consider is the EU. Here the issue of protection of civilians is wrapped up in a much larger process of transformation associated with the halting emergence of a European security and defense identity, its translation into a common European foreign and security policy, and the effort to create institutions and military capability that would implement such a policy. Like so much to do with EU institutional development, this process was, and is, incredibly convoluted. For our purposes, it suffices to highlight the human dimension of the securitization of the EU. The point of origin here lies in the Western European Union (WEU). Again as a result of the rapid deterioration of the security situation in the western Balkans and elsewhere in Europe in the early 1990s, the WEU adopted the Petersberg Declaration, which laid out three ways in which the forces of WEU members might be used in response to crises in its general area of operations: "humanitarian and rescue tasks, peacekeeping tasks, and tasks of combat forces in crisis management, including peacemaking."[93] This set of potential missions underpinned subsequent discussions within the EU on the use of force under a European umbrella that was distinct from NATO and provided the basis for a close, but contested, evolving link between the two European organizations.[94]

The development of an autonomous military capability for the EU was very slow in the 1990s until it received a boost in 1998–1999 from the British and French governments. These states had concluded from the Yugoslav experience that it made sense to explore the possibility of creating the capability at the EU to respond to crises to be used in situations where the United States was not interested in acting and where, consequently, NATO engagement might be problematic.[95] With this push, the European Council proceeded rapidly toward definition of its mission, the identification of necessary capabilities, and procurement and force commitments.[96] In 2000, at its meeting in Feira, the EU added a further element of essential importance to civilian protection— developing the capacity to provide up to 5,000 police officers from EU member states for international missions.[97]

The translation of commitment into capabilities for action has been problematic for several reasons. The United States has made clear its concern that the development of independent EU forces might weaken the transatlantic link. Turkey was not enthusiastic about the prospect of using the NATO infrastructure for EU operations, given the European Union's ambivalent attitude toward Turkey's application for membership. Various EU members have proven to be reluctant to contemplate loss of control over their forces in a larger multilateral arrangement. Honoring concrete commitments of matériel and personnel has proven difficult given budgetary constraints and demands in other operations (e.g., the war in Iraq). It is chronically difficult to secure commitments of large numbers of police for peace operations. More recently, and given the insufficiency of commitments of forces by member states, the EU has moved to consideration of the concept of small battle groups that could be rapidly deployed to address emerging conflict-related humanitarian crises. The outcome of this shift remains to be seen.[98]

However, the potential implications of these developments for the protection of civilians in conflict were evident in Opération Artémis, the 2003 mission to the Ituri District of the Democratic Republic of Congo. Here, in the face of widespread killings that risked destabilizing the fragile peace process and given the incapacity of the UN Observer Mission in the Congo (MONUC) to respond effectively, the European Council asked the special representative of the Secretary-General to consider the feasibility of an EU military operation. The UN responded with a Security Council resolution authorizing deployment of a multinational contingent with a protection mandate for a period of three months.[99] European states operating on the basis of a European Council Joint Action of 5 June 2003 deployed a small but capable force to supplement the UN presence, specifically to halt the mass killing of civilians. After initial hesitation, the French-led force enforced a deadline for Congolese militia to leave the town of Bunia and through armed reconnaissance into the surrounding area significantly reduced violence against civilians in the district as a whole. After a reasonably smooth transition to a reinforced MONUC contingent armed with a Chapter VII mandate, the European forces left at the end of August 2003.

In the meantime, in Sierra Leone the British demonstrated a degree of willingness to backstop UN efforts to protect and assist civilians and to facilitate a settlement of the long-lasting dispute in that country. More broadly, a number of European countries have made real efforts to embed civilian protection in the doctrine and training of their deployable forces, drawing upon their extensive experience in the Balkans. In short, there appears to be in Europe fairly substantial and concrete movement to implement evolving obligations in the area of protection of civilians.

Outside Europe, the record is varied. There has been little effort among Asian regional organizations to address the issue of protection of civilians in conflict. In contrast, the African Union included in its basic document one of the strongest multilateral statements of commitment to the protection of civilians, embracing "the right of the Union to intervene in a Member State pursuant to a decision of the Assembly in respect of grave circumstances, namely: war crimes, genocide and crimes against humanity."[100] This was followed at the AU's Durban meeting in 2002 by the adoption of a protocol establishing a Peace and Security Council.[101] Among other things, the council was empowered to recommend that the assembly intervene in a member state in the event of war crimes, genocide, and crimes against humanity (Article 7.1.e) and to impose sanctions in the event that an unconstitutional change of government took place in a member state (Article 7.1.g).

However, such decisions would have to be taken on the basis of consensus or, failing that, by a two-thirds majority in the council and then the assembly. Given alignment patterns in the region and the preoccupation of many African states with issues of sovereignty, this bar is quite high. The protocol required a simple majority of ratifying members to be put into force.[102] It also called for the establishment of an African standby force, among the stated purposes of which was intervention to protect civilians in harm's way and to provide humanitarian assistance (Article 13.3.c). The training of the national contingents of the force was to emphasize the rights of women and children (Article 13.13), reflecting the AU's awareness of the challenges involved in protection of these particularly vulnerable groups.

Similar considerations are evident in the evolution of subregional organizations in Africa. The Southern African Development Community (SADC) Protocol on Politics, Defence and Security Co-operation establishes an Organ on Politics, Defence and Security. It identifies among its specific objectives the prevention, containment, and resolution of interstate and intrastate conflicts. Where peaceful means fail, it would consider enforcement action in accordance with international law.[103] In its definition of the "significant intrastate conflicts" over which it has jurisdiction, it includes "large scale violence between sections of the population or between the state and sections of the population, including genocide, ethnic cleansing and gross violation of human rights."[104] Decisions on enforcement recommended by the organ fall within the remit of the SADC heads of state and government. In other words, despite the protocol's embrace of sovereignty, territorial integrity, and nonintervention, we see again provision for intervention to address large-scale failures of the state to protect its citizens.

Despite their shortcomings, the AU and SADC initiatives in this sphere are significant for this analysis, particularly with regard to questions about the universality of acceptance that international bodies can interfere in domestic jurisdiction when protection is a significant problem. It has frequently been argued that the interventionist use of force to protect civilians in harm's way was perceived by states in the South to be a western liberal imposition that threatens the sovereignty of weaker states.[105] And in the reactions of the Non-Aligned Movement and other bodies to the notion of humanitarian intervention, there was much evidence to support this contention.[106] However, the statute of the AU and the SADC protocol would suggest that for a considerable number of African states, it was not so much the idea of intervention to address human security challenges that caused concern but the question of ownership—that is to say, the manner in which such actions were (or were not) authorized and implemented. The same appeared to be true of African perspectives on intervention or the use of other coercive instruments to restore democratic authority where there had been an unconstitutional change of government.

This brings us, finally, to Latin America, which falls between Asia and Africa in its perspectives on intervention for protection. As we saw in Chapter 2, the OAS has taken an interest in individual protection within states for some time, generally with a focus on legal and political rights. This interest strengthened in the post–Cold War era, particularly in the area of defense of democracy. In 2001, the OAS adopted the Inter-American Democratic Charter, which affirmed that the peoples of the region had a right to democracy and governments had an obligation to promote and defend that right. The charter also noted that democracy was a necessary condition for exercising fundamental rights and freedoms. It went on to suggest that when a state's democratic order had been "unconstitutionally interrupted," the organization would undertake diplomatic initiatives to reverse this development. If those failed, the state in question would be suspended.[107] There was no mention of enforcing the protection of rights. It is, nonetheless, significant that in this region where the defense of sovereignty has been extremely important to the neighbors of the United States, the OAS as a whole accepted that transfers of power that threatened universal principles regarding the protection of human rights were a legitimate matter of international concern.

In short, norm-building at the regional level parallels that in international society as a whole, if unevenly. Notably, here too we see a growing acceptance that when the state—through omission or commission—does not protect the security of individuals, other states acting multilaterally may have a right to act to ensure that protection.

Addressing Impunity

Organizations, states, and NGOs complemented their consideration of how to protect civilians in armed conflict with normative and institutional change directed at punishing individuals responsible for grave violations of human rights. The underlying logic was not only that people should be held responsible for their actions but that the fostering of lasting peace in fractured societies depended on reconciliation. Reconciliation in turn required justice. As we saw in Chapter 2, the victorious allies in World War II reacted to the commission of crimes of war and crimes against humanity by Axis officials through the creation of war crimes tribunals at Nuremberg and Tokyo. These closed once their business was completed. There was no effort during the Cold War to create permanent institutions to adjudicate such matters.

When international society faced a recurrence of massive crimes against humanity in the 1990s, they reacted in a similar ad hoc fashion. In 1993, the Security Council noted the individual responsibility of persons who committed grave breaches of the Geneva Conventions and the recommendation of the Commission of Experts that a tribunal be established in relation to the events in the former Yugoslavia.[108] The council declared that the human rights situation in the former Yugoslavia constituted a threat to international peace and security and stated its determination to put such violations to an end and bring to justice those responsible.

On that basis, it decided to establish an international tribunal (the ICTY) to address violations of the Geneva Conventions, genocide, and crimes against humanity (including rape). The Security Council specified in the statute of the tribunal that it would have primacy over national courts in the adjudication of these crimes, thereby making clear, in this instance at least, that universal norms regarding the protection of civilians took precedence over norms of domestic jurisdiction.[109] In addition, it emphasized individual responsibility and, following the precedent established by the Nuremberg and Tokyo tribunals, it clearly rejected any immunity that might arise from the claim to have acted at the behest of state authorities.

A year later, the Security Council reacted similarly regarding the crisis in Africa's Great Lakes region, although in this instance the establishment of the ICTR was at the behest of the state in question.[110] Acting under Chapter VII, the council established a tribunal to sit at Arusha to consider the cases of those accused of genocide, crimes against humanity (including rape), and violations of Article 3 common to the Geneva Conventions and Additional Protocol II. As in the case of the ICTY, the statute of the tribunal specified that it had primacy over national courts.

Both of these tribunals have encountered significant problems, which included difficulties in the arrest and transfer of persons indicted, delays in initiating proceedings, and the slow pace of proceedings. However, these courts do indict, prosecute, judge, and imprison. Although the process is far from perfect, the tribunals have gone some distance toward establishing the principle of individual accountability for violations of the Geneva Conventions, genocide, and crimes against humanity. In this respect they provide a useful supplement or alternative to national forms of adjudication. Their success is evident in the establishment (or the attempt to establish) similar tribunals for other conflicts (e.g., Sierra Leone, Liberia, and Cambodia).

However, for many states, the ad hoc nature of the establishment of such bodies had deficiencies. The most obvious was that where the Security Council chose not to act, there would be no institutional process whereby accountability could be reliably ensured. Many states and NGOs were concerned about the selectivity of justice that resulted.[111] These concerns brought an effort to establish an international criminal court with universal jurisdiction.[112] Again, key states, in close collaboration with interested NGOs, played a substantial role in initiating and sustaining this process.[113] Preliminary work on an ICC began in 1994, producing a group of like-minded states that pushed for a conference in 1998 to negotiate a treaty. Their work centered on a preliminary draft statute produced by the International Law Commission in 1994.[114] It continued through an ad hoc committee established at the initiative of the General Assembly, which met twice in 1995. This work culminated in a General Assembly decision to create a Preparatory Committee to move forward on the draft statute. The PrepCom met from 1996 to 1998. This laid the basis for a treaty conference in Rome in 1998, which ultimately produced an agreement on a statute on establishing an international criminal court, signed by 120 states.[115]

Several elements of the statute are of note here. First, it focused on critical dimensions of protection. Its remit was limited to genocide, crimes against humanity, and war crimes. It made considerable progress in specifying and elaborating the content of these categories. In particular, and responding to the protection problems in conflicts of the 1990s, it specified that "rape, sexual slavery, enforced prostitution, forced pregnancy, enforced sterilization, or any other form of sexual violence of comparable gravity" are crimes against humanity,[116] as is the forced transfer of populations.[117] Second, it clearly established individual responsibility.

Third, it extended the ICC's remit to internal conflicts. Provisions regarding genocide and crimes against humanity applied whether the conflict was international or civil. The statute took crimes of war in noninternational armed conflict covered under Common Article 3 of the Geneva Conventions within its jurisdiction (Article 8.2.c) and a broader array of offenses in internal conflict that are covered "within the established framework of international law" (Article 8.2.e). It included protection of women and children and addressed the issue of forced displacement.

Fourth, the statute specified that cases could be brought before the court not only by the Security Council or a state party but by the prosecutor acting ex officio, thereby substantially expanding the potential independence of the court. Fifth, and in contrast to the ICTY and ICTR, the ICC established the primacy of national jurisdiction in the first instance. Where a state had the capacity and the will to deal with violations of the principles of international law within the court's remit, the ICC could not exercise jurisdiction. However, there appeared to be provision for the court to take up cases where the state in question claimed to have exercised national jurisdiction but had not done so in good faith (Article 17.1.b).

The treaty came into force when sixty states ratified it (July 2002). At the time of writing (December 2004), ninety-seven geographically diverse states had ratified the treaty.

However, three of the five permanent members of the Security Council (China, Russia, and the United States) were not parties to the treaty. Significant regional lacunae were also evident. Very few Middle Eastern states entered the agreement. Coverage of the former Soviet republics was sporadic. A number of major southern states (e.g., India and Indonesia) did not adhere to the treaty. The United States rejected any application of international jurisdiction to its military personnel and officials and embarked on an effort to secure bilateral agreements guaranteeing that other states would not put American citizens before the court. Finally, and obviously, since the treaty binds states, it does not include nonstate actors, who constitute a majority of parties to contemporary conflict. Nevertheless, the establishment of the court provides a permanent institutional apparatus for addressing issues of impunity related to crimes against human beings.

Human Security and Disarmament

The Ban on Land Mines

As we have seen, international efforts to control or to prohibit certain categories of weapons have frequently been animated in part by concerns about their effects on human beings. In the post–Cold War era, the logic of human security dramatically extended into the consideration of aspects of conventional disarmament. The most significant was the effort to ban antipersonnel land mines.[118] The case is revealing not only in terms of its relation to the broader question of protection of civilians in and after war but also as an illustration of the limitations of UN instruments in pursuing protection and the consequent bypassing of the UN through innovative alternative diplomacy.

The issue of land mines gained prominence in the early 1990s as a result of the advocacy of the ICRC and medical NGOs, who had become increasingly aware of the threat posed by indiscriminate use of this weapon, especially in Cambodia.[119] The most obvious consequence of widespread laying of mines was a rise in the rate of crippling injury and death among civilians. The practice also had significant economic effects, as large tracts of land could not safely be exploited for agriculture. In response to this growing threat to human security, the NGO community made a sustained effort not only to increase public awareness of the problem but also to establish a large umbrella group to sustain pressure on governments. This turned into the International Campaign to Ban Land Mines (ICBL). At a meeting of interested organizations in London in 1993, the group agreed on the seemingly quixotic agenda of a comprehensive global ban on antipersonnel mines and the establishment of an international fund for mine victims. By 1995, the campaign had grown to some 350 organizations. The group combined their efforts to pressure governments and international organizations with a sustained research effort that produced a series of devastating reports on the human consequences of mines.

In parallel, the ICRC responded to the growing concerns of its medical personnel in the field by beginning its own research and advocacy. Initially, the ICRC focused on ways to ensure responsible use of land mines, but by 1994 it too had concluded that a global ban on use, trade, and production was necessary. In abandoning partial solutions, it also abandoned its discrete and confidential efforts to influence governments and turned to active public global advocacy.

At the UN, the Secretary-General was broadly supportive of the early campaign. Boutros Boutros-Ghali drew attention to the problem as an aspect of peacebuilding in *An Agenda for Peace* and later endorsed the idea of a total ban.[120] In 1993–1994, both UNICEF and the UNHCR recognized land mines as a priority issue, also calling for a total ban. During the same period, both the United States and the European Union (and several of its member states acting separately) pushed for restrictions on exports of mines.

Because of the momentum toward regulation of mines, the question arose as to what multilateral forum was the most appropriate venue for negotiation. In this context, France called for a review of the 1980 Convention on Certain Conventional Weapons (CCCW). The review process graphically displayed the limitations of UN mechanisms for negotiating effective disarmament agreements. It began with expert group meetings in 1994. Here, at the behest of China, significant limits were placed on the participation of NGOs, and these were carried over into the conference itself. The mines conference began in September 1995; it was hamstrung by discussion of the military utility of antipersonnel mines and the possibility of limiting their humanitarian consequences (through, for example, the development and deployment of self-destroying or self-deactivating mines) in the broader context of disagreement between states parties over the desirability of strengthening the protocol. The meeting was suspended until April 1996. In the interim, the ICRC and ICBL increased their pressure for a total ban, rejecting the logic of technological solutions. Despite this pressure, continuing state opposition to comprehensive regulation precluded effective amendment of the CCCW. The NGO community widely denounced the review process as a failure.

Frustrated by the UN's Conference on Disarmament (CD) process, a number of states favoring a comprehensive ban—in close cooperation with concerned NGOs—decided to exit the formal multilateral process. In the context of blockage in the CD, "the principal dynamic of the campaign to ban landmines would be transformed into a strategic partnership between non-state actors and core pro-ban states."[121] After a number of preparatory meetings, the Canadian government held a conference in Ottawa in 1996 to examine the possibility of a global ban in greater detail. At the end of this meeting, after close assessment of the positions of the fifty attending states, the ICRC, and a wide range of NGOs, Canadian foreign minister Lloyd Axworthy called for a negotiation process outside the CD that would lead to a comprehensive treaty banning land mines. He invited participants to return to Ottawa a year later for a signing ceremony. In the interim, a core group of states with diverse regional representation was organized. The number of state participants in the process grew from fifty in October 1996 to 111 at the February 1997 meeting in Vienna on the draft treaty to 120 at the Bonn meeting on verification and compliance to 155 at the June 1997 meeting in Brussels. Ninety states registered for the Oslo final negotiations, and thirty-two observer states attended as well. Ultimately, this process produced the Ottawa Treaty, which was signed by 122 states. It forbade the use, stockpiling, production, and transfer of anti-personnel mines. In September 1998, the treaty entered into force with its fortieth ratification.[122]

A detailed account of the negotiations that led to this outcome is not necessary here. Several general observations are pertinent. One concerns the rapidity of the process. Arms control and disarmament agreements negotiated within the Conference on Disarmament generally take decades to negotiate if success is achieved at all. In contrast, this process took just under two years from the initial call for action from Canada to the time the treaty came into effect. Another is that the treaty was concluded in the face of opposition from the United States. It also was not supported by Russia and China. That is to say, the process proceeded successfully despite the lack of support from a majority of permanent members of the Security Council. Indeed, some have argued that at key points in the negotiation, the U.S. opposition served to stiffen the resolve of participants and produced a treaty that was stronger in key respects than it would have been had the United States taken a more constructive role.[123]

In the absence of support from key Security Council members and in contrast to its successes in the areas of chemical and biological weapons, the UN's multilateral negotiating body for disarmament issues (the CD) proved to be an inefficient mechanism for pursuing this element of the human security agenda. Indeed, the CD was seen as a means of slowing or preventing forward movement by states with reservations about a comprehensive ban. On the other hand, the General Assembly played a key role in legitimizing the process, passing a resolution endorsing a total ban in December 1996 by a margin of 156–0. Furthermore, although some organs of the UN were hamstrung, several specialized agencies actively supported the non-UN process.[124]

The success of the land mine negotiation can be explained in a number of ways. The innovative alliance created between states, multilateral agencies, the ICRC, and NGOs proved to be an extremely effective advocacy mechanism that brought a number of key doubters along (e.g., the UK and France). This group redefined the issue. Land mines were seen initially as one arms control issue among many. NGO activists, the ICRC, and key UN agencies played a key role in redefining the issue as a humanitarian crisis,[125] creating a much more effective platform for civil society advocacy. Also, leadership was crucial at the level of civil society through the efforts of Jody Williams in the ICBL (for which she and the coalition received the Nobel Prize for Peace in 1997) and through the diplomatic risk-taking of Lloyd Axworthy and his colleagues in the Canadian Department of Foreign Affairs and International Trade. Finally, it must be said that had the great powers been truly adamant in their opposition to the process, the outcome might well have been quite different. The fact that the United States in particular did not exercise the power available to it reflects the marginality of land mines as a weapons system. Most military analysts agree that except in certain highly specific circumstances the military utility of antipersonnel land mines was limited while the humanitarian effect was huge. Moreover, there was no substantial civil society constituency in the United States resisting control of this weapon.

Unlike many developments associated with the idea of human security, the Ottawa Treaty has had concrete and measurable practical impact. Suffering and death from mines continues.[126] But the number of countries producing land mines has fallen from fifty in 1992 to fifteen in 2003.[127] More than thirty-five states have destroyed their entire stockpiles of land mines—since 1996, more than 37 million stockpiled land mines have been destroyed. All states (with the exception of Iraq) previously known to have exported land mines have signed formal statements confirming that they no longer do so. Since 2001, there has been no significant international shipment of mines. New mine deployments are increasingly rare. The number of new mine victims is declining steadily.[128] The land mines process has clearly had a substantial and positive impact on human security.

Efforts to Control Small Arms and Light Weapons

This last point brings us briefly to the second major effort of the last decade to control conventional weapons because of their effect on human security; this time the target was small arms and light weapons.[129] The roots of the interest within international and civil society in controlling small arms lie in the fact that most civilian casualties in war are produced by the use of these weapons. The presence of large numbers of small arms in postconflict situations significantly complicates the building of peace. Their uncontrolled presence in large numbers is often associated with widespread criminality and criminal violence against human beings. The human security case for international efforts to regulate and reduce small arms proliferation appears, therefore, to be clear and compelling.[130]

Interest in the impact of small arms and light weapons on civilians affected by conflict grew in the early and mid-1990s, largely as a result of research activities in the United States.[131] Interest extended to Europe in the late 1990s, when the Bonn International Center for Conversion and the British-American Security Information Council conducted numerous studies in the area.[132]

Various parts of the UN system were also interested in the issue, not least because peacekeepers were now frequently operating in areas where substantial proliferation of small arms had occurred. This not only complicated the fulfillment of mandates but also jeopardized the security of UN personnel. In 1995, Boutros Boutros-Ghali highlighted small arms as an important focus in peacebuilding.[133] The General Assembly reacted to the Secretary-General's concern at the end of 1995 by passing a resolution recognizing the significance of the issue, asking the Secretary-General to report regularly on progress in controlling it and calling for the establishment of a panel of experts to assist him in this area.[134] The Commission on Disarmament took up the issue in 1997. The topic also became a major focus of the UN Institute for Disarmament Research (UNIDIR) and an increasingly frequent program component for operating agencies such as the UNDP.[135] Disarmament, demobilization, and reintegration (DDR) programs became an increasingly salient aspect of the UN's postconflict operations throughout the mid- and late 1990s.

The success of the Ottawa Process generated great optimism about the possibility of similar action to produce an effective international arrangement on proliferation of small arms. However, progress has been distinctly limited. A large cluster of NGOs gathered under the umbrella of the International Action Network on Small Arms to coordinate advocacy efforts related to small arms control. In 1998, ECOSOC's Commission on Crime Prevention

and Criminal Justice began to develop a protocol on small arms as an addendum to the UN Convention Against Transnational Organized Crime. Drafting
was again very rapid compared to earlier efforts to produce multilateral arms
control agreements.[136] Negotiation of the protocol was completed in March 2001,
and it was adopted by the General Assembly in June of that year.[137] In July, the
UN convened a global ad hoc conference called The Illicit Trade in Small Arms
and Light Weapons in All Its Aspects, which produced a program of action.[138]

Like the process that produced the Ottawa Treaty, a broad international
NGO coalition played an essential role in partnership with a small group of
interested states. However, this time the protocol was negotiated within a UN
forum (the Vienna Commission on Crime Prevention and Criminal Justice)
and produced a document that was adopted within the UN framework (the
General Assembly) as part of a broader UN convention. The issue was cast
not so much in terms of arms control or humanitarian and human security
issues but in terms of crime control, which no doubt facilitated adoption.

The weakness of the protocol when compared to the land mines treaty is
obvious. It recognizes that the state's inherent right of self-defense implies a
right to acquire weapons. It permits the interstate transfer of such weapons.
While prohibiting illicit manufacture, it permits manufacture of weapons or
components thereof under license or other authorization from the state authorities of the territory in which manufacturing is to take place. Trade in
small arms and light weapons is permitted if it is licensed by state authorities
and if the items traded are marked according to specifications of Article 8 of
the protocol. But parties commit to maintain records of such transfers, and to
ensure, before permitting export, that the state receiving the shipment has
authorized its import.[139] Finally, states can denounce the treaty.

In short, the basic character of the protocol is a defense of the rights of
states with respect to nonstate groups. It makes no effort to address basic
domestic law relating to possession and transfer of small arms and light weapons. Its regulation of interstate transfer is minimal. Its principal utility, in
addition to constraining small arms trafficking, lies in the deepening of cooperation in information exchange and standardization of trading practice.
These are constructive outcomes in the struggle against organized crime, but
for the time being, there is little reason to think that this multilateral process
has had any significant impact on human security. The same might be said of
the cluster of regional instruments that have developed around the issue.[140]
As the High-level Panel commented in 2004, "While concerted action by civil
society organizations and concerned Member States led to a ban on landmines,
efforts to limit the widespread availability of small arms and light weapons
have barely moved beyond rhetoric to action."[141]

The contrast in outcome between these two efforts to control arms is the result of several factors. In the first place, whereas land mines were peripheral to the security concerns of most states, small arms and light weapons are basic elements of their defense and security postures. Second, there are no legitimate nonmilitary uses of land mines. In contrast, small arms have significant law enforcement, recreational, and, in some societies, economic uses. It would be hard to find a strong cultural affinity for land mines. But finding such feelings about guns is not difficult in many societies, not least in the United States, where a very powerful domestic lobby has grown up around the right to possess such weapons for personal use.[142] Given that the United States has found it impossible to come up with a sensible domestic approach to gun control, it is not surprising that it has been strongly opposed to the development of international instruments whose obligations might have domestic political repercussions.

Conclusion

The quotation from the Permanent Court of International Justice that begins this chapter suggests that the meaning of domestic jurisdiction—and the international standing of human beings—is contingent upon broader developments in international relations. In previous chapters, we saw how the emergence of the modern state and the concomitant rise of nationalism fostered a privileging of the state's claims to security at the expense of the claims within states. We then saw how institutional and normative developments during the Cold War era began to draw this statist focus into question.

The analysis of this chapter suggests that the end of the Cold War, the character of post–Cold War conflict and the experience of international society with such conflict, and the maturing of various elements of globalization (the media and the increasing number and influence of transnational civil society organizations) all fostered a much more profound questioning of the balance in security between the individual and the state and the recovery of older discourses on the rights and interests of the individual and the obligations of outsiders to protect when the state was either unwilling or unable to do so. By the end of the 1990s, it was widely accepted that state sovereignty was linked to state responsibility toward its own citizens. For many, when a state failed in these obligations, international actors had a responsibility to do what the state was supposed to do—protect human beings. This acceptance was embedded in Security Council resolutions, in treaties and conventions, in emerging institutions, and in international practice.

This evolution did not prejudice the place of the state in international relations. The major documents analyzed here all make the point that the answer to state dysfunction in the area of protection of civilians is the reconstitution of the state so that it can do its job properly. Yet normative change did widen the scope for intervention into the domestic affairs of states, weakening the principle of nonintervention.

The UN played a central role in much of this evolution, as a generator of ideas, as a forum for advocacy and promotion, as an advocate in its own right, as a legitimizing device, and, to some extent, as an implementer of the human security agenda. Particularly evident in this discussion has been the advocacy role of the Secretaries-General, both Boutros Boutros-Ghali and Kofi Annan, in challenging member states to respond effectively to overwhelming human need.

The case of land mines also displays the inefficiency of some established processes within the UN in translating widespread concern about human security into development of new norms. Similarly, events in the Security Council since 1999 have highlighted the importance of consensus among the five permanent members of the Security Council if the human protection agenda is to move forward.

The case of land mines and the ICISS reflect clearly the agency of particular states and states in coalition with increasingly influential and effective transnational advocacy coalitions. They also display the significance of key leaders in pushing the agenda of ideas forward. It is also clear that those promoting the human protection agenda generally prefer to proceed through the United Nations and regional organizations to ensure inclusiveness and capture gains in legitimacy. Defection from institutionalized multilateral processes occurs when the organization in question proves incapable of generating useful outputs.

Finally, although in many respects the protection agenda is distinct from the development agenda discussed in Chapter 4, those most active in seeking to embed protection norms in international society generally recognized the significance of the development agenda as well:

> Similarly, human security and human development can be understood as mutually reinforcing concepts. Respectively, they address the twin objectives of freedom from fear and freedom from want. Human security provides an enabling environment for human development. Where violence or the threat of violence makes meaningful progress toward development impractical, enhancing safety for people is a prerequisite. Conversely, by addressing the inequalities that are often the root causes of violent conflict, by strengthening governance

structures and by providing humanitarian assistance, human development can also be an important strategy for furthering human security.[143]

Although there has been significant dispute between the "development first" and the "security first" camps in the human security community, the two positions are not mutually exclusive.

6

Human Security and the Protection of Vulnerable Groups

- **The Protection of Children**
- **Women in War**
- **The Protection of Displaced Persons**
- **Conclusion**

The Protection of Children

> More and more of the world is being sucked into a desolate moral vacuum.
> This is a space devoid of the most basic human values: a space in which
> children are slaughtered, raped and maimed; a space in which children are
> exploited as soldiers; a space in which children are starved and exposed to
> extreme brutality.   —*The Impact of War on Children*[1]

The UN's consideration of the impact of war on children dates back to the
Boutros Boutros-Ghali era. The place to start is the World Summit for Children, held in 1990 as the Convention on the Rights of the Child came into
effect. The summit documents are striking in that, although they acknowledged the problems facing children in armed conflict, stated a commitment
to protect children from the scourge of war, and advocated such measures as
periods of tranquility and special relief corridors with this objective in mind,
they embedded physical security issues in a much broader and multifaceted
account of the problems facing children (malnutrition, disease, gender discrimination) and general commitments to address these.[2] In general, the discourse of security—and its application to children—were absent.

The increasing use of child soldiers in post–Cold War conflicts and the
widespread effects of such conflict on children led the UN Committee on the
Rights of the Child to recommend an independent study of the problem in
1993.[3] Boutros Boutros-Ghali appointed Graça Machel to lead the effort, which
was funded and supported by UNICEF and the UN Centre for Human Rights.
Her group consulted widely through 1994 and 1995 and produced its results

in 1996.[4] The report noted that 2 million children had been killed in conflict over the previous decade and three times as many had been seriously injured, often by land mines.

The authors focused in particular on the issue of child soldiers and the sexual abuse of young female combatants and strongly advocated an end to the use of children under the age of 18 as combatants. It also considered at length the situation of displaced children, focusing on the danger of malnutrition and separation from family. In both instances, the report highlighted the vulnerability of children to sexual abuse, including that perpetrated by members of peacekeeping forces, and suggested that rape be codified as a crime under international and national law. The report then considered the threat posed by land mines, noting the particular vulnerability of children to this hazard, suggesting that states enact comprehensive national legislation to ban the production, use, trade, and stockpiling of the weapon and that mine clearance for humanitarian purposes be part of all future peace agreements. The authors highlighted the asymmetric effects of sanctions on children and argued against the use of comprehensive sanctions without clear exemptions for humanitarian reasons. The group also underlined the particular vulnerability of children to disease and psychosocial disruption in situations of conflict and the risks and costs of disruption to childhood education caused by armed conflict.

The report noted the importance of the obligations that the Convention on the Rights of the Child imposed on states but stressed that many of the most serious breaches of children's rights occurred as a result of the actions of nonstate actors and/or when the state in question was incapable of fulfilling its obligations. In consequence, the report called for the deeper framing of the protection of children in conflict not only in terms of local custom and national legislation but also in international law. The report summarized the applicability of the Geneva Conventions and Protocols to the protection of children but noted that operationalizing these provisions (especially Protocol II) in noninternational armed conflicts was problematic, since few governments were willing to concede that any struggle within their borders amounted to an armed conflict. It observed that in contrast to international humanitarian law, international human rights law is generally binding principally on states and so did not apply to many actors in contemporary conflict.

This was also true of the Convention on the Rights of the Child, and the report called for nonstate actors to commit to the provisions of the convention. From the experts' perspective, the convention also fell short by failing to fully address the issue of recruitment of children. Machel's report recommended the adoption of the protocol dealing with this and other matters that was being prepared by a working group commissioned by the Committee on the Rights of the Child in 1994. Noting that legal norms could be effective only if they were broadly understood and if there were effective mechanisms to assess compliance, the authors suggested stronger efforts to disseminate information on children's rights in relation to armed conflict and more robust and child-sensitive monitoring of compliance in armed conflict by the UNCHR and the Committee on the Rights of the Child.

The concluding section of the report addressed the challenges of reconstruction and noted that the security of children in postconflict situations could not be assured without effective bridging from emergency relief to development assistance. Particular emphasis was placed here on education. Another key element of the transitional phase was reconciliation and justice processes that effectively addressed the experiences of abused children. The substantive section of the report ended with an extensive comment on conflict prevention, linking the roots of conflict directly to development and human welfare and insisting that balanced economic social and human development be a central part of addressing the insecurity of children. The report concluded with a wide-ranging set of policy recommendations for states, the UN and its specialized agencies, regional organizations, and the Bretton Woods institutions, all centering on the need to mainstream conflict-affected children in their work. The experts also called for the appointment of a special representative of the UN Secretary-General to advocate on behalf of children.[5]

The report had a seminal effect. It laid out the basic dimensions of the problem of protection of children in conflict and set the parameters of institutional and state response that were followed over the next several years. It is an interesting example of the difficulty of containing the issue of human security within narrow parameters of protection. What began as an analysis of the challenges of protecting children from violent conflict ended up as a very broad account of children's problems ranging from nutrition through education to sexual abuse.

Following the publication of the report, interested states took up the issue.[6] Moreover, having achieved success in the field of land mines, many of the nongovernmental organizations that had gathered around that issue sought new pastures. Interested NGOs grouped themselves into the Coalition to Stop the Use of Child Soldiers with the intention of raising the minimum age for recruitment from 15 to 18.[7] The result was an increasing and surprisingly coordinated effort by states and civil society to advocate regarding the protection of children. Again, context mattered. Media coverage of civil conflict in Sierra Leone and Uganda increased public awareness of sexual slavery, the use of child soldiers, and the mutilation of children.

At the United Nations, the Security Council took up the issue of children in armed conflict in parallel with its growing engagement with the protection of civilians in general. Discussion commenced in 1998 as a result of pressure from the civil society coalition. The Portuguese president of the council recognized the importance of the issue, acknowledged the significance of the work of the special representative of the Secretary-General, and called for further work in the Security Council to respond to the needs of this vulnerable group.[8] A year later, the council adopted resolution 1261, sponsored by Namibia, which then held the council presidency, on the basis of a draft prepared by the special representative. One major aspect of the resolution was the question of the recruitment of children.[9] It drew upon earlier processes in the ILO, notably its Convention 182 on the Prohibition and Immediate Action for the Elimination of the Worst Forms of Child Labour (1999), which prohibits, inter alia, the forced recruitment of children for use in armed conflict. The resolution also drew force from the identification of the use of children in conflict as a war crime in the Statute of the International Criminal Court. The council did not limit itself to the question of recruitment (which had turned out to be highly divisive) but addressed broader issues of child protection as well, recognizing the vulnerability of children in conflict and displaced children and calling upon states and other parties to conflict to honor their obligations in international humanitarian law. The council also suggested that specialized agencies take the special needs of children into account in their programming in situations of conflict and affirmed its intention to ensure that Article 41 (sanctions) mandates took account of the potential impact of sanctions on children.

In parallel with the Security Council process, the Canadian government and the Canadian Red Cross prepared a pledge concerning war-affected children for consideration at the 27th International Conference of the Red Cross in 1999. In addition, in cooperation with the UK, Canada raised the matter in the Group of 8 (G-8). Canada and other concerned states also sought to develop regional initiatives in particularly affected areas, notably the 2000 West African Conference on War-Affected Children, which Ghana co-sponsored and hosted. The conference brought together states, NGOs, and children themselves, producing a Declaration and Plan of Action for War-Affected Children in the region that was adopted by West African participating states, the first interstate agreement to focus on the protection of children in conflict.[10]

The pace increased in 2000 along several tracks. In January, the working group on the optional protocol on child soldiers, drawing on substantial input from the special representative to the Secretary-General, interested UN agencies, and the Coalition to Stop the Use of Child Soldiers, produced a consensus text. The document prohibited the compulsory recruitment of children under 18 and committed signatories to take all feasible measures to ensure that children under 18 serving in their armed forces not be exposed to combat, but (reflecting the customs of a number of major states) it allowed for voluntary recruitment and service by children over the age of 15.[11] Implementation was to be handled primarily by states parties, but the UN Secretariat acted as depositary of the protocol. The UNHCHR Committee on the Rights of the Child was designated to receive and review national reports on measures to implement the protocol. However, the protocol did not identify measures that might be taken by the UNHCHR or by other parties to the protocol in the event of noncompliance.

The required number of ratifications for the protocol to enter into effect was ten. As of December 2004, sixty-six states had ratified. A far greater number had signed. And no great power had failed to sign.[12] More controversially, the Secretary-General recommended that parties commit to a minimum age of 18 for voluntary enlistment.[13] The straight-18 rule was strongly opposed by the United States and the UK in particular; their recruitment of under-18 cadets and the existence of military academies for minors would have put them in violation.

The Security Council's consideration of the needs of children in armed conflict also continued apace. The resolutions discussed above regarding protection of civilians in conflict recognized the specific needs of children in such contexts. In his report of 19 July 2000,[14] the Secretary-General highlighted the significance of the successful conclusion of negotiations on the optional protocol, noting the significant role played by NGOs in that process. He also stressed the central role of UN agencies, the ICRC, and national and international NGOs in monitoring implementation of normative commitments with respect the protection of children. He suggested that monitoring organizations that focus on sanctions and the illicit flow of natural resources, the control of small arms proliferation, and demining extend their remit to consider the effects of their efforts on children and advocated that children's rights be inserted into the Global Compact negotiations.[15]

The Security Council responded to the Secretary-General's report with a second resolution in August 2000.[16] The tone was sharper. The council "strongly condemned" the deliberate targeting of children in war and emphasized the responsibility of states to bring those responsible for genocide and crimes of war (which included crimes against children) to justice without out the possibility of amnesty. The Security Council also recognized the linkage between the small arms issue, illicit natural resources trade, and the protection of children. In language that was consistent with the more general resolutions on protection, it stressed that deliberate targeting of civilians (including children) and systematic violation of international humanitarian and human rights law (including that related to children) might constitute a threat to international peace and security. It thereby placed the issue of protection of children potentially within its Chapter VII remit.

In the resolution, the Security Council continued the effort to mainstream children's issues in conflict management by suggesting that peace settlements include provision for dealing with issues specific to children, that future peace operations include child protection advisers, and that children be involved in peace processes. It strongly encouraged regional organizations to develop their own child protection capacities and to include the protection of children in the mandates of their peacekeeping forces. It also emphasized the significance of gender in child protection, noting the special needs of girls in conflict and suggesting that these needs be included in the structures and programs of the UN and regional organizations.

The Secretary-General filed a second report on the subject in 2001, summarizing progress in pursuing the child protection agenda. He noted the special representative's effort to secure commitments from belligerents that they would respect international obligations to protect children,[17] the success of the UNHCHR in collaboration with the DPKO in embedding child protection concerns in peacekeeping operations, and the increasing efforts of NGOs to monitor compliance with child protection norms in zones of conflict. Annan also emphasized the continuing and deepening role of the Security Council in this area. He noted the council's specification of child protection as a matter of concern in its resolutions on specific conflicts (with what he considered to be concrete results, for example, in the DRC)[18] and its inclusion of child protection in the mandates of peacekeeping forces.[19] This had been complemented by an effort to integrate child protection in the training of peacekeepers. He also stressed the need for further research into the impact of conflict on children and noted the establishment in July 2001 of a research network involving NGOs, a number of research institutions, and UNICEF to bring international expertise to bear in a more focused way.

The Security Council followed the Secretary-General's report with a further resolution that expressed once again the council's determination to protect children affected by conflict and to include child protection issues in the mandates of peacekeeping forces.[20] Paralleling its activities in the general area of civilian protection, the council underlined the importance of establishing and maintaining humanitarian access to children in conflict and noted the importance of ensuring that sanctions regimes were child-sensitive. It reminded parties to conflict of their obligations in law to protect children and encouraged them to include child protection provisions in peace agreements. After a lengthy list of suggestions to UN agencies and the IFIs, it recommended further capacity-building on the issue in regional organizations.

Developments outside the Security Council continued to reflect a somewhat bifurcated approach to the security of children. As with human security in general, two approaches had emerged: focusing on the specific issues of children in violent conflict and situating protection issues in a broader context of welfare and rights.

In the first approach, we find the Winnipeg International Conference on War-Affected Children, which brought together a large number of government ministers, NGO representatives, experts, and children to review the issue of children in armed conflict. The conference was hosted by Canada in September 2000 with a goal of generating a consensual plan of action for presentation to the 2002 General Assembly special session on children. In its background documents, the Canadian government quite specifically situated the issue and the conference within the context of its policies on human security. Its approach typified the narrower, protection-based logic of human security that Canada had embraced in the late 1990s.

The declaration of the conference acknowledged the wider context of children's rights and the consequent obligations of states and other groups regarding health, development, education, and the environment. Nonetheless, its focus lay squarely on the more specific issues surrounding conflict (prevention of the abuse of children in war, the targeting of children in war, child recruitment, abduction, and the need to end impunity and support the consolidation of legal mechanisms—e.g., the International Criminal Court). It also addressed disarmament, demobilization, and reintegration of children as part of peacebuilding. Consonant with similar consideration by the Security Council, the declaration called for peacekeepers to be trained in children's protection issues. In addition, the experts' report called for increased donor attention to children's issues in postconflict peacebuilding. Conference documents called explicitly for regional organizations, nonstate actors in conflict, the corporate sector, and the media to incorporate child protection concerns in their agendas.

In the second approach, we find the special session of the General Assembly that was called soon after the Secretary-General's 2001 report to review progress in implementing the World Summit for Children's (1990) program of action in the context of the UN's Millennium Development Goals. The session document devoted considerably greater attention to the issue of protection but extended its analysis beyond situations of conflict to "war, violence, exploitation, neglect, and all other forms of abuse and discrimination."[21] Discussion of protection in war was embedded in a wider consideration of natural disasters, sexual exploitation, trafficking, kidnapping, economic exploitation, and domestic and sexual violence. The discussion of protection itself was divided between abuse in general and the protection of children in war. Protection issues were sixth and seventh (after universal education and before combating AIDS) in a list of ten objectives, in what seemed to be an effort to ensure that security issues did not overwhelm the broader international agenda relating to children.[22]

The momentum of normative development in this area diminished in 2002–2003. Instead, the council recognized that they had moved into what the Secretary-General referred to in his 2002 report as an "era of application."[23] The point was not so much to build new norms but to implement and ensure compliance with those that had developed already. There is little to argue with in the Secretary-General's 2003 assessment of progress in this area:

> Since 1998, when the issue of war-affected children was placed on the agenda, the progressive engagement of the Council has yielded significant gains for children. These include four resolutions devoted to the issue . . . an annual debate and review, an annual report submitted by the Secretary-General, the incorporation of child-specific concerns into the briefs of Security Council fact-finding missions, an important contribution to monitoring and accountability through the listing of parties to conflict that violate the rights of children and the stipulation for the systematic inclusion of sections devoted to children in country-specific reports. Child protection has been integrated into the mandates of peacekeeping missions and the training of personnel. A significant innovation has been the creation of the role and deployment of child protection advisers in peacekeeping missions.[24]

The Security Council followed up on this report in April 2004, expressing its concern about the continuing recruitment of children and calling upon parties in conflict to make time-bound commitments to cease this practice. It threatened targeted and graduated measures against parties that refused to enter a dialogue on this issue.[25]

Beyond the Security Council, substantial legal limitation on the use of children in war was achieved in the Optional Protocol to the Convention on the Rights of the Child (which had been ratified by sixty-three states at the time of Secretary-General Annan's 2003 report), the Rome Statute of the International Criminal Court (1998), and the ILO Convention No. 182 (1999). As the Secretary-General noted, the desire to limit the participation of children in war extended to the regional level, notably in the African Charter on the Rights and Welfare of the Child (1990; ratified by thirty-one states by 2004), which establishes 18 as the minimum age for compulsory military recruitment and participation in hostilities.

In short, taking the 1990 conference as a point of departure and looking at the evolution in treatment of the security of children in war, we see a gradual but clear securitization of the discourse in the transition from general treatment of the rights of children to more specific consideration of children in war and, finally, to a clear focus on the protection of this vulnerable group in situations of armed conflict. This process of ideational development was quite typical. The issue of child protection came onto the table as a result of growing awareness of the abuse of children in the wars of the 1990s. The report of Graça Machel and her colleagues greatly enhanced the profile of the issue in international society. NGOs and UN organizations (notably UNICEF) mounted sustained advocacy efforts to promote international action to address the problem and provided substantial empirical and analytical input into the evolving UN approach. The UNHCHR and the ILO both had prominent roles in organizing and carrying through legal changes that served the purpose of protecting children in conflict. The Secretary-General played a key promotional role in defining the issue, raising its profile through his reports on the subject, and focusing Security Council discussion of the issue. The council itself made a fundamental contribution, not only in taking on the issue in repeated resolutions but in applying the logic of child protection in other areas of deliberation—notably the wider issue of protection of civilians, sanctions, mandates for peacekeepers, and UN interactions with the global corporate sector. The Secretariat in turn then made an important contribution, both in mainstreaming children's protection issues in agency reporting and in training and monitoring. The special representative of the Secretary-General played a very important role in advocacy at the regional level and with parties to conflict. And, finally, concerned states made a real difference to sustaining and developing the process of weaving children's rights into the fabric of norms of international security.

It is legitimate to ask to what extent these developments made any practical difference to the security of children. Certainly the Secretary-General's list of parties to conflict that were not complying with changing norms[26] is a daunting one. There have been substantial difficulties in promoting the child protection agenda in key cases. The use of child soldiers and the re-recruitment of demobilized children remained common in the DRC, despite the inclusion of child protection advisers in MONUC, whose mandate was to sensitize mission personnel. While the mainstreaming of child protection issues in peace operations is a sound principle, its impact seems small. In the Congolese case, child protection programs in specialized agencies (e.g., UNICEF) were underresourced compared to MONUC's child protection division. Lines of responsibility between MONUC and specialized agencies were unclear and coordination was poor.[27] Regarding the 2004 crisis in Sudan, UNICEF noted: "The unfolding tragedy in Darfur, Sudan, has provided further evidence that the world is not yet able to offer children the protection from armed conflict to which they are entitled."[28]

Close to half of the 3.6 million fatalities in war since 1990 have been children. Hundreds of thousands of children continue to be coerced into participation in conflict. Children continue to be frequent victims of the explosive remnants of war.[29] Changing ideas in this sphere have had a marginal impact on intended beneficiaries.[30]

Even so, it bears stressing that international society moved in fifteen years from a position where there was no substantial normative framework covering or substantial international action related to the participation and protection of children in armed conflict to a position where there is now a substantial set of rules. Ideational change takes time to take root in practice. It is too early to judge what the precise practical impact of this evolution will be.

Women in War

In previous chapters, we described the gradual emergence of women's rights as a matter of international concern. Here, we examine the extent to which a clearer focus on the security of women who are threatened by internal and international conflict emerged in the post–Cold War period. The process of focusing attention on women in war was broadly similar to that just discussed in relation to children. In this case as well, international conferences sponsored by the UN played a key role in advancing understanding and awareness of the issue and promoting adjustment in norms to take it into account. Issues relating to women and security were treated briefly at the 1992 Conference on Environment and Development in Rio de Janeiro and, more substantially, at the 1993 Vienna World Conference on Human Rights. In the first instance, the conference, in its Agenda 21, recognized the salience of the problem of violence against women and enjoined participating states "to consider adopting, strengthening and enforcing legislation prohibiting violence against women and to take all necessary administrative, social and educational measures to eliminate violence against women in all its forms."[31]

In the second instance, the conference expressed its deep concern over "various forms of discrimination and violence, to which women continue to be exposed all over the world" and called for the elimination of gender-based violence and the provision of effective protection and assistance to refugee populations, bearing in mind the special needs of displaced and refugee women. It also expressed its dismay at the violation of human rights in conflict situations, including systematic rape, and called for the perpetrators to be brought to justice and punished. In this context, the conference declared that violations of the human rights of women in war were "violations of the fundamental principles of international human rights and humanitarian law." Recognizing that women's issues had been inadequately addressed in the past, the Vienna Declaration called for the mainstreaming of women's rights in the activities of the UN system.[32]

The next relevant episode was the Fourth World Conference on Women held in Beijing (1995). As was the case for children at the 1990 summit, in Beijing the threat to women in conflict was addressed, but it was embedded in a much larger agenda of women's rights as they related to international and national law, governance, and development. In the declaration of the conference, for example, equality and development were placed ahead of peace in the listing of the goals of participating governments.[33] In its very limited consideration of peace and security, the declaration focused not on the specific problems encountered by women as a potentially vulnerable group in conflict but on the contribution of women as a force for peace.[34]

The Platform for Action adopted by the Beijing conference did somewhat better on the security dimension of gender. It retained the strong emphasis on the broader issues of equality of rights and the significance of gender in development. However, it recognized that the changing character of conflict in the post–Cold War era posed serious threats for the security of women in particular: "Grave violations of the human rights of women occur, particularly in times of armed conflict, and include murder, torture, systematic rape, forced pregnancy and forced abortion, in particular under policies of ethnic cleansing."[35] Moreover, it cited "the effects of armed or other conflict on women" as an area of critical concern.[36]

It is only when one moves to the section on strategies and actions that one encounters a thematic subsection (one of twelve such subsections that deal with identified areas of critical concern) that provided detailed analysis of women and conflict. There was a reasonably full discussion of the legal framework for protection of women in conflict, what constituted violation of international law in this area, and of the fact that women made up a particularly high portion of populations that are displaced or otherwise affected by war. Finally, the document stressed the importance—for these and other reasons—of mainstreaming a gender perspective into all policies and programs addressing armed or other conflicts. The document set out an ambitious agenda for action by states and international organizations that included the strengthening of the legal framework controlling the trade in and use of land mines, the identification and condemnation of rape as a deliberate instrument of war and under some circumstances as a crime against humanity and an act of genocide, the protection of women and children from such acts, the investigation and punishment of the use of systematic rape in conflict, and the training of peacekeeping personnel in general human rights issues with a view to preventing violence against women in particular.[37]

Despite the detail concerning strategies and actions, the issue of women in conflict appears to have been treated at Beijing as a secondary issue.[38] Consideration of the topic covered two out of forty-six paragraphs in the main body of the platform of action, while the area of critical concern just mentioned was one of twelve issues, the bulk of which focused largely on broader economic, social, and cultural rights. The section dealing with protection in detail was buried in paragraphs 131–149.[39] This is somewhat surprising in retrospect, given the widely acknowledged abuse of women (in particular mass rape, forced prostitution, and forced pregnancy) in the former Yugoslavia over the period 1991–1995 and in Rwanda in 1994.

A certain amount of frustration in this and other regards is evident in the NGO Beijing Declaration. After stating their unhappiness with "the watered down position of official documents," the NGO organizations called for:

> Recognition, protection, compensation, financial and other assistance and full legal status for the millions of women and children, and the victims of nuclear and other environmental catastrophes, many of them widows or orphans who have been forced to become immigrants, migrants, refugees, internally and other displaced persons or forced into sexual slavery as a result of war, foreign occupation and political and socio-economic injustices. Every effort should be made to protect civilian populations from the adverse effects of economic sanctions, which impair their economic human rights.

They concluded with a call for an "end to rape, and to all forms of violence, sexual exploitation, and harassment of women and children."[40] However, here too there was little effort to address the specific problems of women in situations of conflict.

Nevertheless, the Beijing conference was an important milestone on the path toward normative change regarding women in conflict in its identification of the need to specify more clearly that rape and similar acts constituted crimes against humanity, in its recognition of the specific protection needs of women and girls in war, and in its insistence that the profile of gender in military and peacekeeping operations needed to be substantially raised.

As the suffering of women in post–Cold War conflict became more clear[41] and as advocacy by human rights organizations, women's organizations, and humanitarian agencies and NGOs became more insistent and effective through the mid-1990s, there was a corresponding deepening of international understanding of and concern over the security of women and girls in conflict. Unlike many issues related to gender and international society (e.g., reproductive rights and equality in national law), this process did not encounter significant cultural obstacles. In 1998, the Commission on the Status of Women submitted a detailed set of recommendations on the subject to ECOSOC.[42] The recommendations focused in the first place on the need to strengthen national and international legal mechanisms to ensure gender-sensitive redress to victims of armed conflict and to establish unambiguously the status in law of the concerns of war-affected women and children. The CSW also called for greater effort to address the health concerns of war-affected women and the special needs of displaced women and girls and to engage women more effectively in postconflict reconstruction. Finally, it highlighted the need to mainstream gender perspectives in peacekeeping operations through recruitment, the design of mandates, and training.

The activities of the international tribunals that dealt with the former Yugoslavia and Rwanda responded to some extent to the CSW's legal concerns by clarifying the status of systematic sexual violence against women in conflict as a war crime and, in certain circumstances, as falling within the category of genocide. This was further codified in the Statute of the International Criminal Court adopted in 1998.

As was implicit in the CSW's recommendations, the challenge was not just to develop norms and enhance awareness. It also involved institutional adaptation in the UN's peace- and security-related activities. In conjunction with the wider effort to mainstream gender in the operations of the UN—and in recognition of the significant shortfalls in the performance of the DPKO in this area—the Secretariat (and, specifically, the DPKO's Lessons Learned Unit) organized a meeting in Namibia in 2000 on the mainstreaming of gender perspectives in peace operations. The conference produced the Windhoek Declaration, which noted that women had been denied a full role in peace-support operations and the failure in the UN system to take adequate account of the gender dimension in peace processes.

The Namibia Plan of Action stressed the need for equal access for women to peace processes and called for the inclusion of women in negotiating teams. It recommended that initial assessment teams include a senior adviser on gender mainstreaming and that the Secretary-General should include the issue in initial reports to the council. It said that mandates of peace operations should include gender mainstreaming, as should follow-up mechanisms for postconflict reconstruction. It asked that all operations include a gender affairs unit and all DPKO-led operational planning teams have a gender specialist. It suggested that the DPKO develop robust structures for gender mainstreaming in its headquarters activities. The plan of action also recommended efforts to recruit women to leadership positions both at headquarters and in the field. Finally, it made a number of specific suggestions for training both at headquarters and in the field and suggested that the DPKO develop a set of gender mainstreaming training guidelines that could be used by member states to prepare national contingents.[43]

Immediately following the Windhoek seminar, the General Assembly took up the issue in detail as part of its Beijing+5 follow-up. The report of the Ad Hoc Committee of the Whole recognized the growing awareness that armed conflict had "different destructive impacts on women and men and that a gender-sensitive approach to the application of international human rights law and international humanitarian law [was] important." On a more sober note, the report stressed the continuing negative impact of armed conflict on gender equality and women's rights, the deepening problems posed by increasing displacement of women and children, and the persisting inadequacy of training in gender issues for those involved in the international response to armed conflict. It also maintained that over the period under review, there had been an increase in crimes committed against women.[44]

In the period following the Windhoek meeting, the Secretariat paid particular attention to the issue of gender mainstreaming in peacekeeping, reflecting a concern that without change in the structure and mandates of peace operations, it would be impossible to effectively address the particular threats to women in conflict. In a panel discussion on the subject, participants stressed the importance of expanding the participation of women in peace operations, including in leadership roles.[45]

Many of the issues raised by the CSW, the Windhoek seminar, and the General Assembly special session fell within the remit of the Security Council. In October 2000, the council held an Arria formula[46] meeting with NGOs, followed by an open session to discuss women, peace, and security. This was the first time the Security Council had held a thematic discussion on the issue. The Secretary-General made a strong plea for the council to take up the issue of protecting women and girls in conflict as a matter of special concern. The response was resolution 1325.[47]

In the resolution, the Security Council took up concerns about gender mainstreaming directly. Recognizing the underrepresentation of women in the area of peace support, it urged states to increase the number of women in national, regional, and international organizations that address conflict. It also encouraged the Secretary-General to pursue his plan to enhance the representation of women in decision-making with regard to peace and called for an increase in the number of female special representatives. It also urged an increase in the number of women in peace operations and expressed its will-ingness to include gender perspectives in the mandates for peace operations. It asked the Secretary-General to provide training materials for member states to use in preparing national contingents and to ensure that civilian participants in operations received similar training. Finally, it requested that the Secretariat prepare a report on the subject for future consideration by the council.

The Security Council met again on the subject a year later and adopted a presidential statement on women and conflict, which reaffirmed its interest in the subject and reiterated its commitment to the agenda laid out in resolu-tion 1325. It also noted its concern that there were still no female special repre-sentatives of the Secretary-General or special envoys and called upon member states to nominate suitable candidates. More pertinently, it called on all par-ties to conflict to abide by international law and international humanitarian law concerning women affected by conflict.[48]

The UN also established an interagency task force on women, peace, and security to oversee implementation of resolution 1325. The task of preparing the Secretary-General's report was devolved to the task force and was com-pleted in 2002.[49] The Secretary-General summarized the findings for the Se-curity Council in October 2002. He began with a comprehensive account of the specific impacts of contemporary conflict on women, stressing in par-ticular their vulnerability to sexual violence, the effect of the absence of men and boys from households on the responsibilities women had to bear in the family, the growth in the number of households headed by girls, the implica-tions of loss of income generated by males for women's engagement in pros-titution and criminal activities, and the discrimination against women victims of conflict in asylum procedures.

Having established the differential impacts of conflict on women, the Secretary-General called for the Security Council to recognize and act upon the specific impacts of conflict on women and girls and in particular to en-sure that these were integrated into Security Council consideration of peace operations. He also noted the increasing responsiveness of the international legal framework to the problems of women in conflict situations and advised the council that these achievements should be built upon in any future ac-tions to create ad hoc tribunals. He suggested that the Security Council en-sure that future tribunals be properly staffed by individuals with specific expertise on gender rights, that amnesty provisions in peace settlements ex-clude crimes against humanity including those based on gender, and that proper monitoring of the performance of tribunals in the area of gender rights be put in place. He also stressed the importance of women's contributions to peace processes and regretted the low rate of inclusion of women in official delegations. In his view, not only did this mean that these processes took insufficient advantage of women's capacities for negotiation; it also meant that their concerns were inadequately represented. In this regard, he declared his intention to establish a database of gender specialists in zones of conflict that the UN could draw upon in its effort to engage this issue.

He also recommended that gender perspectives be integrated into the perspectives of UN fact-finding missions in conflict zones and that the impact of conflict on women be fully considered in UN-mediated peace agreements. He highlighted again the necessity of integrating gender equality issues into the mandates of peace-support operations and recognized continuing difficulties in securing adequate representation of women in operations, in funding appropriate gender sensitization within the DPKO itself, and in ensuring appropriate behavior in the field by UN peacekeepers and officials. He reiterated calls to include systematically gender perspectives in rehabilitation and reconstruction programs and to include women and girls in the planning and implementation of DDR programs. He closed his report by strongly advocating that matters related to gender and conflict not be taken as distinct issues but that they be systematically integrated into the council's deliberations.

Since 2002, much further research and advocacy has been done by UN agencies active in the field of gender. The UN Fund for Women (UNIFEM), for example, has produced a comprehensive study on gender in disarmament, demobilization, and reintegration programming.[50] In short, the UN, its central bodies, and its associated agencies have played a central role in the interplay of forces that produced considerable change in the way in which international society viewed the human security needs of women. Responding to media reports of abuses of women in conflict and the pressures of NGOs and advocacy within the organization (e.g., UNIFEM and the Division for the Advancement for Women), the UN played an important role in defining the problem (as with the identification of rape as a crime of war).

The issue of protection was embedded in a much larger discussion of gender at the beginning of the post–Cold War era. Over time, it emerged as a distinctive focus of the development of norms. It was increasingly recognized that the specific problems and needs of women suffering from conflict were matters of international concern. In particular, considerably greater specificity emerged regarding the legal status of the abuse of women in conflict. In the deliberations of UN bodies and in the statutes and practice of international legal institutions, sexual violence came to be seen far more clearly as a violation of international humanitarian and human rights law and, in some instances, as a crime of war. Systematic behavior of this type came to be seen as a form of genocide. This evolution limited the scope of recognized domestic jurisdiction and provided yet another example of rebalancing the trade-off between the security of the individual and that of the state. Finally, international institutions recognized the need to adjust their practices in view of the security needs of women in conflict, notably in the area of peacebuilding, as part of a much broader effort to mainstream gender in international organizations. In this context, a gender adviser post was established in the DPKO in 2003. All new UN peace operations include gender considerations in their mandates, and gender awareness has been substantially integrated into the DPKO's predeployment training.[51]

In a process that is now familiar, the increased importance of this element of human security had much to do with the course of conflict in the 1990s. Just as the generalized threat to civilians in much of the decade's conflict stimulated a growing interest in the broad issue of the protection of civilians in war, the targeting of women in particularly egregious ways in conflicts such as those in Yugoslavia and Rwanda facilitated a specific focus on the issue of women in war. The Beijing conference enhanced the profile of the issue. Follow-up to the conference and the five-year review in the General Assembly, both of which were strongly influenced by powerful NGO lobbying both within states and at the transnational level, ultimately brought the question to the Security Council. This evolution was facilitated to a considerable extent by the advocacy efforts of the Secretary-General. The new or enhanced understanding of this dimension of human security was translated into law in the activity of ad hoc tribunals created by the Security Council to address criminality in specific conflicts and through the interstate negotiation of the statute of the International Criminal Court.

Again, it is important not to get carried away. The vulnerabilities of women affected by conflict have not disappeared. In late 2004, the Secretary-General's High-level Panel recognized that UN aspirations regarding the protection of women in war had not been fulfilled and called for the Security Council to fully implement the recommendations of resolution 1235.[52] Many would argue that there has been little improvement on the ground. Events in 2003–2004 in Darfur are indicative. As UNIFEM put it recently: "The deliberate killing, rape, mutilation, forced displacement, abduction, trafficking and torture of women and girls continue unabated in contemporary armed conflicts."[53] The effective address of abuse of women both in general and as it relates to conflict has been hampered by budgetary constraints. UN peace and humanitarian operations (e.g., in the former Yugoslavia, West Africa, and the DRC) have themselves on occasion become a threat to the security of women, who have been sexually abused by UN personnel.[54] Significant, and acknowledged, cultural resistance to the mainstreaming of gender in the UN system remains. Efforts to increase the number of women in senior peace-keeping positions have had little effect. In addition, for change to be effective, it must be taken up by member states (for example, in the selection and training of national contingents for peace-support operations). Progress here has been very uneven. Beyond this, to truly have practical impact, normative change concerning women and war must be embraced not only by states but by nonstate parties in conflict. There is little evidence that this has occurred.

Yet there has been potentially significant normative change regarding the problem of protecting women in conflict from their own states, nonstate belligerents, and, for that matter, predatory and opportunistic individuals. People have been prosecuted and convicted by international tribunals for their abuse of women. To the extent that those contemplating such behavior are aware of the potential legal implications, they may take those implications into account in deciding what to do. It is also pertinent to remember where we were at the beginning of the 1990s regarding this issue in peacekeeping. Gender played virtually no part in UN mandates for peace operations. Now it does. There was no gender-sensitivity training for personnel. Now there is. There were no reporting obligations in this matter. Now there are. There were no obvious targets for participation of women in peace negotiations and in peace operations. Now there are. One may argue about whether this glass is half empty or half full, but it is clear that it is more full than it was at the end of the Cold War.

The Protection of Displaced Persons

The last category in the discussion of the protection of civilians in war is one that we have encountered at length in earlier chapters—those displaced by conflict. As we saw in Chapter 2, the basic normative framework for cross-border displacement was well established by the end of the Cold War, both in the Geneva Convention and Protocols and, less evenly, in regional instruments. Many of the responses of international society and the UN to displacement in the 1990s have been discussed earlier, but several issues specific to displaced persons deserve further elaboration here.

First is the changing dimensions of the problem. In 1975, there were 2.4 million refugees.[55] By 1991, the number had grown to 17.2 million before peaking at 18.2 million in 1993. Moreover, after a long period in which the locus of refugee flows had shifted to the Third World, in the 1990s there were significant movements of refugees in Europe. This placed substantial pressure on asylum procedures and, more broadly, on the willingness of states to receive refugees.[56] The commitment of states to their obligations under the refugee regime began to fray. Asylum procedures became tighter, repatriation became more common. In some instances, this repatriation appeared to violate the principle of *nonrefoulement*.[57]

In part for this reason, agencies engaged in refugee issues, such as UNHCR, turned increasingly to the provision of assistance and protection in or near countries where displacement was occurring. Senior UN officials put forward the concept of preventive protection. As UN High Commissioner for Refugees Ogata said: "With increasing emphasis in the UN on preventive diplomacy, I believe UNHCR should equally focus on what I might call preventive protection."[58] This was coupled with a "right to remain"—"the right of people to remain in peace in their own homes and their own countries."[59] Unquestionably, these normative innovations rang hollow after the experiences in the former Yugoslavia, among others. It is one thing to talk about preventive protection and honoring the right to remain; it is another to enforce them.[60] However, from the perspective of this volume, such notions are interesting in that they constitute a further development in the questioning of domestic jurisdiction when the security of individuals is at stake.

Moreover, they point toward the key normative challenge in the post–Cold War era related to displacement—that concerning the internally displaced. As we saw in previous chapters, although substantial progress was made in establishing a normative regime covering those who had been displaced across borders, the matter of internal displacement was not broached. In the 1980s and 1990s, the dimensions of internal displacement grew very rapidly. As Roberta Cohen and Francis Deng have noted: "When internally displaced persons were first counted in 1982, 1.2 million were found in eleven countries. By 1997, the number had soared to more than 20 million in at least thirty-five countries."[61] The countries of concern in this regard spanned all of the world's regions.

The position of the UNHCR and some states regarding preventive protection and the right to remain added further urgency to the question.[62] If displaced people were to remain in their own countries, it was necessary to develop norms and practical procedures to address their needs.[63]

The issue of internal displacement is central to the development of the idea of human security in the post–Cold War era. Generally, those displaced within the frontiers of what purports to be their state are minorities who are perceived as hostile by those who have captured the state apparatus.[64] As they cannot, or have not, crossed frontiers, they enjoy no protection under refugee law. Instead, they fall within the domestic jurisdiction of their own state.[65] As Deng pointed out: "The international community's approach to the crisis of internal displacement and the need for providing protection and assistance to the affected population rests on the fundamental realization that the problem, by definition, is internal and therefore falls under state sovereignty."[66] Their own state, meanwhile, is often the principal threat to their survival. Its policies have often occasioned their displacement. In these respects, the internally displaced are the quintessential example of the tension between the security of the individual and that of the state. They also raise in a particularly stark fashion the question of international rights and responsibilities toward vulnerable human beings within states. In these respects, it is not surprising that consideration of the problem of IDPs was a key source of the gradual rediscovery of the notion that sovereignty involved responsibility.[67]

The problem of internal displacement is to some extent subsumed in the wider development of ideas relating to protection. The general principles discussed above regarding civilians in war and women and children in war all apply to IDPs. However, it was widely felt in the 1990s that IDPs (like the other subgroups of the civilian population discussed above) had particular vulnerabilities and therefore particular protection needs:

> Displacement deprives them of the basic necessities of life such as shelter, food, medicine, education, or employment opportunities. Displaced persons face discrimination and often find their family and communal ties shattered. Worst of all, they are often trapped within the zone of the very conflict which they seek to flee, forcing them to move again and again.[68]

The standard approaches characteristic of the Cold War period were inadequate to address the problem, since they generally relied on relief and protection in contiguous or nearby states. Although provision of relief to such populations was often feasible, if difficult, the key question of how to protect them remained.

The result was a substantial consideration of normative change regarding IDPs. Once again, the UN played a significant role in initiating this process, not least in the appointment of Francis Deng as Representative of the Secretary-General on Internally Displaced Persons by Boutros Boutros-Ghali in 1992.[69] Deng's mandate was initially open ended but gradually focused on advocacy in four areas: the development of a normative framework for responding to the needs of IDPs, the promotion of appropriate institutional mechanisms at international and regional levels, focused attention on specific IDP situations, and the pursuit of further research on the nature and dimensions of the problem. Of these four, the first two concern us most clearly.

As the 1990s progressed, a cluster of concerned NGOs (e.g., the Norwegian Refugee Council) and states (the UK, Sweden, Switzerland, Canada, and Austria) emerged to promote a new set of norms. The first significant contribution was a compilation of international norms relevant to IDPs by a group of international legal consultants.[70] When this was submitted to the General Assembly, the body requested that the special representative develop a normative framework to address the gaps in existing law. This effort culminated in agreement on a set of "Guiding Principles on Internal Displacement" in 1998.[71]

The guiding principles covered behavior by both state and nonstate parties to conflict. They emphasized that the primary duties and responsibilities regarding IDPs are borne by these state and nonstate authorities. They underlined the principle of nondiscrimination: IDPs were to be treated as other citizens were treated. They prohibited arbitrary displacement. Displacement could be deemed necessary (e.g., in the event of natural disasters or impending military action), but such actions by states had to be based in law; where possible, the consent of those affected had to be sought. The right to life, dignity, liberty, and security of those affected were to be respected.

Regarding the protection of displaced persons, the guidelines emphasized the right to life and enjoined protection against genocide, murder, summary execution, and enforced disappearance. They prohibited acts of violence against IDPs not involved in hostilities. Highlighting every human being's right to liberty and security of person, the guidelines prohibited arbitrary arrest, internment or confinement in camps, and hostage-taking. They recognized the particular security and protection needs of displaced women and children and restated international humanitarian law concerning missing persons and the sick and wounded, reunification of families, and the provision of adequate access to the essentials of life. Humanitarian assistance based on principles of impartiality and nondiscrimination was not to be interfered with. The security of those engaged in humanitarian assistance and their transport and supplies were to be guaranteed. The property displaced persons had left behind was to be protected against seizure, illegal and arbitrary occupation or use, or destruction in reprisal.

These principles encapsulated widely accepted obligations of states as they related to the treatment of persons displaced within borders. The purpose was to provide guidance to the UN, to states encountering the problem, to nonstate authorities and groups, and to non-UN intergovernmental organizations and NGOs. The principles were not a binding instrument or new law.[72] But they were endorsed by the UNCHR[73] and the General Assembly[74] and have been integrated into the work programs of agencies of the Secretariat (the Emergency Relief Coordinator and Office for the Coordination of Humanitarian Affairs).

This said, it is noteworthy but not surprising that there has been no substantial consideration of the matter of internal displacement in the Security Council.[75] In the first place, the matter of protection of internally displaced persons is subsumed within the broader consideration by the Security Council of the protection of civilians in war. Second, at least one of the permanent members was in reasonably clear violation of the guidelines.[76] In addition, as the implications of the principles sank in, a substantial backward movement emerged in the General Assembly. At the July 2000 ECOSOC meeting, several states questioned whether a document that had not been drafted or adopted by governments could have standing in the UN system. A year later, the same group of states attempted to have reference to the guiding principles removed from the assembly omnibus resolution on the work of the UNHCR. That these initiatives failed[77] suggests that the guidelines do in some sense represent international society's understanding of existing normative constraints on states' treatment of this category of their own citizens within their own borders.[78]

Conclusion

It is clear that each of the groups discussed above—women, children, and displaced persons—face particular difficulties and have specific needs. As we have seen, the UN and other elements of international society have made substantial efforts to identify, define, and address these needs.

However, there is an intrinsic tension between the universalistic underpinnings of the human security agenda and the group-specific orientation of children and women in conflict and the displaced. The basis of human security is a claim that certain standards of treatment are universal. Advocacy and norm-building for specific groups may involve a claim that their concerns are more important. As such, it may corrode the general principles.

In addition, advocacy for specific groups raises disturbing questions about those who are left out. The elderly, for example, are one of the most vulnerable groups in war, given their dependence on family structures and on public health infrastructure that may be disrupted by conflict. They are less able than many other groups to protect themselves. There is very little international advocacy regarding the threats that conflict poses to them. There has been no specific protective norm-building to address their concerns.

This may reflect the nature of the organization of advocacy networks. Those who focus on the elderly, while they are frequently powerful domestically, are oriented toward their constituents' concerns within particular states and less with the elderly as a category of humanity. They have not expended great effort in the kind of transnational linkages that foster effective international advocacy and action. The result is that—in contrast to children and women—the threats to the old are underrepresented in international discourse on human security. Similar remarks might be made about the disabled and mentally ill, who have frequently been institutionalized and are therefore fully dependent on state health and welfare infrastructures.

The same is true of what is arguably the most vulnerable group in conflict situations: males between the ages of 18 and 40. One might, of course, argue that these people are a source of the problem rather than victims of it. But many young men do not choose to do what they are doing, and their casualty rates are very high.

Moreover, focusing on particular groups may have practical implications for people under threat. One example arises from the war in Chechnya. Here the focus of protection has been on IDPs living in temporary housing, mostly in Ingushetia, supported by an array of international agencies and local NGOs. Their situation became reasonably stable once they settled: it was a "maintenance problem." The real protection problem in this conflict arguably was that pertaining to individuals who had not been displaced from Chechnya or who, willingly or unwillingly, had been returned to what was an active war zone. Targeting the issue of IDPs diverted attention from the heart of the problem.

This is not to say that the problems of specific groups in war are insignificant. They are substantial and deeply troubling. Nor is it to question the motives or achievements of national and international lobbying groups that have managed to greatly enhance awareness of the needs of these groups. But selectivity in dealing with threats to human security may involve ignoring equally disturbing human security issues where advocacy is less effective. The advantage of protection of civilians, as opposed to the protection of women or children or any other specific group in war, is that it avoids this possible dynamic of exclusion.

7

Human Security and the UN: A Critique

- **Promise and Achievements**
- **Whither Human Security?**
- **Conceptual Overstretch and Its Consequences**
- **Human Security as Freedom from Organized Violence**
- **9/11 and the Return of the National Security State?**
- **Conclusion**

Over the course of the twentieth century, it became increasingly obvious that the state was having trouble living up to its end of the bargain in providing for the security of the individual. As noted in Chapter 2, the movement to recover the individual—as opposed to the state—as the primary referent of security was given impetus in the aftermath of World War II with the UN Declaration of Human Rights, the Convention on the Prevention and Punishment of the Crime of Genocide, and other major international agreements and conventions. Chapters 2 and 3 suggest that, with the onset of the Cold War, concrete progress on the human rights–human security front was stymied: in general, the tension between state rights and individual rights in the world arena was resolved in the state's favor. It was only in the waning years of the Cold War that the security discourse began slowly shifting in the direction of the individual. The civil and internal wars unleashed by the end of the Cold War and the ethnic cleansing, genocidal policies, and mass population displacements that accompanied these conflicts refocused international attention on the plight of individuals targeted by, or caught up in, these tumultuous, heartrending events.

Part II of this book demonstrates that by the early 1990s, the idea of human security had begun to make its presence felt in international discourse. Most analysts date the idea's coming of age as 1994, the year in which the UNDP's human development report devoted an entire section to the concept.[1] Combining the UNDP's ideas on the human purposes of economic development with the new security agenda, *Human Development Report 1994* shifted the spotlight away from protecting territory and the national interest to addressing the security needs of the individual. The report merged two hitherto independent streams of thought: the human development approach of the UN and the effort to broaden the meaning of security. The timing of the report was also exquisite: not only did the end of the Cold War afford more room for a people-centered approach but the events of the early 1990s seemed to reinforce the salience of many of the nontraditional insecurities highlighted by the report. As Kanti Bajpai has observed, the report was one of the "two most important sets of writings on the subject."[2] The UN imprimatur enhanced the credibility of the idea and provided an international reach.

The idea did not lie dormant in dusty library shelves. Middle powers such as Canada and Norway appropriated and adapted the human security idea and incorporated it as a prominent aspect of their foreign policy. Canada and Norway are the leaders of the Human Security Network of like-minded states that includes Austria, Chile, Greece, Ireland, Jordan, Mali, the Netherlands, Slovenia, Switzerland, and Thailand.[3] To be sure, the Human Security Network has emphasized the "freedom from fear" component of human security, in contrast to the UNDP's insistence on the importance of the "freedom from want" aspect of human security. In the context of evolving EU security strategy, the Barcelona Study Group of eminent European security specialists elaborated a "human security doctrine" for Europe that emphasized "freedom of individuals from basic insecurities caused by human rights violations."[4] Japan's attempt to incorporate human security notions in its foreign policy, which has a strong emphasis on tackling "freedom from want" (including health) issues, is probably closer to the UNDP's approach. Similarly, NGOs such as the Treatment Action Campaign of South Africa find the UNDP approach salient; it allows them to characterize HIV/AIDS as serious threat to human security.[5]

In May 2003, the Commission on Human Security presented its report, *Human Security Now*, to Secretary-General Kofi Annan.[6] Established in 2000 with principal support from the Japanese government, the remit of the CHS was to "promote public understanding . . . of human security," to develop the concept "as an operational tool for policy formulation and implementation," and "to propose a concrete program of action." As Chapter 4 recounted, the CHS report took a much broader approach than the Human Security Network to human security, bringing under its rubric physical protection, rights, and development. Human security, according to the CHS, necessitated policies that went beyond ensuring people's survival to policies that focused on people's "livelihood and dignity, during downturns as well as in prosperity."[7] Secretary-General Annan convened a high-powered advisory group to consider the best ways of implementing the recommendations of the report.

Outside the UN, institutes and centers dedicated to exploring and implementing the concept are also beginning to dot the landscape. One of the most influential proponents of the idea, former Canadian foreign minister Lloyd Axworthy, became director of the Liu Institute for the Study of Global Issues.[8] The Liu Institute, based at the University of British Columbia, is unique in its tight focus on "expanding the science of human security." The many centers within the institute, such as the Centre for Human Security and the Centre of International Relations, are to varying degrees dedicated to advancing the human security idea. As these developments suggest, the human security idea has not languished: it has been taken up by influential players and institutions, elaborated, and critiqued. It has also informed the foreign policies of countries as diverse as Japan, Canada, Norway, and members of the Lysoen group.[9]

While the preceding chapters have traced the evolution of the human security idea within and outside the UN, this chapter provides a critical assessment of the idea and the attempts to implement it within the world body. We focus on the UNDP's HDR 1994 and the 2003 elaboration of the concept by the CHS, not only because the UN is a primary object of study of this series but also because, together, the reports provide perhaps the most thorough, authoritative, and up-to-date statements on the concept. In recent years, even the Human Security Network has deemed it necessary to go beyond its "freedom from fear" focus to incorporate the "freedom from want" issues emphasized by the HDR.

We begin by acknowledging and commending the idea's contribution to the international security discourse and practice. The most crucial contribution, in our view, is also the most obvious: the unrelenting emphasis on human beings as the ultimate referent of security. Viewed in the light of the struggle between statecentric and individualcentric conceptions of the referent of security, the reports of the UNDP and the CHS represent the culmination of a process that over the course of the twentieth century progressively moved the referent of security in the direction of the individual. This aspect of human security also speaks to many of the post–Cold War security predicaments and it facilitates the invocation of Chapter VII of the UN Charter in cases of serious human rights abuse. The "securitization" of the individual also allows nontraditional security issues such as the environment and health to compete for more policy attention and resources.

Do these initial successes suggest that the human security approach has made serious inroads into the mainstream international security discourse? And is it likely to achieve coequal status with, if not replace, the dominant military and statecentric approach to security? Human security has made important inroads into mainstream security discourse, but it still has some way to go before it can match or dethrone the focus of the major powers on national security. Recent events have conspired to bring national security back to center stage in ways unanticipated by most. But even without the impact of these events, the notion of human security would have come up against a key obstacle to its further progress: conceptual overstretch—the extension of the concept to cover almost every human malady conceivable as a security threat. Such an expansive approach renders the concept analytically incoherent and robs it of its analytical utility. Conceptual overstretch results in three problems: it generates false priorities and hopes, it leads to confusion about the causes of human insecurity, and it may engender military solutions to political problems.[10] To mitigate these problems, we argue for a conception of human security where human beings are retained as the referent of security, but the domain of what constitutes security threats to them is confined to threats against their physical integrity that are planned and perpetrated by states, individuals, or groups that aim to "do them in." This less-expansive notion, because it focuses on organized violence, has a better intuitive fit with what most consider to be "security threats." As such, it is also better poised to enable human security to make further inroads into the mainstream security discourse.

Promise and Achievements

The human security approach has helped redirect our attention to four fundamentals in international relations. First, by reminding us that all our security "doings" are meant for the protection of the individual, not the state, the concept provides a helpful corrective to a mode of thinking that has often reified the state. To the question What is it all for? the human security approach has a clear and appropriate answer: human beings.[11] Second, the concept speaks to the major post–Cold War security predicaments in a way that national security approaches do not. In particular, it provides a vocabulary for describing and understanding the human consequences of internal and civil wars. The latter have emerged as the dominant category of conflict as well as the blight of the post–Cold War era. Human insecurity is an apt and comprehensive term to capture the threat to the physical survival—whether from machetes, bullets, disease, or lack of food and water—of civilians caught in civil wars such as Bosnia, Rwanda, Sudan, Kosovo, East Timor, and Chechnya. Unlike national security approaches that privilege the state—and hence relegate individuals within it to secondary importance—human security compels attention to the threat posed to individual bystanders as others engage in mortal combat to capture power amid a crumbling state. The universality of the term "human," as opposed to "Bosnian Muslims" or "East Timorese," endows international society's concern and consternation with a normative standing or legitimacy that might be otherwise absent.

The third positive payoff follows from the first two. States and regional organizations taken by the concept have incorporated human security initiatives as part of their foreign and security policy. Canada, for example, sees the Landmines Treaty and the International Criminal Court as manifestations of its human security agenda. Encouraged by these successes, Canada is now aiming its human security efforts at controlling small arms and child soldiers. Japan has funded many projects that enhance human security in Southeast Asia under UN auspices. Regional organizations such as the OAS and ASEAN are puzzling about ways to balance state and human security.[12] In our view, these initiatives do make meaningful contributions to increasing the level of human security. As seen in Chapter 5, for example, the treaty on land mines has resulted in a substantial reduction in the production of and trade in these weapons and complete destruction of stockpiles of antipersonnel mines in some thirty-five countries.

Beyond the state and regional level, construing the threat faced by innocent civilians caught in civil wars or those targeted for genocide by their ethnic enemies as a "security" issue increases, in theory, the possibility of action by the UN. Chapter VII of the Charter provides for the use of force by the international community in response to threats to international peace and security. Although the application of Chapter VII is moderated by the prohibition against intervening in matters within the "domestic jurisdiction" of states, Article 2.7 leaves room for the Security Council to override the principle of nonintervention when events within a state constitute a threat to international peace and security. By blurring the distinction between what is domestic and what is international, by drawing attention to the potential link between domestic (human) insecurities and their external ramifications, the human security discourse erodes the robustness of the principle of nonintervention.

To be sure, it is one thing to characterize something as a human security problem and quite another to agree that it is a threat to international peace and security (requiring intervention by the international community). The distance between the two is formidable. But the notion of human security does bring the former a step closer to the latter conceptually. One of the most important conceptual connections (or leaps of faith?) made by the Security Council in the 1990s was that regimes or groups that systematically murdered their citizens were also likely to be threats to international security. During the Cold War, such murderous regimes were tolerated largely because each of the two blocs felt that containing the other was the more pressing security imperative. Without the Cold War overlay, the room for acting against the most vicious regimes expanded, and in numerous cases in the 1990s the Security Council did invoke Chapter VII as the justification for coming to the aid of those who were endangered. The link between human insecurity and international insecurity has been reinvigorated (up to a point), and future serial abusers of human rights (purveyors of human insecurity) will have to factor in the possibility that the threshold of external intervention to end such abuses has been lowered. The most recent manifestation of this normative shift can perhaps be seen in the report of the UN's High-level Panel on Threats, Challenges and Change, which argued that events that lessen life chances, cause large-scale deaths, and undermine states as the basic units of the international system are all threats to international security.[13]

The above does not constitute a paradigm shift on the part of the Security Council. The council was probably right to invoke Chapter VII in the case of the former Yugoslavia. But the implied link between dastardly regimes and threats to international peace and security is not always obvious or sustainable. The Security Council was sometimes willing to define issues that were not strictly threats to international peace and security as such threats. It did so in part because it was normatively appropriate. One would be hard pressed to demonstrate, for example, how the conflict in Somalia posed a serious threat to international peace and security. But calling it a threat allowed a response. The Security Council was not acting on security grounds; it was acting because it was the right thing to do.

Finally, security issues by their very nature are well poised to fight, and win, battles for attention and resources in international organizations such as the UN or national bureaucracies. Security issues are by definition issues that deserve priority, attention, and resources. In the absence of a modicum of security, industry, arts, and intellectual pursuits would not be possible. Hence, the move to "securitize" domains such as economics, the environment, health, and gender is also very much—some would say primarily—about the battle for policy priority and resource allocation. In other words, international organizations, governments, think tanks, and individual scholars engage in this securitization process for both conceptual, policy, and resource-related reasons. As we have suggested earlier, the apogee (or nadir, depending on one's perspective) of this securitization process is the securitization of the individual, or human security.

This description of the achievements of the idea of human security is likely to be contested by some outside of the West. To begin with, some may object to the emphasis we have placed on security from fear as opposed to security from want. As will be obvious later, we have reservations about the horizontal extension of the notion of security to "want" (economic, environment, health) issues. But it may be precisely that horizontal expansion that makes the concept of human security most relevant to the developing world. For example, African officials and activists gave U.S. trade representative Robert Zoellick an earful about HIV/AIDS being a "greater threat to human security across . . . our continent than anything else" when Zoellick was in Mauritius in early 2003 to discuss the creation of a U.S.–Southern Africa free trade zone.[14]

In a similar vein, the ASEAN countries believe that they have been preaching and practicing a form of human security under a different name—comprehensive and cooperative security. Ever since its inception, ASEAN has seen security as multifaceted, incorporating military, economic, cultural, and social dimensions. ASEAN's practice of cooperative security, which involves engaging potential adversaries via regional organizations, was seen as conducive to human security.[15] What differentiates ASEAN's notions of comprehensive and cooperative security from human security is the referent: the state—its resilience, legitimacy, and security—was the primary referent, not the individual or a class of individuals within the state. To be sure, most in ASEAN saw the state and the individuals within it as coterminous: a legitimate and secure state would translate into secure citizens.

Political leaders and analysts from the developing world, including many who won their independence and sovereignty in the 1940s–1960s, may also be more ambivalent about switching the referent (of security) from the state to the individual. As they see it, the implications of this switch for their state sovereignty are especially disconcerting. Having won sovereignty so recently, they worry about its premature erosion; they view human security as the entering wedge of external interference and intervention. This is because their polities are still negotiating the state power–human rights relationship in ways that are reminiscent of the political bargaining between the Leviathan and its subjects in seventeenth-century Europe. Many Third World states remain weak while facing challengers to their authority and legitimacy from groups and individuals within. How far—and with what means—can the rulers of such states go in beating back such challenges? At which point do they forfeit their sovereignty?

Human security advocates argue that their approach does not challenge the principle of sovereignty per se. Sovereignty could be deemed to imply protection responsibilities, they say. If the state does not or is unable to perform these responsibilities, then intervention to make it possible for the state to fulfill its sovereign responsibilities is not a challenge to sovereignty. Yet for some Asian states, it appears that the human security discourse, with its emphasis on protecting the individual, threatens the traditional conception of sovereignty in which the entity to be protected is the state.

These concerns about sovereignty seem more salient in Asia than in Africa and Latin America. In Asia, countries such as China and most members of ASEAN are concerned about the implications of a people-centered approach to international relations if it is at the expense of their hard-won state sovereignty. They felt the first forays against their presumed sovereignty in the early 1990s when their human rights records were subject to increased scrutiny and criticism by the West. Some of the most articulate policymakers from the region countered with an Asian values discourse.[16] Proponents of Asian values questioned the West's emphasis on individual rights; they argued that Asia's history and culture led Asians to privilege community rights over the rights of the individual. It was this emphasis on the community as opposed to the individual, they argued, that facilitated the rapid and successful industrialization of these societies. Most of these writings did not make a strong distinction between the community and the state; for some, the community was the state. Critics countered that this conflation was merely a subterfuge whereby authoritarian states could continue to deny the civil and political liberties of their citizens in the name of the common good. Interestingly, the Asian values argument was taken seriously as long as its advocates had fast-growing economies. The argument lost its force during the Asian financial crisis of 1997–1998. Critics and policymakers turned the Asian values argument on its head by suggesting that Asia's peculiar brand of capitalism condoned "cronyism, corruption, and nepotism," which they saw as the major cause of the crisis.[17] We do not hear as much about Asian values today.

Even within ASEAN, though, some voices were more relaxed about the principle of nonintervention. In the late 1990s, for example, Malaysia's deputy prime minister Anwar Ibrahim and Thailand's foreign minister Surin Pitsuwan were moved by events in their region to suggest that for ASEAN to remain effective and relevant, it might be necessary to relax the principle of noninterference in the domestic affairs of fellow ASEAN members. Anwar Ibrahim called his approach "constructive intervention," while Surin Pitsuwan called his "flexible engagement."[18] Neither made much headway in persuading their ASEAN counterparts. As a regional organization, ASEAN remains rather cautious about relaxing the norm of nonintervention in regional diplomacy. This said, it should be acknowledged that such reservations are not universally and uniformly shared among Third World states, as the normative shifts in the African Union discussed in Chapter 5 suggest.

Overall, we do not see the developing world as opposed to extending the referent of security to the individual. Even ASEAN is showing signs of warming to the idea. M. C. Abad, an adviser to the secretary-general of the organization, has written about "The Challenge of Balancing State Security with

Human Security."[19] The concerns and arguments of regional organizations such as ASEAN are not without merit. Their arguments raise the difficult question of which referent to privilege and at which point in time. In some cases, what is needed is the strengthening of the state in order to provide public goods such as security and order. Political scientist Samuel Huntington observed as far back as the 1960s that in the absence of strong political institutions, widening political participation would lead to political disorder.[20] Even the *Human Security Now* report acknowledges that the "state remains the fundamental purveyor of security."[21]

But the worries of Third World leaders that taking individual rights seriously would open their states to external interference and intervention are probably overblown. In a world where even Myanmar's generals can rest assured that they are unlikely to be deposed by external military force, the threshold for external intervention in the name of human security is so high that only the most murderous of states need worry. We therefore view the argument for switching the referent of security from the state to the individual as one of the key promises of the human security approach, and we believe the change is more conducive to than it is disruptive of international order. Having detailed some of the achievements of the human security approach, we now turn to a discussion of its weaknesses and their implications for the future trajectory of the idea.

Whither Human Security?

In addressing the question Whither human security? it is important to situate the human security idea in its intellectual and policy context. For unlike the concept of genocide, which was created to capture a phenomenon for which there was no existing term, human security emerged in a context in which security was predominantly conceived of in national terms.[22] That is why the opening salvos of those who seek to redefine the concept, from Richard Ullman to the CHS report, aimed their sights at national security—the approach to security that privileged the nation-state and the use of military force/alliances to deter potential aggressors and defend the state's territorial integrity and political sovereignty if deterrence failed. As the proponents of human security acknowledge, "The national security paradigm [with its focus on protecting the state] continues to dominate international relations teaching and research as well as policy practice."[23]

The national security paradigm does seem to be dominant in the G-8 chairmen's summaries of the 2003 and 2004 summits. France's summary of the decisions taken at the Evian Summit in 2003, for example, was organized under four headings: Strengthening World-Wide Growth, Enhancing Sustainable Development, Improving Security, and Regional Issues. Human security was mentioned once as an item under Sustainable Development: "We took note of the report of the Commission on Human Security submitted to the United Nations Secretary-General."[24] This terse one-liner is surprising, because with Canada and Japan as part of the G-8, one would have expected a more involved and positive take on the CHS report. Proponents of human security would probably have liked to see all four of the headings subsumed under the human security umbrella in ways reminiscent of the arguments of the HDR 1994. That the human security report was merely noted, not even endorsed, suggests that the notion has yet to achieve a consensus among the G-8 and that as a group, they prefer to view the human security agenda as part of sustainable development. For the G-8, security was primarily about action plans to counter terrorism and the proliferation of WMD by states such as North Korea and Iran, as the later part of the summary showed.[25]

Similarly, the vast majority of scholars and analysts who teach and write about security—who are based mostly in political science or international relations departments in major universities, think tanks, and military academies—continue to think in national security terms. A select group of these individuals, most of them based in the United States, dominate the leading journals and university presses, thereby facilitating the replication of their approach to security among the younger generation of security studies scholars. These mainstream analysts have not neglected internal and identity conflicts, as some human security proponents assume. In fact, quite a few of the mainstream scholars caught on early and have produced influential works on, for example, how the security dilemma drives ethnic conflicts.[26] Others have sought to incorporate nationalism as part and parcel of their brand of realism.[27] Yosef Lapid and Friedrich Kratochwil have argued that these scholars have not only been quick to address issues of nationalism but are also seeking "inclusionary control"; that is, they seek to incorporate the study of nationalism as part of their security studies agenda so that they can shape the key questions and define the best methods to deal with these questions.[28] Their security studies courses are about national, not human, security. For better or worse, the Cold War—or rather, 300 years of accumulated scholarship on security—may have "hard wired" into these security analysts and professionals the notion that the kind of security that matters is national security. It is not our role to praise or condemn this state of affairs; we merely want to describe it to make the point that all alternatives will have to contend with this dominant view if they seek to complement, compete with, or dethrone it.

Proponents of human security have been rather reticent about engaging the mainstream analysts systematically. Consider, for example, a recent "state of the concept" briefing in *Security Dialogue* that involved twenty-one writers, including some of the concept's most prominent proponents. The bottom line seems to be that there is no consensus about the health, importance, and influence of the concept. Lloyd Axworthy believes that human security has established itself as "a vital part of the international agenda, complementing more traditional notions of nation-based security," while Fen Hampson is of the view that its proponents have failed to "mobilize the requisite level of resources and political support required for the many humanitarian, social, economic, environmental, and developmental challenges that threaten human security." Don Hubert disagrees with Hampson and cites the banning of land mines and the advent of the International Criminal Court as successes attributable to the concept, and he criticizes academics for rejecting it because it "worked in practice, but not in theory." Astri Suhrke, in contrast, argues that the human security initiative, which was championed by Canada and Norway as part of their bid for membership on the Security Council, "appears to have stalled" in the last two years.[29]

Absent from this debate are policymakers from the permanent five (P-5) and mainstream security studies scholars.[30] This is unfortunate because if the concept is to make further inroads into the contemporary security discourse, it should engage and bring on board more of these practitioners and analysts. This is especially urgent in the post–9/11 world. Without this engagement, the human security agenda will be at a disadvantage in making further progress in the shaping of contemporary security discourse and policy. While neither the G-8 nor the P-5 have given their corporate endorsement to human security as a concept, there are promising signs that individual states or issue-specific coalitions within these groupings have already adopted (aspects of) the human security agenda. Hence, G-8 members Canada and Japan are the most active advocates of the human security agenda, even though their emphases differ; the former focuses on "freedom from fear and violence" issues and the latter insists that "freedom from want" issues cannot be neglected. The UK and France—members of the P-5 and the G-8—were prominent and important members of the land mines process. The G-8's Africa Action Plan also reveals that the group is not averse to adopting aspects of the human security agenda in dealing with regional problems. Finally, even the United States has taken on board ideas of economic security—especially those relating to structural economic causes of conflict—in its development assistance policies.

We therefore see an opportunity to mainstream the notion of human security. At the policy level, it means getting more P-5, G-8, and regional organizations to buy into the concept; success would be reached when more aspects of the human security agenda (properly defined) are adopted by the major states and international and regional organizations. At the conceptual level, mainstreaming involves persuading more traditional security analysts of the analytical utility and the normative and policy ramifications of the human security approach. Conceptual success would go in hand with the induction into the community of human security scholars of more analysts such as Richard Ullman, the mainstream scholar who was among the first to argue in favor of redefining security, and the proliferation of articles and debates about human security in mainstream journals and presses.

The first steps in this process have been accomplished: proponents of human security have identified important blind spots in the concept of national security and put forward human security as the more normatively appropriate and analytically more relevant concept. Whether one believes that the idea has made important progress or has stalled in recent years, we believe that the next step is for advocates of the idea to engage in critical self-reflection to see if there are weaknesses in the human security idea, and if there are, how such weaknesses can be rectified. We would not recommend this step if we believed the human security approach to be fundamentally flawed; it is because we see its potential—and its current problems—that we feel the need for advocates of the idea to put their conceptual house in order before pressing ahead. We attempt such a critical examination in the next section.

Conceptual Overstretch and Its Consequences

Advocates of human security have performed a valuable analytical task by problematizing the uncritical privileging of the state in mainstream approaches to security. Once it becomes clear that human beings are the ultimate referents of security, it is also evident that threats to their well-being do not emanate solely from external military attack. Economic deprivation, ecological disasters, deadly diseases, and gender-based violence may be equally serious threats to the well-being of individuals. What are the weaknesses, if any, of this approach to security? Before addressing this question, it is useful to distinguish between the ways in which the human security idea has been put to use.

Conceivably, the human security concept has two purposes, which are not mutually exclusive. First, it may be used as an instrument in the policy battle for attention and resources. A securitized item, so the argument goes, goes right up the policy agenda. Conceptual coherence and meaningfulness are not critical in this usage because it functions as a slogan; its utility is judged by its effectiveness in, for example, capturing the "peace dividend." Analysts who have examined the effectiveness of this instrumental use of the notion are doubtful whether it has been successful in persuading states to divert significant resources from military security to items associated with human security.[31]

Second, the concept is more than a slogan. Its analytical advantage consists in switching the referent from the state to individuals and shifting the focus from military threats to the state to political, economic, environmental, and gender-based threats to individuals. The concept points to a blind spot of mainstream security analysts and policymakers. Revealing this blind spot and privileging the security of individuals facilitates movement on initiatives such as banning land mines and small arms. In other words, by refocusing the referent of security, the human security approach reminds states to accept certain universal norms concerning the protection of individuals within their borders.

Our analysis will focus on the second use of the human security approach because it is premised on the assumption that the concept is analytically coherent and powerful and able to generate positive policy payoffs. These are the grounds on which the concept seems poised to compete with national security approaches. We find that the human security concept comes with its own set of problems. The overriding problem is conceptual overstretch: the concept has been stretched to cover almost every imaginable malady affecting human beings; as such it has lost much of its analytical traction. Conceptual overstretch gives rise to three pitfalls: false priorities, confusion about the causes of human insecurity, and militarized solutions, which are discussed below.

Pitfall I: False Priorities and Hopes

"When the concept of security has been extended (a) horizontally to include economic, environmental, gender, and health issues, and (b) vertically upwards to include international organizations and downwards to individuals, the concept loses all its meaning and coherence." We have often asked our students to discuss this claim in their final examinations; what is our position? We believe the statement contains a kernel of truth and we shall try to uncover that by discussing the pitfalls associated with the horizontal extension of the concept.

The horizontal extension of the concept to almost everything that impinges on the well-being of individuals is primarily responsible for creating false hopes and priorities. For what is *not* a security issue if military, political, economic, ecological, health, and gender-related threats are all lumped together as the many dimensions of human security? And how does one prioritize among all these dimensions?

As noted in the introduction, a major rationale for attaching the label "security" to an issue is to suggest that it is an issue that deserves priority: it needs the focused attention of policymakers and it has prior claim to scarce resources. During the Cold War, security meant almost exclusively the military security of the state; attempts to extend the concept of security horizontally or vertically did not fall on receptive ears until the 1980s. Human and civil rights discourse—which made impressive headway in Europe and within the United States—was conducted without recourse to the label "security." And for good reasons: attempts to explicitly securitize the European Convention on Human Rights or voting rights for U.S. minorities would most likely have backfired. Pitted against the security imperatives of the Cold War state, they would have lost out.

Whatever the disadvantages of the narrow conception of security during the Cold War, it had the benefit of being very clear about the state's priorities: to deter and defend against external military attack. The assumption was that unless one could protect one's territorial integrity and political sovereignty against external encroachment, one's citizens would not be able to enjoy the fruits of a well-functioning economy, a good health system, a sustainable environment, or gender equality.[32] Soviet missiles landing in New York or Washington or American missiles exploding in Moscow or Vladivostok, even if they did not obliterate human life as we know it, would make a mockery of all these other "security" desirables (e.g., a good health system) that competed with state military security for priority.

This emphasis on state military security at the superpower level was replicated at the regional level by the allies and proxies of the two superpowers. Hence the "hot wars" in Asia (Korea and Vietnam); the military standoff between NATO and Warsaw Pact countries in Europe, OAS fears of "another Cuba" in its midst and of Cuban soldiers aiding Marxist revolutionaries in Central and Latin America, the wars in the Middle East, and the Angolan, Mozambican, and Ethiopian/Eritrean conflicts in Africa. Many Third World conflicts had domestic origins, but the Cold War overlay was such that the different sides would generally line up with one or the other of the superpowers. The involvement of the superpowers, more often than not, further militarized the disputes and the contention for state power.

Hence, for the superpowers, the vast resources—financial, human, intellectual, and even cultural—devoted to ensuring and enhancing bipolar stability stemmed from a conviction about its priority status. To give priority to protecting the military security of the state seemed then (during the Cold War) to be the logical policy to pursue. To be sure, while focusing on protecting the military security of the state, the superpowers also had to devote resources to managing the economy, health care, or the environment. But neither the United States nor the Soviet Union characterized issues of the economy, health, and environment as security issues—to do so would have only added confusion to the complicated task of maintaining military security.

A weakness of the human security discourse is willful amnesia about conflict between states as a threat to the values they seek to protect. The claim has often been made that intrastate war and intrastate violence (which is often perpetrated by the government against its people) have claimed more victims than interstate war in the twentieth century.[33] As Andrew Mack, director of the Centre for Human Security at the University of British Columbia, puts it, "In the twentieth century, far more people died as a consequence of the actions of their own governments than were killed by foreign armies."[34] This claim is correct, but the focus on the number of casualties is misleading in two senses. First, the numbers by themselves are not meaningful. Four hundred thousand Americans die every year from smoking-related diseases, but we do not brand smoking as a human security issue. Al Qaeda terrorists killed nearly 3,000 individuals on September 11, and we all agree that the attack is a state and human security problem.

Second, the numbers game begs the question of what was responsible for "low" casualty levels stemming from interstate conflict, especially in the post-1945 period. Could it be that policymakers have finally learned from previous wars and know more about what deters war? If the United States and Russia had not been so focused on balancing each other militarily, might we have witnessed general wars of the kind we saw in the first half of the twentieth century, this time with a nuclear component? In other words, the world of "low" casualties from interstate war is one in which a certain conception of "national security" prevailed. The nuclear powers consciously traded "human security" for "national security." The latter implied a certain kind of military statecraft: nuclear and conventional deterrence among the superpowers and their allies. To be sure, the strategy brought us two "limited wars" in Asia and numerous interventions by the superpowers in other parts of the world, but it also brought us nuclear stability and arguably prevented a direct military clash—the norm in previous bipolar international systems—between the two superpowers. In other words, the fact that "more were killed by their own governments than foreign armies" does not mean that the prevention of interstate conflict is less important or urgent than preventing intrastate conflicts.

A second weakness of the horizontal extension of the notion of human security that also affects its ability to prioritize is the issue of redundancy. Andrew Mack puts it better than most:

Much of the literature on the broad concept of human security is simply an exercise in re-labeling phenomena that already have perfectly good names: hunger, disease, environmental degradation, etc. There has been little serious argument that seeks to demonstrate why "broadening" the concept of security to embrace a large menu of mostly unrelated problems and social ills is either analytically or practically useful.[35]

An analogy to air travel may be useful in articulating the difficulty of prioritization brought about by the horizontal extension of the concept. For many airlines, the luggage of business-class passengers—who pay four to five times the economy fare—are given a priority tag upon check-in. At the destination, these passengers expect their luggage to be among the first to arrive on the carousel. If the airlines were to tag everyone's luggage priority, there would be no way for the handlers to distinguish between those belonging to business-class or coach-class passengers. The luggage would appear randomly at the destination. Business-class passengers would get irritated and switch airlines while some economy passengers would luck out. Or, as one critic of the iPod's ability to hold 10,000 songs put it, "If you can listen to everything, you may end up hearing nothing."[36]

In the world of public policy, the consequences of being unable to prioritize are more serious. All issues cannot be given the priority tag. It matters greatly that policymakers have the ability to discern those that demand priority from those that can wait. It may mean the difference between survival and obliteration. It is not being suggested here that protecting the military security of the state is the only obvious security issue; our point is that the horizontal proliferation of issues that are deemed deserving of the security label creates a situation analogous to that of giving every passenger's luggage a priority tag. The result is an inability to prioritize, or the creation of false priorities. It is not enough for advocates of environmental security, for example, to claim that the environment is a security issue. Like proponents of military security during the Cold War, such advocates need to make their case. How serious a threat to national or individual security would environmental degradation be and how does this rank in relation to other security issues? An approach that lumps together as human insecurity the danger faced by Bosnian Muslims in the former Yugoslavia, the risk to Venetians as a result of rising water levels in the Adriatic, and health risks posed by the depletion of the earth's ozone layer has little value.

Pitfall II: Causal Confusion

While it is possible to treat and mitigate the symptoms of human insecurity, an effective long-term solution must depend on knowledge about its causes.

The problem with putting too many items under the human security umbrella is that it confuses, rather than clarifies, the causes. That is, if military, economic, environmental, health, and gender-related threats to the individual are all lumped as threats to human security, that makes the task of isolating the causes of these threats all the more difficult. This point has not been systematically made and we believe it is important to elaborate on it here.

A major reason for clear delineation of topics of investigation within a discipline is to obtain clarity about how A causes B, or A → B. When B was state/military security, it was difficult and controversial enough. Yet progress was possible because there was a consensus about the outcome to be understood or explained (B = nuclear stability). Thus, during the Cold War, U.S. and Soviet policymakers understood that the condition of MAD was conducive to nuclear stability: insofar as each had the capability to inflict "unacceptable damage" on the other after absorbing a first nuclear blow, both parties would be deterred from initiating an actual nuclear attack on the other. Although the requirements of MAD would constantly evolve—engendering an arms race between the superpowers—both sides felt that they had knowledge of what it took to maintain nuclear stability. In so doing they succeeded in maintaining state and military security.

When B is everything, A becomes impossible to figure out. In other words, throwing everything into pot B renders the outcome to be understood vague and imprecise, and that makes the analysis of A difficult. Why lump economic privation, environmental degradation, gender inequality, and AIDS together as human security threats when their meanings are perfectly clear without the security label? Why economic or health security when economic privation or AIDS will do? Moreover, by incorporating everything under B, A also becomes greatly expanded and what we get is a mishmash of causes. This detracts from the enterprise of understanding the causes of human insecurity.

It is important to understand the separate causes of insecurity because some of the causes may be more amenable to amelioration than others. For example, if one finds that low economic growth leading to economic privation in some parts of the world is primarily due to reluctance or inability to plug into the globalization process, it is unclear what analytical leverage is obtained by characterizing this reluctance as a threat to human security. Labeling it as a policy with human security implications might force politicians to devote more attention and/or resources to it, even though Andrew Mack argues that there are not "many examples of this happening in practice."[37] Even if Mack is wrong, the securitized issue will get more attention only if the advocates of the other issues—the environment, health, gender— do not attach the label of security to their issues and demand equal or greater attention. When everyone embellishes his or her favorite issue with the security label, we are back to confronting the dilemma of how to prioritize among the many causes.

Our point is this: attaching the label of security to an issue does confer the potential that it will get more attention and resources, but this is a praxis-motivated move that does not add to analytical clarity. Quite the contrary. When it is done indiscriminately, it confuses matters because it lumps discrete phenomena with discrete causes under the umbrella of human insecurity. There are many gradations of human insecurity, ranging from hungry stomachs to physical danger to psychological unease. To lump all of them together as security problems detracts from the search for their respective causes.

Pitfall III: Securitization and Military "Remedies"

For better or worse, security problems often imply forceful and military responses. That was how national-military security problems were construed for much of the Cold War, and the traditional responses have involved the military—arms acquisitions, national military service, the formation of alliances, and the stationing of military personnel and hardware in faraway locales. Even at the international level, a similar logic is at work. The term "security" has also been reserved for issues related to the use of force: when a state has acted in ways that threaten international peace and security, the Security Council may invoke Chapter VII, Article 42, which authorizes the UN to use military force to alleviate or solve the problem. At least in the case of intervention under UN auspices, an international consensus must be obtained via the Security Council before the use of force is considered legitimate.

Because states already have a tendency to associate issues with the concept of security so that they can bring force to bear, the human security approach, by introducing and legitimizing a whole new set of issues (e.g., the environment) that can be securitized, may unwittingly lead to military solutions to political or socioeconomic problems. In a perceptive analysis that warns against the oversecuritization of threats, Volker Franke gave examples of how "[s]ecuritizing everything from nuclear missiles to miniskirts and pop music (as in the case in the former Soviet Union, Iran, or the Taliban's Afghanistan) suffocates civil society, jeopardizes democracy, and creates coercive states whose only legitimacy stems from countering increasing security threats."[38] The U.S. government's approach to drug trafficking from Latin America, for example, was heavily securitized from the onset. Under Plan Colombia, the U.S. provided military aid to the Colombian government so that it could interdict the drug traffickers more effectively. According to Franke, U.S. military aid "intensified militarization and provoked a surge in rural violence ... [and] U.S.-backed crop fumigation is destroying small-scale agriculture and highly biodiverse rainforest ecosystems." Hence "policy measures designed to boost U.S. security pose immediate and severe threats to the economic, political and environmental security of the population in that region."[39] Monica Serrano has also written about how the U.S. "war against drugs" led to predominantly military responses with dubious efficacy.[40]

Similarly, crime has become such a serious security problem in Dhaka, the capital of Bangladesh, that Prime Minister Khaleda Zia called in the army to "aid and guide" the police in a nationwide crackdown on crime. While the measure was popular and effective—at least temporarily—in reducing crime, concerns about the truncation of human rights, including the imprisonment of journalists and professors sympathetic to the opposition, have been raised. There are also real concerns about the dangers of immersing the army in societal ills such as crime; calling in the army may undermine democracy, with the army assuming a "national guardianship" role as in countries such as Turkey.[41] As these examples suggest, advocates of making nonmilitary issues security issues may be getting more than what they have bargained for. Or, as Keith Krause and Michael Williams put it, using the example of linking the environment to security:

> Making the environment a national security issue may subvert the goal that proponents of this change seek to achieve. Environmental issues pose significant and pressing dangers, but placing them on the security agenda means subsuming them within concepts and institutions of state security (that is, military responses against a particular "target") that are unlikely to further the agenda of "environmental security."[42]

Human Security as Freedom from Organized Violence

The preceding analysis of the promise and pitfalls of the idea of human security and its various manifestations raises the following question: Is there a way to mitigate the pitfalls while retaining some of the more promising features of the concept? Roland Paris has argued that attempts to improve the analytical utility of the concept are unlikely to be successful because the idea is more a slogan and rallying cry than an analytical notion; moreover, its advocates are keen to keep it vague and comprehensive as a means of uniting the coalition.[43] Paris proposes a taxonomical solution: categorize human security in as one of the four subfields of security studies so that each subfield can be left to its own devices in terms of the central questions, methods, and solutions. He proposes a two-by-two "matrix of security studies" where cell 1 (top left-hand corner) is about military threats to states; that is, the domain of conventional/national security studies. Cell 2 (top right-hand corner) is mainly "non-military threats (instead of, or in addition to, military threats) to . . . states" such as those stemming from the environment and economic scarcity. Cell 3 (bottom left-hand corner) is about military threats to groups within the state; that is, intrastate conflicts such as civil war and ethnic strife. Human security belongs to cell 4 (bottom right-hand corner), which focuses on nonmilitary threats, such as those stemming from environmental degradation to groups and individuals within the state.[44]

Paris's matrix is a bold and helpful attempt to order the various approaches to security studies. Critics of human security may find Paris's relegation of human security to cell 4 deserved, but advocates of the concept will take issue with his arbitrary exclusion of threats in cells 2 and 3 from the human security agenda. Advocates of the concept of human security may be more circumspect about the state, but they acknowledge that the state remains a critical provider of security. Hence they are interested in confronting nonmilitary threats (e.g., economic stagnation) to the state (cell 2) because a "failed state" will have serious implications for those within it. Human security proponents will find the exclusion of military threats against groups and individuals (e.g., Bosnia and Rwanda; cell 3) from their remit even more contentious. A major strand of human security concerns is about the prevalence of intrastate conflicts in the contemporary world and the need to protect such groups and individuals caught up in, or targeted by, those who initiate and seek to gain from such violence. Paris's matrix is controversial, but it helps us make our point: the human security agenda encompasses three of the four categories of security studies. Only interstate war seems out of its remit; everything else is in. Such a broad concept, we have argued, borders on the incoherent. Since we are interested in exploring ways to render the concept more coherent and improve its analytical traction, we will leave the taxonomic approach and embark on a definitional exercise. The task is to see whether it is possible to pare down the security threats that fall within human security's remit without diminishing the concept's relevance and significance.

Two challenges confront those who seek conceptual clarity and analytical traction. The first challenge is whether to accept the sine qua non of the human security approach, that human beings are the most appropriate or irreducible referent of security. Many mainstream national security analysts continue to reject this "vertical (downward) extension" of the referent from the state to the individual on the grounds that every conceivable human malady then becomes a security problem. We believe that this is a legitimate concern and that those, like us, who accept that the referent of security should be human beings must address the concern. The second challenge is to delineate and justify the scope of threats that qualify—on analytical grounds—as threats to human security. Too inclusive an approach will mean the loss of analytical traction; too narrow an approach will mean fixating on military-state security and an inability to comprehend the nature of many of the post–Cold War threats. Can a happy medium be struck? At this juncture in our argument, we owe it to the reader to give it our best try. We proceed by confronting the two challenges described above head on. The conception of human security advanced below is not immune from anomalies or weaknesses, but we have strived to be explicit about our conceptual procedures and commitments. Whether our approach constitutes progress can perhaps be assessed by the extent to which our notion of human security succeeds in mitigating or avoiding the problems of prioritization, confusion about causes, and military remedies discussed above.

Human security, we argue, is about freedom from organized violence. The converse is more easily grasped: humans are insecure insofar as they are in danger of being injured, maimed, or killed by those who organize to harm them. Those who organize to harm are always individuals or a collection of individuals. What moves the latter—whether it is raison d'etat, ideological/ religious fanaticism, ethnic hatred, refusal to brook dissent, or just plain revenge—is less important than the fact they possess the capability and intention to inflict physical harm. The graver the physical harm and the larger the number of people affected, the greater the human insecurity. Others before us have proposed that freedom from violence is central to the idea of human security.[45] Freedom from violence is important, but we also want to direct attention to the source of that violence—a perpetrator—and what makes that violence potent—it is organized. Central to our notion of human (in)security is the existence, out there, of some entity or set of individuals who are organizing to do us in.[46] That is why, despite the massive casualties and horrendous destruction wrought by the tsunami waves of the December 2004, tidal waves are not usefully construed as a human security problem whereas Al Qaeda's premeditated attack against workers in the World Trade Center and the Pentagon is.

Our notion of human security accepts that human beings are the most appropriate referent of security. Put differently, we find the downward extension of the concept from the state to the individual analytically useful and appropriate. Some might argue that this vertical extension robs the concept of security of some analytical value. We acknowledge the danger, but we believe that this risk is more than balanced by an important gain: an approach that focuses on people. Settling on the abstract individual as the referent also means we are wary of efforts to prioritize groups (e.g., women, children, IDPs) because that risks reducing the value of the claims of other types of individuals.

The reification of the state—privileging state security over the security of individuals residing within it—was a result of specific historical circumstances. Changed circumstances require a renegotiation of the position of the individual vis-à-vis the state. Put another way, we may say that the events of the twentieth century have nudged analysts and practitioners toward a recovery of the older understanding of what the state was supposed to do. The principal gain in this movement is that the state is no longer automatically privileged.

While reversing the balance of attention in the individual's favor (at the state's expense) is a healthy corrective, it is important not to overdo it. First, excessive focus on the individual may disempower the state and prevent it from doing what it is supposed to do.[47] The challenge is to find the balance by expecting states to do what they are supposed to do and helping them do it when they cannot (or will not). Second, the derogation of state sovereignty implicit in the human security discourse (especially the protection of individuals) may also erode the principle of nonintervention—which has played a historically useful role in facilitating international stability—and lead to excessive military interventions. Third, there is also the danger that states may employ the discourse of protection in order to legitimize actions they want to take for other reasons. In other words, proponents of human security should be wary about demonizing the state: it remains crucial in delivering the goods, though its legitimacy will always be judged by how well it provides for the physical security of those who reside within it.

Why confine the scope of human security threats to those posed by organized violence? Because as the referent of security expands from "the state" (191 UN members in late 2004) to "humans" (6 billion), there is no other way to impose analytical order on the concept other than what should or should not count as a security threat. When food shortages, deadly diseases, economic privation, environmental degradation, lack of political freedom, and threats to personal and community safety are all considered threats to human security, a huge chunk of humanity is construed to be "imperiled" in the security sense. The broadness and vagueness of these "threats" make it conceivable for almost every individual to be experiencing some form of "security threat." Such an approach risks falling into the three pitfalls discussed above. The office of one of the authors is situated alongside a busy bus route that has been reckoned to be one of the most polluted in England. Being in that part of the city for twenty-four hours, according to research by the clean fuel supplier Calor, is equivalent to smoking sixty cigarettes.[48] The air is certainly polluted, but does that mean that one of us is experiencing human insecurity daily and is oblivious to the danger? If the author with the polluted office is deemed to be facing a security threat, the concept has been stretched to the point of absurdity; such a definition suggests that any and every disturbance of our well-being is a security threat. Under such a formulation, we would all be under some form of a security threat most of the time. The concept becomes, as Lyndon Johnson put it, like grandma's nightshirt: it covers everything. In so doing, it also becomes meaningless and analytically useless.

Hence for those interested in salvaging some meaning and use for the concept of human security, there is a need to distinguish between the maladies that impinge on our well-being and those that threaten our physical survival. This is of course not an either/or distinction. It is more useful to think of it in terms of a continuum of well-being with one extreme (say on the left) representing complete well-being and the other extreme (the right-hand side) representing physical extinction. In our formulation, only threats closer to right-hand side of this continuum qualify as potential threats to human security. Note that even at this corner of the continuum, there are still distinctions to be made between the sources that threaten our physical integrity. Many things can take the life out of us but not all of them are usefully construed as security threats. Our physical integrity can be threatened by our immediate and not-so-immediate surroundings every minute of our existence. Electrical objects, sharp table corners, sunshine, smoking, crossing the road, hurricanes, that midnight knock on the door, and being in a hijacked plane can all threaten our physical integrity in fundamental ways. But few would claim that all these should be considered threats to human security.

The question then is which of the above litany of threats have the best claim to being threats to human security? Only the last two, we argue. Worldwide, tens of thousands of people, especially infants and the elderly, are hurt or killed daily by accidents involving electrical and sharp objects at home. But no serious analyst would consider these household objects to be threats to human security, despite the fact that they cause bodily harm to more individuals than, say, the Gulf Wars of 1990–1991 and the ongoing war in Iraq. The same is true of sunshine (which can cause skin cancer), smoking (whose link to lung cancer is undisputed), crossing the road (where there is always a chance of being knocked down by an oncoming vehicle), and hurricanes: they may kill us, but they are not threats to our security, commonly understood.

We reserve threats to our (individual) security for a different class of phenomena; those exemplified by the midnight knock on the door and the hijacked plane. Consider the midnight knock on the door, the classic fear of individuals living in a police state of being taken away in the middle of the night, tortured, and never heard from again. In this case, the threat to my physical integrity comes from other individuals—the secret police, the Red Guards, American marines, machete-wielding Interahamwe in Rwanda—not inanimate objects or acts of nature. They are almost always acting at the behest of some ideology or executive order, but the victim knows that he or she is likely to be harmed, if not done in. Thus, an important part of our notion of a human security threat is that the source (of insecurity) has to be another individual or individuals. This criterion rules out sharp table corners, tsunami waves, and earthquakes as security threats.

Equally important, the agents of insecurity are organized (e.g., SAVAK, the shah of Iran's secret police, was part of the state apparatus) or they organize themselves (as Red Guards did during the Chinese Cultural Revolution) to hurt people or do them in. The importance of the organization criterion is that it excludes spontaneous individual acts of violence such as road rage or crimes of passion. To be sure, the road rage victim hit by a pipe or the errant lover electrocuted in the bathtub by his jealous partner's hair dryer are just as dead or physically damaged as those forced to jump from high buildings by the Red Guards. But it is the organization that amplifies the ability of the perpetrator to inflict widespread and deadly damage. Without an organization behind him and the ability to coordinate among financiers, suppliers, and allies, the "lone" terrorist would not pose much of a security threat. He would not be able to procure his "dirty bomb," much less detonate it in London or Los Angeles. It is this factor that pushes a threat to the right-hand corner of our continuum of well-being and physical extinction.

Admittedly, conceiving of human security threats as organized violence goes against the trend of the horizontal broadening of the concept advocated in the *Human Development Report 1994* and the CHS 2003 report. The latest manifestation of this broadening agenda can be seen in the HLP report of 2004. It uses human security terminology but seems to go even further by resurrecting the notion of collective security, arguing that it is collective security that needs to be broadened and made more comprehensive so that it incorporates both new and old threats.[49] The report identifies six clusters of threats: economic and social threats such as poverty, infectious diseases, and environmental degradation; interstate conflict; internal conflict; WMD; terrorism; and transnational organized crime.[50] Interestingly—perhaps reflecting the composition of the panel—threats with a strong military dimension seem to have made a comeback, although not at the expense of the economic and social threats.[51] This something-for-everyone approach is, in our view, further complicated by the revival of the term "collective security." Given the dismal record of collective security in responding to interstate aggression during the 1930s and the Cold War, we are very dubious about its efficacy in dealing with the six clusters of threats identified by the HLP report.

Readers will have to decide for themselves whether our approach allows the focus and analytical traction that we find lacking in these three reports and whether those gains are worth the costs of not considering issues such as underdevelopment, HIV/AIDS, and environmental degradation as security issues. The fact that our approach does not consider the latter to be security issues does not mean that they are unimportant or unworthy of significant resource allocations. Far from it—HIV/AIDS, for example, has killed more people since the 1980s than the combined fatalities of all interstate wars since 1945. Saving those infected with HIV/AIDS and devoting the maximum feasible resources to containing the disease must be a priority for governments, NGOs, and the UN.

But HIV/AIDS is a health, not a security, issue. It does not involve individuals organizing to harm other individuals or do them in. It is possible to portray HIV/AIDS as a security issue by arguing that by decimating a significant percentage of a nation's working-age adults, the disease brings about economic dislocation and weakens the state, thereby making the state vulnerable to internal insurrection and external predators.[52] This may be true in some countries, but the role of HIV/AIDS is several steps removed from the final outcome of organized violence. Moreover, whether a country with a serious HIV/AIDS problem will experience conflict depends on a host of other factors, including whether domestic insurgents are opting to use force, the strength of its political institutions, the abilities of its leaders, the strategic calculations of its neighbors, and the interests of other, more distant powers. HIV/AIDS, in other words, may be only one of many relevant factors in fostering violent conflict. When combined with some of the other relevant factors, it may result in a violent outcome; but when combined with a different set of relevant factors (and perhaps in different proportions), the outcome may be placidness and resignation.[53]

The same "several steps removed from the final outcome" problem affects the "root causes of conflict" argument discussed in Chapter 4. In that chapter we traced the arguments of those who saw poverty, inequality, and lack of economic opportunity as important factors that contribute to instability and who portrayed policies that address these economic maladies as security policies. Economic deprivation is undoubtedly correlated with instability and conflict (how strong that correlation is is a matter of dispute), but so are the political and regional variables mentioned earlier. If it is easy to point to cases where poverty and inequality foster conflict, it is just as easy to identify cases where, despite poverty and inequality, conflict was absent. What this suggests is that the peculiar mix of economic, social, political, and international variables that combine to produce conflict remains poorly understood. In formulating our notion of what constitutes security, we have attempted to distance our concept from factors that are susceptible to this "twice removed from the final outcome" problem. In fact, our approach has been to sidestep (though not totally avoid) the causal sequence. The notion of organized violence hones in on two things, whether there are individuals out there with the capability to harm us and whether they are planning and organizing to harm us. (Although it would be nice to know why; it is not essential.)

The "individuals organizing to injure and kill other individuals" criterion would count the following as threats to human security: genocide, internal/civil wars, terrorist attacks, interstate war, ethnic cleansing policies, organized mass rape, torture, and the laying of land mines. Although this is by no means an exhaustive list, what is common to all these cases is the existence of an actor or actors (e.g., states, ethnic, or religious groups) who organize or are organized to inflict physical harm on other individuals. Although the number of individuals harmed tells us about the magnitude of the violence, it is not the numbers themselves that make it a security issue. It is organized individuals with the capability and intent to injure and kill that constitutes the quintessential security threat. That is why it is intuitively clear that the United States and Russia posed a grave security (and existential) threat to one another during Cold War. Their war plans include raining down nuclear missiles on one another to destroy significant percentages of the enemy's population and industry. Similarly, Slobodan Milošević's use of the Serbian army to "cleanse" and eliminate Bosnian Muslims in Bosnia-Herzegovina in the 1990s was a grave human security issue.

In addition to narrowing the scope of security threats to a manageable and coherent range, the focus on organized violence also comes with an analytical insight: if it is sentient individuals organizing to kill that constitutes the core security problem, we can conceivably concoct strategies to deter such individuals and their organizations or at least make it more difficult for them to act. In other words, it seems possible to respond to such security threats by going to the source. Dealing with the source is either impossible or ineffective when it comes to earthquakes, tsunami waves, or incompetent economic policymakers who impoverish their fellow citizens. This prospect of changing or preventing the behavior of the potential perpetrator is not essential to our notion of security, but it gives an added coherence and analytical traction to the concept.

For some, the analytical gains come at too high a price. Objecting to the exclusion of economic insecurity from our approach, they point to the notion of "social security" and the way it has become an accepted part of our vocabulary to show that our criterion of organized violence is unduly restrictive.[54] The passing of the Social Security Act in the United States in 1935 shows that under certain conditions (the Great Depression), it seems appropriate and effective to characterize fears of economic privation—whether in old age or as a result of unemployment—as a "social security" problem. President Franklin Roosevelt named the group of advisers who worked toward the idea of social security the Committee on Economic Security.[55] And today it is second nature to Americans to speak of their mixture of unemployment, retirement, and health benefits as social security.

Indeed, the notion of social security demonstrates that making socioeconomic issues security issues was intuitively compelling and politically effective in the 1930s. But it is also the case that the "security" in social security has little analytical function. The more widely used descriptors of the program are "social insurance" and "social welfare." This can be seen from the indices of works on social security, which often include "insurance" and "welfare" but almost never "security" as a stand-alone descriptor, suggesting that it is the welfare/insurance aspects of "social security" that do most of the analytical heavy lifting.[56] This also explains why outside of the United States, few countries characterize their unemployment and retirement schemes as social security. The preferred description seems to be pensions or insurance. It is not risky for wealthy countries such as the United States to make socioeconomic well-being a security issue because they possess the resources to match the expectations associated with the security rhetoric. As such, the gap between rhetoric and expectation is minimized. For the less wealthy, there are good reasons to avoid securitizing economic well-being. Unemployment and retirement benefits are good things to have, but characterizing their absence as a security threat is likely to widen the gap between expectations and reality. That is one reason why few countries have adopted the label of social security for their unemployment and pension policies. One turns them into security issues at one's own risk.

More important for our purposes is what happened to the term "security" after 1935. Even if the 1920s and 1930s facilitated the wide acceptance of the economic aspects of security, the onset of World War II forced the issue of military security to the top of the international agenda. Unemployment and retirement benefits, while always important to those in need, became less urgent in face of fascist dictators with the capability to attack and overrun their neighbors. The Cold War strongly reinforced this emphasis on military security. In other words, for half a century, from 1939 to 1989, events conspired to equate security with military security. Understanding the way events of the past fifty years have shaped the meaning of security is essential for those who seek to change its contemporary meaning. That is why we believe that in order to succeed, it is essential that proponents of human security arrive at an analytically coherent and appropriately circumscribed notion. The national security way of thinking about security remains dominant and deeply ingrained among mainstream analysts and the great powers.

Another advantage of the organized violence criterion is that it goes further than the UNDP and CHS approaches in building bridges to mainstream thinking on security issues. Protecting the individual from violence is analogous to protecting the state from military attack. In that sense, our notion of human security is akin to national security. National security is about protecting the state from military attack or violence, as when the state's territorial integrity is encroached upon. Human security is about protecting individuals from violent intrusions upon their bodies. Interstate war, terrorism, mass rape, and torture are thus all human security issues because the physical integrity of the potential victim is at risk. In each of these cases, it is the action of an adversary state, terrorists such as Al Qaeda, and/or political groups within states that threatens the physical integrity of the individual. Freedom from this kind of violence—threats against bodily integrity by organized groups that aim to do us in—constitutes human security.

In his perceptive analysis of the notion of human security, Kanti Bajpai observed that "realism's appropriation of the term security rests on the assumption that interstate war is the greatest threat to personal safety and freedom. This may or may not be the case, at any given time." It was the case during the Cold War in an existential sense: if interstate war had broken out between the two nuclear-armed superpowers, there was a distinct possibility that humankind would be obliterated. In that sense, the insecurity associated with the nuclear revolution was felt at the global, state, regional, and individual levels. In the post–Cold War world, this fear of nuclear obliteration has receded. The new maladies and fears had to do with civil war, ethnic cleansing, genocide, terrorism, environmental deterioration, and HIV/AIDS, to mention the most prominent. For Bajpai:

> The expansion of the term security to include a larger set of threats and violence is without doubt discomfiting. Where exactly to draw the line is unclear. What human security proponents have suggested . . . is that security is larger than conventional conceptions would allow. How much larger is the subject of further research. . . . A human security audit should reveal which components are truly important.[57]

We agree in the main with Bajpai. Returning the focus/referent of security to humans is a necessary move, but in order to maintain the coherence and usefulness of the concept, proponents of the concept should be explicit about where they would draw the line. Bajpai believes that a "security audit" would help in deciding where to draw this line. In contrast to Bajpai, we believe that no amount of research can give a clear indication where the line is because the issue is an ontological and a philosophical one. We have made our premises explicit: in our world, the gravest security threats to individuals are acts of violence that are planned and perpetrated by leaders of organized groups (state elites, functionaries, outcasts, or nonstate actors such as terrorists). Hitler's plans and actions against the Jews of Europe; the delicate balance of (nuclear) terror during the Cold War; the genocidal policies of Pol Pot, Slobodan Milosevic, and the Rwandan government; and Al Qaeda's plans and actions worldwide undoubtedly qualify as threats to human security.

Even with these gravest of threats to human security, states and the international community have often remained aloof until the last moment or the killings are over. To throw into this pot issues such as the threat posed to individuals by environmental degradation or unemployment is to commit what Robert Jackson has termed a category mistake.[58] We believe that environmental degradation, unemployment, and infectious diseases are important causes of human misery and that significant resources should be deployed to prevent and eliminate them. But it is a mistake to make these issues security issues, a mistake that not only dilutes the meaning of a useful concept but also complicates the process of prioritizing the more deadly threats to human beings.

9/11 and the Return of the National Security State?

In recent years, passengers who patronize one of Heathrow's restaurants have been confronted with a placard that reads: "We apologize to all of our customers, but for security reasons, metal cutlery is no longer permitted airside." The reason why patrons of the restaurant have to make do with plastic forks and knives is clear. The aim is to deny terrorists an easy source of weapons which they can use—in the same way that the 9/11 hijackers used box cutters—to hijack planes and crash them into high-value and symbolic targets. What makes it easy for us to accept those "security reasons" in this case is knowledge about the existence of organized individuals who are able and willing to kill us as a way to further their goals. The fact that the chances of our being killed by terrorists this way are much smaller than dying in a car accident does not make it less of a security threat.

Using plastic cutlery in airport restaurants is a minor inconvenience. For most, the perceived gain—however slight—in additional security makes it worthwhile. This mundane example of the impact of 9/11 on our existential security raises the question of how 9/11 has affected the human security discourse. Have 9/11 and subsequent events reinforced the insights and policy proposals of the human security approach or have they been a setback to human security by bringing back national security as the number one security imperative?

The murder of close to 3,000 innocent workers from sixty-eight nations at the World Trade Center illustrates the indiscriminate nature of the threat. Al Qaeda and its affiliates elsewhere (e.g., Southeast Asia) do not just threaten Americans or Christians; non-Americans, Muslims, and others are all equally susceptible if they happen to be at the wrong place at the wrong time (e.g., Bali). In this sense, 9/11 and its aftermath reinforce the salience of the idea of human security. As *Le Monde* put it on its front page on September 12, "We are all Americans now."[59] By that the editors meant that all of humankind was under threat from the kind of violence perpetrated by Al Qaeda.

But Al Qaeda did focus its wrath on Americans and the symbols of American economic, military, and political power. It targeted the World Trade Center, the Pentagon, and Capitol Hill (the plane that crashed in rural Pennsylvania was en route to Capitol Hill). The American state and those who lived and worked within it were the primary targets of Osama bin Laden and his associates. America's allies and friends, whether they were Australians holidaying in Bali or Spaniards riding the train to work, were also targeted. The way the United States and others have responded to the terrorist threat is reminiscent of the (Cold War) national security state, where protecting the state is the first line of defense and becomes synonymous with protecting the individuals within it. The notion of "homeland security" reveals a heightened sense of the primacy of territorial defense. The Patriot Act, the creation of a Department of Homeland Security, the appointment of an intelligence czar to oversee all the intelligence agencies have concentrated power in the executive to an unprecedented extent.

Human rights groups bemoan this augmentation of state power and the dangers that it poses to individual rights and liberties. In September 2002, UN High Commissioner for Human Rights Mary Robinson, who characterizes the 9/11 attacks as crimes against humanity, criticized U.S. antiterrorism measures for curtailing human rights at home and abroad. Robinson cited the "use of immigration laws to detain foreigners within its borders for indefinite periods, the racial profiling of people of Arab descent in searches and the prosecution of American citizens as enemy combatants, limiting their rights to legal representation" as examples of infractions of human rights.[60] The return of the national security state also manifests itself in the execution of the two post–9/11 wars: Afghanistan and Iraq. The former was justified in terms of self-defense and going after the perpetrators, a justification accepted by the international community as evidenced by Security Council resolution 1368. The U.S. justifications for going to war in Iraq, namely that Saddam Hussein was in breach of UN regulations in possessing weapons of mass destruction and that he had links to Al Qaeda, were less convincing, and the war was not sanctioned by the UN. "Regime change" in Iraq, the U.S. denial of Geneva Convention protection to fighters captured in Afghanistan and Iraq, and the abuse of the Abu Ghraib prisoners indicate that the American intention to protect "homeland security" may be giving short shrift to the international norms essential in upholding human rights and human security.

Mary Robinson has also lamented the ripple effect of the U.S. position on other countries. Foreign governments with problematic human rights record lost no time in pointing to the United States, reminding her that "standards have changed"[61] when she questioned them about their policies. Witness also the alacrity with which countries such as Russia and China have characterized their respective Muslim dissidents, the Chechens and Uyghurs, as terrorists threatening state security and sovereignty. Even in Britain, the police conducted close to 100,000 house searches under the Prevention of Terrorism Act. According to Robin Cook, Muslim households have borne the brunt of these raids, which, "in the nature of raids looking for suspect terrorists, . . . are often accompanied by the drama of the front door being broken down and the men of the household spread-eagled on the floor." As a former foreign secretary who sought to pursue an ethical foreign policy that focuses on human rights, Cook's verdict on these raids was heavy with sarcasm: "This offensive to trace the enemy within has netted a grand total of seventeen convictions, most of them [having] nothing to do with terrorism."[62]

As the above examples indicate, the imperative of protecting the post–9/11 state reverses some of the momentum of putting human beings first. That imperative, felt most keenly by the United States and its allies[63] but also by states in the "second front" in Southeast Asia, including Indonesia, Malaysia, Thailand, Singapore, and the Philippines, has implications for international relations. Astri Suhrke puts it well: "Terrorism and wars in Afghanistan and Iraq have crowded the policy agenda, and Washington's revival of the early Cold War doctrine of 'either you are with us or you are against us' leaves little room for a coalition of states . . . to promote the security of individuals."[64]

Suhrke's observations reflect the malaise that some feel has descended upon the human security approach since 9/11. Her points are worth reflecting upon because they impinge on the future of the human security idea. First is the issue of Washington. Suhrke points to an assumption we have made throughout, namely that for the idea of human security to compete successfully with the idea of national security, the major—not just middle—powers must buy in. For the purposes of our analysis, the major powers may be construed as the five permanent members of the Security Council, with the United States being the primus inter pares. Wounded and angry, the United States is not in the best condition to move the human security agenda forward, not in the least because some of its own policies—within and outside its borders—may be at odds with putting humans first.

Second, Suhrke's point about antiterrorism crowding the UN policy agenda is revealing. It reinforces the point about America's ability to dominate the UN agenda, and it suggests that when it comes to security, organizations such as the UN and states such as the United States are usually forced to deal with what they perceive to be *the* consuming threat, to which much of their economic, military, and diplomatic resources are devoted. It is clear that the consuming threat for the UN and the United States has not been human insecurity since 9/11. Suhrke has written that her search of the UN database for "Human Security Network" in UN documentation found a total of three entries since 2001.

Third, interstate war is not obsolete, as the cases of Afghanistan and Iraq suggest. The postinvasion difficulties the United States and its allies experienced in Iraq suggest that further preventive wars against Iran, North Korea, and Syria are probably not on the horizon, but none of these states are counting on American restraint. These developments suggest that the CHS report's call for "shielding people from acute threats and empowering people to take charge of their own lives"[65] may prove more challenging than anticipated in the post–9/11 world.

Conclusion

"The state continues to have the primary responsibility for security." So states the CHS report, although it quickly moved, in the next line, to qualify the assertion: "But as security challenges become more complex and various new actors attempt to play a role, we need a shift in paradigm. The focus must broaden from the state to the security of the people—to human security."[66] There is a confusion here between the referent of security (human beings) and the provider of that security (states still have primary responsibility, although other actors are welcome). We agree that the focus must broaden from the state to the security of the people when it comes to the referent, but we are wary of broadening the notion of the provider from the state to human beings. We are wary of throwing the baby out with the bathwater.

It is a positive development to chip away at the state's claim that it is the ultimate referent of security. We believe that the recovery of the individual is a good normative and analytical move. If we agree that human security is about protecting individuals from organized violence perpetrated by others, the question of who we count on for protection arises. The primary answer, as even *Human Security Now* acknowledges, is "states." This answer is endorsed by the more recent report of the Secretary-General's High-level Panel on Threats, Challenges and Change: "If there is to be a new security consensus, it must start with the understanding that the front-line actors in dealing with all the threats we face, new and old, continue to be individual sovereign states."[67]

However, many no longer see states as the end object of security. What this means is that states can no longer form a cocoon around themselves and do whatever they like within that cocoon on the grounds of national security. But it would be erroneous to jump from this to the conclusion that states are no longer the primary providers of (human) security. We need to be careful about undermining the capacity of the state to do its job.

We recognize that our approach is more selective in what it includes under the rubric of human security. But we feel that that is necessary if the concept is to be salvaged and if it is to have any analytical coherence. Our notion allows us to avoid the three pitfalls discussed earlier. By retaining the individual as the referent but by omitting threats that would normally fail the "organize to harm" test, our definition is exempt from the criticism that by covering everything, all meaning is lost. Natural disasters, accidents, diseases such as HIV/AIDS or SARS, and economic privation, for example, are not considered to be threats (or at least grave threats) to human security. They fail the "organized harm" test—tsunami waves, traffic accidents, the spread of viruses, and crop failures are usually not organized by individuals to do their victims in. The issue of prioritization also becomes more tractable because of our restricted focus. Preventing interstate and intrastate war, terrorism, genocide, and human rights abuses such as torture are all issues of the first magnitude for advocates of this approach to human security.

This notion of human security is also theoretically more coherent. In terms of the A → B terminology used earlier, the causes of—though different—have been reduced to a tractable few, and they are related: A can be states, transnational terrorists, or political leaders, but they all share a similar trait, the propensity to inflict violence on others. The policy question is thus similar: How can they be persuaded to desist, deterred, neutralized, or, in extreme cases (such as terrorists), eliminated? The answers will be different depending on whether the perpetrators of violence are states, authoritarian leaders, or terrorists. Different literatures exist on how to prevent interstate war, deal with authoritarian rulers, and track terrorists.

Third, the danger of adopting political and military responses to deal with problems of human insecurity becomes less of an issue. This is because such problems all involve perpetrators who organize to harm; responses that rely on security forces are appropriate and necessary. States with unfriendly neighbors will need matching armies, hardware, and perhaps allies to protect themselves. Without these instruments of deterrence, the basic security of their citizens would be at risk. Governments or leaders who prey on their own citizens for ideological or ethnic reasons are also in danger of forfeiting their sovereignty: the Security Council may authorize the use of force—as in Somalia and Bosnia—to safeguard the security of individuals at risk. Finally, when nonstate actors such as Al Qaeda organize to murder innocent civilians, the use of "all necessary means" to counter such terrorists is both necessary and legitimate.

Finally, in addition to the ability to mitigate the three pitfalls, our notion of human security also goes further in engaging the mainstream analysts who have sought to move beyond explanations of interstate conflict to an understanding of intrastate conflict. Mainstream analysts should find our focus on organized violence akin to their interest in interstate and intrastate conflict.[68] The main difference between us and the mainstream is the referent of security: we view internal wars as a human security problem because we seek clarity about *who* is to be protected, or security for *whom*. Asking these questions prevents us from putting the state—or the existing power holders—on a pedestal; it also clarifies what is at stake should international intervention be called for. Mainstream analysts, in contrast, are less interested in the referent than in the phenomenon of war—whether interstate, intrastate, or between states and nonstate actors. When large numbers of human beings are threatened, injured, or killed by organized violence, it is war, and war is the quintessential security problem. Thus there need be no major tension between the human security approach we suggest here and the mainstream's version of what is a security problem. What the mainstream may have reservations about is the normative impetus behind the human security approach. The case for switching the referent from the state to humans is based in part on the normative assumption that it is right to place human beings at the center of security studies. Mainstream analysts would not deny that, though they would prefer to make a stronger separation between the normative considerations that inform their interest in war and the positive or value-free analysis of its causes and effects.[69]

In sum, the notion of human security proposed here retains an important role for state or military security. In an imperfect world, military security remains a first line of defense if one is serious about preserving the security of one's citizens. One of the most serious weaknesses of the many attempts to define human security is the omission of this traditional dimension. However, our notion also recognizes that the ultimate referent of security has to be the individual. Consequently, states, leaders, societies, or nonstate actors who seek to physically harm the innocent become legitimate targets for forceful dissuasion. Those who allow their environment to degrade, who refuse to recognize the gravity of the HIV/AIDS pandemic, and who are not competent in economic planning are causing a different kind of "human insecurity." Although their misdemeanors inflict serious harm and misery on their subjects, few would advocate invoking Chapter VII and using force to change their ways.

Conclusion

- **Human Security**
- **The Role of the UN**
- **So What?**

In this book, we have attempted to tell two stories. One concerns the evolution of the relationship between the individual, the state, and international society as it relates to the response to threats to individual security. In the post–Cold War era, this evolution has been encapsulated in the idea of human security. However, the themes underlying this contemporary idea are as old as international relations themselves. The second focuses on the role of the United Nations in this evolution. More specifically, how has the organization participated in and influenced this evolution? What does this tell us about the significance of the UN as an incubator, promoter, legitimizer, and vehicle for implementation of ideational change?

Human Security

> The United Nations was created in 1945 above all else "to save successive generations from the scourge of war"—to ensure that the horrors of the World Wars were never repeated. Sixty years later, we know all too well that the biggest security threats we face now, and in the next decades ahead, go far beyond States waging aggressive war. They extend to poverty, infectious disease and environmental degradation; war and violence within States; the spread and possible use of nuclear, radiological, chemical and biological weapons; terrorism; and transnational organized crime. The threats are from non-State actors as well as States, and to human security as well as State security.   —High-level Panel on Threats, Challenges and Change, 2004[1]

In Chapter 1, the point of departure was that the irreducible locus of sovereignty is the human individual. To recall the citation from Charles Tilly that begins that chapter, historically states have largely been justified in terms of their protection of individuals and communities from harm. When the state was problematized, its claim to loyalty was often justified (and its merit often judged) in terms of its capacity to fulfill its responsibility to protect, its willingness to do so, and its performance in so doing. When it could not, or did not, protect its citizens or those resident within its borders, many considered that its sovereign right could justifiably be challenged, either by rebellion from below or, and more contentiously, by intervention from outside.

As discussed in Chapter 1, in the medieval period, although the divine right of the sovereign was frequently claimed and defended, this recognition was often tempered by recognition of obligations on the part of rulers to their subjects and consequent limitations on their power. In modern history, absolute sovereignty pertaining to the state on organic or other grounds was often claimed but frequently contested. Even at its apogee in the nineteenth and early twentieth centuries, the reification of the state was never complete. In liberal theory, the rights of states were balanced against those of individuals. In international law, a set of weak societal constraints emerged on the behavior of states and their agents in war and, internally, toward their minority populations. These normative constraints grew in complexity and strength during the first half of the twentieth century and during the Cold War, when international humanitarian law and its application to internal conflict was clarified in significant ways. More broadly, the period of the Cold War laid down important foundations for the subsequent architecture of human security in the internationalization of human rights norms.

That the normative framework for considering individual security developed at this time in the way it did reflected significant changes in the historical context of the modern state and national and individual security. War became more lethal and engaged ever-larger numbers of people. It became more difficult to insulate civilian populations from the application of force. In some instances, the instruments of the state were used systematically to persecute or murder certain categories of defenseless citizens, with devastating consequences. Normative change that recognized human beings as subjects of international law and international relations was, in some measure, a response to the changing quality of threats to individual human beings and the evolving quality of the relationship between the state and the individual.

The hundred years or so preceding the end of the Cold War also evinced a growing appreciation of the relationship between economic well-being and security. In the late nineteenth century, the nascent social safety nets of European industrial states were conceived in part to address the possibility that widespread impoverishment would produce internal insecurity. The New Deal response to the Great Depression reflected awareness of the threat of social instability rooted in lack of economic opportunity. The drafters of the UN Charter recognized the profound importance of dealing with freedom from want and freedom from fear if a durable peace was to be established. However, making welfare a security issue was not just instrumental; in a more essentialist vein, freedom from want joined freedom from fear as recognized fundamental rights of human beings.

During the Cold War, the trend toward including matters of what has come to be seen as human security in the debates of international forums and in conventions was accompanied, paradoxically, by a further strengthening of norms concerning sovereignty and nonintervention. Also, the protection of human beings was far more impressive on paper than in reality. The paradox is explained in considerable measure by the sensitivity of the recently decolonized emerging majority from the South in the General Assembly to challenges to state sovereignty. It also reflected the constraint imposed by bipolarity on the use of Chapter VII of the Charter and the jealousy with which the superpowers guarded their own sovereignty and their spheres of influence.

The humanizing of security accelerated dramatically in the post–Cold War era. This reflected evolving technological processes and patterns in the international economy that were frequently associated with the concept of globalization. These drew into question the capacity of states to protect their populations. Perhaps more significant, the acceleration of ideational change reflected the disappearance of bipolar competition as the leitmotif of international relations and the consolidation of the hegemony of liberalism in international society. The disappearance of bipolarity was a key condition that enabled the maturation of the idea of human security.

The emerging idea of human security had four fundamental aspects. One was an emphasis on the role of the individual as the ultimate referent of security. The rationale for a preoccupation with the security of individuals, although it maintained its instrumental component (if threats to individuals are not addressed, they will result in social and political instability and conflict), was increasingly based on an essentialist ethic (people are entitled to freedom from fear and want because of their status as human beings).[2] A second was a broadening in the conception of the individual endowed with equal rights to include, more explicitly, women and children and the internally displaced. To put it another way, the notion of the contracting individual was universalized through the inclusion of groups whose rights had in the past been denied (women) or largely ignored (children). The third was the broadening in the conceptualization of threats to individual security highlighted in the quotation that begins this section. The historical preoccupation with violence was joined by an increasing insistence that economic, health, and environmental threats were potentially just as or more deadly and that they should be inserted more completely into discourse about security. This was associated with a gradual reconceptualization of development that moved the focus away from macroeconomic aggregates and toward the lives, fortunes, and possibilities of individual human beings, particularly the economically vulnerable.

The first two aspects enjoy broad agreement among proponents of human security. The third is contentious. Although all proponents of human security accept that both freedom from want and freedom from fear are fundamental human rights, some place the emphasis squarely on protection from violence while others emphasize development issues in their consideration of human security.

There is no intrinsic reason to favor narrow or broad conceptions of human security. It is self-evidently true, for example, that disease and poverty kill more people than does armed conflict. The content and meaning of human security or, for that matter, national and international security are not objectively fixed but are a matter of contestation, not least because the word "security" is ineradicably value laden. However, in our view the merits of the narrow and broad positions on human security can be judged in terms of analytical value added and policy consequences.

In the first instance, it is not obvious what additional analytical traction one gets from redefining human development or health or environmental issues as security issues. Human development, for example, is itself a useful concept. Its emergence is a significant development in humanizing economic policy. Reconceptualizing development in human terms has had concrete and positive impacts for many vulnerable people. The effort to associate it with security presumably reflects an effort to attract resources (e.g., the peace dividend) to the development enterprise. If that is so, then there is little evidence that it has worked. The exercise, in our view, not only fails to add analytical value, it actually detracts from it. The indiscriminate expansion of the scope of security threats stretches the concept to the point of incoherence and meaninglessness. When every human malady is construed as a security threat, nothing is a security threat. For these reasons, we prefer the narrower conception that focuses on protection of individuals from threats of organized violence. Here there is significant movement in the translation of ideational change into normative change and, somewhat less clearly, the translation of normative change into change in the practice of international institutions and states.

The evolving normative landscape of human security raises important questions about the role of the state in security. Have we moved from a situation where the state is the principal guarantor of the security of human beings to one in which other institutions (local, regional, and universal) take on this role? The answer to this question is quite clear: No.

The basic issue common to the reports of the ICISS, the CHS, and the HLP is what to do if states fail to fulfill their fundamental purpose of protection. The answer in these reports, and in most of the broader literature on human security, is that when states and governments fail as a result of incapacity or malign intent to do what they are supposed to do, international society and its institutions have a right and a responsibility not only to protect victims but also to restore states to a position where they do what they are intended to do. Human security is not about transcending or marginalizing the state. It is about ensuring that states protect their people. When they do not, it is about ensuring that there are international mechanisms that can fill the gap ad interim and redesign states so that they will fulfill their purpose in the future. In this respect, it involves a qualification of sovereignty; the rights of sovereign states are conditional upon those states' compliance with international expectations regarding the protection of human beings.[3]

As we have suggested at various points in this volume, this questioning and gradual redefinition of sovereignty is a consistent quality of human security discourse. Here, although we are sympathetic to the principles underlying this problematization of sovereignty, we feel that insufficient effort has been made to flesh out and understand the potential negative consequences of such redefinition. Qualification of sovereignty along these lines may make it more difficult for weaker states to maintain order and achieve the political consolidation necessary for development. It clearly weakens the principle of nonintervention and may produce disorder and attendant suffering. The qualification of sovereignty on human security grounds may be used to legitimize aggressive actions by states against other states, as was evident in the Anglo-American invasion of Iraq. Even with the best of motivations, the postconflict reconstruction of shattered states is a complex, difficult, and long process. The commitment of resources over the long term may be difficult to sustain. The record of such efforts arguably suggests that international institutions are not very good at constructing sustainable, effective, transparent, and accountable state structures.

The Role of the UN

The second thread in this analysis focuses on the significance of the United Nations and other institutions in this development. What was the UN's role in this evolution of ideas and norms? Was it "ahead of the curve"? The answer to this question is mixed. We have seen how UN agencies such as the UNHCR, UNICEF, and UNIFEM played central roles in getting particular issues (refugee issues, the rights of children and women, and human security itself) onto the agenda for discussion. UN-organized conferences (e.g., the Beijing conference) were of great significance in clarifying issues, providing a platform for advocacy, and consolidating coalitions around particular issues. The Secretary-General's reports on women, children, conflict prevention, and the protection of civilians were extremely influential in engaging the Security Council and its key members on central aspects of the human security agenda. The United Nations (both the Security Council in the case of the ICTY and the ICTR and the General Assembly in the case of the ICC) has played a central role in the establishment of judicial institutions intended to deal with the problem of impunity. In the case of humanitarian intervention, the Secretary-General again played a seminal role in pushing things forward by publicly holding states to account in the event that catastrophes such as those in Rwanda and Bosnia recurred. The situation in Darfur at the time of this writing suggests that success here is decidedly modest. In other instances (e.g., the evolution of the laws of war and the ban on antipersonnel land mines), the UN bodies were marginal to, and sometimes dysfunctional in, the process.

Moreover, where matters proceeded toward norm- and institution-building in the area of human security, the key motivating force in the 1990s appears (ironically) to have been, in a number of instances, interested states (e.g., Canada's role in pushing the Security Council toward resolutions 1265 and 1296) or complex entrepreneurial coalitions of interested states, nongovernmental civil society networks, and UN agencies (e.g., the ICC, the agendas that addressed the issues of women and children in conflict, and the ban on land mines). Perhaps the most interesting and significant development in this process of ideational change was the development of coalitions between like-minded states, nonstate actors, and international agencies around human security issues.

The UN (and notably the Security Council, but to a lesser extent the General Assembly) also played a fundamental role in legitimizing the changing preferences of states regarding the protection of individuals. And, finally, it is in the procedures and practices of UN agencies that one sees the most sustained, if still limited, efforts to implement the conclusions of human security debates, as is evident in the issues relative to children and women and in the focus of peacekeeping and peace enforcement mandates and training on the fate of human beings.

Before going on, we should stress the limits on the embrace of human security in international society. Among states, one could easily contrast the seemingly endless reflection on and advocacy of the concept in Canadian, Norwegian, and Swiss documents with the apparent absence of either in the United States.[4] In states that do promote the concept (e.g., Canada), there appears to be a wide variation in enthusiasm among relevant agencies within the state.[5] While Japan sponsored the report of the Commission on Human Security, there was little evidence of any significant debate on the subject within the Japanese academic community and civil society and no obvious effort by government agencies to interrogate the concept. Recognition of the concept is limited in humanitarian agencies within the United Nations, particularly outside New York and Geneva.[6] In the humanitarian community, it is striking that in the two most recent substantial accounts of the humanitarian enterprise in the 1990s, there is no entry on human security in the indexes.[7] And there is little if any recognition of the notion of human security in the dominant strand of security studies. The attacks of 9/11 on the United States and the subsequent struggle against international terrorism have also affected the effort to embed human security in the mainstream security discourse. While they reinforce the message about the importance of human security in our globalized world, they have also brought state and military security back in ways that detract from individual liberty and security. In this context, states, especially the great powers, clearly reserve the right to defect from elements of their human security commitments when it suits them to do so. The U.S. questioning of the applicability of the Geneva Conventions and abandonment of its commitments on the issue of torture in the context of the war in Iraq and Russia's flouting of a wide range of its international commitments (including the laws of war, CSCE and OSCE commitments, and international and regional conventions on torture) in the context of its war in Chechnya are clear examples.

So What?

David Rieff, in criticizing the interventionist strand of liberalism, wrote:

> [I]t seems to me that too often the basis for . . . optimism is not an improvement in people's lives but an improvement in human rights norms. And to me it remains not just an open question, but a question that desperately needs to be asked, what this has actually accomplished for people in need of justice, or aid, or mercy, or bread, and whether it has kept a single jackboot out of a single human face.[8]

The analysis in his work suggests that his answer is negative. Although he provided no methodological basis for answering his questions (after all, one cannot know what would have happened in the absence of the liberal enterprise, let alone compare that alternative history to the one we have lived), Rieff does point to an obvious and disturbing discrepancy between ideational and practical development in the area of human security, as we also do at several points in this volume. His questions are well worth asking. We do not deny the importance of that gap, although we do contest the extremity of Rieff's conclusion.

However, the gap between norms and practice was not our subject. Our primary question was not how ideas are reflected in practice but how and to what extent ideas related to human security have evolved over time. Is there evidence in international society of a rebalancing of the place of the individual and that of the state in the consideration of security? If so, how has this affected understandings of sovereignty, domestic jurisdiction, and international obligation? In short, we are interested in whether, as compared to earlier periods in history, there is evidence that the idea of human security is becoming embedded in international relations.

The answer to this question is, fairly clearly, affirmative. Questions regarding the relationship between the state and the individual and the prerogatives of state power have been present to varying degrees since the advent of political organization of society. Consideration of the rights and obligations of states with respect to suffering within the territory of other states has been with us to varying degrees throughout the history of modern civilization. The state's monopolization of discourse on security is a product of a particular set of historical circumstances: the modern state's rise to preeminence as the principal form of political community and nationalism's associated rise as the dominant doctrine of community. In most theories of the state, the state is justified in terms of its capacity and will to protect its citizens. However, as our discussion of slavery, intervention, and the laws of war in the nineteenth century suggests, this dominance, although extremely strong, was not absolute even then. Individuals continued to have (minimal) rights in international relations and the society of states continued (weakly) to claim a right to interference in domestic jurisdiction when these rights were seriously transgressed. The first half of the twentieth century was one in which the purview of international obligation with respect to individuals and groups within states gradually expanded.

The Cold War era was crucial in laying the normative groundwork for a focus on the human being in security. Largely, but not exclusively, in the UN context, numerous declarations and conventions greatly expanded the sphere of international competence regarding the rights of individuals within states and identified state obligations in the treatment of those who lived within their borders. Protections and obligations in the laws of war were extended to internal conflict. There was growing consideration of, and action upon, the economic rights of individual human beings. These instruments were weak and lacked effective enforcement mechanisms, largely as a result of the bipolar competition between East and West and the value new states attached to sovereign rights. Consequently, the impact of these evolving norms was modest.

In the 1990s there was an explosion of activity around the concept of human security. By the end of that decade, it was widely accepted, and recognized in Security Council resolutions, that the security needs of individuals were a significant and legitimate area of concern for states and international organizations. This transformation involved not merely human beings per se but groups that were deemed particularly vulnerable. The concept of sovereignty was to an extent qualified by what came to be known as a responsibility to protect. As Security Council resolutions 1265 and 1296, inter alia, suggest, when the state was unwilling or unable to fulfill its responsibilities, it was increasingly accepted that international society had obligations with regard to individual victims. Discourse on security expanded in functional terms beyond threats of physical violence to individual and community economic security. Many came to see the health of individuals and their environmental conditions as significant security challenges.

In other words, and looking across the long historical spectrum, we see a rediscovery of the individual as a subject or referent in security, a return in considerable measure to the proposition that the security (and the sovereignty) of the individual is paramount and that states can justify their claim to pre-eminence in the area of security only on the basis of their success in addressing the protection needs of their citizens. This rediscovery exists not only in the scribblings of idealistic academics but in an impressive body of international legislation, from conventions and treaties through Security Council resolutions, and in national laws.

It exists not just in words but has also manifested itself in the practice of states and international institutions. The procedures and practices of the UN and regional organizations, the mandates of peace support operations, the training of military forces involved in such operations, the nature of peace settlements, the behavior of donors and aid organizations, and the production and use of some weapons have all changed.

Perhaps a comparison between 1900 and 2000 is helpful here. In 1900, there was no significant qualification of the sovereignty of states as it related to their own citizens. Now there is. In 1900, there was no consensus about the legitimacy or acceptability of intervention in the affairs of other states when they systematically persecuted their own citizens. There is now evidence that such a consensus may be emerging. There was no international interest in the rights of women or children and how these were affected by conflict. Now there is. There was no question that the recruitment of children to fight in wars was acceptable. Now it is not. There was little significant effort to limit weapons which were particularly destructive of civilian life. Now there is. There was no significant consideration of issues other than military matters as significant aspects of security. Now there is. We may be a long way from utopia, but we are also a long way away from the unchallenged dominance of the state as the principal referent of security.

To return to Rieff's position, the question is not really a matter of optimism or pessimism but a matter of empirical analysis. There has been a profound change in how security is conceived by international organizations and states. This evolution has recognized the security needs of individuals and the responsibilities of states and organizations in attending to those needs. There has been a substantial accretion of norms designed to put that changed understanding into practice. It is reasonable to suppose that this evolving normative framework is reasonably durable in the face of shocks such as the advent of the threat from terrorism.

We are far short of the full implementation of evolving ideas and norms surrounding the notion of human security. Yet there now exists a framework for the international protection of human beings and for holding to account states that fail in their responsibilities in this area. This framework is unlikely to encourage the abuse of people; it is more likely (imperfectly) to deter such abuse. How far the process goes in altering the practice of states and nonstate actors remains to be seen.

Notes

Foreword

1. High-level Panel on Threats, Challenges and Change, *A More Secure World: Our Shared Responsibility* (General Assembly document A/59/565), 2 December 2004, available online at http://www.un.org/secureworld/report.pdf, accessed 3 January 2005.

2. Lloyd Axworthy, "Human Security and Global Governance," *Global Governance* 7 (January–March 2001): 23.

3. Robert McNamara, "An Address on the Population Problem," MIT, Boston, 1977.

4. Commission on Global Governance, *Our Global Neighbourhood* (Oxford: Oxford University Press, 1995); Commission on Human Security, *Human Security Now* (New York: Commission on Human Security, 2003).

5. Lewis Carroll, *Alice's Adventures in Wonderland and Through the Looking Glass* (Baltimore, Md.: Penguin Books: 1972), 274.

6. Kofi A. Annan, *The Question of Intervention—Statements by the Secretary-General* (New York: United Nations, 1999) and *We the Peoples: The Role of the United Nations in the 21st Century* (New York: United Nations, 2000). For a discussion of the controversy surrounding the speech of September 1999, see Thomas G. Weiss, "The Politics of Humanitarian Ideas," *Security Dialogue* 31 (March 2000): 11–23.

7. For an overview, see Mohammed Ayoob, "Humanitarian Intervention and International Society," *Global Governance* 7 (July–September 2001): 225–230; and Robert Jackson, *The Global Covenant: Human Conduct in a World of States* (Oxford: Oxford University Press, 2000).

8. "What Is 'Human Security'?" special section of *Security Dialogue* 35 (September 2004): 347–371, quotes at 347 and 351.

9. Louis Emmerij, Richard Jolly, and Thomas G. Weiss, *Ahead of the Curve? UN Ideas and Global Challenges* (Bloomington: Indiana University Press, 2001), xi.

Introduction

1. Commission on Human Security, *Human Security Now* (New York: Commission on Human Security, 2003), 2.

2. Sadako Ogata, "State Security—Human Security," The Fridtjof Nansen Memorial Lecture, 12 December 2001, 2, available online at http://www.humansecurity-chs.org/activities/outreach/Nansen.pdf, accessed 5 October 2004. See also Arnold

Wolfers, *Discord and Collaboration* (Baltimore, Md.: Johns Hopkins University Press, 1962), Chapter 10; Fen Hampson, John Hay, Jean Daudelin, Todd Martin, and Holly Reid, *Madness in the Multitude: Human Security and World Disorder* (Toronto: Oxford University Press, 2001), 14; and Sadako Ogata, "Globalization and Human Security," Weatherhead Policy Forum, Columbia University, 27 March 2002, 1.

3. Keith Krause and Michael C. Williams, *Critical Security Studies: Concepts and Cases* (London: University College of London Press, 1997), ix.

4. The distinction between vertical and horizontal expansion of security is drawn from Emma Rothschild, "What Is Security?" *Daedalus: Journal of the American Academy of Arts and Sciences* 124 (Summer 1995): 55. For a more general but insightful discussion, see Barry Buzan, *People, States, and Fear: An Agenda for International Security Studies in the Post-Cold War Era* (London: Harvester Wheatsheaf, 1990).

5. Lloyd Axworthy, "Introduction," in *Human Security and the New Diplomacy: Protecting People, Promoting Peace,* edited by Rob McRae and Don Hubert (Montreal and Kingston: McGill-Queen's University Press, 2001), 10. Lest this be dismissed as a purely Canadian phantasm, a leading German analyst of security issues noted similarly that "at the centre of new security thinking in post-international politics is what UN Secretary-General Kofi Annan has called 'human security.'" Hans-Georg Ehrhart, "What Model for CFSP?" Chaillot Papers no. 55 (Paris: EU Institute for Security Studies, October 2002), 17. See also Commission for Human Security, *Human Security Now,* Chapter 1 passim.

6. Louis Emmerij, Richard Jolly, and Thomas G. Weiss, *Ahead of the Curve? UN Ideas and Global Challenges* (Bloomington: Indiana University Press, 2001).

7. Ibid., 3.

8. Ibid., 1.

9. It is curious that while the authors of *Ahead of the Curve?* cite as evidence of the influence of the UN on ideas the fact that numerous Nobel Prize winners in economics have spent part of their careers as UN staff members, they do not mention similar attention paid by Nobel committees to the peace and security apparatus of the UN. UN staff members, state representatives to the UN, and the UN and its specialized agencies have won nine Nobel Prizes for Peace for work in the general area of security (Ralph Bunche, Lester B. Pearson, Dag Hammarskjöld, UN peacekeepers, the UNHCR twice, the International Labour Organization, UNICEF, and Kofi Annan with the UN as a whole). These have been awarded not only for specific achievements in particular conflicts but also for bringing new ideas to the table, such as peacekeeping, and for activities in the economic and social spheres that were seen to have contributed to international peace.

10. Emmerij, Jolly, and Weiss, *Ahead of the Curve?,* 4.

11. See Peter M. Haas, "Introduction: Epistemic Communities and International Policy Coordination," *International Organization* 46 (Winter 1992): 1–36.

12. See, for example, UNDP, *Human Development Report 1994: New Dimensions of Human Security* (New York: United Nations Development Programme, 1994); and UNHCR, *The State of the World's Refugees 1997* (Geneva: United Nations High Commissioner for Refugees, 1997).

13. Emmerij, Jolly, and Weiss, *Ahead of the Curve?*, 6. See also Robert Jackson, *The Global Covenant: Human Conduct in a World of States* (Oxford: Oxford University Press, 2000), 103.

14. These four possible influences of ideas on practice are taken from *Ahead of the Curve*, 13.

15. As Nicholas Thomas and William Tow put it, "In order for human security to be advanced, at least in the short term, it must be embodied by states that overwhelmingly remain the predominant agents of international relations in our time." "Gaining Security by Trashing the State? A Reply to Bellamy and McDonald," *Security Dialogue* 30 (September 2002): 381.

16. *Ahead of the Curve?* defines "global challenges" as "problems that are widely perceived as sufficient threats to upset the economic and social (and eventually also the political) balance worldwide." Emmerij, Jolly, and Weiss, *Ahead of the Curve?*, 14.

17. "One cannot grasp the sense and application of a rule if one misunderstands the context in which it emerged and in which it produces its effects." François Bugnion, *Le Comité International de la Croix-Rouge et la protection des victimes de la guerre* (Geneva: Comité International de la Croix-Rouge, 1986), 3.

18. For a summary account of the recent literature addressing the role of ideas in international relations, see Emmerij, Jolly, and Weiss, *Ahead of the Curve?*, 7–10. For an earlier but extremely useful account of the significance of ideas in human behavior, see Karl Mannheim, *Ideology and Utopia: An Introduction to the Sociology of Knowledge* (London: Routledge, 1991).

19. Emmerij, Jolly, and Weiss, *Ahead of the Curve?*, 8.

20. We are speaking here of wars between the great powers in Europe. Wars conducted by the European powers outside that region were frequently far less discriminating and often had severe consequences for civilians who got in the way.

21. For a useful discussion, see Karma Nabulsi, *Traditions of War: Occupation, Resistance, and the Law* (Oxford: Oxford University Press, 1999), 48–52, 57–59.

22. For a summary of these developments, see William H. McNeill, *The Pursuit of Power* (Chicago: University of Chicago Press, 1982), Chapters 6–8.

23. Rudolph Rummel, *Death by Government* (New Brunswick, N.J.: Transactions Press, 1994).

24. K. J. Holsti, "The Coming Chaos? Armed Conflict in the World's Periphery," in *International Order and the Future of World Politics*, edited by T. V. Paul and John A. Hall (Cambridge: Cambridge University Press, 1999), 302.

25. See Robert H. Jackson, *Quasi-States: Sovereignty, International Relations and the Third World* (Cambridge: Cambridge University Press, 1990).

26. By globalization, we mean "processes whereby many social relations become relatively delinked from territorial geography, so that human lives are increasingly played out in the world as a single place." Jan Art Scholte, "The Globalization of World Politics," in *The Globalization of World Politics*, edited by John Baylis and Steve Smith (Oxford: Oxford University Press, 2001), 14–15.

27. Cross-border environmental problems are not new. However, they are more severe in the era of globalization.

28. An outbreak of severe acute respiratory syndrome in 2003 took the lives of 750 victims. The viral disease started in Asia and spread to more than twenty countries, infecting about 8,000 people before it was contained.

29. For an influential discussion of the changing character of war in the post–Cold War era, see Mary Kaldor, *New and Old Wars: Organized Violence in a Global Era* (Cambridge, UK: Polity Press, 1999). For a critique of Kaldor's argument, see Mats Berdal, "How 'New' Are 'New Wars'? Reflections on Global Economic Change and War in the Early 21st Century," *Global Governance* 9 (October–December 2003): 477–502.

30. For a more complete argument, see S. Neil MacFarlane, "Politics and Humanitarian Action," Occasional Paper no. 41 (Providence, R.I.: Thomas J. Watson Jr. Institute for International Studies, 2000), 27–30; and Mark Frohart, Diane Paul, and Larry Minear, "Protecting Human Rights: The Challenge to Humanitarian Organizations," Occasional Paper no. 35 (Providence, R.I.: Thomas J. Watson Jr. Institute for International Studies, 1999). For data on forced displacement, see UNHCR, *The State of the World's Refugees 2000* (Oxford: Oxford University Press for the UNHCR), Annex 3, available online at http://www.unhcr.ch/pubs/sowr2000/annexes.pdf, accessed 5 October 2004; and UNHCR, *Refugees by Numbers,* 2003 ed. (Geneva: UNHCR, 2003), available online at http://www.unhcr.ch/cgi-bin/texis/vtx/publ, accessed 5 October 2004.

31. For a discussion of the meanings of the term "complex emergency," see Cindy Collins and Thomas G. Weiss, *Humanitarian Challenges and Intervention,* 2nd ed. (Boulder, Colo.: Westview Press, 2000), 4–8; and Andrew Natsios, *U.S. Foreign Policy and the Four Horsemen of the Apocalypse: Humanitarian Relief in Complex Emergencies* (Washington, D.C.: Center for Strategic and International Studies, 1997), 6–14.

32. On this point with regard to the United States, see David Malone, "US-UN Relations in the Security Council in the Post-Cold War Era," in *U.S. Hegemony and International Organizations,* edited by Rosemary Foot, Neil MacFarlane, and Michael Mastanduno (Oxford: Oxford University Press, 2003), 81.

33. On the formation and role of epistemic communities, see Peter M. Haas, ed., *Knowledge, Power, and International Policy Coordination* (Cambridge, Mass.: MIT Press, 1992), originally a special issue of *International Organization* (46 [Winter 1992]). Two examples suffice here: the role of Sadako Ogata in the Commission on Human Security and the move of Andrew Mack, founding director of the Strategic Planning Unit in the Secretary-General's office, first to Harvard and then to the University of British Columbia to continue work on operationalizing the concept of human security.

34. See, for example, UNDP, *Human Development Report 1994: New Dimensions of Human Security*; and UNHCR, *State of the World's Refugees, 1997* (Oxford: Oxford University Press, 1997). The United Nations University has adopted the slogan "Advancing Knowledge for Human Security and Human Development" and has oriented a considerable portion of its research funding efforts within and outside the organization in this direction.

35. Note, for example, Canada's role in sponsoring the International Commission on Intervention and State Sovereignty and Japan's sponsorship of the Commission on Human Security.

36. E-mail communication with UNDP official, 9 October 2002.

37. Interview with Jeff Crisp, UNHCR, July 2002.

38. High-level Panel on Threats, Challenges and Change, *A More Secure World: Our Shared Responsibility* (General Assembly document A/59/565), 2 December 2004, available online at http://www.un.org/secureworld/report.pdf, accessed 3 January 2005.

39. UNDP, *Human Development Report 1994: New Dimensions of Human Security*, 3.

40. Department of Foreign Affairs and International Trade, *Human Security: Safety for People in a Changing World* (Ottawa: Department of Foreign Affairs and International Trade, 1999).

41. Buzan, *People, States, and Fear*, 3–4. Buzan provides a brief but very useful literature review of attempts to address the meaning of security; see 4–7.

42. Ibid., 6.

43. Arnold Wolfers, "National Security as an Ambiguous Symbol," in Arnold Wolfers, *Discord and Collaboration: Essays on International Politics* (Baltimore, Md.: Johns Hopkins University Press, 1962), 147.

44. One UNDP staffer suggested in private communication with the authors that the UNDP's adoption of the term "human security" in 1994 could be explained largely in terms of the organization's desire to secure the post–Cold War peace dividend for development.

45. Fen Hampson, "The Many Meanings of Human Security," in Hampson, Hay, Daudelin, Martin, and Reid, *Madness in the Multitude*, 17–18.

46. For the classic expression of this latter view, see UNDP, *Human Development Report 1994: New Dimensions of Human Security.* The contestedness of the parameters of human security again reflects the value content of the concept and the access to resources that appropriating the language of security may provide.

47. In response, one of our reviewers rightly asks whether the women affected by these practices see seclusion as security.

48. For a discussion of the evolution of basic needs approaches in development studies and policy, see Emmerij, Jolly, and Weiss, *Ahead of the Curve?*, 68–76.

49. See General Assembly resolution S-10/2 (1978); and United Nations Centre for Disarmament, *The Relationship between Disarmament and Development* (New York: United Nations, 1982). This report was prepared by Inga Thorsson and her colleagues.

Introduction to Part I

1. Boutros Boutros-Ghali, *An Agenda for Peace—Preventive Diplomacy, Peacemaking and Peace-keeping: Report of the Secretary-General Pursuant to the Statement Adopted by the Summit Meeting of the Security Council on 31 January, 1992* (General Assembly document A/47/277 and Security Council document S/24111), 17 June 1992, para. 17.

1. The Prehistory of Human Security

1. Charles Tilly, "War Making and State Making as Organized Crime," in *Bringing the State Back In,* edited by Peter B. Evans, Dietrich Rueschemeyer, and Theda Skocpol (Cambridge: Cambridge University Press, 1985), 171.

2. Keith Krause and Michael C. Williams, eds., *Critical Security Studies: Concepts and Cases* (Minneapolis: University of Minnesota Press, 1997). On the dominance of statist realism, see also Michael Doyle, *Ways of War and Peace: Realism, Liberalism, and Socialism* (New York: W.W. Norton, 1997), 42.

3. The problem we set ourselves in this chapter is analogous to that of Daniel Philpott, who began an analysis of the development of sovereignty by noting: "Mine is this task of understanding: If our sovereign states system is crashing, how did it ever come to be?" Daniel Philpott, *Revolutions in Sovereignty: How Ideas Shaped Modern International Relations* (Princeton, N.J.: Princeton University Press, 2001), 3.

4. See Robert Jackson, *The Global Covenant: Human Conduct in a World of States* (Oxford: Oxford University Press, 2003), 12; and Hedley Bull and Adam Watson, *The Expansion of International Society* (Oxford: Oxford University Press, 1984).

5. Vincent suggests the following attributes of statehood: "a continuous public power above both ruler and ruled"; "a geographically identifiable territory over which [the state] holds jurisdiction"; a claim to "hegemony or predominance within a territory over all other associations, organizations or groups within it"; a monopoly of legitimate force; a claim to sovereignty in the sense that the state has no internal rivals and is recognized by other states as a separate unit. Finally, the state is the "source of law" in the sense of compulsory rules. Andrew Vincent, *Theories of the State* (Oxford: Basil Blackwell, 1987), 19–21.

6. As Martin Wight pointed out, division of Western Europeans by nations dates to the organization of students by national origin in the medieval period. The division was replicated, not without controversy, in the affairs of the Church at the Council of Constance in the early 1400s. Wight, *Systems of States*, edited by Hedley Bull (Leicester, UK: Leicester University Press, 1977), 131.

7. Emma Rothschild, "What Is Security?" *Daedalus: Journal of the American Academy of Arts and Sciences* 124 (Summer 1995): 61.

8. Sophocles, *Antigone*, translated by H. D. F. Kitto (Oxford: Oxford University Press, 1998), 9.

9. There were also antecedents in the warring kingdoms of Chinese and Indian history.

10. Thucydides, *History of the Peloponnesian War* (London: Penguin, 1954).

11. Ibid., I: 6–7.

12. Aristotle, *Politics*, translated by William Ellis (London: J. M. Dent, 1947), 3.

13. One could go further to note that there was in classical Greek political thought little conception of the individual as subject. Individualism was alien to the Greek tradition: "The city was prior to any individual." Vincent, *Theories of the State*, 13. It is also important to note that the category of citizen excluded women and slaves.

14. Sophocles, *Antigone*, 24.

15. *Laws* III, para. 691.c–d, in *Plato: The Collected Dialogues*, edited by Edith Hamilton and Huntington Cairns (Princeton, N.J.: Princeton University Press, 1961), 1286. See also *Laws* IV, para. 713.c, 1304.

16. *Laws* IX, para. 875.b–c, 1434.

17. Plato, *The Republic* V, para. 469–471, in *Plato: The Collected Dialogues*, 708–711.

18. More generally, Adam Roberts and Richard Guelff have suggested that "the Greeks and Romans customarily observed certain humanitarian principles which have become fundamental rules of the contemporary laws of war." Adam Roberts and Richard Guelff, eds., *Documents on the Laws of War,* 3rd ed. (Oxford: Oxford University Press, 2000), 3, citing Coleman Phillipson, *The International Law and Custom of Ancient Greece and Rome,* vol. I (London: Macmillan, 1911). That this observance was incomplete is evident in Thucydides' nonjudgmental treatment of the Athenian destruction of Melos.

19. Martin Wight notes that Plato's comment on international relations makes up 3 pages of a 300-page work, suggesting that relations between city-states were not a major preoccupation of Plato or of other Greek writers. Wight, *Systems of States,* 51.

20. Vincent, *Theories of the State,* 48. The Roman view of the powers of the ruler was an important source of absolutist thinking.

21. See the exchange in Matthew 22:17–21 (Revised Standard Version).

22. I Peter 2:13–14 (Revised Standard Version). Bigongiari interprets this as an injunction to cooperate in the efforts of governments to repress violence with violence. *Augustine: Political Writings,* edited by Henry Paolucci and Dino Bigongiari (Chicago: Regnery Gateway, 1962), xix.

23. *Natural Law and Civil Right,* in *Augustine: Political Writings,* 162.

24. In a statement that strikingly prefigures contractarian theory, Augustine declared: "For what is a republic but a commonwealth? Therefore, its interests are common to all; they are the interests of the state. Now what is a state but a multitude of men bound together by some bond of concord?" "The 'Just War,'" in Augustine, *Political Writings,* 74.

25. "'And we, what shall we do?' And he said unto them, 'Rob no one by violence or by false accusation, and be content with your wages.'" Luke 3:14 (Revised Standard Version).

26. *Contra Faustum,* in *Augustine: Political Writings,* 163–165.

27. Vincent, *Theories of the State,* 83.

28. *Contra Faustum,* in *Augustine: Political Writings,* 164, 182–183.

29. D. C. Lau, "Introduction," in Confucius, *The Analects* (London: Penguin, 1979).

30. Confucius, *The Analects,* XIII.11, 120.

31. Ibid., XII.2, XV.24.

32. See Fung Yu-lan, *A History of Chinese Philosophy,* vol. 1, *The Period of the Philosophers* (Princeton, N.J.: Princeton University Press, 1952), 59–61, 73.

33. Chrétien de Troyes, *Perceval, or the Story of the Grail,* translated by Ruth Harwood Cline (Athens: University of Georgia Press, 1983), 51–52.

34. Torbjörn Knutsen, *A History of International Relations Theory* (Manchester, UK: Manchester University Press, 1992), 11.

35. J. M. Wallace-Hadrill, *The Barbarian West, 400–1000* (London: Hutchinson Publishers, 1956).

36. Knutsen, *History of International Relations Theory,* 12.

37. From the *Mishkat al-Masabih,* as cited by John Kelsay, "Civil Society and Government under Islam," in *Islamic Political Ethics: Civil Society, Pluralism, and*

Conflict, edited by Sohail Hashmi (Princeton, N.J.: Princeton University Press, 2002), 14. The similarity between this qualification and similar ones encountered in classical Greek literature is clear.

38. As Kelsay has argued, the *'ulama* and its associated sphere of activities aimed "at providing and protecting an institutional setting for citizen expression regarding social and political, as well as religious, affairs," "a kind of protection for the expression of dissent, in a manner reminiscent of the Lockean tradition." Ibid., 9–10.

39. Ibn Khaldun, *The Muqaddimah,* translated by Franz Rosenthal (Princeton, N.J.: Princeton University Press, 1989), 46–47, 107–108.

40. Ibid., 12–13.

41. Koran 2:189–192 (London: Penguin, 1999), 29.

42. Ibid., 47:3–4; 76:8–9 (357 and 413–414 in the Penguin edition).

43. As cited in Sohail Hashmi, "Interpreting the Islamic Ethics of War and Peace," in Hashmi, ed., *Islamic Political Ethics,* 211. As Hashmi puts it, "The Qur'an and the actions of the Prophet and his successors established the principles of discrimination and proportionality of means." He notes that the question of immunity of noncombatants has been a contentious one in subsequent Islamic legal scholarship.

44. William H. McNeill, *The Pursuit of Power* (Chicago: University of Chicago Press, 1982), 63. Interestingly, McNeill's characterization of the evolution of early feudalism has a distinctly contractarian flavor: local populations provided sustenance to a warrior class in return for protection from "threatening outsiders."

45. George Quester, *Offense and Defense in the International System* (New York: John Wiley, 1977), 32–35.

46. Galbert of Bruges, *The Murder of Charles the Good, Count of Flanders,* translated by James Ross (New York: Columbia University Press, 1960), 291.

47. Knutsen, *History of International Relations Theory,* 21.

48. On this point, see John Finnis, *Aquinas: Moral, Legal and Political Theory* (Oxford: Oxford University Press, 1998), 229, 231, 235. The quotation is from 247.

49. Ibid., 252. This conforms to contemporaneous Islamic notions of the limits of state power in the private sphere.

50. Vincent, *Theories of the State,* 83–84.

51. Aquinas favored constitutional arrangements that limited the power of kings to prevent them from falling into tyranny easily. Finnis, *Aquinas: Moral, Legal and Political Theory,* 261.

52. Henry de Bracton, *On the Laws and Customs of England,* translated by Samuel E. Thorne (Cambridge, Mass: Harvard University Press, 1968).

53. The Magna Carta (British Museum translation), para. 61, available online at www.bl.uk/collections/treasures/magnatranslation.html, accessed 5 October 2004. It is noteworthy that this clause was removed from later versions of the charter.

54. Vincent, *Theories of the State,* 86.

55. Richard Kaeuper, *Chivalry and Violence in Medieval Europe* (Oxford: Oxford University Press, 1999), 8.

56. John Gillingham argues that chivalry had a significant restraining effect in "1066 and the Introduction of Chivalry into England," in *Law and Government in Medieval*

England and Normandy, edited by George Garnet and John Hudson (Cambridge: Cambridge University Press, 1994). For a more jaundiced view, see Kaeuper, *Chivalry and Violence,* 169–175.

57. Gillingham, "1066 and the Introduction of Chivalry," 85. The killing of civilians and the destruction of their property, of course, made strategic sense, since it was from these sources that the power of adversaries was drawn.

58. Kaeuper, *Chivalry and Violence,* 179–180.

59. See the description of the behavior of followers of Robert of Bellême and William of Mortain in Orderic Vitalis, *The Ecclesiastical History,* edited and translated by Marjorie Chibnall (Oxford: Oxford University Press, 1969–1980), VI:96–97.

60. For example, the oath of the knights of the Round Table in Sir Thomas Malory's *Mort d'Arthur.* See Eugène Vinaver, ed., *Malory: Works,* 2nd ed. (Oxford: Oxford University Press, 1971), 75.

61. For example, the distinction between unaccompanied and unattached women and those who, as the spouses of adversaries, were prizes to be won. See Chrétien's *Lancelot,* translated by Kathryn Gravdal in Gravdal, *Ravishing Maidens: Writing Rape in Medieval French Literature and Law* (Philadelphia: University of Pennsylvania Press, 1991), 66.

62. Kaeuper, *Chivalry and Violence,* 24–28.

63. Vitalis, *Ecclesiastical History,* VI:97.

64. "In 1474, Sir Peter von Hagenbach was convicted by an international military tribunal on charges of rape during a military occupation." Thom Shanker, "Sexual Violence," in *Crimes of War,* edited by Roy Gutman and David Rieff (New York: Norton, 1999), 323. The circumstance in question was the siege of Breisach, and the adjudication concerned is said to be the first experience of an ad hoc international criminal court. Sir Peter was stripped of his knighthood and then lost his head in the matter. On this point, see Eduardo Greppi, "The Evolution of Individual Criminal Responsibility under International Law," *International Review of the Red Cross* 835 (1999): 531–553, available online at http://www.icrc.org/Web/Eng/siteeng0.nsf/iwpList106/911763EAA63170C0C1256B66005D85D0, accessed 15 December 2004.

65. Suarez, as cited in Wight, *Systems of States,* 125–126.

66. Commission on Global Governance, *Our Global Neighborhood,* 78.

67. This process spanned the years 1494 to 1715. The time period is bracketed on the one hand by the French invasion of Italy and on the other by the death of Louis XIV. See Wight, *Systems of States,* 111; and David Kaiser, *Politics and War: European Conflict from Philip II to Hitler* (Cambridge, Mass.: Harvard University Press, 1990), 2.

68. Tilly, "War Making and State Making as Organized Crime," 171–173.

69. John Ruggie has referred to this transformation as "the most important contextual change in international politics this millennium." John Gerard Ruggie, "Territoriality and Beyond: Problematizing Modernity in International Relations," *International Organization* 47 (1993): 139–174.

70. As Aquinas put it, no doubt conscious of where he was working: "*Chacun est maître chez soi: personne n'est maître hors de chez soi*" (Each is master of his own house: no one is master elsewhere). Wight, *Systems of States,* 135.

71. Vincent, *Theories of the State,* 70; see also Doyle, *Ways of War and Peace,* 112.

72. It is generally accepted that absolutist theories of the state were a product of civil war and an effort to address the human costs in such wars. Vincent, *Theories of the State,* 48, 52.

73. As he put it: "Sovereignty, then, is not limited either in power, or in function, or in length of time." Jean Bodin, *On Sovereignty* (Cambridge: Cambridge University Press, 1992), 3.

74. The roots of this view in Roman law doctrines of *plenitudo potestas* and *princeps legibus solutus* are clear.

75. It should be noted that the position of Luther and the Calvinists on this point evolved over time, as they came to defend a right to resist the ruler when he or she departed from religious rectitude as they defined it.

76. Contractarian theorists on the whole did not claim that the contract was an historical artifact; instead the concept of contract was a metaphor, reflecting the nature of the relationship between the sovereign and those whom he or she governed. Alasdair MacIntyre has suggested that in the absence of reference to divine authority, "some doctrine of social contract must underlie any claim to legitimacy." In the absence of the web of feudal obligations that tied monarch and subjects together, and given the obviously arbitrary quality of divine right, "the state must fall back, on appeal, implicit or explicit, to social contract." MacIntyre, *A Short History of Ethics* (London: Routledge and Kegan Paul, 1966), 155–156.

77. Thomas Hobbes, *Leviathan* (Oxford: Oxford University Press, 1998), 111. Italics added.

78. Ibid., 84. The similarity of the Hobbes's description to the contemporary conditions facing civilians in much armed conflict is striking.

79. Wight, *Power Politics,* 29.

80. See Simon Chesterman's discussion of this point in reference to the work of Grotius and Pufendorf in *Just War or Just Peace? Humanitarian Intervention and International Law* (Oxford: Oxford University Press, 2001), 15–16.

81. Jackson, *The Global Covenant,* 115.

82. Lentulus, quoted in Niccolo Machiavelli, *The Discourses,* in *The Prince and the Discourses* (New York: Random House, 1950), 527.

83. Vincent, *Theories of the State,* 62.

84. As Bodin put it, "But if the prince forbids killing on penalty of death, is he not then bound by his own law? I say this law is not his law but the law of God and of nature, to which he cannot be dispensed either by the Senate or the people, and for which he is always answerable to the judgement of God." Bodin, *On Sovereignty,* 31.

85. Ibid., 21, 40–42, 81.

86. MacIntyre, *A Short History of Ethics,* 133–134. Hobbes recognizes that when "there is no protection of subjects in their loyalty; then is the commonwealth dissolved, and every man at liberty to protect himself." *Leviathan* XXIX.23. See also XXI.21.

87. See Francis Deng, Sadikiel Kimaro, Terry Lyons, Donald Rothchild, and I. William Zartman, *Sovereignty as Responsibility: Conflict Management in Africa* (Washington, D.C.: Brookings Institution, 1996); and International Commission on Interven-

tion and State Sovereignty, *The Responsibility to Protect: Report of the International Commission on Intervention and State Sovereignty* (Ottawa: International Development Research Centre, 2001).

88. Ernst Troeltsch, "Naturrecht und Humanität in der Weltpolitik," cited in David Southern, "The History of Human Rights in Germany," in *Liberalism, Anti-Semitism and Democracy,* edited by Henning Tewes and Jonathan Wright (Oxford: Oxford University Press, 2001), 173.

89. See Doyle, *Ways of War and Peace,* 214–218.

90. This was not merely a theoretical proposition. Locke, like many constitutionalist thinkers of the period, held that most monarchies in Europe were originally elective. *Two Treatises of Government,* edited by Peter Laslett (Cambridge: Cambridge University Press, 1964), II:106, page 356. On this point, see Richard Ashcraft, *Locke's Two Treatises of Government* (Hemel Hempstead, UK: Unwin Hyman, 1987), 158–160.

91. There is a close connection between this strand of English thought and the earlier accounts of Huguenot thinkers such as François Hotman, who, in *Francogallia,* argued that the Frankish kings had originally been elected and that the Parliaments and the Estates-General had enjoyed a consultative relationship with the monarch. This original constitutional sharing of power and authority had been undermined by later French monarchs. It followed that the Estates had a right, if not a duty, to resist monarchical absolutism. Vincent, *Theories of the State,* 88–89.

92. Ibid., 105. The essence of the natural rights position was well summed up by Immanuel Kant's categorical imperative: to do to others what one would wish and expect others to do to oneself. Immanuel Kant, "Fundamental Principles of the Metaphysic of Morals," as cited in Jackson, *The Global Covenant,* 416. Kant's position here is strikingly similar not only to Christianity's Golden Rule but also to the rule articulated by Confucius some 1,700 years before: "Do not impose on others what you do not yourself desire." Confucius, *Analects,* XII.2.

93. See Immanuel Kant, "The Science of Right," in *Great Books of the Western World,* edited by R. M. Hutchins (Chicago: Encyclopedia Britannica, 1952), xlii, 401, where he stresses the "innate right" of freedom.

94. We are indebted to our colleague, Jennifer Welsh, for this point.

95. Carole Pateman, *The Sexual Contract* (Cambridge, UK: Polity Press, 1988), 1. As she put the point in regard to Locke: "Locke's 'individual' is masculine" (21).

96. It has been suggested that Grotius in particular transformed the law of nature into "an injunction to 'respect one another's rights.'" R. J. Vincent (citing Richard Tuck), "Grotius, Human Rights, and Intervention," in *Hugo Grotius and International Relations,* edited by Hedley Bull, Benedict Kingsbury, and Adam Roberts (Oxford: Oxford University Press, 1990), 241–242.

97. Simon Chesterman, *Just War or Just Peace? Humanitarian Intervention and International Law* (Oxford: Oxford University Press, 2003), 14.

98. Chesterman, *Just War or Just Peace?* 11–16.

99. Jennifer Jackson-Preece, *National Minorities and the European Nation-States System* (Oxford: Clarendon Press, 1998), 56. Jackson-Preece noted that although such provisions could be included as conditions of peace, the international law of the time

did not "sanction intervention by one prince in another's affairs solely on religious grounds" (57).

100. Bull, Kingsbury, and Roberts, eds., *Hugo Grotius and International Relations*, 247.

101. It is noteworthy that Grotius's notion of *temperamenta* does not fall within his treatment of the law of nations. It seems to have been more of a moral exhortation than a legal principle. See G. I. A. D. Draper, "Grotius' Place in the Development of Legal Ideas about War," in Bull, Kingsbury, and Roberts, eds., *Grotius and International Relations*, 197–199.

102. Emmerich de Vattel, *The Law of Nations or Principles of the Law of Nature Applied to the Conduct and Affairs of Nations and Sovereigns* (Philadelphia: T. and J. W. Johnson, 1883), Book 3, paras. 145, 147, 293 and 294, available online at http://www.constitution.org/vattel/vattel_03.htm, accessed 3 January 2005.

103. See, for example, the Swedish Articles of War issued at the outset of the campaign against Russia in the Baltics in 1621. These included rules concerning "assaults on women, unauthorized attacks on towns and villages, theft, and pillage or burning of churches and hospitals." Roberts and Guelff, eds., *Documents on the Laws of War*, 3. More generally, the European powers agreed that ambulances servicing the wounded in battle were neutral and not to be targeted. See Francois Bugnion, *Le Comité International de la Croix-Rouge et la protection des victimes de la guerre* (Geneva: Comité International de la Croix Rouge, 1986), 12, 24.

104. Pateman, *The Sexual Contract*, 94.

105. Cecil A. Spring-Rice, "I Vow to Thee My Country" (1918—of all years!). Available online at http://www.cyberhymnal.org/htm/i/v/ivow2the.htm, accessed 5 October 2003.

106. Carl J. Friedrich, *Transcendent Justice: The Religious Dimension of Constitutionalism* (Durham, N.C.: Duke University Press, 1961), 67.

107. Liah Greenfeld, *Nationalism: Five Roads to Modernity* (Cambridge, Mass.: Harvard University Press, 1992), 3.

108. Wight, *Power Politics*, 28. One of our reviewers noted the choice of the pronoun "she" in this quotation and suggested that the female personification of the state implies vulnerability and a need for protection by males. The echo to the citation that begins this section (where the singer vows *his* love to country) is striking.

109. For an illuminating analysis of the British case, see Linda Colley, *Britons: Forging the Nation, 1707–1937* (New Haven, Conn.: Yale University Press, 1992). In this context, one is also reminded of the French textbooks in use in West Africa from which young African students learned about "*nos ancêtres, les Gaulois.*"

110. See Robert Ergang, *Herder and the Foundations of German Nationalism* (New York: Columbia University Press, 1931), 239, 247, 252.

111. We are grateful to one of our reviewers for this point.

112. According to Marx, the reification of the state through nationalism was a means of creating and sustaining false consciousness in the proletariat. This false consciousness interfered with the proletariat's recognition of their true interests.

113. Karma Nabulsi, *Traditions of War: Occupation, Resistance, and the Law* (Oxford: Oxford University Press, 1999), 111–125.

114. One study from the early 1980s claimed that 92.9 percent of hypotheses tested in the field of international relations derived from realist assumptions. John Vasquez, *The Power of Power Politics: A Critique* (New Brunswick, N.J.: Rutgers University Press, 1983), 165–167.

115. For a useful account of this process, see David Davis, *Slavery and Human Progress* (Oxford: Oxford University Press, 1984).

116. See Lassa Oppenheim, *International Law: A Treatise*, edited by Hersch Lauterpacht, 7th ed. (London: Longmans Green, 1955), II:733–734.

117. Colley, *Britons: Forging the Nation*, 354.

118. Tom J. Farer and Felice Gaer, "The UN and Human Rights," in *United Nations, Divided World: The UN's Roles in International Relations,* edited by Adam Roberts and Benedict Kingsbury (Oxford: Oxford University Press, 1993), 242.

119. Jackson-Preece, *National Minorities and the European Nation-States System,* 60–61.

120. Nicholas Wheeler, *Saving Strangers: Humanitarian Intervention in International Society* (Oxford: Oxford University Press, 2000), 46; S. Neil MacFarlane, "Intervention in Contemporary World Politics," Adelphi Paper no. 350 (London: Oxford University Press for the International Institute for Strategic Studies, 2002), 26–29.

121. Henry Kissinger, *A World Restored: Metternich, Castlereagh, and the Problems of Peace, 1812–1822* (Boston: Houghton Mifflin, 1954), 288–289, 295; MacFarlane, *Intervention in Contemporary World Politics,* 26–29.

122. Jackson-Preece, *National Minorities and the European Nation-States System,* 62.

123. For the text, see Francis Lieber, "Instructions for the Government of Armies of the United States in the Field," available online at http://fletcher.tufts.edu/multi/texts/historical/LIEBER-CODE.txt, accessed 5 October 2004.

124. Roberts and Guelff, eds., *Documents on the Laws of War,* 12–13.

125. Bugnion, *Le Comité International de la Croix-Rouge et la protection des victimes de la guerre,* 12. Bugnion notes that the chances of surviving a war wound were lower under Napoleon III than they had been under Louis XIV.

126. For background, see MacFarlane, "Politics and Humanitarian Action."

127. For the background of this convention, see Eric Myles, "'Humanity,' 'Civilization' and the 'International Community' in the Late Russian Imperial Mirror: Three Ideas Topical for Our Days," *Journal of the History of International Law* 4 (February 2002): 316–318. For the text of the convention, see Roberts and Guelff, eds., *Documents on the Laws of War,* 54–55.

128. Roberts and Guelff, eds., *Documents on the Laws of War,* 55.

129. For the texts, see ibid., 60–61 and 64–65. For background, see Don Hubert, "The Landmine Ban: A Case Study in Humanitarian Advocacy," Occasional Paper no. 42 (Providence, R.I.: Thomas J. Watson Jr. Institute for International Studies, 2000), 1–2.

130. Robert Heilbroner, *The Worldly Philosophers,* 6th ed. (Harmondsworth, UK: Penguin, 1986), 125–126.

131. The number of primary school teachers doubled between 1882 and 1911. Nurses per 10,000 population tripled between 1889 and 1909.

132. For discussion, see David Blackbourn, *History of Germany 1780–1918: The Long Nineteenth Century,* 2nd ed. (Oxford: Blackwells, 2003), 260–262. We are grateful to our colleague, Dr. Jonathan Wright, for this citation.

133. The contrast between the preamble to the Covenant and that to the Charter is striking in this respect. On this point, see Jack Donnelly, *International Human Rights* (Boulder, Colo.: Westview Press, 1993), 7.

134. Farer and Gaer, "The UN and Human Rights," 243.

135. Jackson-Preece, *National Minorities and the European Nation-States System,* 68.

136. For a useful account of the League's role in this area, see Louise Holborn, *Refugees, a Problem of Our Time: The Work of the UNHCR, 1951–1972* (Metuchen, N.J.: Scarecrow Press, 1975), 1:3–20.

137. Gil Loescher, *Beyond Charity: International Cooperation and the Global Refugee Crisis* (Oxford: Oxford University Press, 1993), 33.

138. Ibid., 37–38.

139. Fifty-six governments ratified the 1922 agreement on Russian refugees, eight ratified the 1933 successor convention on Russian refugees, and three ratified a 1938 agreement on refugees from Germany and Austria.

140. Robert Jackson, "International Community beyond the Cold War," in *Beyond Westphalia? State Sovereignty and International Intervention,* edited by Gene Lyons and Michael Mastanduno (Baltimore, Md.: Johns Hopkins University Press, 1995), 78.

141. Simon Chesterman, "Introduction: Global Norms, Local Contexts," in Chesterman, ed., *Civilians in War* (Boulder, Colo.: Lynne Rienner, 2001), 1.

142. Bugnion, *Le Comité International de la Croix-Rouge et la protection des victimes de la guerre,* 94–95.

143. International Labour Organization, *Constitution* (Geneva: ILO, 1919), available online at http://www.ilo.org/public/english/about/iloconst.htm#1ap2, accessed 3 May 2005.

144. For a comprehensive discussion, see International Labour Office, *Social Policy in Dependent Territories* (Montreal: International Labour Office, 1944), 49–61.

145. Franklin Delano Roosevelt, "Inaugural Address," 4 March 1933, available online at http://www.yale.edu/lawweb/avalon/presiden/inaug/froos1.htm, accessed 5 October 2004.

146. In the United States, wages, salaries, and profits from business expansion totaled $15 billion in 1929; in 1932, they were $886 million, having fallen by 94 percent. Heilbroner, *The Worldly Philosophers,* 276.

147. Henry Kissinger, *A World Restored,* 295.

2. The UN and Human Security during the Cold War

1. Clement Atlee, "Statement" at the opening of the first session of the General Assembly, "Verbatim Record of the First Plenary Meeting" (General Assembly document A/PV.1, 41), 10 January 1946, available online at http://www.un.org/Depts/dhl/landmark/pdf/a-pv1.pdf, accessed 22 December 2004.

2. By intervention, we mean coercive intrusion into the internal affairs of a state. For a discussion of the problems of defining intervention, see S. Neil MacFarlane, *Intervention in Contemporary World Politics* (Oxford: Oxford University Press for the International Institute of Strategic Studies, 2002), 13–15.

3. We recognize the possibility that satisfaction of the identity claims of groups may threaten those of individuals or minorities within the territories in question.

4. Edward Stettinius, U.S. secretary of state, cited in UNDP, *Human Development Report 1994: New Dimensions of Human Security* (New York: United Nations Development Programme, 1994), 3.

5. Notably, the drafters of the Charter abandoned the unanimity rule of the League Covenant, taking the view that such a rule would preclude effective collective reaction to aggression by one member upon another. In addition, the great powers were granted a veto on actions to defend international peace and security, reflecting the view that without their support such actions would be fruitless in any case.

6. A similar logic underpinned the major bilateral assistance program of the early Cold War, the Marshall Plan.

7. The Atlantic Charter was the first Anglo-American statement of shared principles guiding the effort in World War II. It was signed by Franklin Roosevelt and Winston Churchill on 14 August 1941 at Placentia Bay, Newfoundland. Available online at http://www.yale.edu/lawweb/avalon/wwii/atlantic.htm.

8. The draft the United States proposed is reproduced in full in Leland Goodrich, Edvard Hambro, and Anne Patricia Simons, *The Charter of the United Nations: Commentary and Documents* (New York: Columbia University Press, 1969) 665–672. The quotation is on page 672. All of this said, the Dumbarton Oaks draft had little to say specifically about human rights.

9. Goodrich, Hambro, and Simons, *The Charter of the United Nations,* 10.

10. Ibid., 92.

11. Adam Roberts and Benedict Kingsbury, "The UN's Roles in International Society," in *United Nations, Divided World: The UN's Roles in International Relations,* edited by Adam Roberts and Benedict Kingsbury (Oxford: Oxford University Press, 1993), 49.

12. There was a hint of instrumentalism in the UDHR in the link the preamble drew between fundamental human rights on the one hand and peace on the other. However, the major thrust of the Declaration suggested a belief that honoring human dignity was right in itself. Moreover, there was no explicit mention of security in the UDHR. This way of thinking appeared even more strongly in the International Covenant on Economic, Social, and Cultural Rights and the Covenant on Political and Civil Rights, both of which asserted that the rights discussed therein "derive from the inherent dignity of the human person."

13. Jack Donnelly, "State Sovereignty and International Intervention: The Case of Human Rights," in *Beyond Westphalia? State Sovereignty and International Intervention,* edited by Gene M. Lyons and Michael Mastanduno (Baltimore, Md.: Johns Hopkins University Press, 1995), 116.

14. UN Division for the Advancement of Women, "Sexual Violence and Armed Conflict: United Nations Response," *Women2000* (April 1998), available online at http://www.un.org/womenwatch/daw/public/w2apr98.htm#part4.

15. *Preliminary Report Submitted by the Special Rapporteur on Violence against Women, Its Causes and Consequences* (ECOSOC document E/CN.4/1995/42), 24 November 1994, para. 27(a), available online at http://www.unhchr.ch/Huridocda/Huridoca.nsf/0/75ccfd797b0712d08025670b005c9a7d?Opendocument.

16. GA resolution 3318 (XXIX), 14 December 1974.

17. Cited in M. G. Johnson and Janusz Symonides, *The Universal Declaration of Human Rights: A History of Its Creation and Implementation, 1948–1998* (Paris: UNESCO, 1998), 32.

18. Michael Ignatieff, "Human Rights as Politics," in Ignatieff, *Human Rights as Politics and Idolatry,* edited and introduced by Amy Gutmann (Princeton, N.J.: Princeton University Press, 2001), 5.

19. For a good discussion of the suspension of Greece, see Andreas G. Papandreou Foundation, "The Council of Europe Fights for Democracy in Greece, 1967–1969," available online at http://www.agp.gr/English/archive/library/historical_series_1.stm, accessed 12 May 2005.

20. Council of Europe, Convention for the Protection of Human Rights and Fundamental Freedoms, Rome, 4 November 1950, preamble, available online at http://conventions.coe.int, accessed 5 October 2004.

21. For a useful account of the powers and procedures of the European Commission and the European Court of Human Rights, see Ralph Beddard, *Human Rights and Europe* (London: Sweet and Maxwell, 1980), 38–50. The commission and court were merged and the powers of the latter were expanded in the 1980s.

22. Protocol 11 (1998) made acceptance of individual complaint compulsory.

23. Donnelly, "State Sovereignty and International Intervention: The Case of Human Rights," 133.

24. Perhaps the most important effect of the Helsinki Process was the impetus it gave to dissident activities within the Soviet bloc because citizens of the socialist countries attempted to hold their governments accountable to the principles of the Helsinki Final Act. These activities may have accelerated the process of political change in the socialist camp.

25. In parallel, regional states adopted the American Declaration on the Rights and Duties of Man (1948). The commission was established in 1959.

26. The lack of attention to economic and social rights in the San José protocol was rectified in the extensive Additional Protocol to the American Convention on Human Rights in the Area of Economic, Social, and Cultural Rights (the Protocol of San Salvador, 1988).

27. For a listing of judgments and opinions of the Inter-American Court of Human Rights, see http://www1.umn.edu/humanrts/iachr/series_A.html, accessed 5 October 2004. All documents referred to in this section on the Americas are available at this site.

28. The text is posted at the Web site of the African Union, available online at http://www.africa-union.org/Official_documents/Treaties_%20Conventions_%20Protocols/Banjul%20Charter.pdf, accessed 22 December 2004.

29. For example, the freedom from compulsion to join an association in Article 10.2 was qualified by reference to Article 29.

30. Such a court was established in the Ouagadougou Protocol to the African Charter on Human and People's Rights on the Establishment of an African Court for Human and People's Rights, June 10, 1998; available online at http://www.africa-union.org/rule_prot/africancourt-humanrights.pdf, accessed 11 June 2005. As this falls into the post–Cold War period, it is not discussed here.

31. Christopher Clapham, *Africa and the International System: The Politics of State Survival* (Cambridge: Cambridge University Press, 1996), 191.

32. Helena Cook, "Amnesty International at the UN," in *"The Conscience of the World": The Influence of Non-Governmental Organisations in the UN System,* edited by Peter Willetts (London: Hurst and Company, 1996), 182. Cook provides an extremely useful account of the multifaceted interaction of Amnesty International with the UN, from which this summary is largely drawn.

33. As Amnesty International's statute notes: "Amnesty International's vision is of a world in which every person enjoys all of the human rights enshrined in the Universal Declaration of Human Rights and other international human rights standards." The statute is available online at http://web.amnesty.org/pages/aboutai-statute-eng, accessed 5 October 2004.

34. One might also note that the award of the prize itself reflected a perception of the linkage between human rights and international security.

35. Gil Loescher, *Beyond Charity: International Cooperation and the Global Refugee Crisis* (Oxford: Oxford University Press, 1993), 48. Loescher notes that this refugee crisis differed from that concerning Russians in the 1920s. In the first period, the home government did not want refugees back, but in the late 1940s, the Soviet government (and its socialist allies) strongly supported return but the refugees themselves were unwilling to go.

36. Ibid., 51.

37. Ibid., 50.

38. Ibid., 53.

39. General Assembly resolution 428 (v), 14 December 1950.

40. See the Convention and Protocol Relating to the Status of Refugees, 28 July 1951, available online at available online at http://www.unhcr.ch, accessed 5 October 2004. *Nonrefoulement* refers to the obligation not to force people to return if they have a reasonable fear of persecution at home.

41. The establishment of the UN Refugee Fund was extremely significant in the evolution of the organization, since it freed the UNHCR of the need for UN appropriations and, over time, of narrow oversight by the General Assembly. The fund was overseen by a committee of donors that became the UNHCR Executive Committee at the end of the 1950s.

42. Loescher, *Beyond Charity,* 63. This attitude changed after the UNHCR successfully managed the refugee flow from the 1956 Hungarian Revolution.

43. See consideration of the European Convention on Consular Functions (1967), Article 48, and the Protocol to the European Convention on Consular Functions Concerning the Protection of Refugees (1967), in "Committee on Legal Cooperation,

Explanatory Report," available online at http://conventions.coe.int/treaty/en/Reports/
HTML/061.htm, accessed 5 October 2004.

44. Convention Governing the Specific Aspects of Refugee Problems in Africa
(1969), available online at http://www.africa-union.org/Official_documents/
Treaties_%20Conventions_%20Protocols/Refugee_Convention.pdf, accessed 5
October 2004.

45. OAS, Convention on Territorial Asylum (1954), available online at http://
www.oas.org/juridico/english/Treaties/a-47.html, accessed 5 October 2004.

46. Cartagena Declaration on Refugees (1984), available online at http://
www.unhcr.ch/cgi-bin/texis/vtx/home/opendoc.htm?tbl=RSDLEGAL&id
=3ae6b36ec&page=research, accessed 22 December 2004.

47. The 1907 Hague Convention IV recognizes the responsibility of the state for acts
committed by its armed forces and contains rather insubstantial references to compen-
sation for such acts. See Adam Roberts and Richard Guelff, eds., *Documents on the Laws
of War*, 3rd ed. (Oxford: Oxford University Press, 2000), 175.

48. It is appropriate to note that there was an element of victors' justice in the
Nuremberg process. Numerous aspects of the behavior of the Allies toward civilian
populations might well have occasioned similar attention had the institutions been
more neutral. Among these might be the firebombing of enemy cities, the first use (on
civilians) of nuclear weapons of mass destruction, the internment of large numbers of
Japanese civilians and the confiscation of their property, and the mass deportation of
entire ethnic groups by the Soviet government.

49. Telford Taylor, *Nuremberg and Vietnam: An American Tragedy* (Chicago:
Quadrangle, 1970), 143.

50. Kirsten Sellars, *The Rise and Rise of Human Rights* (Stroud, UK: Sutton Publishing, 2002), 35.

51. David Forsythe, *Human Rights in International Relations* (Cambridge: Cambridge University Press, 2000), 85–86.

52. Sellars, *The Rise and Rise of Human Rights*, 61.

53. Section A of General Assembly resolution 260, 9 December 1948.

54. Killing, causing serious bodily or mental harm, deliberately inflicting on the
group conditions of life that are calculated to destroy it physically, preventing births
within a group, and forcible transfer of populations.

55. For a summary account, see Roberts and Guelff , eds., *Documents on the Laws of
War*, 179.

56. Part I, Article 3, pertaining to the "case of armed conflict not of an international
character occurring in the territory of one of the High Contracting Parties," prohibited
"violence to life and person, in particular murder of all kinds, mutilation, cruel
treatment and torture; the taking of hostages; outrages upon personal dignity, in
particular humiliating and degrading treatment; and the passing of sentences and the
carrying out of executions without previous judgment pronounced by a regularly
constituted court, affording all the judicial guarantees which are recognized as
indispensable by civilized peoples."

57. Part III, Section I, Article 27.

58. Although some states were willing to recognize international norms with regard to their conduct of internal disputes, few if any were willing to specifically recognize the applicability of Common Article 3 to conflicts in which they were involved. We are indebted to Sir Adam Roberts for this clarification.

59. Reportedly, large chunks of the protocol were dropped in last-minute negotiations in order to achieve agreement on the text. Confidential interview with a leading analyst of the Geneva Conventions.

60. Goodrich, Hambro, and Simons, *Charter of the United Nations,* 34.

61. Ibid.

62. Edvard Hambro, "Preface," in ibid., vi.

63. "Declaration on the Inadmissibility of Intervention in the Domestic Affairs of States and the Protection of Their Independence and Sovereignty," General Assembly resolution 2131, 21 December 1965. See also the "Declaration on Principles of International Law Concerning Friendly Relations and Co-operation among States in Accordance with the Charter of the United Nations," General Assembly resolution 2625, 24 October 1970; and "Definition of Aggression" General Assembly resolution 3314, 14 December 1974.

64. For a summary of relevant literature, see Gene Lyons and Michael Mastanduno, "State Sovereignty and International Intervention," in Lyons and Mastanduno, eds., *Beyond Westphalia?* 272n45.

65. Charter of the OAS, Article 11; Charter of the OAU, Article 3.2.

66. We do not include Security Council actions regarding Palestine here, since Israel had no recognized sovereignty over the territories of Jordan, Syria, Lebanon, and Egypt it occupied in the 1967 war. See Security Council resolution 242, 22 November 1967.

67. This became a serious issue at the UN in 1961, given the large increase in the number of African members, the growing isolation of Portugal in its effort to hold on to its overseas colonies, and the outbreak of a war of liberation in Angola in that year.

68. Security Council resolutions 163 (1961); 180 (1963); 183 (1963); 312 (1972); 322 (1972).

69. See Security Council resolutions 202 (1965); 216 (1965); 217 (1965); 221 (1966); 232 (1966); 253 (1968); 277 (1970); 314 (1972); 318 (1972); 388 (1976).

70. See Security Council resolutions 181 (1963); 182 (1963); 190 (1964); 191 (1964); 282 (1970); 311 (1972); 392 (1976); 417 (1977); 418 (1977).

71. See, for example, the preamble to Security Council resolution 182 (1963), the first substantial resolution on the subject.

72. The preamble of Security Council resolution 418 (1977) that established the arms embargo under Chapter VII "strongly condemns the South African Government for its resort to massive violence against and killings of the African people, including schoolchildren and students and others opposing racial discrimination."

73. UN Security Council resolution 418 (1977).

74. For a good discussion of the tensions surrounding the UN's reluctance to take part in hostilities in support of government forces and the significant problems this caused for UN relationships with African troop contributors, see Jane Boulden, *Peace Enforcement: The United Nations Experience in Bosnia, Congo, and Somalia* (Westport, Conn.: Praeger, 2001).

75. Security Council resolution 361 (1974).

76. Notably, the encouragement of "the fullest possible resumption of normal civilian activity in the buffer zone." See Karl Th. Birgisson, "United Nations Peacekeeping Force in Cyprus," in *The Evolution of UN Peacekeeping*, edited by William J. Durch (New York: St. Martin's Press, 1993); United Nations Department of Peacekeeping Operations, "Cyprus—UNFICYP—Background," available online at http://www.un.org/Depts/dpko/missions/unficyp/background.html, accessed 5 October 2004.

77. See Nicholas Wheeler, *Saving Strangers: Humanitarian Intervention in International Society* (Oxford: Oxford University Press, 2000), 55–138; ICISS, *The Responsibility to Protect* (Ottawa: International Development Research Centre, 2001), 2:49–78; MacFarlane, *Intervention in Contemporary World Politics*, 42–43.

78. Wheeler, *Saving Strangers*, 62–63.

79. Indian representative in the Security Council, cited in Thomas G. Weiss and Don Hubert, *The Responsibility to Protect: Research, Bibliography, Background* (Ottawa: International Development Research Centre, 2001), 55.

80. Wheeler, *Saving Strangers*, 58.

81. Security Council resolution 303 (1971).

82. General Assembly resolution 2793 (1971).

83. Security Council resolution 307 (1971).

84. Wheeler, *Saving Strangers*, 64–65.

85. ICISS, *The Responsibility to Protect*, 2:58.

86. Cited in ibid., 2:59.

87. In subsequent General Assembly debates on Cambodia, justification on humanitarian grounds did appear in the contributions of three of Vietnam's allies—the German Democratic Republic (GDR), Laos, and Afghanistan; ibid., 60. The facts that Laos was dependent upon Vietnam, the GDR made a practice of murdering those of its own citizens that attempted to escape its oppression, and Afghanistan's totalitarian government was engaged (with increasing Soviet assistance) in a massive war against its own population encourage some doubt about the sincerity of these protestations.

88. ICISS, *The Responsibility to Protect*, 2:62.

89. For a very useful account of international aspects of Nigeria's civil wars, see John Stremlau, *The International Politics of the Nigerian Civil War, 1967–1970* (Princeton, N.J.: Princeton University Press, 1977).

90. David Rieff, *A Bed for the Night: Humanitarianism in Crisis* (New York: Vintage, 2002), 71.

91. For a general treatment, see A. Rigo Sureda, *The Evolution of the Right to Self-Determination: A Study of United Nations Practice* (Leiden, Netherlands: A. W. Sijthoff, 1973).

92. For a persuasive account of the influence of the UN on the timing and pace of British decolonization after Suez, see Asahiko Hanzawa, "An Invisible Surrender: The United Nations and the End of the British Empire, 1956–1963" (D.Phil. dissertation, Oxford University, 2002).

93. For a discussion of this shift in Soviet foreign policy, see S. Neil MacFarlane, *Superpower Rivalry and Third World Radicalism: The Idea of National Liberation* (Baltimore, Md.: Johns Hopkins University Press, 1985).

94. "Declaration on the Granting of Independence to Colonial Countries and Peoples," GA resolution 1514 (XV), 14 December 1960.

95. Ibid., operative paragraph 6.

96. Poland and France, in particular, did not appreciate League engagement over Silesia and Saarland. For discussion, see Jennifer Jackson Preece, *National Minorities and the European State System* (Oxford: Oxford University Press, 1998), 87–88.

97. In an introduction to a useful early post–Cold War study of the approach of the Council of Europe to national minority questions, Patrick Thornberry notes: "From 1945 to 1989 international relations were dominated by the perspective of a bipolar world and rival Utopias of development. . . . Societies resolved themselves into classes and the ethnic and religious component of individual and collective identities was ignored." Patrick Thornberry, *The Council of Europe and Minorities* (Strasbourg, France: Council of Europe, 1994), 2.

98. Dwight D. Eisenhower, "The Chance for Peace," 16 April 1953, available online at http://www.eisenhower.archives.gov/chance.htm, accessed 13 March 2005.

99. Independent Commission on International Development Issues, *North-South: A Programme for Survival* (London: Pan Books, 1980), 16.

100. Universal Declaration of Human Rights, preamble and Articles 22–26, available online at http://www.un.org/Overview/rights.html, accessed 15 May 2005.

101. Richard Jolly, Louis Emmerij, Dharam Ghai, and Frédéric Lapeyre, *UN Contributions to Development Thinking and Practice* (Bloomington: Indiana University Press, 2004). The analysis in this section has benefited considerably from this volume's treatment of the subject.

102. For statesmen, the goal of economic development has frequently been the accumulation of power.

103. Paul Streeten, "The Evolution of Development Thought," in Streeten, *Thinking about Development* (Cambridge: Cambridge University Press, 1995), 18.

104. To put it another way: "All good things go together . . . the means [growth] are the means towards the same ends of those who stress the ends [quality of life]." Ibid., 20.

105. Mahbub ul Haq, *Reflections on Human Development* (Oxford: Oxford University Press, 1995), 24.

106. UN, *Technical Assistance for Economic Development* (New York: United Nations, 1949), 8. This report also repeats the linkage between living standards and employment on the one hand and maintaining international peace and security on the other.

107. UN, *Measures for the Economic Development of Underdeveloped Countries: Report of a Group of Experts Appointed by the Secretary-General of the United Nations* (New York: United Nations, 1951).

108. Streeten, "The Evolution of Development Thought," 20.

109. UN, *The Development Decade: Proposals for Action* (New York: United Nations, 1962). Here we see a major precursor to the treatment of the peace dividend in the *Human Development Report 1994*.

110. U Thant, "Foreword," in *The Development Decade*.

111. The ILO launched its World Employment Program in 1969.

112. Independent Commission on International Development Issues, *North-South: A Programme for Survival*.

113. Paul Streeten noted in this context that ideas regarding employment and income distribution formulated on the basis of developed-world experience did not transfer easily to the developing countries, where many of those working remained poor. Streeten, "The Evolution of Development Thought," 18. In this respect, these targets needed to be supplemented by more-targeted efforts to address poverty.

114. Ibid., 19.

115. See the Society for International Development (SID) North-South Roundtable papers: Khadija Haq and Uner Kirdar, eds., *Human Development, The Neglected Dimension* (Rome: SID, 1986); *Human Development: Adjustment and Growth* (Rome: SID, 1987); and *Managing Human Development* (Rome: SID, 1988).

116. International Commission on Development Issues, *North-South: A Programme for Survival*, 14. The Brandt report also shared the view that the focus of development should be on people and that it was important to avoid the confusion between growth and development. Ibid., 23–24, 124–125.

117. World Commission on Environment and Development, *Our Common Future: From One Earth to One World* (Oxford: Oxford University Press, 1987), 43.

118. Ibid., 7, 43–54, 298.

119. The Washington consensus refers to a neoliberal conception of development shared by the U.S. Treasury Department, the IMF, and the World Bank that emphasized privatization of economic assets, the reduction of state-sector deficits, the deregulation of economic activity, and the opening of markets to international competition. For an extensive discussion of the agenda and its impact on developing countries, see Joseph Stiglitz, *Globalization and Its Discontents* (New York: Norton, 2002).

3. The Evolving Critique of National Security

1. Richard Falk, "The Challenge of Genocide and Genocidal Politics in an Era of Globalisation," in *Human Rights and Global Politics,* edited by Tim Dunne and Nicholas Wheeler (Cambridge: Cambridge University Press, 1999), 179.

2. Michael Ignatieff, "Human Rights as Idolatry," in Ignatieff, *Human Rights as Politics and Idolatry,* edited and introduced by Amy Gutmann (Princeton, N.J.: Princeton University Press, 2001), 65.

3. "Source List and Detailed Death Tolls for the Twentieth Century Hemoclysm," available online at http://users.erols.com/mwhite28/warstat1.htm, accessed 21 April 2005.

4. Adam Roberts, "Land Warfare: From Hague to Nuremberg" in *The Laws of War: Constraints on Warfare in the Western World,* edited by Michael Howard, George J. Andreopoulos, and Mark Shulman (New Haven, Conn.: Yale University Press, 1994), 121. The account of pre–World War I constraints on warfare presented here is drawn primarily from the Roberts essay.

5. Tami Davis Biddle, "Air Power" in Howard, Andreopoulos, and Shulman, eds., *The Laws of War,* 142–145.

6. Ibid., 144.

7. Ibid.

8. Roberts, "Land Warfare," 125.

9. "Declaration Renouncing the Use, in Time of War, of Explosive Projectiles under 400 Grammes Weight" (The St. Petersburg Declaration), 14 December 1868, in Roberts and Guelff, eds., *Documents on the Laws of War*, 55.

10. Roberts, "Land Warfare," 125.

11. "Source List and Detailed Death Tolls for the Twentieth Century Hemoclysm."

12. Cited in Biddle, "Air Power," 145.

13. Guilio Douhet, *The Command of the Air* (Washington, D.C.: Office of Air Force History, 1983), 61.

14. Eric Markusen and David Kopf, *The Holocaust and Strategic Bombing* (Boulder, Colo.: Westview Press, 1995), 152–154.

15. See Ronald Schaffer, *Wings of Judgment: American Bombing in World War II* (New York: Oxford University Press, 1985), especially Chapter 5, "The Bombing of Germany: Transition to Douhetian Warfare," for an excellent analysis of the internal debates within the United States that culminated in succumbing to Douhetian warfare.

16. Ibid., 94–100.

17. Biddle, "Air Power," 154.

18. Ibid. See also Schaffer, *Wings of Judgment*, Chapter 7, for a discussion of Japan's vulnerability to firebombing.

19. Michael Walzer, *Just and Unjust Wars* (New York: Basic Books, 1977), 255–263; Geoffrey Best, *Humanity in Warfare* (London: Weidenfeld and Nicolson, 1980), 279–284.

20. Best, *Humanity in Warfare*, 285.

21. Deborah Dwork and Robert Jan van Pelt, *Holocaust: A History* (London: John Murray, 2002), Chapter 8.

22. Daniel Jonah Goldhagen, *Hitler's Willing Executioners: Ordinary Germans and the Holocaust* (London: Abacus, 1996), 420–425.

23. Frank Chalk and Kurt Jonassohn, *The History and Sociology of Genocide* (New Haven, Conn.: Yale University Press, 1990), 325.

24. Ian Kershaw, "The Extinction of Human Rights in Nazi Germany," in *Historical Change and Human Rights*, edited by Olwen Hufton (New York: Basic Books, 1995), 233.

25. Goldhagen, *Hitler's Willing Executioners*, 418.

26. Geoffrey Best, *Nuremberg and After: The Continuing History of War Crimes and Crimes Against Humanity* (Reading, Pa.: University of Reading, 1984), 4–5.

27. Henry Kissinger, *White House Years* (Boston: Little, Brown, 1979), 215.

28. Ibid., 216.

29. McGeorge Bundy, *Danger and Survival: Choices about the Bomb in the First Fifty Years* (New York: Random House, 1988).

30. On the Berlin crisis, see Bundy, *Danger and Survival*, esp. 358–390. On the Cuban missile crisis, see Raymond Garthoff, *Reflections on the Cuban Missile Crisis* (Washington, D.C.: The Brookings Institution, 1989), esp. 154–192; Bundy, *Danger and Survival*, 391–462.

31. See Mark Franchetti, "Cool Hero of Cuba," *The Sunday Times* (London), 20 October 2002, 29.

32. Spurgeon Keeny and Wolfgang Panofsky, "MAD versus NUTS," in *The Nuclear Controversy: A Foreign Affairs Reader,* edited by William Bundy (New York: New American Library, 1985), 3–20.

33. Carl Sagan, "Nuclear War and Climatic Catastrophe: Some Policy Implications," in Bundy, ed., *The Nuclear Controversy,* 117–152.

34. Bulletin of the Atomic Scientists, "1984: Three Minutes to Midnight," available online at http://www.thebulletin.org/doomsday_clock/timeline.htm, accessed 12 April 2005.

35. National Conference of Catholic Bishops, *The Challenge of Peace: God's Promise and Our Response* (Washington, D.C.: United States Catholic Conference, 1983).

36. Ibid., i.

37. Ibid., iii–iv, 56–59.

38. Jonathan Schell, *The Fate of the Earth* (London: Picador, 1982).

39. Ibid., 143.

40. David Krieger, "Nuclearism and Its Insecurities" in *Worlds Apart: Human Security and Global Governance,* edited by Laura Reed and Majid Tehranian (London: I. B. Tauris, 1999), 121.

41. Ibid.

42. Canberra Commission on the Elimination of Nuclear Weapons, *Report of the Canberra Commission on the Elimination of Nuclear Weapons* (Canberra, Australia: Department of Foreign Affairs and Trade, 1996), 18.

43. James Hoge, "'Nuclear Terrorism': Counting Down to the New Armageddon," *New York Times,* Sunday Book Review, 5 September 2004, available online at http://www.nuclearterrorism.org/nyt.htm.

44. Astri Suhrke, "Human Security and the Interests of States," *Security Dialogue* 30 (1999): 266.

45. Geoffrey Robertson, *Crimes against Humanity: The Struggle for Global Justice* (London: Penguin Books, 2002), 39.

46. Ibid.

47. Two classic works are Hans Morgenthau, *Politics among Nations: The Struggle for Power and Peace,* 3rd ed. (New York: Alfred Knopf, 1978); and Kenneth Waltz, *Theory of International Politics* (Reading, Pa.: Addison-Wesley, 1979).

48. Cited in Howard Zinn, *A People's History of the United States from 1492 to the Present,* 2nd ed. (Essex, UK: Pearson Education Limited, 1996), 542.

49. Robertson, *Crimes against Humanity,* 59–63. For a good comparison of the implementation of human rights programs in the United States and Europe, see Kathryn Sikkink, "The Power of Principled Ideas: Human Rights Policies in the United States and Western Europe," in *Ideas and Foreign Policy: Beliefs, Institutions and Political Change,* edited by Judith Goldstein and Robert O. Keohane (Ithaca, N.Y.: Cornell University Press, 1993).

50. The International Committee of the Red Cross, which is neither an intergovernmental organization nor an NGO, had of course existed and done superlative work on casualties and prisoners of war for almost a century before Amnesty International was formed.

51. See Sellars, *The Rise and Rise of Human Rights,* Chapter 1, for an excellent but iconoclastic account of the influence of these NGOs in the making of the UN Charter.

52. Stanley Hoffmann, "The Hell of Good Intentions," *Foreign Policy,* no. 29 (Winter 1977–1978): 3–26.

53. Sellars, *The Rise and Rise of Human Rights,* Chapter 6.

54. Ibid., 134.

55. The Independent Commission on Disarmament and Security Issues, *Common Security: A Blueprint for Survival* (New York: Simon and Schuster, 1982).

56. Mohamad Ayoob, "The Security Problematic of the Third World," *World Politics* 43 (January 1991): 257–283.

57. David Dewitt, "Comprehensive, Common, and Cooperative Security," *The Pacific Review* 5 (1994): 1–15.

58. Dewi Fortuna Anwar, "Human Security: An Intractable Problem in Asia," in *Asian Security Order: Instrumental and Normative Features,* edited by Muthiah Alagappa (Stanford, Calif.: Stanford University Press, 2003), 539.

59. Barry Buzan, *People, States, and Fear,* 2nd ed. (Boulder, Colo.: Lynne Rienner, 1991). The first edition was published in 1982.

60. Ibid., 363.

61. Ibid., 368.

62. Ibid.

63. Richard Ullman, "Redefining Security," *International Security* 8 (Summer 1983): 129–153.

64. Ibid., 129.

65. Ibid.

66. Ibid., 130–131. The trade-off between liberty and security has become most salient in the recent "war against terror."

67. Ibid., 133.

68. Jessica Tuchman Mathews, "Redefining Security," *Foreign Affairs* 68 (Spring 1989): 162.

69. Ibid.

70. Ibid., 165.

71. Ibid., 166.

72. Ibid., 174.

73. Social Science Research Council, "Global Security and Cooperation." Available online at http://www.ssrc.org/programs/gsc, accessed 22 April 2005.

74. The committee member was one of authors of this volume, Yuen Foong Khong. The article he referred to was Richard Betts, "Should Strategic Studies Survive?" *World Politics* 50 (October 1997): 7–33.

75. David Laitin, "Somalia: Civil War and International Intervention," in *Civil Wars, Insecurity, and Intervention,* edited by Barbara Walter and Jack Snyder (New York: Columbia University Press, 1999), 148. Italics added.

76. This account draws from Laitin, "Somalia: Civil War and International Intervention."

77. Daniel Benjamin and Steven Simon, *The Age of Sacred Terror* (New York:

Random House, 2002), 120–122; Jane Boulden, *Peace Enforcement: The United Nations Experience in Congo, Somalia, and Bosnia* (Westport, Conn.: Praeger Publishers, 2001), 51–82.

78. MacFarlane, *Intervention in Contemporary World Politics,* 50.

79. See Thomas Weiss, David Forsythe, and Roger Coate, *The United Nations and Changing World Politics,* 3rd ed. (Boulder, Colo.: Westview Press, 2001), Chapter 3.

80. Robertson, *Crimes against Humanity,* 76.

81. The entire Dutch cabinet resigned in April 2002 when the report of the Netherlands Institute of War Documentation held the government responsible for the cowardly behavior of its peacekeepers in Srebrenica. See Robertson, *Crimes against Humanity,* 82.

82. Ibid.

83. James Fearon and David Laitin, "Ethnicity, Insurgency, and Civil War," *American Political Science Review* 97 (February 2003): 75.

84. MacFarlane, *Intervention in Contemporary World Politics,* 50.

Introduction to Part II

1. Commission on Global Governance, *Our Global Neighborhood* (Oxford: Oxford University Press, 1995), 79.

2. Juan Somavía, *People's Security: Globalizing Social Progress* (n.p., 1999), iv.

3. Boutros Boutros-Ghali, *An Agenda for Peace—Preventive Diplomacy, Peacemaking and Peace-keeping: Report of the Secretary-General pursuant to the statement adopted by the Summit Meeting of the Security Council on 31 January, 1992* (General Assembly document A/47/277 and Security Council document S/24111, 17 June 1992, para. 3.

4. Juan Somavía, "People's Security: From Latin America to the United Nations," in Somavía, *People's Security,* 3. Ambassador Somavía was the chair of the PrepCom for the World Social Summit held in Copenhagen in March 1995.

5. The first major international document to use the concept prominently was UNDP, *Human Development Report 1994: New Dimensions of Human Security* (New York: United Nations, 1994).

6. Ibid.

7. Commission on Human Security, *Human Security Now.*

8. ICISS, *The Responsibility to Protect* (Ottawa: International Development Research Centre, 2001).

9. Thomas G. Weiss, Tatiana Carayannis, Louis Emmerij, and Richard Jolly, *UN Voices: The Struggle for Development and Social Justice* (Bloomington: Indiana University Press, 2005), Chapter 7.

4. The UN and Human Security

1. As time passed, this vector tended to subsume the discussions of other aspects of the functional broadening; environment and security and health and security were seen as part of a relationship between sustainable human development and security.

2. We are indebted to Richard Jolly for bringing this important precursor to the UNDP's *Human Development Report 1994* to our attention.

3. The annual global human development reports are accompanied by numerous national reports. Since their inception, 375 national and subnational human development reports have been published on 135 countries, along with ten regional reports. See UNDP, "Human Development Reports: Measuring Development and Influencing Policy," http://www.undp.org/dpa/publications/ffNHDRe101201.pdf, 14 November 2004.

4. See UNDP, *Human Development Report 1990: Concept and Measurement of Human Development* (New York: United Nations Development Programme, 1990), 11–13.

5. Ibid., 10.

6. Mahbub ul Haq, *Reflections on Human Development* (Oxford: Oxford University Press, 1995), 58.

7. Keith Griffin and Terry McKinley, *Towards a Human Development Strategy* (New York: United Nations Development Programme, 1993), 3.

8. UNDP, *Human Development Report 1993: People's Participation* (New York: United Nations Development Programme, 1993), 1–2.

9. UNDP, *Human Development Report 1994: New Dimensions of Human Security* (New York: United Nations Development Programme, 1994).

10. Ibid., 23.

11. Ibid., iii. Curiously, although the need to reconceptualize security is a prominent theme in the overview of the report, discussion of it is absent from the report's main body.

12. Ibid., 31. This sentiment reflected a widely growing awareness within the UN system of the problems of physical and structural violence against women. See also "Programme of Action of the International Conference on Population and Development" (General Assembly document A/CONF.171/13), 18 October 1994, available online at http://www.un.org/popin/icpd/conference/offeng/poa.html; and *Report of the World Summit for Social Development* (General Assembly document A/CONF.166.9), 19 April 1995, available online at http://www.un.org/documents/ga/conf166/aconf166-9.htm.

13. Commission on Global Governance, *Our Global Neighborhood* (Oxford: Oxford University Press, 1995), 79.

14. The meeting was called at the initiative of ECOSOC, whose recommendation for the convening of a summit on social development was endorsed in General Assembly resolution 47/92, 16 December 1992. The link is clear in the title of the 1994 UNDP Human Development Report overview, which was titled "An Agenda for the Social Summit."

15. Many of these suggestions were also contained in the agenda for action in Mahbub ul Haq's influential contemporaneous work, *Reflections on Human Development*, 85–92.

16. UNDP, *Human Development Report 1994: New Dimensions of Human Security*, 60.

17. Ibid., 77.

18. General Assembly resolution 47/92. The absence of comment on human development in Social Summit official documents is also striking.

19. A point noted by the Egyptian representative, who expressed a desire for concrete commitments of resources for social development on the part of donor countries and for debt alleviation.

20. See former Canadian foreign minister Lloyd Axworthy's comment on the report in Rob McRae and Don Hubert, eds., *Human Security and the New Diplomacy: Protecting People, Promoting Peace* (Montreal and Kingston: McGill-Queen's University Press, 2001), 4.

21. To cite one notable example, it is reported that Lloyd Axworthy first encountered the notion of human security when representing Canada in the summit process as Canada's minister for human resources development. Private e-mail communication. Axworthy himself cites the summit as a turning point for him "in extending this notion of human security into the wider international arena." Lloyd Axworthy, *Navigating a New World: Canada's Global Future* (Toronto: Alfred A. Knopf Canada, 2003), 41.

22. *Note by the Secretary-General* (General Assembly document A/59/565), 2 December 2004, available online at http://daccessdds.un.org/doc/UNDOC/GEN/N04/602/31/PDF/N0460231.pdf?OpenElement.

23. George W. Bush, "Remarks by the President at United Nations Financing for Development Conference," Monterrey, Mexico, 22 March 2002, 1, available online at http://www.whitehouse.gov/news/releases/2002/03/20020322-1.html, accessed 24 October 2004.

24. These mechanisms are the focus of Chapter VI of the UN Charter. See also Boutros-Ghali, *An Agenda for Peace: Preventive Diplomacy, Peacemaking and Peacekeeping,* paras. 23–33.

25. Ibid., para. 26.

26. UNDP, *Human Development Report 1993: People's Participation,* 3.

27. *An Agenda for Development: Report of the Secretary-General* (General Assembly document A/48/935), 6 May 1994, paras. 17–18, available online at http://www.un.org/Docs/SG/agdev.html, accessed 24 October 2004.

28. Edward J. Laurence, *Light Weapons and Intrastate Conflict* (New York: Carnegie Corporation, 1998); and Jeffrey Boutwell and Michael Klare, *Light Weapons and Civil Conflict: Controlling the Tools of Violence* (Lanham, Md.: Rowman & Littlefield, 1999).

29. Carnegie Commission on Preventing Deadly Conflict, *Preventing Deadly Conflict: Final Report* (New York: Carnegie Corporation, 1997), xviii–xix, xxii–xxiii, and 82–89.

30. There is a similar discussion of the structural causes of conflict in Commission on Global Governance, *Our Global Neighborhood,* 95–97.

31. *The Causes of Conflict and the Promotion of Durable Peace and Sustainable Development in Africa: Report of the Secretary-General* (General Assembly document A/52/871 and Security Council document S/1998/318), 13 April 1998, available online at http://www.un.org/ecosocdev/geninfo/afrec/sgreport/main.htm, accessed 24 October 2004.

32. Ibid., para. 2.

33. Ibid., paras. 15, 79–80.

34. Ibid., paras. 80–83.

35. Ibid., paras. 85–89.

36. Ibid., paras. 93–99.

37. UN General Assembly, Declaration and Programme of Action on a Culture of Peace (General Assembly document A/53/243), 13 September 1999, available online at http://www.unesco.org/cpp/uk/declarations/2000.htm, accessed 25 October 2004.

38. *Statement by the President of the Security Council: The Situation in Africa* (Security Council document S/PRST/1998/28), 16 September 1998; *Statement by the President of the Security Council: The Situation in Africa* (Security Council document S/PRST/1998/29), 24 September 1998; Security Council resolution 1209, 19 November 1998.

39. Security Council resolution 1170, 28 May 1998. The working group established in this resolution reported back in September 1998, suggesting that arrangements for cooperation with and support of regional and subregional organizations be enhanced and that the effectiveness of arms embargoes be strengthened. Security Council resolutions 1196 and 1197, 16 and 19 September 1998.

40. *Statement by the President of the Security Council* (Security Council document S/PRST/1999/34), 30 November 1999.

41. The resort to ECOSOC reflected the facts that economic and development issues are generally considered to come under its remit and it oversees most of the agencies that would implement the development aspect of conflict prevention. This points to an institutional ambiguity within the UN regarding the division of responsibility for security when the definition of the term is broadened to include economic issues.

42. *Statement by the President of the Security Council: Role of the Security Council in the Prevention of Armed Conflicts* (Security Council document S/PRST/2000/25), 20 July 2000. See also *Statement of the President of the Security Council* (Security Council document S/PRST/2001/5), 20 February 2001.

43. *Prevention of Armed Conflict: Report of the Secretary General* (General Assembly document A/55/985 and Security Council document S/2001/574), 7 June 2001.

44. Ibid., paras. 7–10.

45. Ibid., para. 100.

46. Kofi Annan, *We the Peoples: The Role of the United Nations in the 21st Century* (New York: United Nations, 2000), 19.

47. The latest consideration of underdevelopment as a source of conflict and the need to address it as part of a collective project of conflict prevention is the report of the High-level Panel, *A More Secure World: Our Shared Responsibility* (General Assembly document A/59/565), 2 December 2004, 12, 25–30.

48. Ibid., 24–31.

49. Regeringskanliet, *Preventing Violent Conflict—A Swedish Action Plan* (Stockholm: Regeringskanliet, 1999), 14, 38, 41–42, 68. See also Ministry of Foreign Affairs, *Preventing Violent Conflict* (Stockholm: Ministry of Foreign Affairs, 1997), 9.

50. See SIDA, "The Funds Were Allocated This Way in 2002—Sectors," available online at http://www.sida.se/Sida/jsp/polopoly.jsp?d=3168&a=22948, accessed 24 October 2004.

51. There are two interministerial conflict prevention pools, one global and the other for Africa. The two pools allocated £600 million between 2001 and 2004. See Greg Austin, Emery Brusset, Malcolm Chalmers, and Juliet Pierce, *Evaluation of the Conflict Prevention Pools: Synthesis Report,* Evaluation Report EV 647 (London: Department for International Development, 2004), 2, available online at http://www.dfid.gov.uk/aboutdfid/performance/files/ev647synthesis.pdf, accessed 24 October 2004.

52. European Commission, "Communication from the Commission on Conflict Prevention," 11 April 2001, 4, 5, 9, 12, available online at http://www.eu2001.se/static/eng/pdf/violent.pdf, accessed 24 October 2004. See also the "EU Programme for the Prevention of Violent Conflict," available online at http://www.eu.int/comm/external_relations/cfsp/news/com2001_211_en.pdf, accessed 24 October 2004. The program, adopted at the Göteborg European Council, sets out a strategy for mainstreaming conflict prevention in the foreign policy and development activities of the EU and provides for regular monitoring and follow-up. The "root causes" logic was also taken up in Council of the European Union in "European Security Strategy, A Secure Europe in a Better World," Brussels, Belgium, 12 December 2003, 2, available online at http://ue.eu.int/uedocs/cmsUpload/78367.pdf, accessed 24 October 2004.

53. "European Security Strategy, A Secure Europe in a Better World," 2, 10. It is noteworthy that the council emphasized that physical security was an essential precondition for development.

54. Frank Columbus, ed., *The National Security Strategy of the United States of America* (Hauppauge, N.Y.: Novinka Books, 2003), Chapters III and IV, available online at http://www.whitehouse.gov/nsc/nss.html, accessed 24 October 2004.

55. Bush, "Remarks by the President at United Nations Financing for Development Conference"; and Bush, "Remarks by the President on Global Development," Inter-American Development Bank, Washington, D.C., 14 March 2002, available online at http://www.whitehouse.gov/news/releases/2002/03/20020314-7.html, accessed 13 May 2005.

56. USAID, *Foreign Aid in the National Interest* (Washington, D.C.: USAID, 2003), Chapter 4, available online at http://www.usaid.gov/fani/cho4/understandingconflict.htm, accessed 24 October 2004. See also USAID, *Strategic Plan, Fiscal Years 2004–2009: Aligning Diplomacy and Development Assistance* (Washington, D.C.: U.S. State Department, 2003), 6, 18, available online at http://www.usaid.gov/policy/budget/state_usaid_strat_plan.pdf, accessed 24 October 2004. The document notes that unequal economic opportunity and neglected social and economic capacity, when coupled with weak or failing state structures, provide fertile ground for terrorist activity and conflict and it stresses the importance of promoting sustainable development to success in the war on terror.

57. African Union, Protocol Relating to the Establishment of a Peace and Security Council, 9 July 2002, Article 4(d). See also the Lomé Declaration's recognition that development is a prerequisite for peace and security. Assembly of Heads of State and Government (AU), 36th Ordinary Session, Lomé Declaration, AHG/Decl.2 (XXXVI), 12 July 2000, 2, available online at http://www.uneca.org/itca/ariportal/lome.htm, accessed 24 October 2004.

58. Assembly of Heads of State and Government (OAU), CSSDCA Solemn Declaration, AHG/Decl.4 (XXXVI), 12 July 2000, 1, available online at http://www.africa-union.org/Special_Programs/CSSDCA/cssdca-solemndeclaration.pdf, accessed 24 October 2004.

59. Ibid., 5–6.

60. See, for example, Peter Uvin, *Aiding Violence: The Development Enterprise in Rwanda* (West Hartford, Conn.: Kumarian Press, 1998); Anton Barré, David Shearer, and Peter Uvin, *The Limits and Scope for the Use of Development Assistance Incentives and Disincentives for Influencing Conflict Situations—Case Study: Rwanda* (Paris: OECD, 1999), 35.

61. For an influential treatment of this issue, see Mary Anderson, *Do No Harm: How Aid Can Support Peace—or War* (Boulder, Colo.: Lynne Rienner Publisher, 1999). For a representative policy statement from the donor community, see OECD Development Assistance Committee, "Policy Statement: Conflict, Peace, and Development Cooperation on the Threshold of the 21st Century," May 1997, available online at http://www.oecd.org/dataoecd/31/39/2755375.pdf, accessed 26 October 2004.

62. See Kaoru Ishikawa, "A New Japanese Approach to Nation-Building: People-Centered Human Security," in *External Factors for Asian Development,* edited by Hiroshi Kohama (Singapore: ASEAN Foundation and Japan Institute of International Affairs, 2003), 212.

63. Amartya Sen, *Development as Freedom* (Oxford: Oxford University Press, 1999).

64. This point harks back to his earlier work on the relationship between famine and governance, where he noted that famines do not occur in democratic political systems. See Jean Drèze, Amartya Sen, and Athar Hussain, eds., *The Political Economy of Hunger: Selected Essays* (Oxford: Oxford University Press, 1999).

65. Sen, *Development as Freedom,* 184–188, quote on 188.

66. See *Statement by Foreign Minister Keizo Obuchi on Japan and East Asia: Outlook for the New Millennium,* 4 May 1998. Available online at http://www.mofa.go.jp/announce/announce/1998/5/980504.html.

67. The Trust Fund for Human Security, *For the "Human-Centred" 21st Century* (Tokyo: Ministry of Foreign Affairs, n.d.), available online at http://www.mofa.go.jp/policy/human_secu/t_fund21/t_fund21.pdf, accessed 4 November 2004.

68. Ibid.

69. Ibid.

70. One of the seven activities in the list of project areas was "protecting people under conflict who are exposed to physical violence, discrimination, and whose destitute situation derives mostly from inequalities in treatment." However, none of the projects on the appended full list of activities that were funded falls into this category. Ibid.

71. Ishikawa, "A New Japanese Approach to Nation-Building," 220.

72. Ibid., 233.

73. The fact that Japan does not participate in the Human Security Network, that there was no substantial dialogue between the CHS and the Norwegian and Canadian governments during the preparation of the commission's report, and that no Human Security Network member contributed to the funding of the CHS study suggests a fundamental difference of view within the community of proponents of human security.

74. Commission on Human Security, *Human Security Now,* 4–12.

75. Ibid., 4.

76. Remarks by some commissioners outside the CHS context suggest a more critical view of the state. See Sadako Ogata, *Statement to the Third Tokyo International Conference on African Development* (TICAD III), Tokyo, Japan, 29 September 2003, 2: "I have come to believe there is a mismatch between the existing machinery for international cooperation and the challenges we are facing. I seriously question whether the assumptions underlying the existing international machinery, such as the primacy of states and national sovereignty, are still adequate today" (mimeo in author's possession). Given Japanese sensitivities to the sentiments of its neighbors, it is not surprising that Ogata's statement is not included on the Web site of TICAD III. See Third Tokyo International Conference on African Development, available online at http://www.ticad.net/speeches.html, accessed 10 November 2004.

77. Commission on Human Security, *Human Security Now*, iv.

5. The UN and Human Security

1. Permanent Court of International Justice, "Advisory Opinion: Nationality Decrees Issued in Tunis and Morocco (French Zone) on November 8, 1921," PCIJ Series B, no. 4, 7 February 1923, 16.

2. Department of Foreign Affairs and International Trade, *Freedom from Fear: Canada's Foreign Policy for Human Security* (Ottawa: Department of Foreign Affairs and International Trade, 2000), 3, available online at http://www.humansecurity.gc.ca/freedom_from_fear-en.asp, accessed 19 November 2004.

3. Department of Foreign Affairs and International Trade, *Human Security: Safety for People in a Changing World* (Ottawa: Government of Canada, April 1999), 3. The similarity of this criticism of the UNDP's broadening of the concept of human security to Mahbub ul Haq's criticism of efforts to include "everything" in the human development index is both obvious and ironic.

4. Ibid., 7. In its security strategy document, the European Union agreed: "Security is a precondition for development." European Union, *A Secure Europe in a Better World* (Brussels: EU, 2003), 2.

5. Department of Foreign Affairs and International Trade, *Freedom from Fear: Canada's Foreign Policy for Human Security*.

6. See the comments on the role of governments in jeopardizing human security in Kofi Annan, "Preface," in UNHCR, *The State of the World's Refugees 1997–98: A Humanitarian Agenda* (Oxford: Oxford University Press, 1997), ix; and on state incapacity in Rob McRae and Don Hubert, eds., *Human Security and the New Diplomacy: Protecting People, Promoting Peace* (Montreal and Kingston: McGill-Queen's University Press, 2001), 19–20. See also the summary of the ICISS in *The Responsibility to Protect* (Ottawa: International Development Research Centre, 2001), 4; the views of UNHCR Sadako Ogata in "Globalization and Human Security," Weatherhead Policy Forum, Columbia University, 27 March 2002, 1, available online at http://www.humansecurity-chs.org/activities/outreach/columbia.html (accessed 13 March 2005); and those of the Commis-

sion on Human Security in *Human Security Now* (New York: Commission on Human Security, 2003), 2.

7. Commission on Global Governance, *Our Global Neighborhood* (Oxford: Oxford University Press, 1995), 92.

8. Southern Rhodesia constitutes a slight exception here because of British use of naval forces to interdict embargoed shipments to its rebel colony via ports in Mozambique.

9. Security Council resolution 688, 5 April 1991.

10. For an insightful analysis of the development of this concept and the role of the Iraq crisis in its inception, see Margaret Jane Hoverd, "Humanitarian Action in Bosnia: A Study of the Office of the United Nations High Commissioner for Refugees, 1991–1999" (D.Phil. Thesis, Oxford University, 2001).

11. Security Council resolution 733, 23 January 1992.

12. Security Council resolution 794, 3 December 1992.

13. Security Council resolution 814, 26 March 1993.

14. For a good account of peacekeeping and peace enforcement in Somalia, see Jane Boulden, *Peace Enforcement: The United Nations Experience in Congo, Somalia, and Bosnia* (Westport, Conn.: Praeger Publishing, 2001), 51–82.

15. Security Council resolutions 757, 30 May 1992; 770, 13 August 1992; 781, 9 October 1992. The ban on military flight was extended to all unauthorized flights in Security Council resolution 816, 31 March 1993. This resolution mandated member states to enforce the ban.

16. Security Council resolution 820, 17 April 1993.

17. Security Council resolution 798, 18 December 1992.

18. Security Council resolution 808, 20 February 1993.

19. Security Council resolution 819, 16 April 1993.

20. Security Council resolution 824, 6 May 1993.

21. Security Council resolution 1031, 15 December 1995.

22. Security Council resolution 929, 29 June 1994.

23. UNPROFOR is a partial exception here. Although the mandate clearly envisaged protection of humanitarian personnel, some aid personnel expressed frustration that the force did not protect the beneficiaries of assistance.

24. The East Timor case raises another important question: If consent is coerced, is it consent?

25. The Non-Aligned Movement, for example, responded by declaring that "we reject the so-called 'right of humanitarian intervention' which has no legal basis in the UN Charter or in the general principles." "Final Communique," Meeting of Ministers for Foreign Affairs and Heads of Delegation of the Non-Aligned Movement, held in New York on 23 September 1999, available online at www.nam.gov.za/minmeet/newyorkcom.htm, accessed 12 November 2004. The quotation is at para. 171. The Declaration of the Summit of the South, a product of the G-77 summit in Havana in April 2000, reiterates the point equally unequivocally.

26. On this point, see David Rieff's comments on the role of Philip Johnston (of CARE USA), in *A Bed for the Night: Humanitarianism in Crisis* (New York: Vintage, 2002), 34–35.

27. A former senior UN official who had responsibilities concerning peace operations in the early 1990s noted that when human security first crossed his screen in the
early 1990s, he was unenthusiastic, feeling that the discussion was too theoretical.
However, the experiences in Somalia and in the former Yugoslavia convinced him
otherwise. He recalled helicopter trips across villages in the former Yugoslavia where he
saw the houses of minority families selectively burned to the ground and concluded
that the organization was paying insufficient attention to the human dimension of
peace operations. Interview, 28 October 2003.

28. Eric Dachy (Médecins sans Frontières-Belgium), quoted in Rieff, *A Bed for the
Night*, 136.

29. UNHCR, *State of the World's Refugees 1997*, 45.

30. José Maria Mendiluce, as quoted in Rieff, *A Bed for the Night*, 144.

31. A UNHCR official involved in drafting the report considered this to be
"symptomatic of the organization's schizophrenic character at that time—wanting to
stretch the mandate beyond traditional refugee-related concerns, but simultaneously
being pulled back into traditional protection issues as defined in the organization's
Statute." E-mail communication, 27 October 2003.

32. Canada's first official use of the term was in a speech by Minister of Foreign
Affairs Lloyd Axworthy to the 1996 session of the UN General Assembly.

33. Department of Foreign Affairs and International Trade, *Human Security: Safety
for People in a Changing World*, 6.

34. The network consists of Austria, Canada, Chile, Greece, Ireland, Jordan, Mali,
the Netherlands, Norway, Switzerland, Slovenia, and Thailand; South Africa was an
observer. See the Human Security Network Web site, available online at http://
www.humansecuritynetwork.org, accessed 12 November 2004.

35. Commission on Global Governance, *Our Global Neighborhood*, 81–82.

36. General Assembly resolution 53/35, 30 November 1998.

37. See his letter to the council, Security Council document S/1999/339, 18 March 1999.

38. See *Report of the Secretary-General Pursuant to General Assembly Resolution 53/
35: The Fall of Srebrenica* (General Assembly document A/54/549), 15 November 1999;
and *Report of the Independent Inquiry into the Actions of the United Nations during the
1994 Genocide in Rwanda* (Security Council document S/1999/1257), 16 December 1999.

39. For the officer's account, see Roméo Dallaire and Brent Beardsley, *Shake Hands
with the Devil: The Failure of Humanity in Rwanda* (Toronto: Random House, 2003).

40. Neil MacFarlane, "Politics and Humanitarian Action," Occasional Paper no. 41
(Providence, R.I.: Thomas J. Watson Jr. Institute for International Studies, 2000), 57–58.

41. The Rwandan-backed rebels took the refugee camps. Most of the refugees
returned to Rwanda. However, a considerable number of Hutu elements most closely
implicated in the genocide of 1994 dispersed westward into the interior of Zaire.

42. *Statement by the President of the Security Council* (Security Council document S/
PRST/1999/6), 12 February 1999.

43. *Report of the Secretary-General to the Security Council on the Protection of
Civilians in Armed Conflict* (Security Council document S/1999/957), 8 September 1999.

44. Ibid., para. 30.

45. Ibid., para. 40. He was careful to qualify this recommendation by suggesting that before such action be undertaken, the council should consider the scope of the violation, whether or not local authorities were able to maintain law and order, whether or not local authorities were complicit in the violations, whether or not peaceful alternatives had been exhausted, the capacity of the Security Council to monitor the situation, and proportionality in the use of force.

46. Security Council resolution 1265, 17 September 1999, para. 10. One Canadian diplomat referred to this paragraph as the Security Council's acceptance of the concept of human security. Interview, 9 November 2002.

47. Security Council resolution 1296, 19 April 2000, paras. 5 and 8. Italics in the resolution.

48. *Identical letters Dated 21 August 2000 from the Secretary-General to the President of the General Assembly and the President of the Security Council* (General Assembly document A/55/305 and Security Council document S/2000/809), 21 August 2000, paras. 41 and 47b.

49. Ibid., para. 62.

50. *Report of the Secretary-General on the Work of the Organization* (General Assembly document A/54/1), 1999.

51. *Report of the Secretary-General on the Work of the Organization* (General Assembly document A/55/1), 2000.

52. *Report of the Secretary-General on the Work of the Organization* (1999), paras. 46 and 52.

53. Ibid., para. 50. See also Kofi Annan, *We the Peoples: The Role of the United Nations in the 21st Century,* 43.

54. *Report of the Secretary-General on the Work of the Organization* (1999), paras. 66–67.

55. Annan, *We the Peoples,* 48.

56. *Report of the Secretary-General on the Work of the Organization* (2000), paras. 30–31.

57. Ibid., para. 37.

58. ICISS, *The Responsibility to Protect,* vii.

59. Francis Deng, Sadikiel Kimaro, Terry Lyons, Donald Rothchild, and I. William Zartman, *Sovereignty as Responsibility: Conflict Management in Africa* (Washington, D.C.: The Brookings Institution, 1996).

60. For a critical evaluation of these principles, see S. Neil MacFarlane, Carolin Thielking, and Jennifer Welsh, "The Responsibility to Protect: Assessing the Report of the International Commission on Intervention and State Sovereignty," *The International Journal* 57 (Autumn 2002): 487–512.

61. See, for example, Alex J. Bellamy and Matt McDonald, "'The Utility of Human Security': Which Humans? What Security? A Reply to Thomas and Tow," *Security Dialogue* 30 (September 2002): 373–377; and Nicholas Thomas and William T. Tow, "Gaining Security by Trashing the State? A Reply to Bellamy and McDonald," *Security Dialogue* 30 (September 2002): 379–382.

62. Namely the reference to the "re-established state"; ICISS, *The Responsibility to Protect,* 41.

63. For further comments on these points, see Welsh, Thielking, and MacFarlane, "The Responsibility to Protect," 496–505.

64. Adam Roberts, "The Price of Protection," *Survival* 44 (Winter 2002–2003): 157.

65. "No one expected that at the end of two days the question of humanitarian intervention would be resolved. . . . The debate was an exercise of enhancing awareness of the issue." "'Un exercice de prise de conscience,' selon Mohamed Sahnoun" ("'An Exercise in Enhancing Awareness,' according to Mohamed Sahnoun"), *Le Monde*, 3 June 2002.

66. "Aide Memoire: For the Consideration of Issues Pertaining to the Protection of Civilians during the Security Council's Deliberation of Peacekeeping Mandates" (Security Council document S/PRST/2002/6), 15 March 2002.

67. High-level Panel on Threats, Challenges and Change, *A More Secure World*, 21–22, 56.

68. See Lisa Martin and Jeffrey Laurenti, *The United Nations and Economic Sanctions* (New York: UN-USA, 1997), 24–25. For an earlier warning along these lines, see Commission on Global Governance, *Our Global Neighborhood*, 107.

69. *Report of the Secretary-General to the Security Council on the Protection of Civilians in Armed Conflict* (Security Council document S/1999/957), 8 September 1999, para. 25.

70. Annan, *We The Peoples*, 50.

71. Security Council resolution 1296, 2000, para. 22.

72. Security Council resolution 1267, 15 October 1999; Security Council resolution 1333, 19 December 2000 on Afghanistan, Security Council resolution 1343, 7 March 2001; and Security Council resolution 1478, 6 May 2003 regarding Liberia.

73. For information on the Interlaken Process, see http://www.smartsanctions.ch, accessed 12 November 2004. One major product of the Interlaken Process was a manual on design and implementation prepared by the Thomas J. Watson Jr. Institute for International Studies at Brown University: *Targeted Financial Sanctions: A Manual for Design and Implementation* (Providence, R.I.: Thomas J. Watson Jr. Institute of International Studies, 2001).

74. This initiative was coordinated by the Bonn International Centre for Conversion with support from the German Foreign Office. Participants produced a substantial study edited by Michael Brzoska, *Design and Implementation of Arms Embargoes and Travel- and Aviation-Related Sanctions* (Bonn and Berlin: Bonn International Centre for Conversion, 2001). See http://www.bicc.de/events/unsanc, accessed 12 November 2004.

75. For background on the Stockholm Process, see http://www.smartsanctions.se, accessed 12 November 2004. The Stockholm Process generated model common law and civil law legislation that spelled out the requirements of national compliance with sanctions regimes in response to the difficulty many states encountered in adopting sanctions legislation on an ad hoc basis. *Making Targeted Sanctions Effective: Guidelines for the Implementation of UN Policy Options* (Uppsala, Sweden: Department of Peace and Conflict Research, Uppsala University, 2003).

76. High-level Panel on Threats, Challenges and Change, *A More Secure World*, 32.

77. CSCE, "Document of the Copenhagen Meeting of the Conference on the Human Dimension of the CSCE," Copenhagen, 5–29 June 1990, available online at http://www.osce.org/docs/english/1990-1999/hd/cope90e.htm, accessed 13 March 2005.

78. See the discussion in William Pfaff, "Shock, Awe and the Human Body," *International Herald Tribune,* 22 December 2004, 6, especially the conclusion of a Department of Defense legal task force in March 2003 that the president, as commander in chief, was not bound by any international or federal law on torture.

79. On the contrary, at para. 37, members declare: "None of these commitments may be interpreted as implying any right to engage in any activity or perform any action in contravention of the purposes and principles of the Charter of the United Nations, other obligations under international law or the provisions of the Final Act, including the principle of territorial integrity of States." "Document of the Moscow Meeting of the Conference on the Human Dimension of the CSCE," Moscow, 15 October 1991, available online at http://www.osce.org/documents/odihr/1991/10/13995_en.pdf.

80. CSCE, "Document of the Moscow Meeting of the Conference of the Human Dimension of the CSCE," Preamble.

81. At the time of writing, there had been five activations of the human dimension mechanism, two of which were requested by individual states wishing external review of their own procedures and three by groups of states concerned about developments in other states. The list of cases where the mechanism has not been activated (Chechnya, Kosovo, Krajina, Abkhazia, Nagorno Karabakh, etc.) is striking.

82. For the London Declaration, see Declaration on a Transformed North Atlantic Alliance Issued by the Heads of State and Government Participating in the Meeting of the North Atlantic Alliance, London, 6 July 1990, available online at http://www.nato.int/docu/comm/49-95/c900706a.htm, accessed 2 December 2004.

83. "The Alliance's Strategic Concept Agreed by the Heads of State and Government Participating in the Meeting of the North Atlantic Council," Rome, 8 November 1991, available online at http://www.nato.int/docu/basictxt/b920604a.htm, accessed 2 December 2004.

84. "Final Communiqué of the Ministerial Meeting of the North Atlantic Council (including the Oslo Decision on NATO Support for Peacekeeping Activities under the Responsibility of the CSCE)," Oslo, 4 June 1992, available online at http://nato.int/docu/basictxt/b920604a.htm, accessed 2 December 2004.

85. The Partnership for Peace (PFP) is a program established by NATO to foster cooperation with nonmembers in Europe and the former Soviet Union.

86. For a useful discussion, see Rachel Kerr, *The International Criminal Court for the Former Yugoslavia* (Oxford: Oxford University Press, 2004), 154–158.

87. This is not to say that protection of civilians was the sole, or possibly even the major, reason for the NATO action.

88. "The Alliance's Strategic Concept Approved by the Heads of State and Government Participating in the Meeting of the North Atlantic Council in Washington, D.C. on 23rd and 24th April 1999," para. 3, available online at http://www.nato.int/docu/pr/1999/p99-065e.htm, accessed 2 December 2004.

89. Ibid., para. 29.

90. Ibid., paras. 31 and 54. Article 5 of the North Atlantic Treaty states the commitment of members to collective self-defense. Non–Article 5 operations refer to military operations that are not responses to aggression (e.g., crisis response).

91. The phrase is taken from Independent International Commission on Kosovo, *The Kosovo Report: Conflict, International Response, Lessons Learned* (Oxford: Oxford University Press, 2000), 4.

92. ICISS, *The Responsibility to Protect*, 55.

93. Western European Union Council of Ministers, Petersberg Declaration, 19 June 1992, para. II.4, available online at http://www.weu.int, accessed 24 December 2004.

94. See Amsterdam Inter-Governmental Conference, Declaration Relating to Western European Union, in European Union, "The Treaties Establishing the European Communities and Related Acts," 10 November 1997, available online at http://europa.eu.int/eur-lex/en/treaties/dat/amsterdam.html#0125030020, accessed 20 November 2004; European Council Declaration on Strengthening the Common European Policy on Security and Defence, Annex III to "Presidency Conclusions: Cologne European Council 3 and 4 June 1999," available online at http://ue.eu.int/en/Info/eurocouncil/index.htm, accessed 21 November 2004; and "Presidency Conclusions: Helsinki European Council 10 and 11 December 1999," available online at http://ue.eu.int/en/Info/eurocouncil/index.htm, accessed 21 November 2004.

95. See British-French Summit, Joint Declaration (the St. Malo Declaration), 4 December 1998, available online at http://www.iss-eu.org/chaillot/chai47e.html#3, accessed 21 November 2004.

96. See "Presidency Conclusions: Cologne" (Annex III), and "Presidency Conclusions: Helsinki." The Helsinki conclusions envisaged a force of some 50,000–60,000 soldiers "capable of the full range of Petersberg tasks."

97. "Presidency Report on Strengthening the Common European Security and Defence Policy," Annex I to "Presidency Conclusions: European Council, Santa Maria da Feira, 19–20 June 2000," para. III.3(d), available online at http://www.iss-eu.org/chaillot/chai47e.html#26, accessed 21 November 2004. All of the European documents cited in notes 94 through 97 are also available in hard copy in Maartje Rutten, "From St. Malo to Nice—European Defence: Core Documents, Chaillot Papers no. 47 (Paris: Institute for Security Studies, Western European Union, May 2001).

98. For an early and positive assessment, see "EU Agrees to Develop Battle Group Teams," *International Herald Tribune,* 23 November 2004, 3.

99. Security Council resolution 1484, 30 May 2003.

100. "The Constitutive Act [of the African Union]," Lomé, Togo, 11 July 2000, Article 4h, available online at http://www.africa-union.org/About_AU/Constitutive_Act.htm.

101. Protocol Relating to the Establishment of the Peace and Security Council of the African Union, Durban, South Africa, 9 July 2002, available online at http://www.africa-union.org/Official_documents/Treaties_%20Conventions_%20Protocols/Protocol_peace%20and%20security.pdf, accessed 21 November 2004.

102. Ratification of the protocol was achieved in December 2003. See "Decision on the Operationalization of the Protocol Relating to the Establishment of the Peace and

Security Council," 16 December 2003, Assembly/AU/Dec.16 (II), available online at
http://www.africa-union.org/Official_documents/Decisions_Declarations/
Assembly%20AU%20Dec%2016%20II.pdf, accessed 21 November 2004. As of December
2004, thirty-seven member states had ratified the protocol.

103.   SADC, Protocol on Political, Defence and Security Co-operation, Blantyre,
Malawi, August 14, 2001, Article 2.2.e and f, available online at http://www.sadc.int/
index.php?lang=english&path=legal/protocols/&page=p_politics_defence_and_
security_cooperation, accessed 21 November 2004.

104.   Ibid., Article 11.2.b.i.

105.   See the analysis by one of the two co-authors in S. Neil MacFarlane, "Intervention in Contemporary World Politics," Adelphi Paper no. 350 (London: Oxford
University Press for the International Institute for Strategic Studies, 2002), 58–60.

106.   See the reactions of the Non-Aligned Movement and the G-77 to the intervention in Kosovo cited in note 25.

107.   "Inter-American Democratic Charter," Lima, Peru, 11 September 2001, Articles 1,
7, and 21, available online at http://www.oas.org/charter/docs/resolution1_en_p4.htm,
accessed 21 November 2004.

108.   In resolution 780 (6 October 1992), the council established a Commission of
Experts to assess breaches of the Geneva Convention and other violations of international law committed in the territory of the former Yugoslavia.

109.   Security Council resolution 808, 22 February 1993; Security Council resolution
827, 25 May 1993, annex.

110.   Security Council resolution 955, 8 November 1994.

111.   On this point, see Darryl Robinson, "Case Study: The International Criminal
Court," in *Human Security and the New Diplomacy: Protecting People, Promoting Peace,*
edited by Rob McRae and Don Hubert (Montreal and Kingston: McGill-Queen's
University Press, 2001), 171.

112.   The idea of the International Criminal Court originated in a proposal by
Trinidad and Tobago to the United Nations calling for the establishment of an international criminal organ to try cases related to drug trafficking. The experiences of the
early 1990s shifted the focus to war crimes and crimes against humanity. See Coalition
for the International Criminal Court, "A Timeline of the Establishment of the International Criminal Court." Available online at http://www.iccnow.org/pressroom/
factsheets/CICCFS_Timeline_Sept04.pdf, accessed 14 May 2005.

113.   Namely, the NGO Coalition for an International Criminal Court, which
grew ultimately into a network of over 2,000 NGOs. For background, see http://
www.iccnow.org, accessed 12 November 2004.

114.   The International Law Commission was established by the UN General
Assembly in 1947 to develop and codify international law.

115.   "Rome Statute of the International Criminal Court" (General Assembly
document A/CONF.183/9), 17 July 1998.

116.   Article 7.1.g. The Rome Statute is available online at http://www.icc-cpi.int/
library/basicdocuments/rome_statute(e).html, accessed 12 November 2004.

117.   Ibid., Article 7.1.d.

118. The best general study of the evolution of the ban on land mines is Don Hubert, "The Landmine Ban: A Case Study in Humanitarian Advocacy," Occasional Paper no. 42 (Providence, R.I.: Thomas J. Watson Jr. Institute for International Studies, 2000). This study is the principal source for our summary of the ban on land mines.

119. See the particularly influential report that was sponsored by Asia Watch/Human Rights Watch and Physicians for Human Rights: Eric Stover and Rae McGrath, *Landmines in Cambodia: The Coward's War* (New York: Asia Watch/Human Rights Watch and Physicians for Human Rights, 1991).

120. Boutros Boutros-Ghali, *An Agenda for Peace—Preventive Diplomacy, Peacemaking and Peace-keeping: Report of the Secretary-General Pursuant to the Statement Adopted by the Summit Meeting of the Security Council on 31 January, 1992* (General Assembly document A/47/277 and Security Council document S/24111), 17 June 1992, para. 58; and Boutros-Ghali, "Foreword," in Kevin Cahill, *Cleaning the Fields: Solutions to the Global Landmines Crisis* (New York: Basic Books, 1995), xiv.

121. Hubert, *The Landmine Ban*, 17.

122. As of November 2004, 143 countries have ratified or acceded to the treaty. See "States Party to the Ottawa Treaty," available online at http://www.icrc.org/Web/Eng/siteeng0.nsf/iwpList108/3418BAA4D78AE8ACC1256B66005B33B7, accessed 21 November 2004.

123. Hubert, *The Landmine Ban*, 25.

124. For example, the UN Department of Humanitarian Affairs and UNICEF participated in preparations for the initial Ottawa meeting, while UN agencies participated in the October 1996 meeting as observers.

125. Hubert, *The Landmine Ban*, 20.

126. Land mines continue to produce 15,000 to 20,000 new casualties each year. Carol Bellamy, *The State of the World's Children 2005: Childhood under Threat* (NY: UNICEF, 2004), 46, available online at http://www.unicef.org/sowc05/english/sowc05_chapters.pdf, accessed 14 December 2004.

127. Ibid.

128. For further details, see "Canada's Guide to the Global Ban on Landmines," available online at http://www.mines.gc.ca/III/III_B-en.asp, accessed 14 December 2004.

129. This category includes revolvers, self-loading pistols, rifles and carbines, submachine guns, assault rifles and light machine guns, and light weapons such as heavy machine guns, hand-held under-barrel and mounted grenade launchers, portable anti-aircraft guns, portable antitank guns, recoilless rifles, portable launchers for antitank missiles and rocket systems, portable anti-aircraft missile systems, and mortars (<100mm). These weapons are manufactured to military specifications for use as lethal instruments of war. *Report of the United Nations Panel of Government Experts on Small Arms* (General Assembly document A/52/298), 27 August 1997.

130. For a representative statement of concern, see the International Action Network on Small Arms (IANSA), "Founding Document of IANSA," available online at http://www.iansa.org/about/m1.htm, accessed 12 November 2004.

131. See the work of Jeffery Boutwell, Michael T. Klare, and Laura W. Reed, eds., *Lethal Commerce* (Cambridge, Mass.: American Academy of Arts and Sciences, 1995); Aaron

Karp, "Arming Ethnic Conflict," *Arms Control Today* 23 (September 1993): 8–23; Jasjit Singh, ed., *Light Weapons and International Security* (New Delhi: Indian Pugwash Society and British American Security Information Council, 1995); Michael Renner, "Small Arms, Big Impact: The Next Challenge for Disarmament," Worldwatch Paper 137 (Washington, D.C.: Worldwatch Institute, October 1997); and various British American Security Information Council occasional papers on light-weapons issues by Edward Laurance.

132. See David DeClerq, "Destroying Small Arms and Light Weapons: Survey of Methods and Practical Guide," BICC Report 13 (Bonn: Bonn International Centre for Conversion, 1999); Sami Faltas and Holger Anders, "Combating the Excessive and Uncontrolled Accumulation and Spread of Small Arms: A Compilation of Policy Recommendations," BICC Paper 17 (Bonn: Bonn International Centre for Conversion, 2000); British American Security Information Council, "Small Arms and Light Weapons: An Issue for the OSCE?" (Washington, D.C.: BASIC, 1998).

133 "Supplement to the *Agenda for Peace*" (General Assembly document A/50/60 and Security Council document S/95/1), 25 January 1995, paras. 47 and 60–63.

134. General Assembly document A/50/70, 12 December 1995. The panel reported in 1997: Panel of Governmental Experts on Small Arms, *Report of the Panel of Governmental Experts on Small Arms* (General Assembly document A/52/298), 27 August 1997.

135. See the series of reports produced by the project of the UN Institute for Disarmament Research called "Managing Arms in Peace Processes." For a full list of UNIDIR publications on small arms, see http://www.unidir.ch/bdd/focus-search.php?onglet=5, accessed 14 December 2004.

136. Geraldine O'Callaghan and Sarah Meek, "The UN Firearms Protocol: Considerations for the UN 2001 Conference," British American Security Information Council–International Alert–Saferworld, Briefing 4, 4, available online at http://www.international-alert.org/pdf/pubsec/btb_brf4.pdf, accessed 12 November 2004.

137. "Protocol against the Illicit Manufacturing of and Trafficking in Firearms, Their Parts and Components and Ammunition, Supplementing the United Nations Convention against Transnational Organized Crime" (General Assembly document A/55/255), 8 June 2001, available online at http://www.unodc.org/pdf/crime/a_res_55/255e.pdf, accessed 12 November 2004.

138. See Keith Krause, "Facing the Challenge of Small Arms: The UN and Global Security Governance," in *The United Nations and Global Security*, edited by Richard M. Price and Mark W. Zacher (New York: Palgrave Macmillan, 2004), 21–38; and Keith Krause, "Multilateral Diplomacy, Norm Building and UN Conferences: The Case of Small Arms and Light Weapons," *Global Governance* 8 (April–June 2002): 247–263.

139. Protocol against the Illicit Manufacturing of and Trafficking in Firearms.

140. The Economic Community of West African States, the EU, the OAS, the OSCE, and the SADC have all adopted instruments on regulation of small arms.

141. High-level Panel on Threats, Challenges and Change, *A More Secure World*, 36.

142. The bizarre spectacle of the 2004 U.S. presidential candidates competing to demonstrate their prowess in killing animals with guns is testament to the strength of the constraint of domestic opinion in this matter.

143. Department of Foreign Affairs and International Trade, *Freedom from Fear*, 3.

6. Human Security and the Protection of Vulnerable Groups

1. General Assembly, *Promotion and Protection of the Rights of Children: The Impact of War on Children, Note by the Secretary General* (General Assembly document A/51/306), 26 August 1996, para. 3.

2. World Summit for Children, "World Declaration on the Survival, Protection and Development of Children," 30 September 1990, available online at http://www.unicef.org/wsc/declare.htm; "Plan of Action for Implementing the World Declaration on the Survival, Protection and Development of Children," 30 September 1990, available online at http://www.unicef.org/wsc/plan.htm#Protection.

3. General Assembly document A/48/157, 20 December 1993.

4. General Assembly, *Promotion and Protection of the Rights of Children: The Impact of War on Children.*

5. In September 1997, the position of special representative of the Secretary-General for children was established and Olara Otunnu was appointed to the post.

6. For Canada's policy response, see Carmen Sorger and Eric Hoskins, "Protecting the Most Vulnerable: War-Affected Children," in *Human Security and the New Diplomacy: Protecting People, Promoting Peace,* edited by Rob McRae and Don Hubert (Montreal and Kingston: McGill-Queen's University Press, 2001), 135–151. The experience of Foreign Minister Axworthy as Canada's minister for human resources development seems relevant here as well. His interactions with the UN in the area of social policy greatly enhanced his awareness of threats against children (e.g., child labor and sexual exploitation). In the context of his general embrace of human security and his focus on protection issues, it was logical to hone in on the protection needs of children.

7. As stipulated in Article 38 of the Convention on the Rights of the Child. The text of the convention is available online at http://www.unhchr.ch/html/menu3/b/k2crc.htm, accessed 15 May 2005.

8. See *Statement by the President of the Security Council* (Security Council document S/PRST/1998/18), 29 June 1998. See also *Statement by the President of the Security Council* (Security Council document S/PRST/1999/6), 12 February 1999, and *Statement by the President of the Security Council* (Security Council document S/PRST/1999/21), 8 July 1999.

9. Security Council resolution 1261, 30 August 1999.

10. Accra Declaration on War-Affected Children, available online at http://www.waraffectedchildren.gc.ca/declaration-en.asp; "Conference on War-affected Children in West Africa—Plan of Action," available online at http://www.waraffectedchildren.gc.ca/planofaction-en.asp, accessed 12 May 2005.

11. However, the protocol did contain a commitment from states to raise the minimum age for voluntary recruitment. Article 4 extended the provisions of the protocol to armed groups other than those associated with states. The text of the protocol is available at http://www.unhchr.ch/html/menu2/6/crc/treaties/opac.htm, accessed 2 December 2004.

12. As of 14 November 2003, China and Russia had signed but not ratified. Curiously, the United States, although it had signed and ratified the protocol, had not

ratified the convention to which the protocol was attached. The United States and Somalia are the only two states that have not ratified the convention.

13. *Children and Armed Conflict: Report of the Secretary-General* (General Assembly document A/56/342 and Security Council document S/2001/852), 7 September 2001, 2.

14. *Children and Armed Conflict: Report of the Secretary-General* (General Assembly document A/55/163 and Security Council document S/2000/712), 19 July 2000.

15. The Global Compact, launched in July 2000 at the UN, is a voluntary network of corporations that have agreed to advance responsible international corporate citizenship and support universal human rights, the rights of workers, and environmental principles.

16. Security Council resolution 1314, 11 August 2000.

17. At the time the report was submitted, Mr. Otunnu had obtained child protection commitments from fifty-nine governments and representatives of armed groups. *Children and Armed Conflict: Report of the Secretary-General* (General Assembly document A/56/342 and Security Council document S/2001/852), 7 September 2001, para. 11.

18. See, for example, Security Council resolution 1332, 14 December 2000, which led to the release of children in the DRC to UNICEF. In Annan's view, this was a good example of the leverage that could be exercised through resolutions on this issue. The extent to which Security Council resolutions produced positive effects in this case is open to question. Demobilization of child soldiers was incomplete, and many were re-recruited. The DRC case underlines the difficulty of translating normative commitments into practical results in this sphere.

19. Security Council resolution 1355, 15 June 2001, concerning MONUC. At the time of the report, two peacekeeping operations (MONUC and UNAMSIL, UN Assistance Mission in Sierra Leone) included child protection in their mandates and child protection advisers among their personnel, while several others were engaged in issues relating to child protection.

20. Security Council resolution 1379, 20 November 2001.

21. See the declaration of the assembly, 10 May 2002, in *A World Fit for Children* (New York: UNICEF and the General Assembly, 2001), para. 7, available online at http://www.unicef.org/specialsession/docs_new/documents/wffc-en.pdf, accessed 14 May 2005.

22. *A World Fit for Children*, paras. 41–44.

23. *Report of the Secretary-General on Children and Armed Conflict* (Security Council document S/2002/1299), 26 November 2002. This report was remarkable for its identification of parties in conflicts of which the council was seized who were violating norms on the recruitment of children. On council perspectives, see Security Council resolution 1460, 30 January 2003.

24. *Children and Armed Conflict: Report of the Secretary General* (Security Council document S/2003/1053), 10 November 2003, paras. 4 and 5; and *Children and Armed Conflict: Report of the Secretary-General* (Security Council document S/58/546), 20 February 2004.

25. Security Council resolution 1539, 22 April 2004.

26. *Report of the Secretary-General on Children and Armed Conflict* (Security Council document S/2002/1299), 26 November 2002.

27. *Children and Armed Conflict: Report of the Secretary-General* (General Assembly document A/58/546 and Security Council document S/2003/1053), 8 October 2004, 8–10. This passage also draws on correspondence with Tatiana Carayannis.

28. Carol Bellamy, *The State of the World's Children 2005: Childhood under Threat* (New York: UNICEF, 2004), 39.

29. Ibid., 10, 43–44, 46.

30. For a useful set of case studies indicating the state of play at the time of writing, see *Children and War: Impact, Protection and Rehabilitation* (Edmonton: University of Alberta, 2004), available online at http://www.humansecurity.info/Conferences/childrenandwarreport_3.pdf, accessed 13 March 2005.

31. United Nations Conference on Environment and Development, "Agenda 21," 14 June 1992, para. 24.2, available online at http://www.unep.org/Documents/Default.asp?DocumentID=52&ArticleID=72, accessed 2 December 2004.

32. World Conference on Human Rights, "Vienna Declaration and Programme of Action," 14–25 June 1993, preamble and paras. 18, 23, 18, 29, 37, available online at http://www.unhchr.ch/huridocda/huridoca.nsf/(Symbol)/A.CONF.157.23.En?OpenDocument, accessed 2 December 2004. One major impetus for the Vienna Conference's recognition of the threats women faced in war was the sustained advocacy by women in the UN system and the associated efforts of women's NGOs to bring these issues onto the agenda. It is improbable that these issues would have been treated as they were in the absence of this effective lobbying.

33. "Fourth World Conference on Women: Beijing Declaration," September 1995, para. 3, available online at http://www.un.org/womenwatch/daw/beijing/platform/declar.htm, accessed 15 October 2003.

34. The only specific mention of protection of women in conflict was at para. 33, which expressed participants' determination to "ensure respect for international law, including humanitarian law, in order to protect women and girls in particular." Ibid.

35. "Fourth World Conference on Women: Platform for Action," September 1995, para. 11. Available online at http://www.un.org/womenwatch/daw/beijing/platform/plat1.htm.

36. Ibid., para. 44.

37. Ibid., paras. 131–149.

38. In this judgment, we differ from the conclusions of the UN Division for the Advancement of Women and the Department of Economic and Social Affairs. Their publication, "Sexual Violence and United Nations Response," *Women2000*, April 1998, is available online at http://www.un.org/womenwatch/daw/public/w2apr98.htm#part4, accessed 24 December 2004.

39. And, in this section of the declaration, it was mixed with comment on the role of women in the peace movement, their role in building a culture of peace, the need to reduce defense expenditure and divert resources to development, and so forth.

40. "The NGO Beijing Declaration," 15 September 1995, available online at http://www.twnside.org.sg/title/declar-cn.htm, accessed 24 December 2004.

41. See, for example, the discussion of crimes against women in the experts' report on the crisis in Rwanda: *Final Report of the Commission of Experts Established Pursuant to Security Council Resolution 935 (1994)* (Security Council document S/1994/1405), 9 December 1994, paras. 136–137.

42. The Commission on the Status of Women, "Agreed Outcomes on Women and Armed Conflict: Report on the 42nd Session," 2–13 March 1998, ECOSOC Official Records, 1998, Supplement No. 7, available online at http://www.peacewomen.org/un/UN1325/CSWOutcomes.html, accessed 2 December 2004.

43. The Windhoek Declaration and Namibia Plan of Action on "Mainstreaming a Gender Perspective in Multidimensional Peace Support Operations," 31 May 2000, available online at http://www.peacewomen.org/un/pkwatch/WindhoekDeclaration.html, accessed 2 December 2004.

44. *Report of the Ad Hoc Committee of the Whole of the 23rd Special Session of the General Assembly* (General Assembly document A/S-23/10/Rev.1, June 2000), paras. 15–19.

45. "Summary of the Panel Discussion on Mainstreaming a Gender Perspective in Peacekeeping Operations," 8 June 2000, available online at http://www.un.org/womenwatch/daw/followup/panels.html#peacekeeping, accessed 2 December 2004.

46. Arria formula meetings began in 1992; they enable a council member to invite an outside expert or experts to meet with council members informally. These meetings are held outside the council chambers and are chaired by the inviting member.

47. "Women and Peace and Security," Security Council resolution 1325, 31 October 2000. The Women's International League for Peace and Freedom maintains an extremely useful chronologically organized database on the resolution available online at http://www.peacewomen.org/un/UN1325/1325index.html, accessed 2 December 2004.

48. *Statement by the President of the Security Council* (Security Council document S/PRST/2001/31), 31 October 2001.

49. United Nations, *Women, Peace and Security* (New York: United Nations, 2002), available online at http://www.un.org/womenwatch/daw/public/eWPS.pdf, accessed 3 December 2004.

50. See United Nations Development Fund for Women, *Getting It Right, Doing It Right: Gender and Disarmament, Demobilization and Reintegration* (New York: UNIFEM, 2004). The study includes a useful set of standard procedures for gender-aware DDR.

51. For a substantial discussion of gender mainstreaming in humanitarian and peace operations, postconflict reconstruction, and DDR, see *Women, Peace, and War: Report of the Secretary-General on Women and Peace and Security* (Security Council document S/2004/814), 13 October 2004, 7–15, available online at http://daccessdds.un.org/doc/UNDOC/GEN/N04/534/14/PDF/N0453414.pdf?OpenElement, accessed 13 March 2005.

52. High-level Panel on Threats, Challenge and Change, *A More Secure World,* 63.

53. UNIFEM, "Women, Peace and Security," available online at http://www.unifem.org/index.php?f_page_pid=35, 3. See also *Report of the Secretary-General on Women and Peace and Security,* 16 and 24.

54. For comment on this subject, see *Report of the Secretary-General on Women and Peace and Security,* 20–21. At the time of writing, a UN investigative group was documenting sexual misconduct by peacekeepers in the DRC. Their report assesses accusations of pedophilia and prostitution. The investigating group has been threatened with retaliation while witnesses have allegedly been bribed to alter their testimony. The draft report remains secret. See "Secret Report Alleges UN Abuses in Congo," *International Herald Tribune,* 18 December 2004, 4. For a broader assessment of the (lack of) protection of women in war, see the incisive analysis of Irene Khan, "Violence against Women: Justice for the Unacknowledged Casualties of War," *International Herald Tribune,* 18 December 2004, 6.

55. By refugees, we mean people who have crossed an international frontier and been granted asylum. The figure does not include Palestinian refugees from Israel.

56. See Adam Roberts, "More Refugees, Less Asylum: A Regime in Transformation," *Journal of Refugee Studies* 11 (December 1998): 375–395.

57. On this point, see, for example, the treatment of Rwandan refugees in Burundi and Tanzania in mid-decade, as discussed in Neil MacFarlane, "Politics and Humanitarian Action," Occasional Paper no. 41 (Providence, R.I.: Thomas J. Watson Jr. Institute for International Studies, 2000), 58–60.

58. See, for example, *Statement by Mrs. S. Ogata, UN High Commissioner for Refugees, to the 48th Session of the Commission on Human Rights,* 20 February 1992, 2, available online at http://www.unhcr.ch/cgi-bintexis/vtx/home/ +EwwBmeqCZ69wwww9wwwwwwwh, accessed 16 January 2004.

59. S. Ogata, *Statement by the UN High Commissioner for Refugees at the World Conference on Human Rights,* 16 June 1993, 5, available online at http://www.unhcr.ch/ cgi-bintexis/vtx/home/+6wwBmeMCZ69wwwwewxwwwwwwh, accessed 16 January 2004. For comment on the right to remain from a legal perspective, see Guy Goodwin-Gill, "The Right to Leave, the Right to Return and the Question of a Right to Remain," in *The Problem of Refugees in the Light of Contemporary Law Issues,* edited by Vera Gowlland-Debbas (Dordrecht, Netherlands: Martinus Nijhoff, 1995).

60. For an extensive account of the efforts to implement preventive protection and the problems therewith, see Margaret Jane Hoverd, "Humanitarian Action in Bosnia: A Study of the Office of the United Nations High Commissioner for Refugees, 1991–1999" (D.Phil. thesis, University of Oxford, 2001).

61. Roberta Cohen and Francis Deng, "Introduction," in *The Forsaken People,* edited by Roberta Cohen and Francis Deng (Washington, D.C.: The Brookings Institution, 1998), 1. In 2003, the Global IDP project estimated that 25 million individuals were IDPs. See Norwegian Refugee Council, Global IDP Project, "Global Overview" (2003), available online at http://www.db.idpproject.org/global_overview.htm, accessed 4 December 2004.

62. For a recent example, see "New International Approaches to Asylum Processing and Protection," Correspondence from Tony Blair, Prime Minister of the United Kingdom, to Costas Simitis, Prime Minister of Greece and President of the European Council, UK submission to the European Council, 10 March 2003. Reprinted in Select Committee on European Union, *European Union: Eleventh Report* (London: House of

Lords, 2003), Appendix V. Available online at http://www.publications.parliament.uk/pa/ld200304/ldselect/ldeucom/74/7415.htm, accessed 15 May 2005.

63. *Statement by Mrs. S. Ogata, UN High Commissioner for Refugees, to the 48th Session of the Commission on Human Rights,* 1–2.

64. There are, of course, exceptions. In both Georgia and Azerbaijan, the majority of those displaced internally are members of the majority population who have been removed by insurgent minorities with the assistance of a neighboring great power (Nagorno Karabakh in Azerbaijan, Abkhazia and South Ossetia in Georgia). For extended treatment of these cases, see S. Neil MacFarlane, Larry Minear, and Stephen Shenfield, "Armed Conflict in Georgia: A Case Study in Humanitarian Action and Peacekeeping," Occasional Paper no. 21 (Providence, R. I.: Thomas J. Watson Jr. Institute for International Studies, 1996); and S. Neil MacFarlane and Larry Minear, "Humanitarian Action and Politics: The Case of Nagorno-Karabakh," Occasional Paper no. 25 (Providence, R.I.: The Thomas J. Watson Jr. Institute for International Studies, 1997).

65. International humanitarian law does provide some protection to civilians affected by war, including the displaced. See Common Article 3 of the Geneva Conventions of 1949 and Part IV of Protocols I and II Additional to the Geneva Conventions. However, this presumes a recognized status of belligerence. Many internally displaced persons may not be displaced by officially recognized war and they may not be located in officially recognized war zones.

66. Francis Deng, "The Global Challenge of Internal Displacement," *Washington University Journal of Law and Policy* 5, no. 141 (2001): 144. See also 145.

67. See Roberta Cohen and Francis M. Deng, *Masses in Flight* (Washington, D.C.: The Brookings Institution, 1992), 275–280.

68. Deng, "The Global Challenge of Internal Displacement," 142.

69. The initiative originated in the UN Commission on Human Rights because international refugee law did not apply and the commission was the principal UN agency that dealt with the human rights of individuals within states. Deng notes that the initiative by the UNCHR was the result of intensifying NGO pressure. See "1998 Jean Mayer Global Citizenship Award: Dr. Francis Deng," *EPIIC Newsletter Online,* Fall 1998, available online at http://www.epiic.com/newsletter/deng.html, accessed 4 December 2004.

70. See Francis Deng, *Compilation and Analysis: Report of the Representative of the Secretary General* (ECOSOC document E/CN/4/1996/52/add. 2), 22 February 1996; *Report of the Representative of the Secretary-General on Legal Aspects Relating to the Protection against Arbitrary Displacement* (ECOSOC document E/CN.4/1998/53/add. 1), 11 February 1998; and *Report of the Representative of the Secretary-General, Mr. Francis M. Deng, submitted pursuant to Commission resolution 1997/39, Addendum, Guiding Principles on Internal Displacement* (ECOSOC document E/CN.4/1998/53/Add. 2), 11 February 1998.

71. *Guiding Principles on Internal Displacement* (extract from ECOSOC document E/CN.4/1998/53/Add.2), 11 February 1998, available online at http://www.unhchr.ch/html/menu2/7/b/principles.htm, accessed 15 May 2005.

72. See Francis Deng, "Introductory Note," in ibid. The author of the guidelines, Walter Kalin, has since replaced Deng as special representative.

73. See UNCHR resolution 2001/54, 24 April 2001. Available online at http://www.unhchr.ch/html/menu2/2/57chr/resolutions.htm.

74. See General Assembly resolutions 54/167, 54/168, and 56/164, 20 February 2002.

75. However, the needs of IDPs are mentioned briefly in the Security Council's *aide mémoire* on the relation between protection of civilians and peacekeeping mandates. See the section on "Effects on Women" in *Statement by the President of the Security Council* (Security Council document S/PRST/2002/6), 15 March 2002.

76. Contrast, for example, principle 14 on liberty of movement and freedom to choose place of residence and principle 15 (d) regarding protection against forcible return or resettlement where life or safety might be at risk with Russia's approach to those displaced by the war in Chechnya. But then, Russian authorities claim that it is not a war.

77. As Deng points out, the omnibus resolution was voted on at the insistence of Egypt. The poll produced no opposing votes but thirty abstentions. Deng, "The Global Challenge of Internal Displacement," 149. Deng also notes the irony that the states questioning the guideline had voted for the earlier assembly resolutions that encouraged the development and dissemination of the guidelines.

78. For a very useful assessment of the decade-long effort to protect IDPs, emphasizing both progress made and remaining shortcomings, see Thomas G. Weiss, "Background Paper: International Efforts for IDPs after a Decade: What Next?" in Brookings Institution–SAIS Project on Internal Displacement, "International Symposium on the Mandate of the Representative of the UN Secretary-General on Internally Displaced Persons: Taking Stock and Charting the Future" (Washington, D.C.: The Brookings Institution–SAIS Project on Internal Displacement, 2002), 43–67.

7. Human Security and the UN

1. UNDP, *Human Development Report 1994: New Dimensions of Human Security* (New York: United Nations Development Programme, 1994).

2. Kanti Bajpai, "Human Security: Concept and Measurement," Kroc Institute Occasional Paper no. 19 (Notre Dame, Ind.: University of Notre Dame, August 2000), 4. Bajpai identified the Canadian government as the other importance source; to that we may now add the 2003 CHS report *Human Security Now*.

3. "Chairman's Summary," Second Ministerial Meeting of the Human Security Network, 11–12 May 2000, available online at http://www.humansecuritynetwork.org/docs/Chairman_summary-e.php, accessed 19 November 2004.

4. Study Group on Europe's Security Capabilities, *A Human Security Doctrine for Europe: The Barcelona Report,* 15 September 2004, 1, available online at http://www.lse.ac.uk/Depts/global/Human%20Security%20Report%20Full.pdf, accessed 3 January 2005.

5. Elizabeth Becker, "U.S. Trade Representative Will Get an Earful in Africa," *International Herald Tribune,* 11 January 2003, 3.

6. Commission on Human Security, *Human Security Now* (New York: Commission on Human Security, 2003).

7. Ibid., iv.

8. Axworthy has since become president of the University of Winnipeg.

9. In 1998, Canada and Norway signed the Lysoen Declaration, which committed both countries "to a framework for consultation and concerted action in the areas of enhancing human security, promoting human rights, strengthening humanitarian law, preventing conflict, and fostering democracy and good governance." The bilateral undertaking was subsequently expanded to include eleven countries, including Austria, Chile, Ireland, Jordan, the Netherlands, Slovenia, Switzerland, and Thailand. See Department of Foreign Affairs and International Trade press release, "Canada and Norway Form New Partnership on Human Security," 11 May 1998, available online at http://www.nisat.org/export_laws-regs%20linked/Norway/lysoern.htm; and Department of Foreign Affairs and International Trade, "Axworthy Announces Progress on Human Security Agenda," 20 May 1999, available online at http://webapps.dfait-maeci.gc.ca/MinPub/Publication.asp?publication_id=375020&Language=E.

10. An early version of this critique can be found in Yuen Foong Khong, "Human Security: A Shotgun Approach to Alleviating Human Misery?" *Global Governance* 7 (July–Sept. 2001): 231–236.

11. Michael Walzer's *Just and Unjust Wars* (New York: Basic Books, 1977) has often been criticized for privileging states' rights (as in his legalist paradigm) over individual rights. However, even he recognizes that "individual rights (to life and liberty) underlie the most important judgments that we make about war." He also acknowledges that "states' rights are simply their collective form" (54).

12. For OAS interest in promoting peoples' rights to democracy, see Inter-American Democratic Charter, Lima, Peru, 11 September 2001, especially Articles 1, 7, and 21, available online at http://www.oas.org/charter/docs/resolution1_en_p4.htm, accessed 21 November 2004. On ASEAN, see M. C. Abad, "The Challenge of Balancing State Security with Human Security," available online at http://www.aseansec.org/14260.htm, accessed 21 December 2004.

13. High-level Panel on Threats, Challenges and Change, *A More Secure World: Our Shared Responsibility* (General Assembly document A/59/565), 2 December 2004, available online at http://www.un.org/secureworld/report.pdf, accessed 3 January 2005, 12.

14. The remarks on HIV/AIDS were made by Zackie Achmat, president of the Treatment Action Campaign of South Africa. See Becker, "U.S. Trade Representative Will Get an Earful in Africa," 3.

15. David Dewitt, "Comprehensive, Common, and Cooperative Security," *The Pacific Review* 5, no. 2 (1994): 1–15.

16. See Bilahari Kausikan, "Asia's Different Standard," *Foreign Policy* 92 (Fall 1993): 24–41; and Fareed Zakaria, "A Conversation with Lee Kuan Yew," *Foreign Affairs* 73 (March/April 1994): 109–127.

17. See Rodney Bruce Hall, "The Discursive Demolition of the Asian Development Model," *International Studies Quarterly* 47, no. 1 (2003): 71–100; and Robert Rubin and

Jacob Weisberg, *In an Uncertain World: Tough Choices from Wall Street to Washington* (New York: Thomson Texere, 2003), 230–256.

18. See Roger Milton, "ASEAN Loses Critic Anwar," *Asiaweek.com,* available online at http://www.asiaweek.com/asiaweek/98/0918/nat6.html, accessed 23 December 2004.

19. Abad, "The Challenge of Balancing State Security with Human Security."

20. Samuel Huntington, *Political Order in Changing Societies* (New Haven, Conn.: Yale University Press, 1967).

21. Commission on Human Security, *Human Security Now,* 2.

22. See Samantha Power, *A Problem from Hell: America and the Age of Genocide* (London: Flamingo, 2003), Chapters 2–4, for a fascinating analysis of how Raphael Lemkin coined the term "genocide" and fought for its inclusion as part of international law.

23. Canadian Consortium on Human Security, "What Is Human Security?" available online at www.humansecurity.info/CCHS_web/About_Human_Security/en/index.php, accessed 19 November 2004.

24. "G-8/Evian Summit," available online at http://www.diplomatie.gouv.fr/actu/article.gb.asp?ART=35184, accessed 9 November 2004; see also Sea Island Summit Documents, "Chair's Summary," available online at http://www.g8usa.gov/d_061004m.htm, accessed 9 November 2004.

25. The G-8 Africa Action Plan, on the other hand, suggests that the group is not averse to adopting the human security concept for regional endeavors.

26. See Michael Brown, *Ethnic Conflict in International Politics* (Princeton, N.J.: Princeton University Press, 1993); Barry Posen, "The Security Dilemma and Ethnic Conflict," *Survival* (Spring 1993): 27–47; Barbara Walter and Jack Snyder, eds., *Civil Wars, Insecurity, and Intervention* (New York: Columbia University Press, 1999).

27. Stephen Van Evera, *Causes of War: Power and the Roots of Conflict* (Ithaca, N.Y.: Cornell University Press, 1999); John Mearsheimer, *The Tragedy of Great Power Politics* (New York: W.W. Norton, 2001), 365–366.

28. Yosef Lapid and Friedrich Kratochwil, "Revisiting the 'National': Toward an Identity Agenda in Neorealism?" in *The Return of Culture and Identity in International Relations Theory,* edited by Yosef Lapid and Friedrich Kratochwil (Boulder, Colo.: Lynne Rienner, 1996), 110–120.

29. Lloyd Axworthy, "A New Scientific Field and Policy Lens," 348–349; Fen Hampson, "A Concept in Need of a Global Policy Response," 349–350; Don Hubert, "An Idea That Works in Practice," 351–352; and Astri Suhrke, "A Stalled Initiative," 365, all in *Security Dialogue* 35 (September 2004).

30. Three of the twenty-one participants in the debate—Neil MacFarlane, Barry Buzan, and Roland Paris—may be considered mainstream by some but not others. It is probably less contentious to claim that the mainstream security studies scholars include those who write or serve on the editorial boards of journals such as *International Security, World Politics, Security Studies, Journal of Conflict Resolution,* and the Cornell University Press security series.

31. Andrew Mack, "Human Security in the New Millennium," *Work in Progress: A Review of Research of the United Nations University* 16 (Summer 2002): 4.

32. See Walzer, *Just and Unjust Wars*, xv–xvi and 51–55 for a rights-based defense of territorial integrity and political sovereignty.

33. Ramesh Thakur, "Human Security Regimes," in *Asia's Emerging Regional Order: Reconciling Traditional and Human Security*, edited by William Tow, Ramesh Thakur, and In-Taek Hyun (Tokyo: United Nations University Press, 2000), 250.

34. Mack, "Human Security in the New Millennium." Mack, it should be noted, is a critic of the broad conception of human security.

35. Ibid., 6.

36. Bernard Holland, "Music at a Wheel's Click, but Do We Really Hear?" *New York Times*, 6 November 2004, B13.

37. Mack, "Human Security in the New Millennium," 6.

38. Volker Franke, "The Emperor Needs New Clothes: Securitizing Threats in the Twenty-First Century," *Peace and Conflict Studies* 9 (December 2002): 10.

39. Ibid., 16.

40. Monica Serrano, "Unilateralism, Multilateralism, and U.S. Drug Diplomacy in Latin America," in *Unilateralism and U.S. Foreign Policy: International Perspectives*, edited by David Malone and Yuen Foong Khong (Boulder Colo.: Lynne Rienner Publishers, 2003), 117–136.

41. Philip Bowring, "On Dhaka's Streets, Two Radical Changes," *International Herald Tribune*, 15 January 2003, 9.

42. Keith Krause and Michael Williams, "Broadening the Agenda of Security Studies: Politics and Methods," *Mershon International Studies Review* 40 (October 1996): 247. Krause and Williams's example is drawn from Daniel Deudney, "The Case Against Linking Environmental Degradation and National Security," *Millennium* 19 (1990): 461–476.

43. Roland Paris, "Human Security: Paradigm Shift or Hot Air?" *International Security* 26 (September 2001): 87–102.

44. Ibid., 98. See Figure 1. The 2x2 matrix locates human security in the bottom right-hand corner.

45. See, for example, Department of Foreign Affairs and International Trade, *Freedom from Fear: Canada's Foreign Policy for Human Security* (Ottawa: Department of Foreign Affairs and International Trade, 2002).

46. Robert Jackson's *The Global Covenant* contains one of the most lucid discussions of the idea of security. For him, "Personal security is our individual insulation from threat, danger, or harm, the source of which is always *other people*." *The Global Covenant: Human Conduct in a World of States* (Oxford: Oxford University Press, 2000), 186, italics in original.

47. Muhammed Ayoob, "The Security Problematic of the Third World," *World Politics* 43 (January 1991): 257–283.

48. "Oxford Tops UK Air Pollution List," available online at http://www.lpg-vehicles.co.uk/lpg_news/oxford_tops_uk_air_pollution_list.htm, accessed 23 December 2004.

49. High-level Panel on Threats, Challenges and Change, *A More Secure World*, 2.

50. Ibid., 12.

51. Ibid., 117–118. The sixteen-member HLP, which is chaired by former Thai prime minister Anand Panyarachun, includes top politicians, heads of international and regional organizations, ex-generals, and ex-civil servants.

52. See Celia Dugger, "Devastated by AIDS, Africa Sees Life Expectancy Plunge," *New York Times,* 16 July 2004, A3.

53. It is interesting in this regard that while the relevant section of the HLP report does link poverty and conflict, it discusses concerns about infectious diseases without positing a link to violence. See High-level Panel on Threats, Challenges and Change, *A More Secure World,* 26–27.

54. We thank Richard Jolly for bringing this point to our attention.

55. See Roy Lubove, *The Struggle for Social Security, 1900–1935* (Cambridge, Mass.: Harvard University Press, 1968); and Edward Berkowitz, *America's Welfare State: From Roosevelt to Reagan* (Baltimore, Md.: Johns Hopkins University Press, 1991).

56. Lubove, *The Struggle for Social Security,* 265–276; Berkowitz, *America's Welfare State,* 209–216.

57. Bajpai, "Human Security: Concept and Measurement," 51.

58. Jackson, *The Global Covenant,* 195.

59. Jean-Marie Colombani, "We Are All Americans," *Le Monde,* 12 September 2001; translation available online at http://www.worldpress.org/1101we_are_all_americans.htm, accessed 12 December 2004.

60. Julia Preston, "Departing Rights Commissioner Faults U.S.," *The New York Times,* 12 September 2002.

61. Ibid.

62. Robin Cook, "No One Still Thinks We're Soft on Crime," *The Guardian,* 19 November 2004, 28.

63. Among the more prominent states in such a list are the UK, the other NATO members, Saudi Arabia, Egypt, Jordan, Israel, Russia, Pakistan, China, Japan, and Australia.

64. Suhrke, "A Stalled Initiative," 365.

65. Commission on Human Security, *Human Security Now,* iv.

66. Ibid. The HLP, in contrast, seems to place greater emphasis on the importance of "sovereign States" and in seeing them as "the front-line actors in dealing with all the threats we face." High-level Panel on Threats, Challenges and Change, *A More Secure World,* 11.

67. Ibid., 11, 15.

68. See essays in Walter and Snyder, eds., *Civil Wars, Insecurity, and Intervention.*

69. Ibid.

Conclusion

1. High-level Panel on Threats, Challenges and Change, *A More Secure World,* 11, 21–22.

2. The combination of moral principle and interest underlying the pursuit of human security is well expressed in Study Group on Europe's Defence Capabilities, *A Human Security Doctrine for Europe: The Barcelona Report,* 15 September 2004, 9–10,

available online at http://www.lse.ac.uk/Depts/global/
Human%20Security%20Report%20Full.pdf, accessed 3 January 2005.

3. For the latest iteration, see ibid., 21–22.

4. As one of the authors' correspondents put it when asked how much resonance human security had in Washington: "No one in Washington who is in the 'power loop' is talking about human security. It is all anti-terrorism and anti-rogue state. The hardliners run the show here—intellectually as well as politically. The liberal-left or alternative thinkers are not a factor at all. Zero. There is a little bit of discussion among UN-oriented internationalists but nothing beyond this." Private e-mail communication.

5. For example, in the case of Canada, there appeared to be little interest in the "responsibility to protect" within the Department of National Defence. Moreover, some within the Department of Foreign Affairs felt that Axworthy's approach to foreign policy was "romantic" and that his priorities distracted Canada from what should be the central dimension of its foreign policy: the economic relationship with the United States. See Michael Hart, "Lessons from Canada's History as a Trading Nation," *The International Journal* LVIII, no. 1 (2002–2003): 25–42; and the comment on Hart in Jennifer Welsh, "Canada in the 21st Century," *The Round Table* XC, no. 376 (September 2004): 590.

6. In late 2002, when a senior UN field official was asked about the impact of the concept of "human security" on the work of his agency (which is involved in humanitarian response in a conflict zone), he responded that he wasn't sure what human security meant and had not run into it. Private e-mail communication.

7. Fiona Terry, *Condemned to Repeat: The Paradox of Humanitarian Action* (Ithaca, N.Y.: Cornell University Press, 2002); and Larry Minear, *The Humanitarian Enterprise: Dilemmas and Discoveries* (Bloomfield, Ill.: Kumarian Press, 2002). This also applies to the major critics of humanitarianism. See David Rieff, *A Bed for the Night: Humanitarianism in Crisis* (New York: Vintage, 2002). An eminent analyst of humanitarian action, when asked whether the lens of human security made any difference to how humanitarian practitioners approach their work, replied that "the term, and perhaps to a lesser extent the concept, has found its way into the vocabulary of practitioners, but it doesn't yet play a very discernible role in decision-making." E-mail communication with Larry Minear, 12 January 2004.

8. Rieff, *A Bed for the Night,* 15.

Index

Abad, M. C., 232–233
absolutism, 36–40, 58, 281n91. *See also* state
    sovereignty
Abu Ghraib scandal, 255
accountability. *See* responsibilities of states
acquired immune deficiency syndrome
    (AIDS). *See* HIV/AIDS
Ad Hoc Committee of the Whole, 215
Afghanistan, 117, 182, 242, 254–256, 290n87
Africa. *See also specific countries*
    Cold War conflicts, 238
    and conflict prevention, 155–156, 299n51
    HIV/AIDS epidemic, 231
    and refugee issues, 78, 80
    and regional organizations, 73, 188–190
Africa Action Plan, 235
African (Banjul) Charter on Human and
    Peoples' Rights, 73–74, 287n30
African Charter on the Rights and Welfare of
    the Child, 209
African Commission on Human and Peoples'
    Rights, 73
African Union (AU), 157, 188–189
Agence de Genève, 56
Agenda 21, 211
An Agenda for Development, 151
An Agenda for Peace, 194
Ahead of the Curve? UN Ideas and Global
    Challenges, xiii, 3, 272n9
aid agencies. *See specific institutions*
Aideed, Mohamed, 134–135
air exclusion zones, 185
Al Qaeda, 135, 239, 245, 252–254, 258
Algeria, 78
Allende, Salvador, 125
American Civil War, 6–7
American Convention on Human Rights, 72
American Federation of Labor (AFL), 125
American Revolution, 41
Amin, Idi, 94
Amnesty International, 64, 75, 94, 125–126,
    287n33
Angell, Norman, 46
Angola, 89, 182, 238
Annan, Kofi
    advocacy role, 200

and conflict prevention, 150, 152
embrace of human security, 163, 272n4
Human Security Now report, 226
and ICISS, 161
on individual sovereignty, xi–xiii
and the Nobel Peace Prize, 272n9
and protection of children, 207, 313n18
and sustainable human development, 159
on threats against populations, 175
Antigone (Sophocles), 26, 27
antinuclear movement, 118, 120
anti-Semitism, 114. *See also* Holocaust
apartheid, 64, 84, 88–89, 166
Aquinas, Thomas, 32, 33, 278n51
Arab-Israeli War, 127–128
Arias, Oscar, 144
Aristotle, 27, 28
Arkhipov, Vasilii, 117
arms controls, 89, 109
arms race, 103, 117, 241
Army Air Force (AAF), 112
Arria formula, 215
Asia, 74, 78, 80, 188, 231–232, 239. *See also*
    specific countries
Asian financial crisis, 157–158, 232
Association of Southeast Asian Nations
    (ASEAN), 93, 128, 229, 231–233
Atlantic Charter, 65, 285n7
Atlee, Clement, 61
atomic weapons. *See* nuclear weapons
Augustine, 28, 30, 32, 277n24
Australia, 93, 120, 221
Austria, 55, 226, 284n139, 319n9
authoritarianism, 232. *See also* state sovereignty
Axworthy, Lloyd
    critiques of, 323n4
    experience with the UN, 312n6
    on human security, 172, 235
    and land mine bans, 195–196
    and the Liu Institute, 227
    and the Social Summit, 298n21
    on state security, x–xiii
Azerbaijan, 317n64

Bajpai, Kanti, 226, 252–253
Balkans, 185. *See also specific countries*

325

About the Authors

S. Neil MacFarlane is Lester B. Pearson Professor of International Relations and Head of the Department of Politics and International Relations at the University of Oxford, and Professorial Fellow at St. Anne's College. A native of Montréal, he is a graduate of Dartmouth College and received his doctorate in international relations from Oxford University, where he held a Rhodes Scholarship. He was formerly Associate Professor of Government and Director of the Center for Russian and East European Studies at the University of Virginia and Professor of Political Studies and Director of the Centre for International Relations at Queen's University, Canada. MacFarlane has held research posts at the International Institute for Strategic Studies in London, Harvard University, the University of British Columbia, and the University of California (Berkeley). He has written extensively on nationalism and national liberation, humanitarian action and its relationship to peacekeeping, the responses of states and international organizations to civil conflicts, and Russian and American foreign policy.

Yuen Foong Khong is John G. Winant University Lecturer in American Foreign Policy and a Fellow of Nuffield College, Oxford University. He is also Senior Research Adviser to the Institute of Defence and Strategic Studies (IDSS), Nanyang Technological University, Singapore. A former Director of Oxford's Centre for International Studies, he has also served as Deputy Director and Director of IDSS Singapore. He received his Ph.D. from Harvard University, where he was Assistant/Associate Professor of Government until he joined Oxford. His publications include *Analogies at War: Korea, Munich, Dien Bien Phu and the Vietnam Decisions of 1965* (1992), which won the 1994 American Political Science Association's Political Psychology Book Award. In 1996, he received the Erik Erikson Award for distinguished early career contributions to political psychology. Recent books include a multi-authored volume on *Power in Transition: The Peaceful Change of International Order* (2001) and a co-edited volume with David Malone on *Unilateralism and U.S. Foreign Policy: International Perspectives* (2003).

About the United Nations
Intellectual History Project

Ideas and concepts are a main driving force in human progress, and they are arguably the most important contribution of the United Nations. Yet there has been little historical study of the origins and evolution of the history of economic and social ideas cultivated within the world organization and of their impact on wider thinking and international action. The United Nations Intellectual History Project is filling this knowledge gap about the UN by tracing the origin and analyzing the evolution of key ideas and concepts about international economic and social development born or nurtured under UN auspices. The UNIHP began operations in mid-1999 when the secretariat, the hub of a worldwide network of specialists on the UN, was established at the Ralph Bunche Institute for International Studies of The CUNY Graduate Center.

The UNIHP has two main components, oral history interviews and a series of books on specific topics. The seventy-three in-depth oral history interviews with leading contributors to crucial ideas and concepts within the UN system provide inputs into these volumes. Complete and indexed transcripts will be made available to researchers and the general public in 2006.

The project has commissioned fifteen studies about the major economic and social ideas or concepts that are central to UN activity, which are being published by Indiana University Press.

- *Ahead of the Curve? UN Ideas and Global Challenges,* by Louis Emmerij, Richard Jolly, and Thomas G. Weiss (2001)
- *Unity and Diversity in Development Ideas: Perspectives from the UN Regional Commissions,* edited by Yves Berthelot with contributions from Adebayo Adedeji, Yves Berthelot, Leelananda de Silva, Paul Rayment, Gert Rosenthal, and Blandine Destremeau (2003)
- *Quantifying the World: UN Contributions to Statistics,* by Michael Ward (2004)

- *UN Contributions to Development Thinking and Practice,* by Richard Jolly, Louis Emmerij, Dharam Ghai, and Frédéric Lapeyre (2004)
- *The UN and Global Political Economy: Trade, Finance, and Development,* by John Toye and Richard Toye (2004)
- *UN Voices: The Struggle for Development and Social Justice,* by Thomas G. Weiss, Tatiana Carayannis, Louis Emmerij, and Richard Jolly (2005)
- *Women, Development and the UN: A Sixty-Year Quest for Equality and Justice,* by Devaki Jain (2005)
- *Human Security and the UN: A Critical History,* by S. Neil MacFarlane and Yuen Foong Khong (2006)

Forthcoming titles:

- *The UN and Human Rights Ideas: The Unfinished Revolution,* by Sarah Zaidi and Roger Normand (2006)
- *The UN and Development Cooperation,* by Olav Stokke (2006)
- *The UN and the Global Commons: Development Without Destruction,* by Nico Schrijver (2006)
- *The UN and Transnationals, from Code to Compact,* by Tagi Sagafi-nejad, in collaboration with John Dunning (2006)
- *The UN and Global Governance: An Idea and its Prospects,* by Ramesh Thakur and Thomas G. Weiss (2007)
- *The United Nations: A History of Ideas and Their Future,* by Richard Jolly, Louis Emmerij, and Thomas G. Weiss (2007)

The project is also collaborating on *The Oxford Handbook on the UN,* edited by Thomas G. Weiss and Sam Daws, to be published by Oxford University Press in 2007.

For further information, the interested reader should contact:

UN Intellectual History Project
The CUNY Graduate Center
365 Fifth Avenue, Suite 5203
New York, New York 10016-4309
212-817-1920 Tel
212-817-1565 Fax
UNHistory@gc.cuny.edu
www.unhistory.org